D1563130

In the Cause of Freedom

In the
Cause of
Freedom

Radical Black

Internationalism from

Harlem to London,

1917–1939

MINKAH MAKALANI

The University of
North Carolina Press

Chapel Hill

Designed by Jacquline Johnson
Set in Minion
by Tseng Information Systems, Inc.
Manufactured in the United States of America

The paper in this book meets the guidelines for permanence
and durability of the Committee on Production Guidelines for
Book Longevity of the Council on Library Resources.

The University of North Carolina Press has been a member of
the Green Press Initiative since 2003.

Library of Congress Cataloging-in-Publication Data
Makalani, Minkah.
In the cause of freedom : radical Black internationalism from Harlem to London, 1917–1939 /
Minkah Makalani.
p. cm.
Includes bibliographical references and index.
ISBN 978-0-8078-3504-3 (cloth : alk. paper)
1. African Americans—Politics and government—20th century. 2. Blacks—Great Britain—
Politics and government—20th century. 3. Racism—Political aspects—United States—History—
20th century. 4. Racism—Political aspects—Great Britain—History—20th century. 5. African
Blood Brotherhood. 6. International African Service Bureau. 7. United States—Relations—
Great Britain. 8. Great Britain—Relations—United States. I. Title.
E185.61.M23 2011
323.1196′073—dc23   2011016834

15 14 13 12 11   5 4 3 2 1

In memory of my brother,
Eric Narville "Nobbie" Mathews

Contents

Illustrations

Acknowledgments

It was an undergraduate class on black nationalism. My fellow student activists and I fashioned ourselves Marxist-Leninists, revolutionary nationalists, proletarian intellectuals, artists, and intellectuals who were interested in the history of black nationalism for what, in our grandiose minds, we could use to reshape the world. In this context, the professor, Sundiata Cha-Jua, almost in passing mentioned the African Blood Brotherhood as the left wing of the Garvey movement and the black cadre of the Communist Party. Myths fueled our passion about the past, and I clung to this one with dogged tenacity. My initial efforts to track down information on the ABB turned up only a facsimile reprint of *Crusader* that carried Robert Hill's introductory essay on Cyril Valentine Briggs, the ABB's founder and the editor of the *Crusader*. What I read in the magazine and Hill's essay did not comport with my lecture notes, but my interest remained. At around this time, C. L. R. James passed away, and another professor, David Roediger, organized a remembrance that our student group and a radical history student group cosponsored. A sophomore, I knew nothing of James, though I was thoroughly impressed, to say the least. After nearly twenty years of reading his writings and essays about him and more than a decade of research on the ABB, this volume is my homage to those organizations and the people and period that brought them to my attention.

The myths that have kept the ABB alive in the historical memory of activists, scholars, community organizers, and archivists I have encountered while researching this book have served the Brotherhood well. The ABB has lived a vibrant life in those memories, the minor and at times routine efforts to reconcile what little people knew of or remembered about the organization with their political commitments, convictions, and visions for the future. Foremost, I wish not merely to acknowledge but thank (and even this is an inadequate word) those people who have given freely (or reservedly) of their time, memories, ideas, and insights into the ABB, its members, and their experiences. Those remembrances have been far more valuable and important to this story than the archives, magazines, correspondence, and other ephemera of historical scholarship I have mined to write this book. I hope that I have set to paper a story that has survived in the archive of a collective black radical memory for nearly a century now. I depart from many of the myths that I have been given and take issue with some of the stories that have been told. I hope that any myths that I have created along the way complement what so many other people have said and done, thought and written about these figures and events and that they aid future scholarship on this subject.

I owe a special debt of gratitude to Joyce Moore Turner. Joyce presented herself after my first conference presentation on the African Blood Brotherhood. The daughter of Richard B. Moore, one of the central figures in the ABB, I was amazed and honored that she would come listen to my paper. As is her style, she corrected my anglicized pronunciation of the Afro-Dutch Otto Huiswoud's surname (Hees-WOUD, rhymes with "loud"), then corrected my various mistakes in research and argument. I assumed that I would never see her again. Instead, she has remained an enthusiastic if still critical supporter of my research, helping with occasional sources and providing insights into the archive that have helped make this process much easier. I hope that even if she does not precisely agree with what I have written, she finds my work something that she can appreciate as having been crafted with her gentle, critical gaze in mind.

While in graduate school at the University of Illinois at Urbana-Champaign, I had the good fortune of a committee whose members ensured that I pushed my thinking beyond well-worn arguments and easy conclusions. Juliet E. K. Walker, James Barrett, Sundiata Cha-Jua, and Dave Roediger poured an immeasurable amount of time and energy into that effort, entertaining my questions and emerging ideas. Each brought his or her unique historiographical and political perspective to my work, which forced me to write with a wide readership in mind. A series of conversations with Antoinette Burton about the international contours of black radicalism prompted me to look seriously outside the United States and planted the seeds of what eventually became the final half of this book. And Robin D. G. Kelley has been a constant source of support, criticism, and feedback from afar. His feedback, criticisms, and suggestions about argumentation, framing, and sources have been invaluable. While I am not among the fortunate graduate students who have worked with Robin, the debt of gratitude I feel for his openness, collegiality, and support is no less great.

Landing in the history department at Rutgers has been a blessing. I have the rare fortune of a score of colleagues who always seemed to understand what I was trying to do (at times perhaps better than I did) and were willing to engage me on those terms as well as push my thinking in new and innovative ways. Mia Bay, Jackson Lears, Keith Wailoo (now at Princeton), and Deborah Gray White read the manuscript at different stages, freely offering their expertise and insights. Each, in his or her own way, has gone beyond the call of duty to help usher me through this process. I thank others who have read sections of the manuscript, especially Kim Butler, Indrani Chatterjee, Barbara Cooper, Ann Fabian, Sumit Guha, Jochen Hellbeck, Nancy Hewitt, Al Howard, Alison Isenberg, Seth Koven, Aldo Lauria-Santiago, Julie Livingston, and Donna Murch. Keith Wailoo went beyond the call of duty and mentorship to encourage me to share my work. Temma Kaplan helped me decode the finer points of historical writing and inspired me to work at telling the kind of story I wanted to tell. Marc Matera, then a graduate student, shared his research on black activist intellectuals in London and helped direct me to the Public Records Office there. His commentary on the final two chapters improved them greatly. Steven Lawson offered a good sounding board as well as a sympathetic ear for complaining about the Yankees when it seemed that Red Sox fans had overrun New York in 2004.

A fellowship at the Institute for Research in Women on the Douglass Campus introduced me to a range of people from various departments at Rutgers who fostered a healthy model of scholarly engagement and constructive criticism. I especially want to acknowledge Roberta Goldberg, Tanya Kateri Hernandez, and Ana Y. Ramos-Zayas for their feedback on a paper presented to that workshop and their continued friendship. Nancy Hewitt, who ran the IRW during my fellowship year, offered and continues to offer a keen historical eye, and a model of mentorship. Others at Rutgers (some no longer here) were equally important in making this an intellectually rich and personally enjoyable experience: Herman Bennett, Christopher Leslie Brown, Abena Busia, Carlos Decena, Zaire Dinzey-Flores, Brent Hayes Edwards, Nicole Fleetwood, Paul Hanebrink, Yolanda Martínez–San Miguel, Carter Mathes, Jennifer Morgan, Sonali Perrera, Jasbir Puar, Stéphane Robolin, Evie Shockley, Cheryl Wall, and Edlie Wong.

A one-year postdoctoral fellowship at the University of Illinois at Chicago provided me much-needed time to finish my research and think about reshaping the manuscript into its current form. Along with the great folks at UIC, the colleagues, and now new friends who make up what has been aptly dubbed the New Chicago School provided a vibrant intellectual community: Ana Aparicio, Martha Biondi, Michelle Boyd, Nicholas Brown, Sherwin Bryant, Corey Capers, Ainsworth Clarke, Madhu Dubey, David Embrick, Tyrone Forman, Lorena García, Michael Hanchard, Barnor Hessee, Richard Iton, Amanda Lewis, Dwight McBride, Charles Mills, Barbara Ransby, Beth

Richie, Kerry Ann Rockquemore, Mérida Rúa, David Stovall, Bill Watkins, and Paul Zeleza.

Over the past ten years, I have accumulated many friends and even more debts. Davarian Baldwin, Corey Capers, Clarence Lang, and Jessica Millward helped me talk through ideas, read parts of the manuscript, and most important, took my calls and patiently talked me down from my plans to ditch academia for a career as a barista or a job in a paper mill. Their sage advice has made the past several years enjoyable. Marika Sherwood spent several hours talking with me about George Padmore, C. L. R. James, and the Comintern. Hakim Adi graciously took my phone call and pointed me toward key sources in the British Library. I thank Margaret Stevens, Barrymore Bogues, Susan Pennybacker, Horace Campbell, and all those present for the honor of participating in the graduate students' symposium on Early Twentieth-Century Black Radicalism at Brown University in April 2008. Many other longtime and newfound friends, and other generous souls that I have met along the way, read parts of the manuscript, offered advice, helped translate documents, shared their own research, or inspired me to continue plugging away at the project. I especially thank Carole Anderson, Jacqueline Nassy Brown, Robin Bryson, Adrian Burgos, Derrick Burleson, Rod Bush, Tina Campt, Jung-Hee Choi, Jelani Cobb, Jon Coit, Sika Dagbovie, Sace Elder, Sujatha Fernandes, Johanna Fernandez, Unique Frasier, Jeremy Glick, Frank Guridy, Jennifer Hamer, Hasan Kwame Jeffries, Kelly Josephs, Scott Kurashige, Naa Oyo Kwate, Ferentz LaFargue, Leshane Lindsey, Erik McDuffie, Quincy Mills, Richard Mizelle, Helen Neville, Jeffrey Ogbar, Eddie Paulino, Jeffrey B. Perry, Richard Pierce, Jemima Pierre, Millery Polyné, Sherrie Randolph, Samuel Roberts, Nikhil Singh, Mark Solomon, Sharan Strange, Anantha Sudhakar, Benjamin Talton, France Winddance Twine, Michael Walsh, Monica White, Fanon Che Wilkins, and Chad Williams. Melissa Cooper graciously took time from her graduate studies to help put together the bibliography. Joshua Guild gave valuable feedback on parts of the manuscript and helped clarify some of the finer points of black British history. Christiana Oladini-James deserves a special note of thanks for her tireless work translating several hundred pages of French documents. The insights she provided into the nuances of these documents made writing the latter part of this book possible.

I owe Tom Wells a great debt for his critical eye, attention to detail, and willingness to tell me that the story I wanted to tell did not need to say absolutely everything. He helped me shape a rather unwieldy manuscript into a far more readable book than I could have hoped for. At the University of North Carolina Press, Sian Hunter has provided a kind ear, patiently answered what must have seemed like one series of anxious questions after another, and gently pushed me to let go of my work so that the process could go forward. Her ability to see value in this book despite my doubts helped convince me that I did have a contribution to make. UNC Press's Kate Torrey has been phenomenal, providing much-needed support and a firm editorial hand. I also thank the anonymous readers whose critical insights and encouraging feedback on earlier drafts of the manuscript greatly improved the work. I hope I have met their exacting standards.

Among the many archivists and librarians who helped me as I researched this book, I especially want to thank Steven Fullwood, Diana Lachatanere, and the late Andre Elizee at the Schomburg Center for Research in Black Culture. Mieke Ijzermans at the International Institute of Social History tracked down a wealth of materials during my visit as well as offered an affordable, immensely comfortable room for rent in her home. I also thank Simon Elliott at the Manuscripts Division of the University of California at Los Angeles Library, Department of Special Collections, for copying the Ralph Bunche Diary, and Chris Laico and Tara Combs at Columbia University's Rare Book and Manuscript Library. Karen Bouchard at Brown University's Art and Architecture Library reproduced a hard-to-find photo at the eleventh hour. I also thank the staff at the Moorland-Spingarn Research Center at Howard University; the Library of Congress Reading Room and Eastern European Reading Room; Yale University's Beinecke Library; the Labour History Archive and Study Center at the People's History Museum in Manchester, England; the Manuscript, Archives, and Rare Books Library at Emory University; and the Tamiment Institute, New York University.

Finally, I thank the members of my family, who have supported me through several years of missed holidays and missed phone calls. My cousins and aunts, too many to name here, have been supportive throughout, and they are greatly appreciated. My mother, Evelyn Mathews, always offered her time and conversation when I was down and somehow knew to call just when I needed a pick-me-up. My grandmother, Narvis Penn, has been my biggest supporter, always having far more faith in me than I could ever have had in myself. My grandfather (daddy), Charles Penn, has never quite understood why I could not work a second job since I teach only twice a week; I hope this book will help him make sense of my career choice and seemingly lazy ways. My sisters, April and Sheila, and my niece and nephew, Loren and Solace, have been great distractions from work and writing (and the marathon phone conversations with April helped, too).

To my older daughter, Cheyenne Alexandria Williams, I hope so much for you and your future. So many of these pages were written with you in mind. And despite the fact that you dislike Brooklyn, play questionable practical jokes, have dubious musical tastes (Mike Jones is not real Hip-Hop), and have a dismaying belief that I am old, watching you grow up over nearly twenty years has been one of my greatest joys. I hope you will find something in here useful or enjoyable.

The Sanchez family—my in-laws, Julio and Carmen; my sister-in-law, Renee; y todos mis primos nuevo—have welcomed me into their lives even though I do not know how to play dominos, I ran that wicked Boston on cats, and I obviously can't handle more than two cups of coquito. Thank you all for helping make Brooklyn home.

Delida Sanchez came into my life midway through my writing of this book and has made it an immensely better experience, even if it did not always seem like I appreciated the sacrifices she made. She has changed my life, encouraged me when I did not believe in what I was doing, and opened me up to a new world that I had never imagined. Without her classic smile, bubbly personality, ability to find the positive in what often seemed an abyss, and her tireless support, this book would have remained an interesting idea. In addition to reading multiple drafts, she helped bring into the world and care for our beautiful daughter, Yesenia Ziza Makalani. Watching Yesenia's first steps, hearing her first words, and seeing her flash an infectious smile (almost as brilliant as her mother's) have been indescribable experiences. I look forward to watching our lil' Ladybug grow in the coming years and to the adventures she is sure to take us on.

Abbreviations

ABB	African Blood Brotherhood for African Liberation and Redemption
ANLC	American Negro Labor Congress
BBNT	Black Belt Nation Thesis
BSL	Black Star Line
CDRN	Comité de Defense de la Race Nègre (Committee for the Defense of the Black Race)
CEC	Central Executive Committee
CPA	Communist Party of America
CPGB	Communist Party of Great Britain
CPUSA	Communist Party of the USA
ECCI	Executive Committee of the Communist International
FNF	Friends of Negro Freedom
HEF	Harlem Educational Forum
HLW	Hamitic League of the World
HTL	Harlem Tenants League
HUAC	House Un-American Activities Committee
IAFE	International African Friends of Ethiopia
IASB	International African Service Bureau
IBNW	International Bureau of Negro Workers
ICNW	International Conference of Negro Workers
ILP	Independent Labour Party
ISH	International of Seamen and Harbour Workers
ITUCNW	International Trade Union Committee of Negro Workers
KUTV	University of the Toilers of the East

LAI	League against Imperialism
LCP	League of Coloured Peoples
LDRN	Ligue de Defense de la Race Nègre (League for the Defense of the Black Race)
NAACP	National Association for the Advancement of Colored People
NCBWA	National Congress of British West Africa
PAC	Pan-African Congress
PCF	Parti Communiste Français (French Communist Party)
PEF	People's Educational Forum
Polcom	Political Committee
RILU	Red International of Labor Unions
SMM	Seamen's Minority Movement
SPA	Socialist Party of America
UFC	United Front Conference
UNIA	Universal Negro Improvement Association
WASU	West African Students Union
WP	Workers (Communist) Party

Introduction

In July 1929, the black radical lawyer William Patterson boarded a train from Moscow to Frankfurt, Germany, to attend the Second International Congress against Imperialism. Patterson was a student at the University of the Toilers of the East (KUTV), the school run by the Communist International (Comintern) for training Asian and African activists. His route to Frankfurt (and Moscow before that) had begun a decade earlier, when he completed law school at the University of California in San Francisco but failed the California bar examination. Even as a student, Patterson nursed a nascent radicalism, attending Socialist Party meetings, criticizing World War I as "a white man's war," and reading every black and left periodical he could find. Indeed, while in law school, he first considered leaving the United States for Africa, which he believed "needed young men who were hostile to colonialism and the oppressors of Black people." Failing the bar was the perfect excuse to make his way across the Atlantic, but he got only as far as London. The dreary metropolis thrived with colonial subjects from throughout the British empire; its intellectual energy appealed to Patterson and convinced him of how little he knew of the world. Among London's radical papers, he was particularly impressed with the British Labour Party's *Daily Herald*, and he visited the offices of its editor, George Lansbury, only a few days after arriving in the city. Talking with Lansbury convinced Patterson that rather than continue on to Liberia, his original destination, he should return to the United States and join the struggle against racism there.[1]

Patterson traveled to New York City, where he took a room Uptown, in the same Striver's Row building as Eslonda Goode (the future wife of Paul Robeson), with whom he would become good friends. After passing the New York bar exam, he took a position in a small, upstart Harlem law firm. But Uptown's political and cultural ferment stoked his nascent radicalism, and he soon began meeting in his office with local radicals, discussing politics, racial oppression, and communism. Among those who gathered there and debated well into the night were longtime Harlem radicals Richard B. Moore, Cyril Valentine Briggs, and Grace Campbell, all of whom were prominent black Communists and former members of the African Blood Brotherhood for African Liberation and Redemption (ABB), a small radical organization established in 1919 that advocated socialism as the solution to racial oppression and colonialism. Moore and Briggs especially challenged Patterson's thinking about racial oppression, and Moore convinced the young lawyer that it was futile "for a Black American to rely solely on U.S. laws . . . as liberating instruments." Briggs gave Patterson a copy of the *Communist Manifesto*; although Patterson had previously read the book, only now did he feel that he could grasp what it was saying. He ultimately joined the Communist Party and rose rapidly within its ranks, gaining the attention of party leaders, who selected him to study in Moscow.

At the KUTV, he met black radicals from throughout the United States and Africa as well as Asian and Indian anticolonial radicals, including the son of Chinese nationalist Chiang Kai-shek and a niece of India's Jawaharlal Nehru. Yet Patterson's mind and political commitment remained on fighting racial oppression and colonialism. He received the opportunity to help outline a program against racial oppression and colonialism when his fellow KUTV students nominated him to go to Frankfurt for the International Congress against Imperialism.[2]

Patterson traveled to Germany with James Ford, the era's most prominent black Communist and an Alabama native. Although they would attend the Frankfurt Congress as observers, they left Moscow "hoping and expecting to speak with as many delegates as possible and, above all, to talk with the Black delegates from Africa and the Americas, North and South," Patterson recalled. Moore had participated in the first International Congress against Imperialism, held two years earlier in Brussels, and had worked with several Francophone African and Caribbean radicals to draft a resolution on the Negro question, an experience he surely related to Patterson and Ford. In Frankfurt, Patterson and Ford found themselves in conversation with a range of diasporic radicals, among them future Kenyan president Johnstone (Jomo)

Kenyatta and Garan Kouyaté, a West African anticolonial activist living in Paris. The meeting marked just the second time that diasporic radicals in the international communist movement had met to discuss their struggles and ways of linking them. Thus, when Ford announced that the First International Conference of Negro Workers would meet the following summer, those present believed, as Patterson put it, that it would be the "gathering of Black men from all parts of the world [that] was necessary if a united anti-imperialist position was to be taken."[3]

The International Conference of Negro Workers convened in Hamburg, Germany, and established the International Trade Union Committee of Negro Workers (ITUCNW). Patterson and Ford worked closely with George Padmore, a young Trinidadian radical active in the Communist Party's Harlem branch, to organize the conference. Padmore quickly assumed leadership of the ITUCNW and from Hamburg directed efforts to organize black maritime workers in Europe, West Africa, and the Caribbean. He also edited the group's journal, *Negro Worker*, and built a network of contacts throughout the African diaspora. The ITUCNW provided the institutional apparatus through which a black international would take shape. Indeed, those involved in the ITUCNW went on to work with others in African national liberation movements, anticolonial organizations, and struggles against racial oppression. Padmore rose to international prominence, building lasting relationships with Kouyaté, Kenyatta, the South African labor organizer and Communist Albert Nzula, and a host of other African, Caribbean, and Indian radicals. After leaving the Comintern in 1933, Padmore and Kouyaté worked on the abortive Negro World Unity Congress, and with Kenyatta and others, Padmore would establish the anticolonial organization, the International African Service Bureau (IASB) in London in 1937.

Patterson's brief account of his route to Frankfurt provides a window onto the history of interwar radical black internationalism that *In the Cause of Freedom* seeks to narrate. This story travels from the heights of 1920s Harlem radicalism to the summit of anticolonial activism and black international organizing in 1930s London, encompassing the ideas, activities, organizations, and networks of the black radicals who made this history. This volume focuses particularly on their thinking about race, colonialism, and class struggle in their pursuit of a worldwide movement centered on pan-African liberation. Early-twentieth-century black radicals were witness to a world that they believed teetered between revolution and repression, self-determination and ever-expanding empires. In the wake of a destructive world war that itself proved the catalyst for the movement of black laborers into cities and industries around the world, the growing crisis over the European colonial presence around the globe, and the rise of socialist and communist alternatives to Western democracy, black radicals sought alternative forms of political activism and began to forge links to other African diasporic radicals. These activists were convinced that whether humanity enjoyed greater freedoms or suffered even harsher colonial regimes hinged on the struggles that peoples of African descent in the United States, Caribbean, and Africa would wage against racism, colonialism, and capitalism and on their ability to link these struggles with similar movements in Asia, Latin America, and Europe. Briggs captured this sentiment in 1920 when he proclaimed simply but profoundly, "The cause of freedom, whether in Asia or Ireland or Africa, is our cause."[4]

This book tells a new kind of story about those radicals who found the Comintern efficacious for building such a movement. Their thinking about race and colonialism led them to embrace organized Marxism and to theorize African and Asian liberation as the driving forces of proletarian revolution.[5] It accords special attention to the nuances of radical internationalism as it emerged both from these activists' immediate circumstances and through an array of transatlantic exchanges that they carried on through pamphlets and periodicals, correspondence, and debates. These exchanges allowed black radicals to build important ties and connections that would reverberate throughout much of the century.

In the Cause of Freedom follows these black radicals on their odyssey in search of a worldwide movement. Beginning with those radicals who established the ABB in 1919 in Harlem, it tracks their role in the rise of an independent black radicalism within the intellectual and political institutions and social interactions of Harlem. Uptown boasted a rich intellectual culture whose study groups, lyceums, intellectual forums, and formal debates constantly brought to the surface questions of race, colonialism, and liberation. A walk down the street in Harlem or a lunch break in a park often brought one within earshot of a speaker who unraveled the relationship between southern lynchings, unsanitary tenement housing, and global conflicts over African colonies. In social clubs, fraternal lodges, beauty salons, and barbershops as well as at local sporting events, people would discuss a dynamic minister's proselytizing about poor southern migrants and Caribbean immigrants or W. E. B. Du Bois's most recent *Crisis* editorial. For those black radicals from the Socialist Party of America who joined black nationalists in creating the ABB, these were the venues where they carried out their intellectual work. This history is essential to any understanding of black radicals in the Communist International. For within these institutions, ABB radicals were already elaborating an internationalist politics that saw struggles in Asia, Latin America, Ireland, and Europe as essential to black liberation and world revolution. But in 1919, when the Comintern declared its support for Asian and African anti-colonial struggle, it became, as historian Hakim Adi notes, "perhaps, the era's sole international white-led movement . . . formally dedicated to a revolutionary transformation of the global political *and* racial order." This position made the Comintern appealing to many black radicals.[6]

Indeed, when the first ABB radicals became Communists, they had not so much joined "the American Party, they had joined the Comintern."[7] Yet this is not a simple matter of the ABB's anti-imperialism leading its members, almost naturally, to the Comintern. A full account of the period leads one to ask, for example, why ABB radicals were initially hesitant about the Bolsheviks. And why, during a nearly three-year run, did the ABB's magazine, the *Crusader*, only mention the Comintern in three of its final five issues? Answers to these questions do not lie in overdrawn debates about Kremlin intrigue, black naïveté, and the antiracism of the American communists that has guided a great deal of the writing on blacks in organized communism.[8]

What has gone largely unremarked in the scholarship on blacks in organized communism is how Asian radicals opened up the Comintern so that it might be seen as a vehicle for pan-African liberation. Almost at its inception, Asian radicals challenged the privileged position that Comintern leaders accorded white workers in socialism, proposing instead that Asian liberation would signal the hour of liberation for European workers. Indeed, black and Asian radicals were engaged in parallel debates about race and nation within Marxism. And black radicals entered the theoretical breach opened by Asian radicals to raise the importance of race in socialist thought. Bringing Asian radicals into a history of early-twentieth-century radical black internationalism alters the standard narrative arc of accounts by allowing black radicals in communist parties in England, France, and the United States a history outside the white Left.[9]

If black radicals plotted their internationalism through the corridors of international communism, organized Marxism represented less the source and more the moment of their politics. With their entrance into the international communist movement, black radicals abandoned their independent organizations and relinquished a great deal of autonomy. They confronted a U.S. Communist Party leadership that repeatedly proved either indifferent to questions of race or openly hostile to black radicals' organizing initiatives and ideas. It is not without irony, then, that U.S. black radicals realized a global network with other black radicals through the Comintern's networks and international meetings, as in Frankfurt. U.S. based blacks radicals would likely not have made these global contacts had they remained outside the U.S. communist movement.[10]

Of those institutions of black internationalism that black radicals created within the Comintern, the most exciting was the ITUCNW. Through his work with this committee, Padmore built an international network of contacts that reached from the British Isles, France, and Holland to the Caribbean and from the coastal ports of West Africa further inland to Cameroon. He maintained this network after 1935, when he moved to London and found a vibrant anti-colonial and antifascist movement that in important ways revolved around the social and political organizing of Amy Ashwood Garvey, Marcus Garvey's first wife. Ashwood's long history of radical political organizing led to her involvement in the West African Students Union and made her a center of black London's social life and intellectual activity. Padmore drew on Ashwood's work with C. L. R. James in the International African Friends of Ethiopia (IAFE) to help establish the IASB. With the IASB, black radicals encountered the limits of engaging organized communism, demonstrating in the process their tendency to judge the value of white leftist formations based on how those formations approached racial oppression and colonialism. Indeed, the bureau had a broad, almost ecumenical political orientation, at times working with black and white Communists in England but overall working far more closely with the Independent Labour Party and British Trotskyists.

These black radicals came from an array of intellectual backgrounds and social movements, including labor movements and intellectual circles in the Caribbean and Africa. But 1930s London boasted a much different black community than was subsequently the case. Although the colonial metropole had long-term black residents, especially those engaged in maritime work, most of the activist-intellectuals were students, writers, itinerant labor organizers, and advocates who came to London to argue before the Privy Council. Unlike black folk in Harlem—both African American and Caribbean—those in London were not preoccupied with questions of citizenship rights, access to public space, the rise of urban ghettos, or the pervasiveness of white racial violence. These were not the black British intellectuals of a later generation but rather were colonial intellectuals concerned with bringing an end to empire and colonial domination. IASB radicals used periodicals largely as organizing and propaganda tools while producing important works on anticolonial liberation, rebellion, and socialist revolution. In this period, James wrote *World Revolution*, his study of the Bolshevik revolution and the decline of the Communist International; his classic study of the Haitian revolution,

The Black Jacobins; his play *Toussaint L'Ouverture*; and the pamphlet, *A History of Negro Revolt*. Padmore penned *How Britain Rules Africa* and *Africa and World Peace*, and Kenyatta wrote *Facing Mount Kenya*. For these radicals plotting an end to empire from within the metropole, the rise of fascism and Italy's invasion of Ethiopia (Abyssinia) in October 1935 showed the vacuity of racialized Western liberal democracy, belying the claim to any differences between Hitler, Mussolini, and the British and French empires. "The fight against fascism," Padmore wrote in 1936, "cannot be separated form the right of all colonial peoples and subject races to Self-Determination."[11]

The ABB and the IASB encapsulate the intellectual and political complexities of interwar radical black internationalism. Although both organizations were short-lived, their respective roles in early-twentieth-century African diasporic politics help limn intellectual and political complexities and provide much of the focus of the story told here—how the motivations, agendas, and structures of radical black internationalism took form within black social movements and then created room in organized Marxism for the emergence of a black international. Black radicals recognized both the immense possibilities in international communism and its extreme limitations. Although contemporaneous movements such as Marcus Garvey's Universal Negro Improvement Association and W. E. B. Du Bois's Pan-African Congresses held out similar possibilities for an international field of struggle, the Comintern offered a structure purportedly able to bring oppressed people in Asia, Africa, Europe, and the United States into a single movement.

As Michael West and William Martin note in their discussion of black internationalism in this period, when the Comintern declared "the Negro Question integral to the world revolution it sought to promote, [it] broke new ground." Indeed, this story continues to get fleshed out in studies that explore how international communism reverberated throughout twentieth-century social movements and national liberation struggles and established its spheres of influence so that it could shape critical aspects of anticolonial thought.[12] This process adds further weight to Robin D. G. Kelley's observation that the American Communist Party "offered African Americans a framework for understanding the roots of poverty and racism, linked local struggles to world politics, and created an atmosphere in which ordinary people could analyze, discuss, and criticize the society in which they lived."[13] Yet the role that the Comintern and its member parties played in black life resulted not simply from their actions but also from the activities of black radicals who pushed international communism beyond its focus on European nations and white workers to address the non-Western world and oppressed racial groups. Black radicals exerted the same influence on socialist and Trotskyist formations linked to the Fourth International, in which James played so integral a role: His activities in 1930s British socialism as they relate to independent black radical politics are only now being told.[14]

In examining what brought black radicals into white Left formations and then what led them out, *In the Cause of Freedom* provides a new understanding of the history of black radicalism. A critical element of this history involved a heretical intellectualism—what political theorist Walter Mignolo calls the colonial fracture in Marxism—that caused a series of ruptures in the earliest encounters between black radicals and organized Marxism. Marx, Mignolo observes, "misses the colonial mechanism of power underlying the system he critiques," and it was this lack that early-twentieth-century black radicals picked up on. In their attention to race and their insistence on the centrality of anticolonial liberation to a socialist future, ABB and IASB radicals "unfold[ed] the colonial matrix of power" both within the capitalist world order, and how within organized Marxism that matrix had created "a fracture in the hegemonic imperial macro-narratives" that continued to center on a modern Europe—in this instance, a European proletariat bringing liberation to Africa and Asia. In plotting a new narrative arc for this history, I explore the limitations of that anticolonial move and black radicals' willingness to move outside international communism and the white Left more generally. Such departures from communist formations—representative of a willingness to pursue black liberation through organized socialism or wholly outside the structures of the white Left—allowed for precisely the international circuits of heretical intellectualism that could connect a small group of Caribbean and African American radicals from 1920s Harlem with Caribbean and African radicals in 1930s London as well as link anticolonial struggles in the Caribbean to those in Africa that would capture the imagination of peoples of color for the next several decades.[15]

The central figure in this story is George Padmore, who followed a path that is particularly revealing about the history of interwar black radicalism. He arrived in the United States from Trinidad in 1924 to study medicine, then gravitated to radical politics and joined the Communist Party, working briefly in Harlem with former ABB radicals on housing issues before moving on to head the Comintern's Negro Bureau in Hamburg. In August 1933, barely a year and a half later, however, Padmore resigned from the Comintern. He eventually relocated to London, where he worked with several former ITUCNW members as well as Amy Ashwood Garvey and C. L. R. James in the IASB. The concern here is not one of filiation. Rather, how did the work of ABB radicals initiate a process by which Padmore could build an international of black workers, thereby laying the foundation for the IASB?

Padmore's political and intellectual journey highlights the complex terrain over which New Negro internationalism traveled. In exploring Padmore, I depart from the periodization of his political biography that seems to issue from the title of his major autohistorical essay, *Pan-Africanism or Communism?* I thereby join a new crop of scholars who do not argue for two Padmores — the Padmore who pushed Comintern policies and the later Padmore who broke with the Comintern to take up pan-Africanist causes. That dichotomy is overdrawn. Padmore grew increasingly critical of communists and much later in life would come to despise "the pretentious claims of doctrinaire Communism, that it alone has the solution to all the complex racial, tribal, and socio-economic problems facing Africa."[16] Yet Padmore left the Comintern because he believed it had abandoned the cause of African liberation from British and French imperialism, a cause he had pursued through the ITUCNW. Rather than marking a turn to pan-Africanism, his break with the Comintern reflected a long-standing concern with pan-African liberation that took on a different valence in his writings but that had informed his activism well before 1933.[17] In other words, Padmore's arguments, proposals, and organizational efforts evidence a greater continuity than has generally been assumed.

When Padmore helped establish the IASB, in a way it continued the intellectual project initiated by the ABB more than a decade earlier. The bureau emerged out of the political milieu of 1930s London, which took on particular force with Italy's 1935 invasion of Ethiopia. C. L. R. James and Amy Ashwood Garvey created the IAFE, which focused on defending Ethiopia but came to have much broader concerns regarding British colonialism and anticolonial struggles in Africa, China, and India.

Problem-Space and the Black Marxist Archive

The ABB and IASB show how organized Marxism provided the institutions through which black radicals in diaspora were able to work with one another as well as with Asian radicals to articulate a vision of linked struggles that altered, if only for a time, the character of the white Left. But this book parts with previous works on blacks and communism that tend to see communist and socialist parties as, on the whole, a necessarily positive force in antiracist and anticolonial struggles. While recognizing that the white Left made valuable contributions to African diasporic struggles, this work brings into focus the contradictions, inherent limitations, and strictures that such formations placed on black radical thought and activity. This work also does not focus on a single national or party context (for example, African Americans in the Communist Party of America), an approach that is structured substantially by the archives on which one draws to tell such stories. Drawing together the ABB and the IASB, Harlem and London, and the various formations and metropolitan nodes in between suggests the possibilities at hand in placing various other metropolitan and colonial points within a single historical frame. Black radical intellectuals never limited themselves to the realms of struggle sanctioned by organized Marxism, regardless of its variant or attraction.

To reorient the story in this way is to assume, in the words of anthropologist David Scott, a different "problem-space" from which to write a history of radical black internationalism. Scott defines a problem-space as the "conceptual-ideological ensembles, discursive formations, or language games that are generative of objects, and therefore of questions." Within such a field or discursive context, specific problems are posed and certain questions are deemed worthy of being asked and answered. Yet one must always remember that over time, "the problem-space in which a question has emerged as a question demanding an answer may have altered, thereby altering the critical . . . status of the question—leaving it recognizably coherent but largely academic."[18] The question of Russian control versus American communist autonomy that has dominated much of the work on blacks and communism is now largely academic; to the extent that it still provides a logic for ordering histories of the Left, it forecloses attention to what early-twentieth-century black radical activism and thought suggests about a new way for conceiving of the future.[19]

The problem-space from which one writes, the questions one asks, and the mode in which one casts the narrative that answers those questions performs a dual task of opening an archive of inquiry and enacting a historical silence. Anthropologist Michel-Rolph Trouillot sees these processes as simultaneous and inherent in one another, and he therefore implores historians to recognize the silencing that occurs as part of any historical narrative, a process spanning fact creation (sources), assembly (archives), retrieval (narratives), and the "moment of retrospective significance (the making of *history*)."[20] According to Trouillot, any event "enters history with some of its constituting parts missing. Something is always left out while something else is recorded." As a result, "there is no perfect closure of any event. . . . Thus whatever becomes fact does so with its own inborn absences, specific to its production."[21]

If any narrative, in the process of opening up an archive of inquiry, necessarily silences a part of its past, then the writing of a history involves a set of choices about what to include and what to leave out, decisions that at times depend on the sources available to "the making of history." However inevitable silences may be, as Trouillot's discussion of a little-known Haitian revolutionary, Colonel Jean-Baptist Sans Souci, reveals, the histories that one silences are not always left out in order to judiciously tell a story. Rather than reflecting literary economy, silences often reflect value judgments and power relationships that inhere in the creation of sources and the structures of archival holdings as well as the problem-space one assumes in determining what questions should be asked and answered.

In the Cause of Freedom breaks from the narrative archive that has guided much of the writing on black radicalism, although many other authors are already narrating this history in new ways.[22] I propose charting a narrative arc that stretches beyond what I want to call the "archive of black Marxism" — that conceptual-ideological ensemble of concerns and questions that sets the range of arguments and conclusions deemed acceptable about black radicalism. While source materials from which to write such stories have serious historical limitations, of greater import has been the "retrospective significance" assumed when ordering those sources to construct a narrative. As Trouillot explains with regard to his approach to Sans Souci's story, the "evidence required to tell" the story of black radicals in organized Marxism from 1920s Harlem to 1930s London "was available in the corpus I studied, in spite of the poverty of the sources." To be sure, I have benefited from newly available sources, but this book equally reflects a process of repositioning evidence "to generate a new narrative" and a refusal to follow the narrative arc dictated by the prevailing archival grain.[23]

In the Cause of Freedom deploys diaspora as an analytic to rescue radical black internationalism from the narrative sutures of international communism. The volume opens up room in which to analyze black radicalism as issuing from the colonial fracture in Western radical thought, an outgrowth of the questions and concerns that preoccupied black activist-intellectuals in the New Negro movement that pushes us beyond the confines of the Harlem Renaissance. The New Negro movement frame suggests a new range of questions and possible answers if the frame is broadened to include not merely Harlem and London or Harlem and Paris but also Chicago and Paris, Lagos and Hamburg, Liverpool and Marseilles, Cardiff and Accra, Port-au-Prince and Dakar, and Port-of-Spain, Georgetown, and Bridgetown.

Black Heretics

In retelling this story without taking organized Marxism as the principal or originary frame, it is important not to negate that encounter, not to silence the discourses that grew up in the interstices of black radicals' engagement with Marxist assumptions and terms of analysis. When ABB and IASB radicals extended or innovated on Marxism to discuss Africa, Asia, colonialism, and racial oppression, they were pursuing precisely what the Martinican Aimé Césaire subsequently imagined as an African communism that might "shade or complete a good many of the doctrine's[Marxism's] points."[24] The distinction between Marxist theory and organized Marxism may be too fine, and I do not want to imply that there is a "true" Marxism easily distinguished from the "corrupted" versions articulated by socialist or communist parties. Marxism's currency is the ability of activist-intellectuals to theorize it in a given time beyond its initial elaborations and points of analysis, its refusal to remain static and unchanged and thus easily identified in sacred texts by Marx and Lenin.

But in discussing the various modes of black intellectual production, political theorist Anthony Bogues offers the especially useful notion of the black heretic. Bogues defines the black heretic as one who "engages in a double operation—an engagement with Western radical theory and then a critique of this theory."[25] While I find this notion useful for thinking about how black radicals developed a politics out of Marxism's colonial fracture, I remain somewhat hesitant about the disjuncture Bogues suggests between the black radical intellectual and Western radical thought. Mignolo echoes this disjuncture; more important, however, it resonates with Cedric Robinson's argument in *Black Marxism*. Bogues allows for a critical engagement between black radicals and Western radicalism, but Robinson, writing in the early 1980s against the prevailing trend that saw black radicalism as an outgrowth of Western radicalism, does not. Instead, he sees black radicalism as issuing from a long historical process of black self-activity and the institutions and developments in black communities that gave rise to it. Therefore, black radicalism must be understood not as "a variant of Western radicalism whose proponents happen to be Black," but as a "specifically African response to an oppression emergent from the immediate determinants of European development in the modern era and framed by orders of human exploitation woven into the interstices of European social life from the inception of Western civilization."[26] One of those "immediate determinants" Robinson identifies in Western civilization is racialism, "the legitimation and corroboration of social organization as natural by reference to the 'racial' components of its elements." Racialism existed elsewhere in the world, but its codification "into Western conceptions of society was to have important and enduring consequences."[27] Building on the work of Oliver Cox, especially *Capitalism as a System*, Robinson locates the emergence of racialism in the initial orderings of the West, which in turn structured "the relations of European to non-European peoples" that "permeate[d] the social structures emergent from capitalism." Part of Cox's project entailed challenging Marx's labor theory of value; Cox situated the rise of capitalism several centuries earlier than did Marx, in the Venetian maritime trading empire. The source of value under capitalism was thus exchange rather than labor exploitation.[28]

Instead of exploring this point in Cox's work, Robinson summons a wealth of scholarship on the Venetian empire to sustain his claim that racialism informed all aspects of European life in its earliest iterations. It would have therefore been "exceedingly difficult and most unlikely," Robinson maintains, "that such a civilization in its ascendancy . . . would produce a tradition of self-examination [Marxism] sufficiently critical to expose its most profound terms of order"—racialism.[29] Robinson argues that because Marx developed historical materialism through an analysis of European societies, its "analytical presumptions, its historical perspectives, its points of view" were equally informed by racialism.[30] He thus offers black radicalism as an African cosmological worldview, a negation of Western civilization that twentieth-century black activist-intellectuals who operated in the orbit of organized Marxism did not develop but rather discovered after breaking with Marxism, finding radicalism "first in their history, and finally all around them."[31]

Robinson's work has informed how a new generation of scholars thinks about black radicalism, though they have gone on to treat with greater nuance and insight the lives, ideas, and intellectual production of black radicals.[32] But his central claim that black radicalism and Marxism are incongruent and that the former is an epistemic negation of Western civilization and thus a critique of the latter is difficult to follow.[33] His detailed biographies of W. E. B. Du Bois, Richard Wright, and C. L. R. James conclude that all three men critiqued Marxism, which led them to "a radical Black consciousness" and to "their eventual encounter with the Black radical tradition." Yet Du Bois and James, at least, never rejected Marxism; James saw himself extending its contours and analyses—an intellectual biography mirroring that of African diasporic activist-intellectuals such as Amílcar Cabral, Claudia Jones, Louise Thompson Patterson, Aimé Césaire, and Frantz Fanon.[34]

Whether Venice was a racialized society that exported racialism to the rest of Europe is doubtful. What seems more important, however, is Robinson's conception of racialism as an idea that renders race an eternal feature of European social life—an idea always present—rather than specific social relationships whose determinants grew out of specific historical contexts and were thus constitutive of the very structures of modernity.[35] But if Marx, Engels, and Lenin were unwilling or unable to address racial oppression and racial ideologies (or coloniality), and if this lack contributed to a Eurocentric diffusionist strain of Marxism, African diasporic, Asian, and Latin American radicals approached that very lack as an opening in which they could perform what Fanon called a stretching of "Marxist analysis . . . every time we have to do with the colonial problem."[36]

Robinson's point that black Marxism and black radicalism are not synonymous raises important questions about how we think about both. While I would agree that we must avoid seeing the two as essentially identical, they are not necessarily incongruent. Consequently, I would not employ Robinson's notion of black radicalism as a negation of Western civilization that issues from the long train of black self-activity extending back to the fifteenth century. Robinson overextends C. L. R. James's discussion of the revolutionary character of black struggles and assigns it a specific quality, a definite politics. This approach renders Robinson's conception of black radicalism so broad as to lose theoretical coherence and analytical value. James never claimed a particular political character for black liberation movements, only their ability to crystallize the particular historical form of struggle in a particular racialized society. James insisted on a historicity to studying black liberation struggles that is absent from Robinson.[37] We must treat black radicalism as something that took shape over time, changed at varying moments, and addressed different concerns in different societies. Black radicalism did not assume a permanent form once for all time with the first racialized encounters between Africans and Europeans—the rise of Africa and Europe itself was a process rather than an event. By attending to how black radicalism looks in one moment and how that picture differs from other moments and by focusing on its historical, intellectual, and political influences, we can provide critical insight into what Robinson calls the "black radical tradition" by highlighting how black radicals have always been concerned with particular historical realities.

During a 1956 radio address, Moore, a former ABB radical, offered an instructive view of black radicalism: When "radical" qualified politics, it signaled a project that "proposes basic change in the economic, social, and political order." A radical is always historically contingent, Moore argued. For example, he offered, "a 'radical' in relation to chattel slavery . . . was one who advocated [the] abolition of the system of chattel slavery and its replacement by another system such as the free wage labor system. In respect to the system of capitalism," the emphasis shifts, and "a 'radical' is one who advocates the replacement of the capitalist system by a socialist order of society."[38] Moore spoke against a Cold War understanding of radicalism as "a horrible and violent extremism" that threatened "everything good and decent in human life." Moore's lecture expressed the views of a socialist equally committed to ending racial oppression and labor exploitation. Although New Negro radicals included more than just black socialists, communists, and anarchists, Moore's comments provide a sense of how those in the New Negro movement who considered themselves radicals understood what was distinct about their politics.

The approach taken here builds on Moore to treat those who considered restructuring the dominant political economy a central feature of ending racial oppression and considered some form of socialist economic organization essential to racial liberation and national self-determination for colonial Africa and Asia. The list of radicals with such beliefs would probably be far greater than Moore or other former ABB radicals would likely allow, especially when one includes the scores of black workers, farmers, and community members whose lives, actions, and cultural practices created the topsoil out of which intellectuals articulated a radical politics.

In his address, Moore went on to discuss the means by which New Negro movement activist-intellectuals arrived at a radical politics: public lectures by black Socialists such as Helen Holman and Hubert H. Harrison; the work of independent black political organizations; study groups that read such Marxist works as the *Communist Manifesto* and *Socialism Utopian and Scientific*; formal lectures and debates on an array of topics; repeated encounters with—and rejections of—white radicals' doctrinaire views of Marxism focused solely on industrial workers; a black radical print culture; organizing among black workers and community members in Harlem and Chicago; and in response to the repressive Cold War policies of the 1940s and 1950s. This view gives attention to the relationship that black radicals believed they had with organized Marxist groups and how those radicals differentiated between the programs those groups put forward and the theory that they claimed to represent.

Diaspora and the Localities of Race

This books looks largely at Caribbean radicals who entered the U.S. communist movement, were active in the Comintern, and ultimately left organized communism to pursue an anticolonial politics in London. Such a focus neither makes a claim for Caribbeans' supervening radicalism with regard to African Americans or Africans nor suggests Caribbeans' determining influence on and shaping of radical black political culture in the United States or Europe. Indeed, I would take issue with any notion of Caribbean prominence or preeminence in either U.S. or international black radical discourses. One can easily point to African American radicalism before the New Negro movement, outside those metropolitan areas that received large waves of Caribbean immigrants in the 1910s and 1920s, and among black workers in places such as Chicago, Milwaukee, Liverpool, Gambia, the Gold Coast, Cleveland, Baltimore, Birmingham, Oklahoma, Bogalusa, Hamburg, Rotterdam, and Elaine, Arkansas who lacked the time and possibly the inclination to put their ideas on paper but whose activism nonetheless produced a rich black radical political and intellectual tradition.[39] Caribbeans' centrality in the story told here stems from my desire to chart the ties between 1920s Harlem and 1930 London. Caribbean radicals in Harlem who came into the international communist movement are central to this narrative.

While for the Comintern race existed only within the precincts of the Negro, black radicals constantly stretched the insights on race gained from black struggles in the Caribbean and United States to see race in Asia, India, and South America as a component part of colonialism. White radicals considered American and West Indian Negroes the most advanced by virtue of their location at the center of the American empire—saw them as modern Negroes possessed of the intellect, ability, and class-consciousness necessary to lead their "backward" African kin. Black radicals, in contrast, came to challenge the idea that they were a vanguard who should lead in redeeming Africa and the race. ABB radicals thus pushed the boundaries of thinking about race within the Comintern, articulating a notion of global black liberation that resisted any simple conception of black unity. And those efforts led to the formation of the American Negro Labor Congress, proposals for a World Negro Congress, and ultimately the meetings that led to the formation of the ITUCNW, all of which sought to bring black radicals in the United States, England, France, Germany, and the Francophone and Anglophone colonial world into an international organization under the auspices of the Communist International. In other words, the intellectual work that those (largely Caribbean) black radicals in the United States carried on within the Comintern helped create the context for the series of interactions and exchanges through international communism that allowed Padmore to create a network that could give rise to such a dynamic organization as the IASB.

This narrative looks at how black radicals developed a diasporic identity and politics out of their experiences with race, class, gender, and color in distinct historical contexts. One aspect of this broad question is how these experiences informed black radicals' involvement in organized Marxism and their entrance into the organized Left in general; another is how such experiences factored into their disillusionment with and eventual abandonment of those same institutions. If diaspora represents a transnational formation, a condition and an ongoing process, and a project that must actively be pursued across the multiple structures of race, class, gender, and color, we are inevitably led to ask how those multiple realities were understood and experienced. How did black radicals make sense of the similarities and dissimilarities between diasporic populations? In what ways did they respond to the persistent "failure to translate even a basic grammar of blackness?"[40] The localities of race are central here, for race reveals the local as a series of historical processes and power relationships that allows for discordant vernaculars of blackness that structure diaspora as hierarchies as much as a transnational mode of affinity and unity. Part of my concern, to borrow from anthropologist Jacqueline Nassy Brown's discussion of black Liverpool, is how a radical black internationalism emerged out of the complex interplay of the "geopolitics of diverse Black histories, experiences and constructions of race and identity." In other words, how was reconciling the diverse histories of racialization generative of a radical politics?[41]

ABB radicals were themselves products of diaspora. Largely African Caribbeans, many had fair complexions that rendered them racially mulatto or colored in their home countries. But in the United States, they experienced what historian Winston James calls "racial downgrading," a process whereby they became black and existed within a racial discourse of blackness that harbored little room for differentiations of complexion, nationality, or ethnicity.[42] Drawing on their experience of race in two societies, with dissonant racial formations and varying dominant forms of social control, these radicals stressed the political character of race; they described it as a power relationship that both was affected by and informed processes of capital, labor organization, and national citizenship. Color differences among African diasporic populations were salient to how race was structured in each society. In their journalism, public debates, and discussions of race, human evolution, and culture, U.S.-based black radicals contemplated the challenges that color differences presented to pan-African liberation, especially as it suggested multiple national histories of race. The ABB stressed that race, class, nationality, and color marked critical points of difference, what we can call the fault lines of diaspora, points of difference that, if unacknowledged, have the potential to obscure how diasporas get structured as hierarchies equally available to oppressive political projects and liberatory ones. ABB radicals' efforts to unify African-descended populations entailed outlining a politics that could move between divergent idioms of race, between the dissimilar vernaculars of blackness that existed in the Caribbean, the United States, and Africa.[43]

One solution rested in a political notion of blackness where the ties between peoples racialized as black were historical, economic, and political rather than biological. Cyril Briggs, W. A. Domingo, and other ABB radicals stressed that African peoples living in diverse racial formations occupied similarly subordinate positions in the racial hierarchy. Although intended to identify a political basis for racial unity in a common liberation struggle, this orientation nonetheless tended to elide those differences that made such unity elusive. For an earlier generation of black intellectuals (and many of the ABB's contemporaries) concerned with the destiny of the race, racial unity and uplift dovetailed with civilizationist appeals to reclaim Africa and redeem "her" in order to create "a better manhood" for the race.[44] To be sure, radicals in the African Blood Brotherhood for African Liberation and *Redemption* were hardly immune to such notions. Yet their calls for racial unity always confronted the potential for such unity to replicate the structures of capital and empire.

ABB radicals grappled with this dilemma in contemplating the relationship between Africans of the dispersion, to use their phrase, and Africans on the continent, racialized political groups whose struggles, while tied to one another, were not identical. In fact, interactions among diasporic groups were often rife with conflict and betrayed intradiasporic tension and hierarchies.[45] In time, the ABB came to resist the tendency to ignore differences while also resisting hierarchies, especially the idea that the modernity of New World Negroes made them the natural leaders of Africans. At crucial moments and in important ways, these activist-intellectuals resisted what historian Arif Dirlik argues is a tendency in diasporic projects to erase the social relations that create difference and hierarchies within a diaspora.[46] ABB radicals instead insisted that African-descended populations struggle against capitalism, imperialism, and racial oppression where they were located in accordance with particular on-the-ground conditions.

In London and other colonial metropoles, interactions between Caribbeans and Africans raised similar questions about any singular notion of blackness on which to hinge diasporic political projects. In radical political circles, debates and conflicts routinely erupted between Caribbeans, who considered themselves more educated and thus more modern than Africans, and Africans, who often accused Caribbeans of mimicking whites. In Paris, these conflicts ultimately splintered several black radical formations.[47] In London, as I will show, those conflicts were generative for such figures as C. L. R. James, who drew on the discourses of race in that small diasporic community to reconceptualize pan-African liberation and black radical identity as centered on African liberation struggles, not on the modernity or fitness of New World blacks for self-government.

By delimiting the scope of diasporic struggle, black radicals in Harlem and London recognized the dissimilarities between diverse colonial contexts and racial oppression and understood that movements designed to address one did not neatly address the other. As literary scholar Rajagopalan Radhakrishnan observes, no theoretical calculus exists where "the different politics of ethnicity, sexuality, class, gender, and nationality add up into one unifiable political horizon."[48] Radical notions of racial unity entailed remaining alert to how the differences making up diaspora simultaneously marked its limits. But these radicals also saw African diasporic struggles as linked to one another and considered anticolonial struggles in Asia, the Pacific islands, South America, and Europe as well as working-class movements against capital important to African diasporic liberation. Radicals believed that the movements, though not identical, were intertwined and were important to one another's success.

Outline

Chapters 1 and 2 explore how black radicals understood the relationship between diverse groups in the African diaspora through their attention to race and how their intellectual labor on these questions occurred within black cultural and political institutions and social interactions in Harlem, leading to a better understanding of how such labor led these radicals to Marxism. Moreover, under V. I. Lenin, the Comintern took an explicit anti-imperialist stance supporting African and Asian liberation that appealed to Asian radicals as well. As chapter 3 demonstrates, black radicals saw their participation in the Comintern as an opportunity to join an international struggle of all oppressed races for socialism. While for the Comintern race applied only to the Negro, black radicals saw race as a component of colonialism. At the Comintern's Fourth Congress in 1922, ABB and Communist Party members Otto Huiswoud and Claude McKay met with Asian radicals and augmented their discussion of national liberation by insisting on the importance of race to socialist revolution. Within the space of Comintern policy debates, Huiswoud and McKay established links to Asian radicals and other black radicals from around the world. Rather than serving as apparatchiks, they worked to shape international communism, especially on questions of racial and national oppression.

Chapter 4 follows the aftermath of the Second Comintern Congress, especially the failed organizing attempts led by black radicals now operating solely within the Workers (Communist) Party. The chapter also examines how the strictures of organized communism ironically allowed black radicals greater opportunities than did existing black organizations for building the kinds of international linkages they had long desired. At the Fifth Comintern Congress, held in 1925, former ABB radical Lovett Fort-Whiteman met Guadeloupean lawyer Joseph Gothon-Lunion, a member of the Parti Communiste Français (French Communist Party), and the two discussed the possibility of coordinating their efforts in the United States, France, and elsewhere in the diaspora. At each Comintern Congress, black radicals trod a delicate path between exhibiting a commitment to proletarian class struggle and challenging the Comintern to see the Negro question beyond the particularities of the United States and to approach race as a global question.

Chapter 5 tracks how the encounters between U.S. black radicals and radicals overseas opened up modes of exchange that both shifted the organizational focus from the United States to Europe and began to move some key black Communists away from the Comintern as others became more ensconced. At the International Conferences against Imperialism, held in 1927 and 1929, radicals found much-needed room to outline a politics whereby a radical internationalism could assume institutional form.

Chapter 6 shows how Comintern institutions provided diasporic radicals with opportunities to organize a black international. Those opportunities initially resulted in the International Trade Union Committee of Negro Workers, the organization that propelled Padmore onto the world stage. Chapter 7 follows Padmore out of the ITUCNW to London, where he worked briefly in the International African Friends of Ethiopia and later replaced it with the IASB, whose focus broadened to include fascism, colonialism, trade union organizing, and the importance of a Marxist notion of class struggle that would situate Africans at the center of world revolution. This discussion situates the

IASB within the political moment of 1930s London, which included a growing antifascist movement and a relatively strong British socialist movement that is especially important to any understanding of C. L. R. James. Yet as with Harlem, the politics enunciated by IASB radicals, especially James, owed a great deal to London's uniquely diasporic black population. While James and many other Caribbeans in the imperial metropole insisted on their modernity and fitness for self-governance, some, including James, began to question the value of that modernity.

Straight Socialism or Negro-ology?

Diaspora, Harlem, and the Institutions of Black Radicalism

By the second decade of the twentieth century, one did not have to walk far in Harlem to find black Socialists among the scores of activist-intellectuals who transformed the neighborhood's street corners into public lecterns from which to put forward their political programs. Alongside the nationalists, religious proselytizers, social reformers, and self-anointed race seers, black Socialists had a reputation as skilled orators with keen intellects who were just as willing to debate passersby as other activists. Harlem streets provided a relentlessly democratic public forum in which residents could engage a wide range of ideas and organizations. And the ideas one put forth were rivaled in importance only by one's facility with the spoken word, a would-be leader's political value measured in large part by his or her ability to bring into relief the circumstances of black people's racial subordination. At the dawn of the Great Migration, such concerns were especially acute for black southerners who now enjoyed the freedoms offered by the urban North yet nevertheless recognized the all-too-familiar limitations, proscriptions, and social norms that subordinated blacks to whites. Tellingly, when black Socialists prepared for their public meetings, they routinely asked one another, "What shall we expound tonight, straight Socialism or Negro-ology?"[1]

The dilemma seemed false for black Socialists frustrated by the white Left's tendency either to treat race as a facade masking the more fundamental class struggle or to claim that as workers, black people's liberation would issue seamlessly from socialist revolution. Black Socialists realized that both claims freed white Socialists from thinking deeply about race or the difficulties of organizing black people alongside white workers. Black radicals had long rejected these views. Peter H. Clark, a Reconstruction-era educator and one of the first black Socialists in the United States, took the failure to address racial oppression as evidence that that "the welfare of the Negro" was not among late-nineteenth-century Socialists' guiding concerns. At the founding convention of the Socialist Party of America (SPA) in 1901, three black coal miners, William Costley, John Adams, and Edward McKay, presented a resolution on the "Negro Problem" that demanded equal rights, including the franchise, and condemned lynching: The resolution was adopted only after all references to lynching and the right to vote had been removed. Two years later, the iconic Eugene V. Debs, who opposed segregated unions and had refused to address segregated southern audiences, implored the SPA to "repeal [its] resolutions on the negro question." Since black people were workers, he wrote, their oppression would end with socialism. Thus, the SPA had no need for special resolutions on race or any other question and had "nothing special to offer the negro."[2]

The African American and Caribbean radicals drawn into the SPA in the 1910s believed, like those before them, that Marxism best explained social inequality and racial and national oppression and helped them make sense of the U.S. South, the vagaries of the urban North, and social and political life in the Caribbean islands. Yet these radicals rejected any suggestion that class and race were theoretically incongruent terms or that class so thoroughly explained every other social ill that race was rendered a mere distraction. They understood that such class conceit diminished the importance of race by ignoring racism, which led to a refusal to organize black people as a racial group and to a general indifference toward black Socialists' initiatives. If black radicals desired an integrated approach to race and class that did not yet exist, they would have to develop it themselves.

The politics of Caribbean radicals setting up street-corner platforms grew out of a complex history of race and intellectual and political engagements of which socialism was merely a part. Harlem's intellectual ferment — its political organizations, periodicals, debates, and intellectual forums — provided the spaces in which Caribbean immigrants could work out their ideas about race, colonialism, class, and the place of African and Asian liberation in proletarian revolution. These radicals' thinking about the global character of race, the imbricated structures of white supremacy and empire, and the relations of different African diasporic populations in pan-African struggle grew from personal experiences with race and colonialism in the Caribbean, which they believed gave them a unique perspective on American empire. Indeed, their thinking about these issues preceded their entrance into organized Marxist groups, and their conclusions outstripped the thinking of white leftists. The articulation of a black radical politics that reconciled the dichotomy between "straight Socialism or Negro-ology" occurred largely independent of the SPA's institutions and initiatives, though it was hardly inconsequential to such an elaboration. Rather, they carried on such intellectual work in their own institutions and through their own political projects; at critical junctures, they did so in conversation with Asian radicals who had similar concerns that rested beyond the boundary of white radical thought. Possibly most important for Caribbean radicals, though few scholars have given the subject much attention, is the fact that their radicalism arose from their attempts to reconcile their experiences with the racial logics and systems of the Caribbean with a much different U.S. racial hierarchy, especially as it was experienced in Harlem's unique diasporic community.

Race, Difference, and Diasporic Harlem

By the 1920s, the Harlem section of Manhattan grew into one of the most vibrant black communities in the world, leading contemporaries to dub it the Mecca of the New Negro. By 1900, Caribbeans began immigrating to New York, settling primarily in Manhattan and Brooklyn and ultimately comprising the largest group of foreign-born blacks in Manhattan. While in 1900 only 5,000 of the 60,000 black people in New York had been born outside the United States, that number grew rapidly over the next two decades. By 1910, nearly two-thirds of the 40,339 foreign-born blacks in the United States were Caribbeans, and most lived in Manhattan. In 1920, the percentage of Caribbean-born blacks in the city peaked at 33 percent before dropping to 16.7 percent ten years later.[3] Caribbean immigrants had been drawn by the labor demands of U.S. industries during World War I, but the implementation of immigration restrictions in 1924 slowed the flow considerably. By that time, however, Harlem had transformed from simply an African American community into an African diasporic community that confronted a myriad of problems and conflicts but that also offered tremendous hope and possibility. Langston Hughes's reflections on his early days in Harlem capture this complex tapestry:

Harlem—Southern Harlem—the Carolinas, Georgia, Florida—looking for the Promised Land—dressed in rhythmic words, painted in bright pictures, dancing to jazz—and ending up in the subway morning rush time—*headed downtown*. West Indian Harlem—warm rambunctious sassy remembering Marcus Garvey. Haitian Harlem, Cuban Harlem, little pockets of tropical dreams in alien tongues. Magnet Harlem, pulling an Arthur Schomburg from Puerto Rico, pulling an Arna Bontemps all the way from California, a Nora Holt from way out West, and E. Simms Campbell from St. Louis, likewise a Josephine Baker, a Charles S. Johnson from Virginia, an A. Philip Randolph from Florida, a Roy Wilkins from Minnesota, an Alta Douglas from Kansas. Melting pot Harlem— Harlem of honey and chocolate and caramel and rum and vinegar and lemon and lime and gall.[4]

Claude McKay wrote in equally moving prose, though a bit more soberly in describing his return to the New Negro Mecca after more than a year in London, where his literary interests began to merge with radical politics:

Ellis Island: doctors peered in my eyes, officials scrutinized my passport, and the gates were thrown open. . . . The elevated swung me up to Harlem. At first I felt a little fear and trembling, like a stray hound scenting out new territory. But soon I was stirred by familiar voices and the shapes of houses and saloons, and I was inflated with confidence. A wave of thrills flooded the arteries of my being, and I felt as if I had undergone initiation as a member of my tribe. And I was happy. Yet, it was a rare sensation again to be just one black among many. It was good to be lost in the shadows of Harlem again. . . . Spareribs and corn pone, fried chicken and corn fritters and sweet potatoes were like honey to my palate.

McKay found his way back to old haunts and explored new places, including Sanina's, a 7th Avenue speakeasy he remembered "always humming like a beehive with brown butterflies and flames of all ages from the West Indies and from the South."[5]

But while many young male intellectuals and artists were excited about Harlem and took comfort in the security provided by living in such a large enclave of black people, the experiences of African American migrants and Caribbean immigrants in Harlem could be trying. Racial and class dynamics Uptown were complex, often revealing internal conflicts that strained the ties binding its diverse peoples. Caribbeans created numerous organizations and social institutions that not only helped them adjust to the United States but also helped them sustain their national identities and demarcate themselves from African Americans. Class differences between the two groups exacerbated national differences. Early-twentieth-century Caribbean immigrants usually worked various jobs until they could secure work commensurate with their skills. Between 1911 and 1924, when African American migrants from the South worked primarily as unskilled laborers, approximately 14 percent of African Caribbeans held professional or white-collar jobs, while 55 percent worked as skilled laborers; only 31 percent worked as unskilled laborers.[6]

Caribbeans also had to adjust to race in America, as many who had light complexions and thus occupied an intermediary social position between blacks and whites in the Caribbean became undeniably black in the United States. And as Winston James argues, the experience of racial downgrading along with occasionally working menial jobs combined to radicalize many African Caribbean immigrant intellectuals.[7] As historian Ula Taylor explains, for example, Amy Jacques, who became Marcus Garvey's second wife, arrived in the United States and encountered racism, white supremacist organizations growing in popularity, and race riots, leading her to join the Universal Negro Improvement Association. Her decision constituted a clear indication "that she had by then relinquished some of her culturally *colored* attitude and embraced her 'blackness' in a new way."[8] According to racial identity theorists, such encounters disrupt people's sense of the salience of race in the world, potentially leading to a reevaluation of their racial identity, or how they make sense of their racial group classification. Each person resolves such encounters in a unique way, although the process never follows a simple linear path and does not necessarily result in a black identity.[9]

For many Caribbean activist-intellectuals, however, their response to such encounters was part of a larger effort to mitigate the impact of national and class differences. They had to reconcile their most basic understanding of race in the Caribbean with the reality of the U.S. racial formation. And one could hardly have grown up in the Caribbean without confronting the complexities of race.

C. L. R. James's well-known discussion of his choice of cricket clubs in Trinidad demonstrates both the importance and the particularity of race in the Caribbean. Around 1920, James, a dark-skinned but middle-class Trinidadian, had to choose whether to play for "Maple, the club of the brown-skinned middle class," for which "class did not matter so much . . . as colour";

for the much better Shannon club, "the club of the black lower-middle class"; or for the Stingo club. Maple did not welcome dark-complexioned players regardless of their class, but James had gone to school with and knew well many of the club's players, so it was an option in his case. He easily dismissed the idea of playing for Stingo, which was "too low." Its members "were plebeians: the butcher, the tailor, the candlestick maker, the casual labourer, with a sprinkling of unemployed. Totally black and no social status whatsoever." The choice between Maple and Shannon, however, was agonizing. Ultimately, despite the appeal of playing "the brilliant cricket Shannon played," he joined Maple. The incident clearly demonstrates the salience of race in the Caribbean: Socially, James "was not bothered by my dark skin and had friends everywhere"; however, "the principle on which the Maple Club was founded . . . stuck in my throat." Grant Farred considers James's decision to join Maple a reflection of his social distance from those who formed Shannon. Moreover, James later recognized that his choice "delayed my political development for years. But no one could see that then, least of all me." All the implications for a radical politics to which James would later dedicate his life inhered in that racial decision.[10]

Scholarly claims that race was less salient in the Caribbean than in the United States often overlook how race was (and is) understood in the islands. What in the United States are coded as color differences within a black/white binary may in the Caribbean be understood along a continuum of racial distinctions. Writing in the early 1930s, just before leaving Trinidad for England, James explained the complex nature of race in the Caribbean:

The Negroid population of the West Indies is composed of a large percentage of actually black people and about fifteen or twenty per cent of people who are a varying combination of white and black. . . . There are the nearly white hanging on tooth and nail to the fringes of white society, and these, as is easy to understand, hate contact with the darker skin far more than some of the broader-minded whites. Then there are the browns, intermediates, who cannot by any stretch of imagination pass as white, but who will not go one inch towards mixing with people darker than themselves. . . . Associations are formed of brown people who will not admit into their number those too much darker than themselves, and there have been heated arguments in committee as to whether such and such a person's skin was fair enough to allow him or her to be admitted without lowering the tone of the institution. . . . Should the darker man, however, have money or position of some kind, he may aspire, and it is not too much to say that in a West Indian colony the surest sign of a man having arrived is the fact that he keeps company with people lighter in complexion than himself.[11]

African Americans made similar color distinctions, but they generally lacked the institutional and juridical armature necessary to elevate them to a racial distinction. Many Caribbean immigrants whose racially privileged position no longer obtained in the United States had to rethink themselves racially and adjust to a racial system that cast them as undeniably black. Racial downgrading entailed adjusting to a different register of blackness, being black in a new way, or being undeniably black for the first time.[12]

James's contemplation of the political implications of his cricket decision involved his racial position as mediated by his class mobility. As a black Trinidadian, the racial politics of middle-class life struck James in a particular way. And though he downplayed the importance of race in his life, the fact that this episode plunged James "into a social and moral crisis which had a profound effect on [his] whole future life" suggests that race in the Caribbean had a far greater impact than much of the social science research might suggest.[13]

Few of Harlem's black radicals in the mid-1910s left such rich and revealing accounts of their lives in the Caribbean. Also, most of those discussed in this book immigrated to the United States in their teen years, while James remained in Trinidad until he was past thirty. We therefore have relatively little information on how those radicals who were considered colored in the West Indies might have come to understand race in the Caribbean and on their adjustment to the United States and its radically different racial grammar. But one indication of their rejection of Caribbean racial mores is found in their response to the salience of national and color differences in Harlem. Black radicals gathered around the Socialist Party probed the complexities of race and confronted racial differences among Caribbeans that affected both social life and politics in Harlem.

Otto Huiswoud, Richard B. Moore, and Cyril Briggs were among the most important of these radicals. Huiswoud was born in 1893 in Paramaribo, Dutch Guiana (present-day Suriname). Huiswoud's father apprenticed the boy to a printer at a young age; during his apprenticeship, he developed an interest in books and began dreaming of traveling to Amsterdam. At sixteen, Huiswoud convinced his father to let him work as a seaman on a ship set to sail for the Netherlands. However, the ship's captain soon proved tyrannical, and after the vessel left port, he gave no indication that they would ever reach Amsterdam. On January 17, 1910, the ship docked in Brooklyn, and Huiswoud and two Surinamese shipmates walked across the Williamsburg Bridge into Lower Manhattan, where they quickly found lodging. Huiswoud found work as a printer and met and became friends with Socialist organizers. He also began taking classes at the Rand School for Social Science, where he met the Japanese Socialist Sen Katayama. Conversations with Katayama helped Huiswoud developed a sense of the importance of socialism for workers as well as anticolonial struggles in the Caribbean and antiracist struggles in the United States.[14]

Though Huiswoud's father had been born a slave, he possessed a fair complexion, which suggests that his mother was a colored woman. Huiswoud enjoyed a certain social mobility in his home country, but soon after arriving in the United States, he suffered a series of slights and other experiences with racial discrimination that would inform his later radical politics. According to Joyce Moore Turner, "he was barred from becoming an accredited printer because the union did not accept African Americans in the trade. When he lost his job in the printing house he was forced to work in a variety of menial temporary jobs."[15] Seeking to improve his English in hopes of expanding his employment options, Huiswoud began spending his lunch hours listening to public lectures at Madison Square Park and Union Square. Those lectures, his reading regimen, classes at Rand, and his conversations with Katayama ultimately led Huiswoud to join the SPA in 1916.[16]

Richard B. Moore was born in Barbados in 1893 and arrived in New York in 1909. Moore's family was solidly middle class: His father built custom homes and ran a bakery and grocery store, and the Moores' fair complexions placed them in Barbados's colored racial group. The death of Moore's father, however, spelled financial crisis. After Richard completed his education at Lynch's Middle Class School in Bridgetown, he gained work as a junior clerk in a department store. When his stepmother realized that the family could no longer sustain itself in Barbados and decided to join her sister in New York, the fifteen-year-old Moore eagerly went along. He worked numerous jobs before securing steady work as a clerk at a silk manufacturing company. Yet he also confronted the daily realities of race in New York: segregation, insults, personal attacks, and seemingly constant reports of lynching, all of which led him, his daughter remembered, on a "quest for an understanding of [race] relations . . . and a basic philosophy by which he might guide his behavior." In 1917, Moore joined Huiswoud in the SPA after listening to Socialist speakers in Madison Square Park and reading radical literature.[17]

Unlike the fair-complexioned Huiswoud and Moore, Cyril Valentine Briggs looked white. He was born in 1888 on the small Leeward Island of

Nevis, a British West Indies plantation colony involved primarily in sugar cultivation. His mother was a rather fair-skinned colored woman; his father, a white plantation overseer. Despite his appearance, Briggs lived on the margins of the island's tiny white elite, though he did enjoy the social latitude available to Nevis's colored population. Briggs excelled in school, but his colonial education came with its own problems. Briggs recalled that it "aimed to turn out Black Anglo-Saxons, glorify whites, denigrate Africans." As a schoolboy, Briggs was required to memorize Cecil Frances Alexander's largely unremarkable hymn, "All Things Bright and Beautiful," which includes a stanza attributing class divisions to providential design. The words stayed with Briggs for more than half a century:

> The rich man in his castle,
> The poor man at his gate,
> God made them, high or lowly,
> And order'd their estate.[18]

But Briggs's colored racial status and attendant education also exposed him to radical anti-imperialist thought.[19]

Sometime in his teens, he went to work as an assistant in the library of a Reverend Price, pastor of the Baptist church that ran the parochial school he attended in Nevis's capital, Basseterre. The position offered Briggs the opportunity to read from Price's considerable collection, especially the works on imperialism. Robert Green Ingersoll's speeches particularly impressed the young Briggs. Ingersoll advocated civil rights for blacks in the United States and called the South and the Democratic Party "uncivilized" for segregating former slaves. He also maintained friendships with both Frederick Douglass and Eugene V. Debs and merged free-thought agnosticism with liberal anti-imperialism. In Ingersoll, Briggs found an intellectual heretic willing to challenge dominant thinking. He subsequently left Nevis for neighboring St. Kitts, where he worked for the *St. Kitts Daily Express* and the *St. Christopher Advertiser*, harnessing his talent as a writer and earning a scholarship to study journalism. If reading Ingersoll fostered in Briggs a nascent anti-imperialism, his time in St. Kitts showed him the possibilities of politically charged journalism.[20]

But Briggs turned down the scholarship and instead joined his mother, who had immigrated to the United States. When the seventeen-year-old Briggs arrived in New York in 1905, he found himself part of a small Caribbean-immigrant community that lacked the institutions that might have helped Briggs and others confront race in the United States. In Nevis and St. Kitts, he was colored, a racial designation below whites but above blacks in the racial hierarchy. In the United States, however, he either had to identify himself as black or pass for white. However white he may have looked, it seems unlikely that he would have seriously considered passing. The small-scale communities in Nevis and the privileges afforded coloreds in the Caribbean had made passing unnecessary there, and attempting to do so in New York might have required Briggs to distance himself from his mother and the city's slowly growing Afro-Caribbean population, a likely impossibility given the Caribbean lilt of his English. The U.S. racial hierarchy, particularly his classification as black within it, probably confused him.

What is most intriguing about the biographies of Huiswoud, Moore, and Briggs is their age and lack of political experience when they immigrated. All three came to New York in their teens and were not politically active in the Caribbean. But all three entered into radical politics in part in response to their experiences with racial oppression in the United States. Color differences in the United States were not racial distinctions as in the Caribbean. Mulattos and fair-complexioned U.S. blacks in the mid-1800s populated the black middle class out of proportion to their numbers in the black community as a whole, but all those of African descent were members of the same social, religious, recreational, and political organizations.[21] Debates regarding color differences had raged at least since the nineteenth century, and these patterns persisted into the twentieth.[22] But as color became increasingly contentious, many New Negro movement activist-intellectuals, especially in Harlem, voiced concern about the importance many blacks attached to color.

Taking up the question of color, Wilfred Adolphus (W. A.) Domingo, a black Jamaican radical who worked alongside Marcus Garvey in Jamaica in his teens and later worked with A. Philip Randolph in the United States, was acutely aware of how race in the Caribbean tended to serve the interests of white supremacy. He was concerned that using the term "colored" for black people in the United States might introduce a Caribbean-style racial hierarchy. He pointed out that in the West Indies, "colored" was a classification for "a more or less exclusive or distinct group with definite . . . group interests" that set them apart from people classified as Negro. The nature of racism in the United States, he argued, required that black people abandon any term that could politically fragment their antiracist struggle. "The so-called colored or Negro race" was not reducible to a given phenotype. He considered Negroes "neither black, yellow nor brown" but rather "a composite people carrying in their veins the blood of many different types of the human family" held together by "the pressure exerted from the outside upon them by a dominant and domineering stronger race." This pressure, he argued, had "produced oneness of destiny and for that reason the 'race' is developing a sentiment and consciousness of unity." Domingo's argument suggested a certain political expediency to the U.S. racial system, which he believed united all peoples of African descent into a single Negro race. This idea broke with prevailing racial thought by rejecting notions of biological purity, which undermined the claim that the future of the race rested on reproducing a pure racial stock. Biological purity explained little about racial oppression, he added, and obscured the more important set of power relationships whereby whites defined and oppressed subordinate groups. Further, he warned that the "colored" label threatened to exacerbate intragroup antagonisms and introduce a racial logic and structure where Negro "connotes . . . a status lower than that connoted by the word colored."[23]

When Briggs turned to Moore, Domingo, and Grace Campbell to establish the ABB, among the founders' driving concerns was how the ABB might help end the divisions of "the race into light and dark . . . West Indians, Southerners, Northerners, and so forth."[24] But these activists also knew quite well, both from the Caribbean and from their experiences in the United States, that class marked another important fault line among black people. Indeed, the question of the relationship between race and class was paramount for black radicals. And it seemed that no one had more to say on this topic than Hubert Henry Harrison.

Black Intellectual Institutions and Theorizing Race and Class

Born in St. Croix, Danish West Indies, to a working-class black family in 1883, Hubert Harrison arrived in New York in 1900, a highly intelligent, mature seventeen-year-old. In New York, he had a typical Caribbean immigrant experience, working odd jobs until he gained employment commensurate with his skills, training, and education. After graduating from Manhattan's De Witt Clinton High School in 1906, Harrison went to work as a postal clerk, married, moved his new family to Harlem, and embarked on a vigorous reading regimen that at one point included nearly four books a week. He also participated in reading lyceums, where he met such prominent figures as black journalist John E. Bruce and the bibliophile Arturo (Arthur) Schomburg and honed his public-speaking skills. In addition, Harrison gravitated to radical free-thought literature, began writing editorials for the socialist *Truth Seeker*, and joined the SPA. He would lose his postal clerk job, however, for criticizing Booker T. Washington in two letters to the *New York Sun*. Nevertheless, Harrison was emerging as an adept organizer and formidable intellect within the SPA. With recommendations from W. E. B. Du Bois and others in the SPA's Harlem branch, the party offered him work as a paid speaker and organizer. Harrison jumped at the opportunity.[25]

He threw himself into his new job, drawing especially on his skills as a gifted orator. Stepladder speaking, a practice that grew out of a Caribbean political tradition that developed in response to elite control of the press in the islands, proved his most effective tool. In Harlem, the stepladder offered a democratic space to articulate an alternative politics and ideologies without the money required to publish a newspaper or magazine or to print pamphlets.[26] Combining the stepladder with the printed word, Harrison became one of the better-known and most revered New Negro activist-intellectuals in the 1910s. A. Philip Randolph remembered him as having "a very fine mind . . . that reached in all areas of human knowledge." W. A. Domingo described Harrison as "a brilliant man, a great intellect, a socialist and highly respected." Even the *New York Times* called him "an eloquent and forceful negro speaker [who] shattered all records for distance in an address on Socialism."[27] His public lectures in Madison Square Park drew many future ABB members, among them Domingo, Moore, and Campbell, into the SPA.

Harrison's keen grasp of Marxism was on full display when he offered what biographer Jeffrey Perry has identified as the first Marxist analysis of race by a black radical. In an effort to justify special organizing among black people by the SPA, Harrison published a series of articles in Socialist periodicals between 1911 and 1913 on the Negro problem and socialism. The SPA had a long history of ignoring the complexities of race among workers and in the larger society. In 1908, the Jewish Socialist Isaac M. Rubinow, writing under the pseudonym I. M. Robbins, attempted to broaden socialist thinking about race in a series of fifteen articles insisting that economics alone did not explain racial prejudice. Rubinow urged the Socialist Party to confront black people's unique experiences and warned party members that race would not simply vanish with socialism, as the "connection between race prejudice and socialism is not self evident."[28]

Harrison extended Rubinow's work to discuss the confluence of race and class in black people's experiences, outlining what Harrison considered the social, economic, political, and educational aspects of racism and highlighting how white workers contributed to racial oppression. Though at one point he argued that "when this system of vicarious production relations disappears, the problem which is its consequence [racism] will disappear also," he ultimately rejected that view.[29] Harrison believed that black workers experienced both racial oppression and the highest levels of economic exploitation, but he lamented that the white Left continued to ignore blacks. Black people were class-conscious, he argued, but had no allegiances to the whites who barred them from labor unions, supported segregation, and terrorized them at night. The Negro was right to be suspicious of socialism and "everything that comes from the white people of America," Harrison told his comrades. For Harrison, one could not sequester race from questions of class or assume that it had no impact on notions of freedom and liberation. Indeed, white-led movements for "the extension of democracy" usually broke down "as soon as [they] reached the color line." He therefore believed that Socialists faced a choice between "Southernism or Socialism," between organizing "the white half of the working class against the black half," or organizing "all the working class." The SPA could cast itself as the party of white labor or could tap into the reservoir of black labor radicalism through industrial organization.[30]

Harrison ultimately failed to persuade the SPA to alter its organizing activities. Over the next couple of years, the party continued to pursue an economically deterministic view of race that drove out many black members. By 1912, Harrison realized that the SPA would never offer adequate support to black liberation, and his criticisms of party leaders and his support for industrial organization grew increasingly pronounced. The SPA's conservative executive committee responded by suspending him for three months in 1914. Rather than accept his punishment, Harrison resigned, convinced that socialists would neither bring about socialism nor contribute to black liberation.[31]

Before he resigned, however, Harrison had already begun to work outside the SPA. In 1914, he launched the Radical Forum, a lecture series that met six nights a week, using it as a venue to continue working out a theory of race and class. Many of those who attended the Radical Forum later joined his Liberty League, which he established in 1917. That same year, Richard Moore, a member of the Cosmo-Advocate Publishing Company's executive board, worked with Harrison to publish his articles from Socialist periodicals in a small pamphlet, *The Negro and the Nation*. The pamphlet became something of a primer for Harlem radicals and continued to circulate well into the 1920s. At times, these radicals drew on Harrison's work; at other times, they moved beyond it to think about racial oppression globally, especially the relationship between Africans of the dispersion and continental Africans. Along with black periodicals, lyceums, reading groups, and other intellectual forums, Harrison's Liberty League, Radical Forum, and writings were institutions outside the purview of the white Left, proving essential to the elaboration of a black radical politics in Harlem. One of the more impressive activist-intellectuals drawn into this current was Cyril Briggs.[32]

Cyril Briggs and Radical Journalism

Around the time that Harrison left the SPA and began thinking about the Liberty League, the editorials of Cyril Briggs, who would go on to found the African Blood Brotherhood, were gaining the attention of Harlem radicals. Though never a member of the Socialist Party, Briggs interacted with many of the people Harrison recruited into the SPA. By 1912, Briggs had secured a position as a society reporter covering local weddings, cotillions, and lyceums for Harlem's major black weekly, the *Amsterdam News*. Although an inauspicious start, the job provided him with an entrée into Harlem politics and introduced him to Uptown's burgeoning black elite.[33] He quickly built a reputation as a race man and journalist, catching the attention of Jamaican real estate broker E. Touissant Welcome, who was then preparing to launch a Harlem-based business magazine, the *Colored American Review*. Welcome wanted to promote local black businesses and encourage an entrepreneurial spirit based on Booker T. Washington's philosophy that "at the bottom of education [and] politics . . . there must be for our race . . . an economic foundation, economic prosperity, economic independence." Welcome believed that he had found in Briggs a more-than-capable editor.[34]

But Briggs edited just three issues of the *Colored American Review*. His early editorials displayed the conservative racial uplift ethos that guided the thinking of the black elite, urging black people to pursue self-help in response to racial oppression and to support black businesses. Indeed, Briggs believed that the destiny of the race depended on the creation of a sound economic base for future generations. Yet for the editor of a black business magazine, he did rather little to promote local black businesses, often showing greater concern for the day-to-day issues confronting poor and working-class black people. Rather than instructing readers on comportment, morals, or respectability, he enjoined them to engage in organized political action and to think politically about where they shopped. In his most strident tones, Briggs criticized "ignorant" and "foolish" black people who patronized white businesses. Showing little compassion for black families torn between patronizing race businesses and stretching their meager incomes, he called such people unaware "of the crime [they] are committing against the coming generation." If black people shopped with greater regularity at black businesses, he reasoned, those businesses would have greater revenue and could stock their shelves, lower their prices, and provide better service.[35]

At their core, these editorials attended to a politics of consumption that revealed the contradictory impulses in Briggs's thinking. These impulses were most apparent when he turned his attention to black women. On the one hand, he could dismiss the idea that women's place is in the home and urge black men to support the enfranchisement of black women. On the other, he took particular aim at black women who shopped at white stores, describing black housewives as having "even less intelligence and race pride [than] the average mortal." He saw their shopping habits not as a domestic activity but as part of "this great fight that must be waged unceasingly and courageously for the salvation of the race." He also turned from supporting black businesses to emphasizing jobs for and the treatment of black people. Rather than shop at sparsely stocked black stores that charged higher prices than their white competitors and disrespected black customers, readers should ask white store-owners "if there is any colored person employed with the firm." If not, go "find some other place for our patronage—and money." He even provided a list of white stores that employed black people.[36]

Although Briggs never translated his ideas into a direct campaign, his *Colored American Review* editorials contained the seeds of the radical politics he would soon embrace, especially in condemning racial oppression, U.S. imperialism, and white racial violence. Showing signs of the anti-imperialism that soon became his journalistic hallmark, he included two pieces on the U.S. invasion of Haiti that equated U.S. barbarity with Belgian imperialism. That nascent radicalism appealed to many Harlem radicals. Harrison hailed the *Review* as "just what we have needed for years," expressing the hope that Briggs would "rapidly become a power in the community." In response, Briggs made Harrison and John E. Bruce contributing editors to the *Review*.[37]

Welcome could hardly have been pleased to see Briggs listing white companies in Harlem that deserved black patronage. Further, after Briggs published an editorial criticizing Booker T. Washington's support of the U.S. invasion of Haiti, which had the unfortunate timing of appearing the same month that Washington died, Welcome had little reason to retain Briggs as editor. Nevertheless, Briggs's brief tenure at the *Colored American Review* established him as a major figure in Harlem's intellectual circles.[38]

He returned to the *Amsterdam News* with the experience to function as editor in all but name, a role that allowed him to continue developing his anti-imperialist and antiracist politics. He returned to the paper just as the United

States expanded its military presence in the Caribbean and prepared to enter World War I. Briggs and many other black radicals saw an irony in President Woodrow Wilson standing at the helm of an ever-expanding American empire while asserting that the United States should enter the war to help make the world "safe for democracy." Along with the U.S. military presence in the Caribbean and Pacific islands denying self-government to people of color there, Wilson failed to protect the lives and rights of black people in America, at times even endorsing racial segregation.

In his two surviving *Amsterdam News* editorials, Briggs questioned Wilson's commitment to self-government in Eastern Europe in light of continued European colonial holdings in Africa and Asia, doubting whether a government that had consistently failed to stop racial violence within its borders could ensure international peace. He discussed American racial oppression in a colonial framework and characterized African Americans as a "nation within a nation" with a right to self-determination. In response to Wilson's Fourteen Point Program for peace, especially Point 13's call for the establishment of an "independent Polish state" composed of "territories inhabited by indisputably Polish populations," Briggs noted the incongruity of Wilson's tacit support of racism in the United States. Black people constituted "an oppressed nationality as worthy of . . . a separate political existence as any of the oppressed peoples of Europe," he argued. As far as Briggs was concerned, Wilson's arguments brimmed with hypocrisy. "Can America demand that Germany give up her Poles, and Austria her Slavs, while America still holds in the harshest possible modern bonds of moral, intellectual, political and industrial bondage a nation of over ten million people . . . a nation within a nation . . . oppressed and jim-crowed, yet worthy as any other people of a square deal or failing that, a separate political existence?"[39]

Although Briggs wrote in what might be seen as the "Wilsonian moment" for anticolonial discourses of self-determination, his criticism of Wilsonian self-determination grew from a black anticolonial discourse. Briggs likely had not yet read Lenin's writings on self-determination, but his editorials anticipated both the Socialist Party's proposal to extend Wilson's notion of self-determination to the "race question in the South" and the Communist International's policy on the Negro question a decade later.[40] Moreover, he joined over a century's worth of black intellectuals who believed that national separation was the only solution to racial oppression.

Writing for Harlem's most widely read weekly, Briggs reached both the Uptown coterie of activist-intellectuals and the scores of southern migrants and Caribbean immigrants trying to make sense of the new world around them. Through his growing relationship with Harrison, Briggs also began to work with Domingo, Moore, and Campbell in the Liberty League. Here, Briggs found a group of intellectuals who were attentive to the complexities of race and had pored over the most advanced theories of class; while they disagreed with Briggs on black separation, they still urged him to further develop his understanding of race and national oppression. The League thus marked Briggs's initial involvement in a group committed to organizing the black community and reinforced his desire to fuse intellectual activity with political struggle.[41]

The People's Educational Forum and the Black Left

Many of the black radicals whom Harrison had recruited into the SPA remained Socialists after his resignation, though they continued to find the party disinclined to support work regarding race. While the SPA had established a Colored Socialist Club in 1912 under Harrison's leadership, party leaders closed it within two months, and another six years passed before the SPA opened the largely black 21st Assembly District (AD) in Harlem.[42] And while most black Socialists likely agreed with the SPA that class exploitation lay at the heart of racial oppression, they took exception to claim that it was more important for black people to "join revolutionary organizations of the general proletariat than the special organizations of their race."[43] Frustrated with choosing between "straight Socialism or Negro-ology," Moore, Huiswoud, Campbell, Domingo, and Frank Crosswaith began meeting on Sunday mornings to discuss contemporary issues and read classic Marxist works, including the *Communist Manifesto* and Frederick Engels's *Socialism — Utopian and Scientific.*[44]

In the summer of 1917, under Campbell's and Louise Jackson's leadership, black radicals in the SPA launched the People's Educational Forum (PEF) on Sunday afternoons. The forum augmented the study group by sponsoring public lectures and debates for the wider Harlem public at Lafayette Hall at 7th Avenue and 131st Street. Campbell, a black social worker and secretary of the 21st AD, secured guest speakers, among them W. E. B. Du Bois and the anthropologist Franz Boas, various nationalist political activists, labor organizers, and other Socialists. Lecturers discussed such practical concerns as "How to Meet and Defeat the K.K.K." as well as more theoretical questions—for example, Boas's lecture on "Supposed Racial Inferiority." The forum encouraged participants to engage speakers and their ideas rather than merely listen. "Unlike other organizations of Negroes in Harlem," declared a 1920 advertisement in Domingo's *Emancipator* newspaper, "the proceedings of the PEF are absolutely democratic."[45] The forum was an "intellectual battleground" whose very structure challenged the elitism of Harlem's black leadership class and the autocratic structure of many black organizations. Such open exchanges, however, could aggravate guests. In October 1920, when Du Bois lectured on "The War and the Darker World" and suggested that black workers should take a middle ground between capital and labor, forum participants attacked what they called his suicidal program. Possibly embarrassed and certainly infuriated, an imperious Du Bois admonished the audience, "I didn't come here to engage in this sort of exchange. I thought you wanted to learn something but you know everything." Du Bois never returned.[46]

The PEF provided black radicals a venue in which to engage race and class outside the SPA, allowing them to cultivate a leadership cadre and, as Moore later recalled, see "socialist theory as a method of social analysis of the Afro-American situation and [the] oppressed colonial peoples in Africa, the Caribbean, and elsewhere."[47] The forum thus enabled these activists to work to transform the SPA's approach to organizing around race, ultimately leading to a rift between black Socialists and party leaders that corresponded to the internecine struggles between the party's left and right wings. Black Socialists saw that struggle as less important than how the party would organize black people, though it did offer an opportunity to try to reshape the SPA's posture toward black people.

One of the more important attempts came from Domingo, a skilled pamphleteer, who in the early months of 1919 circulated within the party a pamphlet, *Socialism Imperiled or, the Negro—A Potential Menace to American Radicalism*. Domingo's work echoed Harrison's earlier concerns with the Socialist Party's reductionist approach to race and similarly stressed the need to organize black people as a group. Yet where Harrison had stressed industrial organization, Domingo insisted that organizing black agricultural laborers would focus the party's efforts on the majority of blacks and demonstrate the importance of organizing around race. He criticized the SPA's focus on northern industries and its rejection of the Industrial Workers of the World's model of organizing workers regardless of race and saw the party's emphasis on skilled white workers as promoting a view of blacks as "an enemy of that organization and the scab of America." He argued that black people had acted sensibly in developing a racial consciousness in light of the fact that they were restricted to poor jobs and excluded from unions, and the SPA did nothing to help "transmute their race consciousness . . . into class-consciousness." Socialists might find a model in the Bolsheviks, who under Lenin showed a willingness to organize oppressed nationalities and to "extend the principle of self-determination to . . . Africa, Asia and all the colonies." The Socialist Party's success among black people, he concluded, would come through affirming its commitment to black liberation, denouncing lynching, giving blacks greater prominence in its publications, financially supporting black radical initiatives, fighting to admit black workers into labor unions on equal terms, and explaining how socialism would benefit black people.[48]

Although some SPA leaders responded to the concerns that Domingo and other black radicals raised, most were unmoved. Domingo's negative portrait of the party's stance on race prompted at least one official to call for "missionary work [among] colored people" and to echo Domingo's warnings that if black workers remained unorganized, they would be used by capitalists against a socialist revolution.[49] Still, the SPA's leadership showed little interest in challenging segregated southern party locals, a continuing source of frustration for many black Socialists, who felt that the party had to focus on black agricultural workers. This view did not represent a mere difference of opinion regarding the division of limited resources between agricultural and industrial organizing. To organize black agricultural workers would require the SPA to dedicate intellectual energy and organizational time to studying debt peonage, Jim Crow, and the effects of racial violence on black life in the South, issues and problems for which, Robin D. G. Kelley reminds us, the writings of Marx or Lenin contained no ready-made answers.[50]

One PEF episode clearly demonstrated that the Socialist Party would do little to seriously address the Negro problem. In an effort to find redress on the party's program, PEF organizers invited Algernon Lee, the director of the Rand School, to speak. Black Socialists saw this as an opportunity to force the SPA to clarify its position on southern blacks. After asking Lee a series of well-planned questions, organizers posed their most direct query: "What program does the Socialist Party have for organizing [Negroes], especially in the South?" Lee responded in a classically doctrinaire fashion, arguing that when Marx wrote about the proletariat, he meant industrial workers; thus, regardless of any need to organize Negroes, the Socialist Party had no program for southern black agricultural workers. Forum participants pounced on Lee so vehemently that he later complained to the party's district committee, which eventually brought PEF participants up on disciplinary charges. For black Socialists, however, this incident was the proverbial last straw. Many left the Socialist Party in 1919, convinced, like Harrison before them, that it would never speak to black people's concerns.[51] The forum had highlighted a fundamental problem with how the white Left approached a subject black Socialists considered essential to socialist revolution.

Black radicals continued thinking about socialism's utility for black people, sponsoring a series of lectures on socialism in the spring of 1920. Along with two lectures by David Berenberg from the Rand School's Correspondence Department, Elizabeth Gurley Flynn discussed "Progress and the Price We Pay," while a group of Socialists discussed "Debs and Other Martyrs of To-Day." Other lecturers included Chandler Owen; E. Ethelred Brown, who spoke on "Religious Liberalism and the Negro"; and William H. Ferris, editor of the *Negro World*, who addressed the "Four Phases of Negro Radicalism." The series also included an open symposium on "The Fallacy of a Negro Empire" and a discussion on "The Relation of the Race Problem to the Proletarian Movement."[52] On this last point, black radicals drew ties between black liberation and self-determination in Africa and Asia. Indeed, black Socialists were well situated to turn to Asia in thinking about a global struggle against the color line and to highlight the similarities between African diasporic and Asian liberation.

By the summer of 1919, a small group of Japanese radicals in New York had begun to stress the importance of Asian workers and Asian national liberation to socialism. This group had coalesced around Katayama, who had become a central figure among California Bay Area Issei radicals before relocating to New York in 1916. In Manhattan, he worked with fellow radical Taguchi Unzo to form the Japanese Socialist Group in America. Katayama's long-standing interest in the Negro problem extended back to his student days in Tennessee, where he first witnessed and experienced white supremacy. He came to see the United States as a "country of . . . race prejudices and racial hatred," and subsequently sought to discuss labor in Asia as well as Japanese and Chinese workers in America in racial terms, an effort that drew black Socialists to his lectures at the Rand School. As Turner notes, many of these radicals shared Katayama's experiences as a racialized immigrant on the margins of both American society and the white Left, as well as his beliefs regarding the need to stretch socialist thought to address colonialism and racial oppression. Katayama's friendship with Huiswoud, Moore, Campbell, and the African American Socialist Lovett Fort-Whiteman involved long discussions of socialist politics and theory, conversations that likely included other radicals from the Japanese Socialist Group of America, which by the autumn of 1919 had renamed itself the Japanese Communist Group and sought affiliation with the Communist International.[53]

Various black radicals were pondering the international dimensions of black liberation and the ties between African diasporic struggles and non-African struggles as well as between various diasporic populations. In his 1920 collection of articles, *When Africa Awakes*, Harrison turned his attention to the international contours of racial oppression and the "international fact to which Negroes in America are now reacting, . . . the social, political and economic subjection of colored peoples by whites."[54] Black people existed within an "international of the darker races," where "black, brown and yellow peoples [are] stretching out their hands to each other and . . . seeking to establish their own centers of diffusion for their own internationalism."[55] He urged black people to link their struggles to similar struggles elsewhere, advocating an intercolonial approach where, for example, African Caribbeans could see the importance of Indian national liberation to their own independence.[56]

In a series of articles in the *Messenger* that appeared over the course of a year,[57] Domingo also continued to think about the role of socialism in anti-racist and anticolonial struggles, asking in the penultimate article, "Will Bolshevism Free America?" Although seemingly focused on the United States, he took as his purview a much broader field. The spread of "Bolshevism into Egypt and into the heart of Africa via Arabia constitutes the greatest danger to imperialism and the greatest hope to the Negro race everywhere." Rather than relying on the white Left, Domingo proposed an international anticolonial struggle of all oppressed races for socialism in Africa and Asia, noting in particular that "the forces of freedom, represented by Soviet Russia and guided by impersonal economic laws are on the side of the Negro." Socialism thus represented "the only weapon that can be used by Negroes effectively to clip the claws of the British lion and the talons of the American eagle in Africa, the British West Indies, Haiti, the Southern States and at the same time reach the monsters' heart (they have a common one) in London, Paris, New York, Tokio and Warsaw."[58] Many New Negro radicals, like their counterparts in the Japanese Communist Group, remained optimistic about the white Left and socialism in light of the Communist International's 1919 declaration to colonial Africa and Asia that "the hour of the proletarian dictatorship in Europe will strike for you as the hour of your own emancipation." Less obvious in Domingo's pronouncement, though possibly more important, is his assertion that African diasporic struggles and Asian liberation movements, not the European proletariat, would usher in socialism.[59] He tied diasporic liberation to non-African movements, linking pan-African liberation to anticolonial and anticapitalist struggles worldwide. Rather than remaining focused on the United States or even solely on a pan-African struggle, black radicals hoped to realize the international of darker races that Harrison had so powerfully suggested in his writing and that was beginning to emerge from interactions with Asian radicals.[60]

BLACK RADICALS IN HARLEM spent considerable energy theorizing the nature of racial oppression and class exploitation. The SPA's appeal, however, did not lie in its class analysis or the analytical force of scientific socialism. Many of the black Socialists who later worked in the ABB had to confront, on a deeply personal level, the discord between the vernaculars of blackness they knew in the Caribbean and how those idioms were largely unintelligible in the United States. Such differences presented myriad problems in efforts to fight racial oppression and to build racial unity. In working through those experiences, these African-Caribbean radicals entered into dialogues with an array of black and Asian radicals about race, class, and the role of oppressed groups in socialist revolution. This kind of intellectual work occurred largely, though not solely, through institutions and intellectual networks outside the purview of organized Marxism. When black radicals joined the SPA, their understanding of race and the stakes at hand in socialist revolution for African and Asian peoples far exceeded the horizons of Socialist Party programs and policies.

Though Moore, Campbell, Domingo, Randolph, and Owen remained members of the SPA into the 1920s, few black radicals stayed beyond the 1919 split between the party's left and right wings. Some blacks gravitated to the communist parties that emerged from that split; others took some time to become Communists; and others still, like Domingo, remained outside the organized white Left and worked solely with black radicals such as Briggs in the newly formed ABB.[61] Those black radicals committed to socialism confronted the special demands of organizing in the uniquely African diasporic community of Harlem while focusing on the changing conditions facing African Americans in both the rural South and the urban North. In the process, they developed a sense of racial oppression that linked the plight of blacks in the United States to anti-imperialist and working-class struggles in Africa, the Caribbean, and the non-African world. Black radicals pursued their international projects in a number of different political formations, perhaps none more important than the ABB. And through the ABB, many radicals believed, they could best build an international movement against racial oppression, capitalism, and imperialism, further transforming the international white Left's thinking about socialist revolution.

Liberating Negroes Everywhere

Cyril Briggs, the African Blood Brotherhood,
and Radical Pan-Africanism

Early in 1919, Cyril Valentine Briggs joined a group of black Socialists in Harlem to establish the African Blood Brotherhood for African Liberation and Redemption (ABB). They fashioned themselves a secret paramilitary organization but in fact functioned as a group of activist-intellectuals intent on guiding the black freedom movement toward a pan-Africanist proletarian revolution. They believed that they would achieve nothing less than liberating Africa, ending colonialism and racial oppression, and contributing to the cause of freedom everywhere.

As a national organization, the ABB could hardly compare in size and reach to its more notable contemporaries, the National Association for the Advancement of Colored People and Marcus Garvey's Universal Negro Improvement Association (UNIA). Outside New York, the ABB's membership consisted largely of workers—skilled laborers in Chicago; coal miners in West Virginia; World War I veterans in Tulsa, Oklahoma; Anglo-Caribbean migrant laborers in the Dominican Republic and Panama. At its height, it would claim no more than eight thousand members, and the Harlem branch, Post Menelik, never consisted of more than a handful of activist-intellectuals. But the ABB's size belied its significance to the New Negro movement and black radical thought more generally. It embodied alternative political currents. As black Socialists continued to flesh out the idea of socialism so that it responded to the particularities of race and colonialism, Briggs sought to infuse class into black nationalist thought. Further, the ABB's small size lent itself to the kind of institution building it believed would foster radical change. Though they never constituted a mass movement, ABB members clearly carried out their labors within the context of a social movement. Indeed, Briggs established the Brotherhood as a result of his sense that existing organizations were inadequate to the task of "the ultimate liberation of Negroes everywhere."[1]

Briggs remains one of the more storied if poorly studied black radical intellectuals of the New Negro movement. He is among a score of casualties of the scholarly habit of limiting intellectuals to those who left behind a corpus of easily accessible and archived writings—novels, poetry, scholarly articles, essays, diaries, and so on. Yet recent scholarship on the New Negro movement has begun to expand the realm of the "intellectual" beyond men and women of letters to include a broader range of people engaged in self-reflective, creative critical activities and knowledge production.[2] Briggs occupied a middle ground, leaving a substantial body of journalism but never producing a sustained scholarly work or piece of literature, though he did venture into fiction with two serialized short stories that ran in his radical magazine, the *Crusader*. A speech impediment prevented him from engaging in Harlem's stepladder-speaking and street-strolling traditions, where public intellectuals without the backing of major political organizations and mainstream publications tested their intellectual mettle and built movements outside the normative realms of black middle-class leadership. As if recognizing his limitations, Briggs concentrated on journalism, crafting politically engaged editorials and articles less concerned with reporting than with analyzing contemporary issues, struggles, and events, always with an eye turned toward the cause of pan-African liberation.

Along with his activism, his writings reveal a kind of political daring and imagination that one might consider essential to a public intellectual.[3] Briggs spoke to multiple publics in addition to the coterie of Harlem's New Negro intellectuals. The consensus among scholars who have written on Briggs is that his signal importance lies in having joined elements of black nationalist and socialist thought, which the ABB then held in balance until its demise in 1925.[4] Yet this view glosses over what brought Briggs to a sustained critical reflection on both black nationalism and socialism and the array of institutions and political relationships in which he developed intellectually. The idea that he merely merged two mutually exclusive political currents understates his historical importance. In fact, Briggs and the ABB left an indelible imprint on both frameworks, ultimately producing something quite new.

Briggs had been a member of black nationalist organizations and had worked for a few black periodicals before launching the *Crusader* in September 1918. His earliest known writings reveal a conservative bent and gendered, racialist worldview whereby blacks and whites were natural enemies with no hope of peaceful coexistence. But those writings were also concerned with building a movement to liberate the race. Briggs attributed black people's social subordination to whites in the United States, the Caribbean, and Europe to racial differences, yet he believed racial oppression could be ended. With the *Crusader*, he plumbed the complexities of slavery, exploitation, and racial violence, arriving at an understanding of race and imperialism that focused on power relationships, class struggle, and systems of domination spanning the globe. This understanding ultimately stood in tension with his racialist worldview.

In many ways, Briggs is an enigmatic figure. His ideas do not lend themselves to any easy ideological taxonomy. One of his short stories envisioned blacks annihilating whites with a "Ray of Fear" yet also imagined that the race war in which this annihilation would occur would build political bonds among Africans, Asians, and the Irish.[5] He could insist that blacks and whites would never live together peacefully but nevertheless argue that an independent black nation would both liberate Africa and protect black people in the United States and Europe from white violence. He once penned an editorial insisting on a race-first politics but followed it directly with an editorial that offered possibly his most elegant argument for why class struggle was the only way to end racism and colonialism. At his most perplexing, he simultaneously called socialism the only solution to racial oppression and maintained that white worker racism would persist in a socialist society. Briggs was an intellectual who pursued a political vision that drew on both socialism and black nationalism but who refused to be restricted by them. He embraced an expansive if at times nebulous notion of freedom and covered a range of black thought.

Briggs approached the American racial landscape through the prism of his experiences in the Caribbean. He had long contemplated the impact of European colonialism on the West Indies, an examination that informed his initial efforts to understand race in the United States. He drew on race in the Caribbean to analyze the points of difference between African diasporic populations. What distinguished Briggs was not simply that he joined black Socialists in elaborating a radicalism that drew on but ultimately moved beyond socialist and black nationalist thought; rather, he paid attention to the relationship between Africans on the continent and its diaspora, insisting that racial unity or pan-African struggle was not a foregone conclusion. When he turned his attention to class, he began to expand his understanding of race, seeing races as political groupings and racial oppression as a power relationship between them. He thus approached the relationship between various diasporic populations as involving distinct racialized political groups whose futures, while linked, were equally tied to nondiasporic racialized groups as well as working-class struggles, a view that by 1920 characterized the ABB's program.

While serving as the executive head of the ABB and editor of its magazine, Briggs produced writings that provide a window into the Brotherhood's program and the roots of its radical black internationalism. Briggs and the Brotherhood balanced concerns about racial oppression with attention to class exploitation and envisioned ties between various segments of the African diaspora that moved beyond national and color differences. Never a blatantly masculinist group, it nonetheless replicated contemporary gender notions of women as wives and mothers of the race who should be concerned with maintaining their physical beauty and raising future revolutionaries. In that sense, the ABB was no better than the world its members hoped to change.

Briggs and the ABB understood that any attempt to unite diasporic liberation movements had to confront varying structures and ideologies of domination, which meant confronting the multiple structures of race and other realities of color and national difference within the diaspora. In the ABB, Briggs also devoted greater attention to the relationship between capitalism and racial oppression and how it explained black people's position in the U.S. political economy. The group sought to build alliances not only between people of color fighting racial and national oppression but also between nonwhite peoples and class-conscious white workers committed to an antiracist, anti-imperialist politics. And alongside the call for an independent black nation, Briggs and the ABB criticized what they considered the structures of the nation that led to empire, particularly with regard to Garvey and the UNIA. The ABB, like many Harlem New Negro movement organizations, entered into heated conflicts with Garvey, even though many ABB members, especially Briggs, initially viewed Garvey favorably and supported the UNIA.

Rather than produce a coherent theory of race easily identified in a series of articles and editorials, Briggs lodged his conception of race in an ongoing discussion of self-determination and racial unity in the *Crusader*. Racial unity would come, he argued, from establishing either a separate nation-state for American blacks or an independent African nation. It would not issue from simply acknowledging a set of common experiences or a common racial destiny. Instead, one had to build such unity, giving special attention to how the different movements in the African world related to one another. In other words, Briggs and the early ABB gave as much attention to the limits of racial unity as they did to pan-African liberation. They focused on how the structures of class, nationality, and color presented challenges to building a pan-African movement and forging solidarity between diasporic populations. Briggs drew on and added to the efforts of black Socialists who were theorizing race and class. The product was an anticolonial politics that saw the struggles of black workers; liberation movements in Asia, the Pacific islands, and Europe; and working-class struggles as tied to pan-African liberation.

Race Radicalism and the *Crusader*

In his unofficial capacity as editor of the *Amsterdam News*, Briggs continued to criticize U.S. foreign policy, the League of Nations, and the U.S. rationale for entering World War I. In response, federal officials pressured the *Amsterdam News* to rein in Briggs's editorials, but he refused to be tempered and was forced to leave the paper. That decision bolstered Briggs's reputation as a principled, uncompromising journalist and a radical.[6] It also gave him the chance to launch his own magazine.

Briggs started the *Crusader* with financial support and other help from Harlem businessmen, other people impressed with his writings, and his former colleagues at the *Amsterdam News*. The *Crusader* reflected his preoccupation with political struggle and racial pride in extolling the glories of ancient African civilization. He planned for its coverage to span the diaspora—supporting African liberation, examining the position of blacks in South America and the Caribbean, providing the "necessary Historic Background . . . to eradicate the evils of Alien Education," and demonstrating black people's readiness for self-government. Guided by a commitment to self-government and "Africa for the Africans," the *Crusader* would engage in "an uncompromising fight for Negro rights" in the United States and help ensure the safety of African-descended peoples throughout the world.[7]

The *Crusader*'s earliest issues struck a delicate balance between political struggle and a racialist focus on culture. Among its first articles were discussions of "Advertisements That Insult," education, lynchings, political parties, and liberation movements around the world.[8] The first issue displayed the range of Briggs's intellectual inclinations with his "Race Catechism," a short piece praising the virtues of race patriotism: "The Negro Race [is] the most favored by the Muses of Music, Poetry and Art, and . . . possessed of those qualities of courage, honor and intelligence necessary to the making of . . . the most brilliant development of the human species."[9] Briggs believed that race determined aesthetic sensibility, temperament, and artistic talents,[10] not unlike many New Negro artists and theorists at the time who were convinced that black artistic achievement would demonstrate the Negro's humanity and thus compel white acceptance. But Briggs went beyond Renaissance thinkers to suggest that the racial qualities of the Negro were essential if the world were ever to achieve a higher level of humanity. Thus, those committed to freedom must join their art with political organizing and social insurgency.

Briggs used the *Crusader*'s editorial page to explore these and other questions, though he pursued a sort of heretical politics that joined seemingly contradictory impulses. For example, in the inaugural issue he began a three-part series on "The American Race Problem," arguing that the only "honorable solution" entailed combining political struggle in the United States with the establishment of a separate black nation that was militarily capable of defending the race everywhere. He emphasized black artistic and cultural genius while endorsing the entire Socialist Party ticket for New York state and municipal elections. The SPA ticket included several black radicals, including Dr. George Frazier Miller, A. Philip Randolph, and Chandler Owen, activists with whom Briggs had political relationships. Briggs urged readers to abandon the Democrats and Republicans, as the SPA was the only party working "to insure political justice [for] the Negro masses." Like his friends from the PEF and those on the ticket, he argued that any approach to racial oppression had to address class exploitation. Despite the SPA's spotty record on race, its sometime promotion of working-class interracialism signaled a commitment to racial equality absent from other parties.[11]

The decline of Hubert Harrison's Liberty League had left Briggs searching for an organization in which he might translate his vision of pan-African freedom into a political program. He turned to the Hamitic League of the World (HLW), a small intellectual organization founded by George Wells Parker in 1917 in Omaha, Nebraska. Parker was a lay historian and local activist who believed that when black people recognized their greatness in the annals of Africa's past, they would reject social subordination to whites and redeem Africa. To that end, Parker committed himself to demonstrating that "no race can lay claim to such glory as can the African race," and created the HLW. The HLW's program centered on producing a body of knowledge to "inspire the Negro with new hopes; to make him openly proud of his race and of its Great contributions to the religious development and civilization of mankind." The HLW declared that the "Negro race is the greatest race the world has ever known."[12] In an April 1917 address to the Omaha Philosophical Society, Parker cited numerous examples from the works of European historians, Herodotus, Homer, and others to argue that Africa had provided the basis for Greek culture and civilization and by extension Western civilization.[13]

The HLW offered Briggs an opportunity both to bridge intellectual and political activity and to make connections with a group of diasporic radicals with similar ideals. Although Briggs later downplayed his involvement with the HLW, historian Robert A. Hill points out that Briggs's name appeared as a founding member, and in December 1918 he was listed as the HLW's vice president. In fact, he held a leadership position alongside the Puerto Rican activist Grace Hutten, the Haitian intellectual Francisco Callas, and the noted African nationalist and future Garveyite J. E. Casely-Hayford of the Gold Coast. The following summer, Briggs joined John E. Bruce, Arturo (Arthur) Schomburg, Augusta Warring, and Anselmo Jackson in organizing a Harlem branch of the HLW, and by its fourth issue the *Crusader* had become the Hamitic League's publicity organ.[14] The group's diasporic scope and commitment to detailing the superiority of the African race appealed to Briggs, though he would push the HLW toward political activism. Although Parker was active in Omaha's black community, his racialist vindicationism steered the organization away from community organizing and political struggle. But Harlem's more activist-oriented members encouraged the group to address issues of social equality, and Briggs helped shape its anti-imperialist politics, as seen in the HLW's call for self-determination for African nations.[15] Briggs's political vision was outgrowing the HLW.

After the first few issues of the *Crusader*, Briggs began thinking about creating an organization to pursue pan-African liberation. Political organizations in Harlem were notoriously ephemeral, and while starting them was common enough, sustaining them presented obvious challenges. With the Liberty League, Harrison had shown quite impressively, if only briefly, that it was possible to pursue a progressive community organizing agenda with a goal of linking local and global struggles. While Garvey's UNIA had drawn in several Liberty League and HLW members (most notably Bruce and Schomburg), some radicals saw major flaws in Garvey's program. In this context, Briggs and some core Liberty League members came together to fashion an organization that could address the immediate, day-to-day concerns of blacks in the United States and link these concerns to anticolonial movements around the world.[16]

Gender and the African Blood Brotherhood

Briggs and his colleagues established the ABB a few months after the *Crusader* first appeared. When Briggs published an advertisement in the October 1919 issue announcing the group's founding, he struck a chord with his readers, especially black men who saw it as a way to involve themselves in a struggle for the manhood of the race. The ABB required "no dues, fees or assessments," the ad said, only that applicants "are willing to go the limit!" From Philadelphia to Chicago, the Panama Canal Zone to the Dominican Republic, black men, largely workers, wrote to Briggs seeking membership. Several inquiries emphasized the need for race men to fight to redeem Africa and "pledge ourselves to rescue our women and children."[17] Others stressed their roles as family men and skilled laborers, while still others wrote simply seeking "to go to Africa and do all in my power for my race."[18]

By 1923, Briggs would claim that the ABB had more than eight thousand members, though only three thousand were considered fully active. He privately disclosed that two thousand members were women.[19] As historian Ula Taylor notes, black women in this period commonly joined male-dominated organizations, but within those groups often challenged their masculinist structures and patriarchal relationships in the larger black community.[20] While the ABB never outlined clearly defined gender roles for men and women, it replicated contemporary gendered notions of race struggle.

The covers of many issues of the *Crusader* carried photos of black women that conveyed their respectability, fine dress, comportment, and intellect. Many of these women had dark complexions. In part, this practice represented an attempt to challenge the black community's negative valuations of African physical features and light-skinned standards of beauty. Briggs's phenotypic white appearance and his cultural nationalism gave him a clear sense of the problems with complexional conflicts among black people. In the context of the urban North, where generally darker southern blacks entered black communities dominated by people with lighter complexions, the photos challenged a white supremacist cultural logic that undergirded black cultural values. However, by focusing on black women's beauty to challenge internalized racism, the *Crusader* limited black women to the corporeal.

Black women's importance to racial progress centered on their roles as wives and mothers. ABB Supreme Council member Theo Burrell called on black women to give birth and prepare Negro "manhood" for race struggle by nurturing scholars and philosophers and by bringing "us other Hanni-

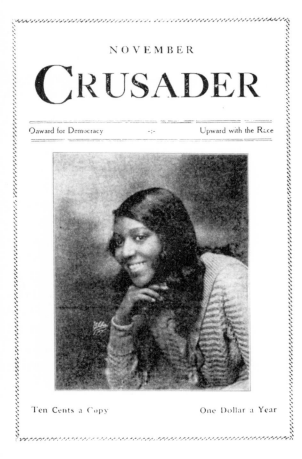

NOVEMBER

CRUSADER

Oaward for Democracy -:- Upward with the Race

Ten Cents a Copy   One Dollar a Year

bals and Dessalines to be the unified commander of the race."[21] The *Crusader*'s "Women's Department," a two-page spread that ran for nearly a year, reinforced the limited notion of black women in racial progress. In a practical vein, the spread offered suggestions to help "lighten as far as possible the burden that every housewife must carry through these strenuous times," providing recipes for using leftovers and stretching meager household budgets. But such concerns were dwarfed by its attention to the maintenance of physical beauty. Its regular instructions on grooming, the proper application of cosmetics, how to dress and adorn the "stout woman," and maintaining a buxom figure were of a piece with the belief that cooking was just as important to racial liberation as were art and literature.[22]

Grace Campbell, a social worker, parole officer, and clubwoman, was the only woman among the ABB's founders and the only woman on its Supreme Council. As such, she played a pivotal role in organizing the Brotherhood's daily activities.[23] In 1905, Campbell moved to New York from Washington, D.C., and quickly became ensconced in the local black club network. In 1911, she began working as a probation officer for the New York Court of General Sessions, and by 1916 she had established the Empire Friendly Shelter, a Harlem home for unwed mothers. Like other black radicals, she was drawn to Harrison's public lectures, and she became one of the first African American women to join the SPA.

In addition to her social work, Campbell lectured widely around the city, sponsored lyceums, and in 1923 held a position on the local school board, where she maneuvered to have Harrison lecture to the board on education and racial progress.[24] She also held multiple positions in radical organizations: secretary for the SPA's 21st Assembly District in Harlem, treasurer of the ABB, and president and organizer of the PEF. She handled all the ABB's logistical concerns and oversaw its activities from her home at 133rd Street and 8th Avenue. And when she could not meet or fell ill, the Brotherhood canceled its meetings. By 1923, the Uptown branch of the Communist Party held many of its meetings at her home. Equally important, Campbell's national reputation as a clubwoman ensured that black weeklies from Harlem to Chicago carried stories on the ABB.[25]

Such a high level of activity left Campbell little time to develop her ideas in print. Rather, she represents what Taylor calls a community feminist, a woman who joined feminism and nationalism "in a single coherent, consistent framework" that "provided a means of critiquing chauvinistic ideas of women as intellectually inferior."[26] Campbell would have pursued such work in discussions and debates within the ABB and the PEF, though she never deflated the myth of black women as mothers. Still, Campbell initiated a process where questions and concerns about race opened up space for thinking about issues related to women and the home as key to black revolutionary struggle. The small number of black women that Campbell recruited into the 21st AD in 1920 — women who likely formed the core of what Briggs identified as the ABB's most dedicated members — brought with them into these radical formations a concern for raising families and for sanitary living conditions and a sense of their political importance to revolutionary activism. Indeed, Briggs's editorials on housing in Harlem reflected not only his reading of Friedrich Engels's *The Housing Question* but also, and perhaps more important, discussions with Campbell. Indeed, such thinking ultimately led Campbell and Elizabeth Hendrickson to form the Harlem Tenants League in 1928.

The ABB and Black Internationalism

Briggs envisioned the ABB as an intellectual vanguard capable of directing the course of pan-African liberation. The Brotherhood began under a shroud of secrecy, and as befitted its name, functioned much like a fraternal order, replete with blood rituals and death oaths, yet it also emulated the Liberty League and HLW by fusing intellectual rigor with political organizing. In its initial iteration, the ABB reflected Briggs's racialist belief that people of African descent were joined together by primordial bonds. And it embraced the civilizationist impulse of racial uplift, seeking not merely to liberate Africa but to redeem it from its lowly place in the brotherhood of nations. At the same time, the Brotherhood's Socialist members sought to translate their theorizing about race and class into a program of community organizing.[27] The Brotherhood thus represented converging impulses, concerned both with an independent black nation-state and with elaborating a theory of race and class. Briggs shaped the ABB's early program and propelled it forward as he developed an internationalist pan-Africanist perspective in which he drew connections between the African world and Asia, Latin America, and Europe. At the same time, he thought through the relationship between black nationality in the United States, pan-African liberation, anti-imperialism, and socialism.

That Briggs rooted his internationalist politics in a desire for a stable, militarily solvent nation underscores the paradox of internationalism—its dependence on the nation. Briggs lacked the theoretical language to outline a political vision where pan-African liberation could conclude in a political reality other than the nation. Indeed, it would have been extraordinary had black internationalists in this era imagined a future without the nation as the ideal social organization.[28]

What tied New World blacks and continental Africans together was the fact that each was "born a Negro," which for Briggs hinged on his sense of the Negro as a *racialized* political being rather than a *biological* racial being. In discussing U.S., Caribbean, and African struggles, he offered possibly his clearest conception of an African diasporic identity, insisting that "the status of one section of the race surely affects the status of all other sections, no matter what ocean rolls between."[29] Racial unity represented a political response to the circumstances confronting different diasporic populations, he argued. What bound together those in Jamaica, Alabama, the Gold Coast, and London who were racialized as Negroes was not the "fact" of their blackness but the social, political, and economic realities that made them black, the racial hierarchies that "denied [Negroes] equal rights and the merest justice under any of the existing white governments."[30]

In regarding African diasporic populations as racialized groups occupying similarly subordinate positions in diverse racial formations, Briggs was concerned with highlighting how the dissimilar forms of oppression required seeing local struggles as constituting a global movement. Nonetheless, he put forward a diasporic identity that presented fundamental problems. On the one hand, he implied that pan-African unity required ignoring real social differences among African-descended populations and the complex of racial identities that arose from those differences. On the other, by insisting that local struggles would contribute to pan-African liberation, he sought to balance local and global concerns.

The black nation-state that Briggs believed essential to diasporic liberation would come out of the political movements of continental and New World Africans, he asserted, though the two did not constitute a single struggle.[31] Diasporic liberation therefore required asking how differently situated racial groups would relate to one another. Through this inquiry, Briggs came to see a need to build ties to non-African social movements. Histories of racialization had provided the basis for people of African descent to develop ties to one another. But if racialization was broader than the African world and represented political structures rather than biological groupings, it could also serve as a basis for building ties to liberation struggles in Asia, India, and the Pacific.

After World War I, many black radicals were concerned above all with the future of Germany's former African colonies and European empires. Du Bois had planned the Pan-African Congress of 1919 as a way to lobby for Africa's eventual freedom at Versailles. Briggs helped draft the HLW's resolution to the United States and the Allied nations, demanding that the "full rights of citizenship be granted to all people of Color, that all discrimination because of Color be made illegal," "that self-determination be extended to all nations and tribes within the African continent and throughout the World, and that the exploitation of Africa and other countries belonging to people of Color herewith cease."[32] Briggs continued to criticize Wilson's proposed League of Nations, which Briggs did not believe would bring freedom to the "Subject races" in Africa, the Americas, and the Pacific. Unless England and France were "prepared to give up their millions of square miles of African territory" and America would end its occupation of Haiti and Dominican Republic, grant Filipinos independence, and "apply self-determination" to Negroes in the South, Wilson's League would do little more than strengthen the "thieves and tyrants" whose interests lay in "the exploitation of the darker races."[33]

Less than a year after founding the *Crusader*, Briggs began devoting greater attention to class in his discussions of racial oppression and colonialism. In some respects, his understanding of the relationship between race and class seemed to share the socialist assumption about the primacy of class, but it went beyond race as an epiphenomenon. For example, when writing about the series of race riots that took place during the Red Summer of 1919, he dismissed the claim that Communists were solely responsible for black people defending themselves; rather, he argued, Negroes needed no prodding from white radicals to protect their lives or insist on social equality. Still, he considered racial oppression and lynching rooted in the same system that produced "wage slavery," "exploitation," and "imperialism" in Africa, Asia, and the Caribbean. Briggs connected black people's antiracist struggles to anticolonial and working-class movements. Black people suffered higher rents and lynching, he wrote, because they were "almost wholly of the proletariat" and had good reason "to be dissatisfied with the present system by which the white capitalists exploit the black and white masses and spread imperialism throughout the world."[34] Though blacks' economic exploitation did not negate the reality of racial oppression, class offered a basis on which to unite black people, white workers, the Irish, and oppressed African and Asian nations against white supremacy and capitalism.[35] Yet the hierarchies of diaspora, especially those relating to class, limited the possibilities for racial unity.

So did complexion. More than a decade after arriving in New York, Briggs continued to grapple with his white appearance, and he was bothered that many U.S. blacks considered his complexion a status symbol—a situation not unlike what he had known in the Caribbean. It troubled him that those blacks described as "brownskin" and "high yellow" considered themselves superior to "pure blacks" and sought to connect themselves "with the 'best white blood' of the South and North." Revealing something of the source of his race nationalism, Briggs expressed regret at being "as light as any light-skinned Negro possibly can be" and rejected the privileges his color afforded him. Nevertheless, if he could suggest that light-skinned blacks in the United States embrace blackness, the racial structures of Caribbean societies held no such possibility. There, light and dark skin were markers of racial differences that had definite consequence for class. But Briggs was convinced that black workers in the Caribbean would some day "question the wisdom of tilling the soil at starvation wages [so] that a few whites, near-whites and would-be-whites may live in luxury"; one day, he predicted, these workers would "become class-conscious as well as race-conscious." He recognized the problems in seeing race in one location as identical to another and believed that race in the diaspora reflected the interplay between distinct structures of racial oppression and histories of class.[36]

Briggs's attention to the constitutive structures of diaspora underscored the importance of the fight against imperialism in Asia to pan-African liberation. European imperialism could endure in Africa only as long as it survived in Asia, he argued, and "any action of the Asiatics in 'booting' the European thieves will be reflected by similar action in Africa and other parts of the world."[37] But the Brotherhood's thinking about Asia not only grew from some abstract sense of intercolonial connections but also resulted from exchanges with Asian radicals. ABB radicals traveled in the same circles as Indian radicals in the West Coast–based Ghadar Party, immigrant Chinese Communists, and the Japanese radicals gathered around Sen Katayama. Many in the Brotherhood had taken classes with Katayama at the Rand School in New York, where he studied in part as a result of his interest in the Negro problem. Katayama thus provided a bridge between ABB and Asian radicals.[38] This helps explain why Briggs devoted such considerable space in the *Crusader* to movements in China, Japan, and India, while W. A. Domingo ran stories in the *Emancipator* about Indian workers organizing in Trinidad and hailed a Hindu union movement in India as a model for black struggle.[39]

Given that the organized Left facilitated such intercolonial exchanges, it makes sense that Briggs also considered the Bolsheviks' position on national oppression in thinking about the global dimensions of race. In an editorial written two months after the 1919 Chicago race riot, he dismissed the red-baiting of New Negro radicals by declaring that if to fight for "one's rights is to be Bolshevists, then we are Bolshevists." In another editorial, Briggs described Bolshevism as the sole possibility for a racially egalitarian social order. Taking a rather romantic view of the new socialist society, he declared that "in Soviet Russia pogroms are no more because, for one thing, there are no reactionary capitalist influences at work to put worker against worker and race against race." In echoing a notion of race as an epiphenomenon of class exploitation, he suggested that he had moved away from his earlier racialist views of white supremacy and toward a perspective that emphasized relations of domination. Russia's appeal thus lay in the Bolsheviks' attitude toward anticolonial struggles, with Russian anti-imperialism and the illusion of racial equality representing for Briggs a challenge to Western imperialism and Western "'principles' of 'democracy'" as those principles are applied by England in India, Africa, Ireland . . . and by France in Africa and Indo-China."[40]

But Briggs remained keenly attuned to the differences between African peoples and the obstacles those differences posed to black internationalism. If races were primarily political groups, then racial unity could not simply be invoked; rather, it was a goal to be achieved based on similar experiences of social subordination. Briggs realized that the situation facing blacks in the United States did not explain the reality of all African peoples. As historian Arif Dirlik observes, such an overgeneralization would have meant an "erasure of the social relations that configure difference within and between groups" and their specific historical realities.[41] For Briggs, class marked one of the more important lines of intradiasporic difference by shaping the varying structures of race, determining the divergent social and political histories that limited racial unity, and creating hierarchies within the diaspora.

If the HLW, Liberty League, and intense discussions and debates that were the hallmark of the PEF provided Briggs and other black Socialists with venues in which to explore how class informed the structures and idioms of race, the ABB was the institutional context in which they explored how race informed the structures and histories of class. In 1921, the ABB published its organizational program, which emphasized the centrality of the international black working class to a pan-African liberation movement. The black workers in the United States and Africa who would lead this revolution would align with other forces struggling against oppression. The Brotherhood saw the end of racism and colonialism as central goals of proletarian struggle, pointing to Soviet Russia as the only world power opposing "the imperialist robbers who have partitioned our motherland and subjugated our kindred." Liberating Africa and its diaspora therefore required connecting the proletarian revolution sweeping through Europe with national liberation movements in the colonial world. The ABB envisioned an international force of anti-imperialist, antiracist, and working-class struggles ending oppression everywhere.[42]

To organize Africans and American blacks into an international movement, the ABB proposed bringing "all Negro organizations [in the United States] together on a Federation basis" to build "a united, centralized Movement" as well as combining "all Negro organizations in each of the African countries into a worldwide Negro federation." Each segment of this worldwide federation would work with a central body yet retain its local autonomy, basing its activities on local conditions. In the United States, the ABB believed that the needs and struggles of working-class blacks should take precedence, urging all "Negro organizations and all New Negroes [to] interest themselves in the organizing of Negro workers into labor unions for the betterment of their economic conditions and to act in close cooperation with the class-conscious white workers for the benefit of both." For its part, the international pan-African federation would form alliances with "small oppressed nations who are struggling against the capitalist exploiters" and with "class-conscious white workers who have spoken out in favor of African liberation and have shown a willingness to back with action their expressed sentiments." Their ultimate ally would be "the Third Internationale and its millions of followers."[43]

The ABB's program reflected both Briggs's efforts to infuse class into a pan-African politics and the efforts of black Socialists to expand class analysis around questions of race and national oppression. ABB radicals championed socialism not simply as an alternative to capitalism but as the basis of pan-African liberation, which they believed would only come with liberation struggles elsewhere. Their desire for racial unity led them to pursue alliances with other New Negro movement organizations, although disagreements at times arose about important political questions.

One of the more striking and historically important examples was Garvey's UNIA. Several ABB radicals were among Garvey's early supporters, believing, as did many others, that his organization offered black people a much-needed international organization with a largely working-class membership and that he was a charismatic leader capable of distilling the aspirations of millions of African peoples into a coherent program. The UNIA's support for Irish and black longshoremen who led a 1920 series of wildcat strikes against British shipping lines in the United States increased the group's appeal.[44] But Brotherhood radicals tempered their enthusiasm with skepticism about Garvey's vision of an African empire centered on capitalist development, a plan that they feared would replicate precisely the structures of power and domination that they opposed.

Garvey, Empire, and Racial Liberation

After World War I, when the world raged with revolution, the UNIA "burst into prominence," in the words of C. L. R. James, as a black working-class movement that benefited from the black masses who "felt the stir of the period."[45] With a program that made sense of their experiences and a message that resonated with a disenfranchised population, Garvey drew to the UNIA large numbers of rural southern blacks, African Americans in various urban areas in the North, and scores of Caribbean immigrants living in the Northeast.[46]

A great deal of mythology has grown up around the history of the ABB's opposition to Garvey and his UNIA that leaves the two groups' differences largely unexplained. The ABB was not a Communist-front group directed by Moscow to infiltrate and undermine the UNIA, as some have argued. Equally misleading is the suggestion that Briggs's criticisms of Garvey, even if part of a struggle over the direction of the black liberation movement, reflected personal jealousy regarding Garvey's success and the UNIA's international stature.[47] Some black radicals certainly envied Garvey,[48] but little evidence suggests that Briggs was among this group. Indeed, he and other ABB radicals had principled disagreements with Garvey about the African diaspora, pan-African struggle, and their visions of a liberated future.

When Hubert Harrison introduced Garvey at a 1917 meeting of the newly formed Liberty League, Garvey had already established the Universal Negro Improvement Association and African Communities League in Kingston, Jamaica. In the United States, Garvey concluded that he had a greater opportunity to build the UNIA among American blacks than in Jamaica, and he received considerable support from black radicals. His speech to the Liberty League, coming on the heels of the 1917 East St. Louis race riot, launched his U.S. political career. He established a New York branch of the UNIA and in 1918 moved its headquarters from Kingston to Harlem. Garvey then launched the *Negro World*, a weekly newspaper that served as the UNIA's publicity organ, with his old friend W. A. Domingo as editor. In Jamaica, both men had been officials in Sandy Cox's National Club, and they shared its commitment to Jamaican self-government. While Domingo became a Socialist after moving to the United States, Garvey increasingly embraced a pro-capitalist approach to liberation. Neither could have known of the other's politics when they met up again in Harlem. And when Domingo introduced Garvey to local activists, they had little reason to believe that they held such divergent political perspectives.[49]

Domingo's role as editor of the *Negro World* gave him considerable sway over the UNIA's public image. Though none of the issues that Domingo edited have survived, his writings in other Harlem periodicals make it easy to see why Garvey soon deemed Domingo's editorials too radical. In the July 1919 *Messenger* magazine, under the byline "W. A. Domingo, Editor of *The Negro World*," Domingo began a series of articles on socialism in pan-African struggles by lamenting that "Negroes do not embrace the philosophy of socialism . . . in greater numbers." He considered this situation a consequence of both the Socialist Party's failure to organize adequately among black people and black leaders' support for the critical institutions of racial oppression (that is, capitalism). In response to this and other pieces where he argued that socialism represented the Negro's best hope in the fight against racism and colonialism, Garvey had Domingo tried by the UNIA's executive committee for writing editorials in the *Negro World* inconsistent with UNIA goals. Domingo responded by resigning and publicly distancing himself from Garvey, criticizing his authoritarian leadership, and ridiculing the UNIA's "various business projects."[50]

Nevertheless, black radicals still welcomed Garvey's popularity and leadership. Briggs counted Garvey among the leaders on whom the race could "pin our faith,"[51] though Briggs stood largely alone among ABB radicals in praising the *Negro World* and supporting the UNIA's proposal for a black shipping line that would provide a commercial link among blacks in the United States, the West Indies, and Africa. Briggs believed that the Black Star Line (BSL) was "a most entrancing opportunity" for blacks in the West "to establish commercial relations with his kith and kin across the seas and to make millions of dollars trading with them and for them."[52] He still supported black businesses if their profits funded political struggle and would buy "big guns" to sit atop "the decks of modern battleships." The BSL thus appealed to his desire for an independent black nation with an economic base and the military ability to protect black people everywhere.[53]

By all appearances, Briggs admired Garvey and respected him as an organizer, supporting the UNIA's general program and defending Garvey's integrity against what Briggs at times considered overly harsh criticisms. Far from exhibiting envy or resentment, Briggs told his readers that Garvey had suffered enough for the race to be considered "a martyr" who had earned "a full-grown niche in Ethiopia's hall of fame."[54] Yet such praise, glowing as it often was, never blunted Briggs's criticism of Garvey. Briggs openly questioned Garvey's business practices (the BSL concept aside) and leadership style, urging Garvey to recognize "the peculiar circumstances and environment affecting this race of ours" and to allow greater transparency and judiciousness in his business dealings. In a glimpse of what would become his principal criticism, Briggs concluded that Garvey had been "too imperialistic and arbitrary in the past."[55]

Other black radicals considered Garvey an imperious leader with a troubling program. When Domingo left the *Negro World*, a reluctant Harrison took over as editor, hoping he might "give [the paper] a little 'tone'" but admitting privately that he did not want to be too closely associated with Garvey's program. Harrison disagreed vehemently with Garvey's vision of an African empire modeled after European modernity and rejected the idea that advanced, Westernized Negroes would lead and civilize backward Africa. In fact, Harrison saw nothing redeeming about Garvey and dismissed his intellect, a low opinion that sank further while Harrison edited the *Negro World*. In that position, he became convinced that Garvey suffered from delusions of grandeur and had changed the UNIA's "policy from Negro self-help to invasion of Africa."[56] While Domingo respected Garvey's propaganda skills and ability to tap into black people's latent frustrations and desires, Domingo, too, thought little of Garvey's intellect and leadership. When Domingo launched the *Emancipator*, he devoted considerable space to challenging the BSL as the basis of racial liberation, still convinced that racial equality and national liberation would come only through class struggle.[57]

In the spring of 1920, the *Emancipator* ran a serialized analysis of the BSL by Anselmo Jackson as well as a report by Briggs on the BSL's holdings. The report found that the line owned virtually none of the ships that it claimed to own. In response, Garvey filed a two-hundred-thousand-dollar lawsuit, and UNIA members physically attacked newsboys selling the *Emancipator* and destroyed copies of the paper on newsstands.[58]

Many black radicals found Garvey's proposal for an African empire even more troubling. An array of Harlem radicals publicly criticized the imperial elements of Garvey's program. When former UNIA secretary-general Bryant C. Buck addressed the opening of the local chapter of the London-based African League (a small, characteristically ephemeral New Negro movement organization), he warned black people to "beware of autocrats who . . . are engaged in the futile but self-enriching task of Empire-building." Domingo echoed Buck's concerns.[59] Many radicals saw empire as indelibly linked to imperialism, with its hierarchical social structures and international relations of power. In one editorial, Domingo cautioned, "The desire for [empire] on the part of some Negroes is compounded of ignorance, ambition and a desire for revenge. It is not rational. Appeals having imperialism as a basis reach down to the bottom of group life and rouse the dormant consciousness of race. . . . It is the road to decay, disaster and destruction."[60] An African empire would be just as oppressive as the British empire, and racial oppression, poverty, and hunger would continue unabated, with black people simply exchanging "our white parasites and profiteers for black parasites and black profiteers," concluded the Afro-Caribbean socialist Frank Crosswaith. At a session of the PEF, Victor Daily, who worked on the *Messenger* staff, in his lecture on "The Fallacy of a Negro Empire," called Garvey "a fool, a lunatic or a swindler who hoped to profit from misleading the people."[61]

Briggs, too, found Garvey's call for an African empire troubling, though when the UNIA announced its plans for the August 1920 International Convention of the Negro Peoples of the World, which would bring together African peoples from throughout the diaspora to plot a course for African liberation, he was initially supportive. Briggs even called Garvey's idea for a supreme leader of the race necessary as long as that person was elected and derived "his powers and authority from the race" rather than by fiat. Briggs asked that Garvey invite organizations outside the UNIA's influence so that they could determine their own future and select their own leaders. Garvey responded with a letter praising Briggs for providing "the most intelligent explanation of the real purpose of our Convention" and invited him to attend. Although Briggs appreciated the letter, he still cautioned that without adequate representation "from all the Negro communities of Africa and the New World," choosing such a leader could threaten any hope for racial unity and "engender enmity and division."[62]

In July, however, Briggs disparaged the idea of an African empire and called the International Convention "a noble concept" that suffered from "selfishness and smallness of mind" and would "approach the proportions of a gigantic farce."[63] He was now concerned that a supreme leader of the race might pose serious problems for a program of African liberation. The ABB had long argued for the importance of local leadership in diasporic struggles. In an editorial titled "Africa's Redemption," Domingo echoed Harrison's criticism of the period's racial uplift ethos to argue that Africans would liberate Africa: "Africans of the dispersion" could best help in African liberation through their local struggles, by "striving to the limit to break a system that is responsible for the present political degradation of Africa and their own oppression in the West Indies, Central and South America and the United States." Doing so called "for clear thinking and recognition of the fact that Africans are not the only ones who are the victims of capitalis[m]."[64] Domingo scoffed at the tendency among New Negro intellectuals to criticize imperialism in Africa yet remain silent about the ravages of capital in the United States. Black struggles in the Americas could affect African liberation without imposing themselves on Africa, he argued. Moreover, Asia, Latin America, and white workers also suffered under capitalism, a view that insisted on seeing racism as bound to global capital and that required building ties between African diasporic and non-African liberation struggles.

The International Convention of the Negro Peoples of the World, coming as it did amid massive global upheavals, captured many people's imaginations. Briggs saw it as "the most important event in the history of the Negro" since the Civil War, though the convention was "fraught with catastrophic dangers to the Negro." According to Harrison, who attended as a delegate from the Virgin Islands, only a fraction of the reported twenty-five thousand participants actually attended. Moreover, he claimed that Garvey arrived without a program for racial liberation, dictated the convention's resolutions, and manipulated the election of officers. And only one delegate, Gabriel M. Johnson of Liberia, was from Africa; most were, like Harrison, Caribbean residents of New York whom Garvey "called in to pose as delegates *sent* from the West Indies and Africa."[65] While Briggs believed that the convention had the potential to build ties among blacks in America, the West Indies, and Africa, he felt that Garvey's election as the provisional president of Africa threatened to undermine that solidarity. The main problem, as Briggs saw it, was that the convention was "'packed' for Mr. Garvey." Briggs questioned whether "the African peoples will relish the idea of a New World leader in preference to the very many able native leaders," suggesting that Africans might "resent this almost autocratic election of a New World leader for them." Garvey's only chance to salvage the effort was to appoint a cabinet of race men and to give "numerical preference to the African group" in leadership positions.[66]

In the ensuing months, Briggs came to argue with greater frequency that socialism was essential to ending racial oppression and imperialism. For that year's New York state and municipal elections, the *Crusader* again endorsed the Socialist Party ticket, which included A. Philip Randolph and ABB Supreme Council member Grace Campbell, claiming that it was the only ticket that supported the Negro's class and racial interests. Later, when Briggs began to openly dismiss the SPA as yet another of the "eminent respectables of American politics," he continued to advocate socialism when reiterating the links between African diasporic and other liberation struggles.[67] But although Briggs saw racial equality as impossible under capitalism, he was not entirely optimistic that it would come about under socialism. Worldwide socialism, he told *Crusader* readers in April 1921, "is only one way whereby oppressed *races* may save themselves from the oppression engendered by the functioning of imperialist capitalism." Briggs had little faith that white workers would entirely abandon their racist ideals.[68]

The nascent communist movement appealed to some ABB members who had left the SPA as a consequence of its deficiencies on race, national oppression, and especially the "Negro Question," among other issues. U.S. communism would provide a link to the Communist International, whose support of national liberation in Africa and Asia impressed ABB members.[69]

Around the same time, Briggs severed all ties with the HLW. In June 1921, the *Crusader* ended its run as the HLW's organ and became the ABB's publication. During the same month, the Brotherhood published its constitution, which declared the group's purposes as opposing racist terror, propaganda, and education and strengthening the struggles of blacks in the United States.[70] The ABB's emphasis on self-defense became more than idle rhetoric later in the summer when a race riot ravaged Tulsa, Oklahoma.

In early June 1921, a rumor had spread that a Tulsa bootblack, Dick Rowland, had assaulted a white female elevator operator in a downtown building. Local officials moved quickly, arresting Rowland and placing him in the county courthouse. When word that local whites were talking of lynching Rowland reached Tulsa's black residents, seventy-five armed men, almost all of them World War I veterans, stood guard outside the courthouse to protect Rowland, preventing the lynching. Angered by such audacity, local whites unleashed a wave of violence that claimed hundreds of black lives and burned thousands out of their homes. When word got out that only a few months earlier black veterans had organized a local ABB post and that this post was at the forefront of the black community's defense — indeed, had even taken the violence into white sections of town — the ABB was thrust into the international spotlight.[71]

In the national press, Briggs affirmed black people's right to defend themselves from white violence, though he denied that the ABB had fomented the riot. The unfortunate publicity gave the ABB a level of political currency it had not previously enjoyed. Seizing the opportunity to reach hundreds of Harlem residents, the ABB held a series of public meetings on the riot, allowing survivors to tell their stories and raising money to help the newly homeless. In one flyer announcing a public meeting, the ABB urged "every [N]egro tired of lynching, peonage, jim-crowism and disfranchisement, to come out and hear our plan of action for removing these injustices which we suffer, with others, as workers." During one street-corner meeting, Domingo reasserted black people's right to self-defense: "Our aim is to allow those who attack us to choose the weapons," he told listeners from his stepladder; "if it be guns, we will reply with guns."[72] The events in Tulsa also presented ABB leaders with a chance to drive home an internationalist take on racial violence. In the *Crusader*, Briggs reminded readers that Russian Jews had received similar treatment "until the workers of all races arose and overthrew the capitalist Czarist combination, and set up the Soviets." Tulsa provided black people yet another example of the need to "line up . . . with the radical forces of the world that are working for the overthrow of capitalism and the dawn of a new day."[73]

Briggs also tried using Tulsa to forge a coalition with Garvey and the UNIA.

Many ABB activists still believed that they could influence black people globally through the UNIA. During the second International Convention of the Negro Peoples of the World, held in August 1921, Briggs wrote to Garvey that the two men shared "the same aims and ideals" and that it therefore behooved them to consider "what we might be able to do for the race through conscious co-operation." Briggs proudly claimed that reports from Tulsa, though erroneous, confirmed the Brotherhood's ability to protect black life. But the attempt at a coalition bore little fruit. Garvey made it clear that neither the UNIA nor the convention would embrace communism.[74] What Briggs and the ABB could not have known is that Garvey had made a sharp political turn the previous summer. Robert Hill notes that when the Department of Justice kept Garvey out of the United States for nearly five months for alleged seditious utterances, Garvey gained readmission "only after much political wire-pulling in Washington, D.C." This, Hill argues, led Garvey to begin openly attacking radicals and urging moderation. Although ABB members had seen little that they considered radical in Garvey, they were not prepared for his starkly conservative turn.[75]

During the second International Convention, the ABB's criticisms of Garvey grew increasingly barbed. The organization published a pamphlet that carried a contemptuous title, *To New Negroes Who Really Seek Liberation*, and called any anticolonial struggle not committed to destroying capitalism counterproductive. With regard to Garvey's call for black people to return to Africa, the ABB argued that it was futile to "imagine that by moving from one 'colony' to another our people can escape oppression." When European workers overthrew capitalism, blacks would have the "opportunity to conquer power and seize control on the continent of Africa." The ABB also distributed a *Negro Congress Bulletin and News Service* outside the convention hall. Garvey, already annoyed with Briggs and the ABB, became irate when he saw the third issue's headline: "Negro Congress at a Standstill—Many Delegates Dissatisfied with Failure to Produce Results." He then publicly expelled the ABB delegates from the convention, dashing any remaining hopes for an alliance.[76]

Garvey was convinced that Briggs and the ABB were Communist pawns directed to infiltrate and undermine the UNIA. But although both the American Communist Party and the Communist Labor Party were recruiting Briggs, he was not yet a Communist, and neither party exercised any kind of control over the Brotherhood. Nevertheless, Garvey and many others saw sufficient evidence to suspect a conspiracy. After the convention, the enmity between the ABB and UNIA turned personal. Garvey told a Harlem crowd that Briggs was a white man masquerading as a Negro and made disparaging remarks about his mother. A furious Briggs launched into an impromptu two-hour speech on a Harlem stepladder, excoriating Garvey, the UNIA, and their supporters, reportedly without stuttering once. In addition, Briggs filed and won a slander suit against Garvey and began a series of editorials and articles in the *Crusader* criticizing the UNIA's failures. All but one of the editorials in the October 1921 issue attacked Garvey, as both men abandoned what civility remained in their exchanges and pursued personal vendettas, attempting to bring federal pressure to bear on the other man. Garvey supplied the Justice Department with a copy of Briggs's midconvention letter as evidence of the ABB's plans to overthrow the government. An infuriated Briggs responded by publishing his letter to Garvey in the *Crusader* under the title "Garvey Turns Informer."[77] Rather inexplicably for a purported revolutionary, however, Briggs also supplied federal agents with information from his investigation into the BSL and visited the New York office of the Department of Justice with former UNIA secretary-general James D. Brooks, reportedly to find out "when the Government intended taking action."[78]

Briggs devoted the final issues of his magazine almost entirely to Garvey and the UNIA. Cyril A. Crichlow, former UNIA resident secretary in Liberia, criticized Garvey's plans for a UNIA settlement in that country, questioning how those plans would affect native Liberians. Citing the history of African Caribbeans coming to Africa as "the tools of the British capitalistic and military interests," he asked what good could come of Garvey's plans. Much of the *Crusader*'s last issue reported on Garvey's January 12, 1922, arrest by federal agents for using the mail to defraud, charges that stemmed from the sale of fraudulent BSL stock. Briggs virtually gloated over Garvey's arrest and the UNIA's failures, and he admonished Garvey's followers for their "blind, fanatical allegiance *to the individual above the Cause.*" Rather ungraciously, he pointed out that "for the past five months *The Crusader* has been warning its readers and the public in general against the manifold financial schemes of Marcus Garvey." People who ignored those warnings "have no one but themselves and Marcus Garvey to blame for their loss." Briggs even took credit for helping expose the BSL and facilitating Garvey's arrest, showing no empathy for the UNIA's rank and file and certainly no political tact.[79]

Following Garvey's arrest and the UNIA's decline, ABB radicals continued to pursue a united front of New Negro organizations, with black working-class struggles in the United States at the center of their vision of pan-African liberation. Yet they rejected the idea that New World blacks would bestow modernity on and thus civilize Africa and Africans. At the same time, although few ABB members were actually Communists and Garvey had exaggerated the Communist influence on the group, the relationship between the ABB and American communism slowly became crucial to the development of radical black internationalism. The thinking of black radicals about race and nation would ultimately push the Comintern to step up its support for black liberation worldwide.

3

With All Forces Menacing Empire

Black and Asian Radicals Internationalize the Third International

The African Blood Brotherhood's global vision was not unique. The belief that a pressing need existed for a global movement of black people was widely held and had existed for some time. Alexander Walters, the African Methodist Episcopal bishop who presided over the 1900 London Pan-African Conference convened by the Trinidadian barrister Henry Sylvester Williams, echoed the sentiments of many when he said that the race needed "a great National and International organization" that could "incorporate in its membership the ablest and most aggressive representatives of African descent in all lands."[1] Such sentiment prompted W. E. B. Du Bois to resurrect the Pan-African Congress (PAC) movement and Marcus Garvey to create his UNIA.

The ABB saw in Garvey's UNIA a movement that had a significant presence in the Caribbean and parts of Africa (especially Liberia) and that drew much of its membership from the black working class, which ABB leaders considered vital to black liberation. But the Brotherhood never contemplated merging with the UNIA, hoping instead for collaboration. Coalitions with larger organizations, however, had not proven productive, and ABB radicals had seen in Garvey the danger of an imperious leadership that would impose itself on Africa. Whereas Garvey's African empire failed to seek African input while plotting the course of pan-African liberation, the Brotherhood sought to draw diasporic organizations into a pan-African federation.

But although the ABB believed organizational alliances offered the best chance of achieving a global reach, a working relationship with the UNIA never materialized. Cyril Briggs, Richard B. Moore, and W. A. Domingo were often so caustic in their criticisms of Garvey that many observers became convinced that they had facilitated the arrest of the single black man capable of mounting a serious challenge to European imperialism. And, indeed, not only had Briggs urged the Justice Department to take action against Garvey, but several ABB members had published reports about Garvey that they openly claimed led to his arrest. As a result, the ABB went into decline, marginalized by recriminations toward it and other New Negro activist-intellectuals who had called for the government to arrest Garvey and destroy the UNIA.

ABB radicals' experiences with Garvey raised difficult questions: What would a global movement of black people look like? How might an organization spanning the globe attract rather than merely propose to speak for black people in Africa, the Caribbean, Europe, and the United States? And, most important, could they in fact build such a movement?

ABB radicals realized that with their small numbers, marginal popularity, and inadequate resources to send their members outside the United States, the black international they desired was more an ideal than a genuine possibility. Still, their arguments about pan-African liberation were beginning to resonate with other New Negro radicals. When Du Bois convened the second PAC in 1921 in London, Brussels, and Paris, nearly one-third of the participants were African,[2] and the London resolution called for self-government in Africa, Asia, and the "isles of the sea." It also advocated creating institutions to foster interracial exchange among suppressed people and urged race leaders to align with black workers. Further, Du Bois, departing somewhat from the racial uplift ethos of the era, argued that "Africa for Africans" meant that at some point, Africa should be administered by Africans, not, as so many believed, "by West Indians or American Negroes."[3]

But the PAC movement soon found itself in disarray, riven by conflict. The ABB had previously been highly critical of Du Bois and had derided the 1919 PAC's resolution as calling "merely for 'better' white government of the black man." ABB leaders believed that Du Bois had overlooked African anticolonial movements and failed to relate them to Indian liberation struggles against the British empire, and by 1921 the PAC echoed many of their concerns. Still, Du Bois's conflict with the conservative Francophone African contingent in 1921 limited the possibility that the PAC might offer ABB radicals a vehicle for pursuing a black international.[4]

Amid such limited options, key members of the ABB turned increasingly to international communism to link pan-African liberation with anticolonial struggles in the non-African world. Several ABB members came from the Socialist Party and had developed relationships with American Communists. By the summer of 1921, these ABB members were entering the communist movement, primarily because of its international potential. Of particular importance was the support that the Third Communist International, headquartered in Moscow and led initially by V. I. Lenin, expressed for Asian and African anticolonial struggles. Briggs had originally considered the white Left insignificant to black liberation, but after reading the Comintern's position on anticolonial struggles, he began to read the works of Karl Marx and Friedrich Engels and to devote more attention to Russia in his writings.[5]

Still, Brotherhood radicals initially hesitated to embrace both the Communist Party of America (CPA) and the Bolsheviks as a consequence of the Left's approach to race and national oppression, and the doubts radicals had about working in a white-dominated organization. For Briggs, "the Negro was the acid test of any program." And it was not clear to anyone in the ABB that the Comintern's anti-imperialism would easily translate into a program that addressed African people's struggles.[6] So what had changed?

The entrance of ABB radicals into organized communism lies in a history outside the white Left. Operating mainly within the New Negro movement, the ABB had put forward a program and undertaken political activities based on its sense of the circumstances facing black people around the world. But given its problems sustaining itself, such efforts had produced few if any tangible results. Hence, weighing the practical concerns of a movement against their organization's shortcomings led Briggs, Grace Campbell, Richard Moore, and others in the ABB to contemplate entering the communist movement. They came to the communist movement, however, as they came into the Socialist Party—as activist-intellectuals willing to stretch the boundaries of a political theory so that it might address racial oppression and colonialism.

What has gone unnoticed in scholarship on blacks in organized communism is how Asian radicals opened up the Communist International so that it seemed to black radicals a vehicle for African diasporic liberation. At the same time that the ABB was pursuing an alternative, non-European route to socialism and challenging the notion of white workers liberating Africa and Asia, Asian radicals were arguing for the centrality of Asian national liberation to socialism. Their argument had little impact on the Comintern's 1920 resolution on national liberation but nonetheless informed how the Comintern approached anticolonial struggles and prompted the establishment of communist parties throughout Asia. When ABB radicals joined the communist movement, they were joining not merely an international elaborated by the Bolsheviks but an international in which Asian anticolonial radicals had created important theoretical openings.

Through theorizing the international dimensions of race, black radicals from the ABB connected African and Asian diasporic struggles. At the Comintern's Fourth Congress, held in 1922, ABB members Otto Huiswoud and Claude McKay, who were also Communists, met with Asian radicals, drawing on their treatment of national liberation to discuss the Negro question and describe race as an international system of oppression linking the African diaspora to Asia. The ABB and Asian radicals thus introduced race and nation into international communism at its inception. These two radical traditions converged to put forward what Brent Hayes Edwards calls intercolonial internationalism, an "alternative universality" in which African and Asian anticolonial struggles represented the "horizon to an emergent Comintern discourse of internationalism" that centered on white workers in Europe and the United States. Edwards's treatment of Nguyen Ai Quoc (later known as Ho Chi Minh) and Lamine Senghor in Paris highlights their sense of the linkages between Asian and African colonial peoples within the French empire.[7] Within the institutional space of Comintern policy debates, ABB radicals articulated a vision of similar linkages across empires through the prism of race and alongside Asian radicals theorized the centrality of Asian and African diasporic struggles to socialism. In the process, they internationalized the Third International.

Race and American Communists

The internationalism that black radicals praised in the Bolsheviks was not reflected in the U.S. communist movement. In fact, the initial years of American communism offered little evidence that those calling themselves Communists would approach race any differently than they had when they were Socialists.

Both the CPA, which consisted largely of foreign-born members, and the heavily native Communist Labor Party, rivals formed within a day of one another,[8] seemed to believe that the Negro problem was simply a class problem that proletarian revolution alone would solve. Only the CPA counted among its charter members a black radical, Otto Huiswoud. Huiswoud's activism in the SPA and his successful leadership of striking black workers on New York's Fall River boat line had earned him a delegate seat on the SPA's left wing in February 1919, a position he used to build ties to those foreign-born Socialists who later formed the CPA.[9] Huiswoud may have found the CPA's program appealing because it included a paragraph on the Negro problem: "In close connection with the unskilled worker is the problem of the Negro worker. The Negro problem is a political and economic problem. The racial oppression of the Negro is simply the expression of his economic bondage and oppression, each intensifying the other. This complicates the Negro problem, but does not alter its proletarian character. The Communist Party will carry on agitation among the Negro workers to unite them with all class conscious workers."[10] Although the CPA intended to convey its opposition to segregation and commitment to organizing black and white workers without distinction, for black radicals this paragraph merely made explicit white radicals' general inability to consider seriously how race affected the lives of black people.

An editorial in the independent monthly *Liberator*, published just after the CPA's founding convention, did not make black radicals feel any better. The editorial looked forward to the day when Negroes would "realize that the economic problem, the problem of exploitation and class-rule in general, lies at the heart of the race-problem" and patronizingly explained that it was of greater importance for Negroes to join revolutionary proletarian organizations than racial organizations. Yet during the abortive attempt to merge the CPA and the Communist Labor Party the following summer, native-born Communists criticized the CPA for giving "undue prominence" to the Negro problem.[11]

Black radicals had already rejected such thinking by Socialists and were loath to join a new movement that offered more of the same. Brotherhood radicals at first showed no desire to join the growing communist movement, though Communists had targeted them following the publicity over the Tulsa race riot. ABB publications initially carried no commentary about any Communist party and even publicly criticized white radicals on questions of race. Domingo questioned white leftists whose "radicalism in many cases doesn't extend to colored peoples"; few understood that "in America the Negro question is the touchstone, the measure by which the sincerity of American radicalism can be measured." Echoing his previous warnings to the SPA, Domingo implored white radicals to recognize that the Negro possessed enough power to either "maintain or destroy American radicalism." He argued that the Negro was central to socialist revolution and that achieving socialism in Africa and the Caribbean was essential for socialist revolution in Europe.[12] Domingo also criticized Bolsheviks who could support "the oppressed of all races" yet tended to bungle the race question. After learning that Leon Trotsky openly feared that Western empires might use Asians and Africans as soldiers against Soviet Russia, Domingo lamented that "everywhere Bolshevism brings terror to the heart of imperialism . . . yet, the chieftains of this liberating doctrine are afraid of some of the very races whom they would free."[13]

While the Bolsheviks appealed to most black radicals, they at times appeared little better than the Socialists. Despite their support of anticolonial struggles, the Bolsheviks seemed to view the Negro as backward and easily manipulated by the bourgeoisie. Only after changes in both American communism and the Comintern would appreciable numbers of black radicals become Communists.

Asian Radicals, Intercolonialism, and the Second Comintern Congress

In the months leading up to the Communist International's Second Congress in 1920, Lenin submitted his "Preliminary Draft Theses on the National and Colonial Question" and requested from those comrades "who possess concrete information on any of these very complex problems" their opinions and suggestions for improving his proposals. Lenin developed an agenda that he believed would foster greater unity among the international proletariat. If Communists recognized the progressive character of national liberation movements, the Comintern would be compelled to support those struggles that chipped away at capitalism. Of Lenin's twelve theses, two proved particularly important to black radical participation in international communism: one required Communist parties to "render direct aid to the revolutionary movements among the dependent and underprivileged nations (for example, Ireland, the American Negroes, etc.) and in the colonies"; the other directed parties to "assist the bourgeois-democratic liberation movement" in "backward states and nations."[14] Lenin sought to broaden the discussion of national liberation beyond its normative European terrain and draw Asia, Africa, and American blacks into Comintern organizational work. He thus raised the widespread condemnation of nationalism that many felt had undermined the earlier Socialist Second International and reiterated his earlier criticism of the SPA's position that the Negro question was merely a class question. Others within the Comintern echoed Lenin's concerns. In his report for the Second Congress, Gregory Zinoviev, chair of the Comintern's executive committee, noted that because the Third International had focused solely on Europe and America, "all which has been done by it up to now on the Eastern question is very far from sufficient."[15]

Lenin's invitation to discuss his theses sparked a series of debates that would prove critical to how radicals of color around the world perceived the Comintern. Much scholarly attention to Lenin's theses, however, has been pre-occupied with whether, in his parenthetical reference to American Negroes alongside Ireland, he intended to argue that blacks in the United States were an oppressed nation, thus anticipating (and for some observers validating) the 1928 Black Belt Nation Thesis. Long-standing debates have concerned whether the thesis came in response to conditions in the United States or was imposed by Moscow and whether it comprehended the workings of race in a capitalist political economy. Participants in these debates generally have failed to note Comintern theorists' inability to deal with racial oppression as a system of domination.[16] However suggestive Lenin's overture may have been, however laudable its intent, its appeal rested on applying the theory and rhetoric of national oppression and imperialism to address, if only cursorily, racial oppression as a species of national oppression. In this sense, it resonated with a political intellectual project that many anticolonial activist-intellectuals were already pursuing and that black radicals in the ABB were attempting to outline. Indeed, both Ho Chi Minh and Briggs credited Lenin's theses with prompting their entrance into international communism.[17] Still, it is striking that so little of the scholarship on Lenin's theses has considered precisely how he approached national liberation outside Europe, the historicism guiding his proposal, or the challenges that Asian anticolonial radicals mounted to his thinking in the Comintern.

Possibly the most important critical response came from Manabendra Nath (M. N.) Roy, who came to the Second Congress representing the Partido Comunista Mexicano (Mexican Communist Party). Born Narendra Nath Bhattacharya in Arbelia, Bengal, in 1887, the young Brahmin had established the Bengali revolutionary Jugantar Party in 1913, when he was in his mid-twenties, and had helped to organize a plot to procure weapons from Germany for an armed uprising. He was joined in that effort by the Berlin Committee of Indian Revolutionaries, a conglomerate of various Indian revolutionary groups formed in 1914 by a nationalist in exile, Champakram Pillai. The Berlin Committee had created an international network of Indian radicals to facilitate the plan, which along with procuring arms was to include training and coordinating the return to India of more than five thousand Indians in diaspora. This network included the San Francisco–based Ghadar Party, a Punjabi revolutionary society formed in 1913 by Sikh peasants and Hindu students whose radicalization grew from their experiences of being racialized in the Bay Area. But the plan failed when British authorities intercepted shipments and boats with returning revolutionaries and arrested several returnees. Bhattacharya immediately went into exile, settling for a time in the United States.[18] In San Francisco, he assumed the name M. N. Roy, began contemplating the colonial situation in India, and met for the first time Ghadar radicals as well as white liberals and radicals sympathetic to Indian national liberation. Among these was Evelyn Trent, a white woman studying at Stanford University whom he married.[19]

Roy and Trent moved to New York, where they befriended noted exiled Indian nationalist Lala Lajpat Rai. Lajpat Rai and Roy spent many hours discussing India's independence and debating white Socialists and anarcho-syndicalists about Marxism. Lajpat Rai and Roy rejected Marxism's materialism as contrary to Indian spirituality and felt that white radicals' concerns about the Indian masses were a ruse to avoid supporting anticolonial struggles and self-rule. Yet when Lajpat Rai declared that Indians should first be masters of their own house and that it "make[s] a great difference whether one is kicked by his brother or by a foreign robber," Roy wondered if "there was something wrong in our case." Seeking an alternative to Indian nationalism, Roy began studying Marxism in earnest.[20]

After only a few months, he was thinking about Asian and African anticolonial struggles in relation to Marxism. He wrote a small pamphlet that indicted British colonialism and questioned Woodrow Wilson's commitment to self-determination.[21] Roy also showed signs of departing from Marxist historicism when he attributed the "industrial supremacy of present day England" to "the plundering done in India" rather than to internal class struggle, economic development, or the rise of a new mode of production. Roy declared that the lasting peace envisioned by Wilson could come only through "the complete liberation of all countries and subjected people, not only in Europe, but also in Asia and Africa."[22]

The British had enlisted American authorities' aid in tracking Ghadar radicals associated with the attempt to obtain German arms for an uprising, and on March 7, 1917, in what became known as the Hindu Conspiracy case, Roy was arrested while walking home from a Lajpat Rai lecture at Columbia University. Convinced that he would be prosecuted and deported to India, Roy, accompanied by Trent, left New York for Mexico City in the spring of 1917.[23] If the United States provided him the opportunity to rethink revolution and political activism, Mexico brought him "into contact with a mass revolutionary movement" that allowed him to implement those ideas.[24] Roy quickly rose to prominence in the Mexican Left, editing the Socialist Party's *La Lucha* newspaper and working with the Bolshevik Mikhail Borodin and the American expatriate Charles Francis Phillips to establish the Partido Comunista Mexicano. Most important, Roy had the opportunity to discuss Marxism's theoretical nuances with Borodin and to clarify his understanding of national liberation in socialist revolution.[25]

Yet few Communists would have recognized in Roy's writings on nationalism what they understood as "scientific socialism." In an August 1919 article, "Hunger and Revolution in India," Roy offered an approach to Indian national liberation that departed from what political theorist Sanjay Seth has identified as a division in Marxism between "backward" (non-Western) and "advanced" (Western) nations. If, as Seth argues, Lenin saw imperialism bringing the East into capitalism's orbit "and *thereby* within the ambit of Marxism," Roy worked at reformulating Marxism "to include the East, in its specificity."[26] Roy argued against any notion of Indians as preproletarians whose nationalist struggles would bring them into historical proximity to the West and "real" (that is, proletarian) revolution. Inverting Frederick Engels's 1882 declaration that "the half-civilized countries will follow" proletarian victory in Europe and North America,[27] Roy maintained that India's independence would weaken the British empire and signal "a long step towards the redemption of the world from the jaws of the capitalistic system," setting the stage for socialist revolution, which he believed English workers would never undertake.[28]

Roy arrived in Moscow for the Second Comintern Congress in 1920 with the aid and support of Borodin, who was so impressed with Roy that he interceded to ensure he attended as a representative of the Partido Comunista Mexicano.[29] Roy thus came to the Second Congress with the sanction of a high-ranking Bolshevik revolutionary. He also brought an internationalism that centered on the "backward" peoples of Asia and Africa.

When Roy read Lenin's draft theses, he believed that the commitment to national liberation outside Europe would be "popular in Asia and Africa" but feared that in practice it would collapse class differences and ignore radical elements in Asia likely to embrace class struggle. In a rare personal meeting with Lenin, Roy found the leading Bolshevik gracious; Lenin readily admitted that he knew little about Asia and Africa and willingly engaged in a long discussion of national liberation in Asia. Roy pointed to Lenin's proposal for wholesale support of bourgeois nationalist movements as the critical flaw of his draft theses. Roy maintained that the oppressed bourgeoisie "even in the most advanced colonial countries" groped for a feudalism that kept their movements from becoming "a bourgeois democratic revolution." The importance of Europe's Asian colonies to the global capitalist economy meant that the Comintern should recognize class differences in Asia and "develop the national liberation movement . . . as part of the World Proletarian Revolution."[30]

At Lenin's behest, Roy drafted a supplementary set of theses, which he submitted to the National and Colonial Commission. In them, Roy positioned Asia and the global South at the nexus of proletarian revolution. In his mind, communism would realize its global ambitions only if the Comintern turned its attention to the East.[31] Although Lenin had called on Communists to support national liberation, Roy distinguished between national liberation movements, which fostered class consciousness among colonial peasants and workers, and nationalism, which served the interests of the colonial elite. The Comintern's responsibility, he continued, was to foster the radical elements in Asia, not to support the bourgeoisie. The colonial world's revolutionary potential equaled Europe's, and ignoring the importance of Asian national liberation to socialist revolution would replicate the Second International's failure "to appreciate the importance of the colonial question" and would result in a continuing pursuit of socialism as if "the world did not exist outside Europe." The Third Communist International, he claimed, had outgrown such "pure doctrinarism" but had to recognize that "without the breaking up of the colonial empire, the overthrow of the capitalist system in Europe does not appear possible."[32] In opening discussion of his supplementary theses, Roy argued even more forcefully that Europe's colonies were "the foundation of the entire system of capitalism," and colonial liberation movements would "lead to the downfall of European imperialism, which would be of enormous significance for the European proletariat." Roy thus encompassed within proletarian revolution a broader field of activity than previously envisioned by the Comintern—both anticolonial struggles against imperialism and workers' struggles against capital.[33]

Members of the National and Colonial Commission responded forcefully to Roy's heretical arguments. Some complained that his theses would require European Communists to assign their members to work in the "backward" colonies, which, according to one, would distract from proletarian class struggle in Europe. Avetis Sultanzade, an Armenian Communist who helped organize the Iranian Communist Party, scoffed at Roy's arguments, insisting that even if "communist revolution [had] begun in India," it would survive only with "the help of a big revolutionary movement in England and Europe."[34] But other Asian radicals agreed with Roy. Lao Hsiu-Chao of the Chinese Socialist Workers Party stressed the importance of "the Chinese revolution . . . for the revolutionary movement of the entire world." The Communist Party of Korea's Pak Chin-sun argued that socialist revolution would come "only when the western European proletariat deals the deathblow to its bourgeoisie" and "the colonial peoples strike the western bourgeoisie in the heart."[35]

Asian radicals' ability to use Comintern policy debates to put forward an intercolonial internationalism that went beyond proletarian class struggle in Europe showed the possibilities of international communism. In seeing the colonial world as the fulcrum of socialist revolution, they suggested a reordering of the terms of Marxism that would bring race into greater focus. But although Lenin called for adopting portions of Roy's theses, the "Theses on the National and Colonial Question" adopted by the Comintern contained few of the insights of its Asian members. The National and Colonial Commission even redacted those passages of Roy's supplementary theses that stressed the Comintern's outgrowing "pure doctrinarism" and approaching socialism as a world struggle with the fulcrum in Asian liberation movements, and distinguishing between bourgeois nationalism and national liberation.[36] Officially, at least, the Comintern would focus on the European proletariat, though it urged white workers to see common cause with the oppressed peoples of "backward" nations.

Despite Asian radicals' limited impact on the "Theses on the National and Colonial Question," they shaped the Comintern's approach to anticolonial struggles in important ways. In its "Statues" adopted at the Second Congress, the Comintern announced its break with the "traditions of the Second International, for whom in fact only white-skinned people existed," and declared that its ranks included "the white, the yellow, and the black skinned peoples." In closing out the congress, Zinoviev acknowledged that the discussions on national liberation made it clear that the Comintern did not "only want to be an International of the toilers of the white race but also an International of the toilers of the black and yellow races, an International of the toilers of the whole world."[37] And at the subsequent Baku Congress of the Peoples of the East, Zinoviev hinted at a departure from Marxist historicism when he announced that the Comintern no longer believed that Asian countries must pass through capitalism to achieve socialism.[38] Indeed, the Comintern organized Communist parties in Japan, China, Turkey, and Egypt and at its Third Congress proclaimed anticolonial liberation movements just as important to socialism as European class struggles. And Roy gained considerable influence within the Comintern, heading its newly formed Eastern Commission.[39]

Lenin had shown with the Comintern's resolution his resolve to address the Negro question in terms of the national question. On this point, the Comintern ignored the reductionism of white Communists from its member parties. The only substantive discussion of the Negro question at the Congress came from John Reed, the Communist Labor Party's representative, who argued against Lenin. Rejecting out of hand the idea of national liberation or self-determination for Negroes, Reed claimed that black people in the United States "hold themselves above all to be Americans," thus requiring Communists to support social and political equality as a way to make clear that the "only effective means of liberating the oppressed Negro people" was proletarian revolution. Though race received far less attention than nation, Lenin still included language explicitly directing American Communists to conduct work among American Negroes and to adopt an internationalist politics to combat "race hatred," "national antagonisms," and "anti-semitism."[40]

Black Radicals Respond

When black and Asian radicals responded to what they viewed as the Communist International's unequivocal support for Asian and African liberation struggles by joining the communist movement around the world, they were essentially responding to the work of Asian radicals in the Second Congress. But Lenin's writings also appealed to their anticolonial sensibilities. The Vietnamese radical Nguyen Ai Quoc (Ho Chi Minh) recalled the transformative effect of reading Lenin's "Theses" in a radical Paris weekly, *L'Humanité*, the summer before the Second Congress. Despite its somewhat opaque political terms, Nguyen read the theses repeatedly until "finally I could grasp the main part of it. What emotion, enthusiasm, clear-sightedness, and confidence it instilled in me! I was overjoyed to tears." And although "sitting alone in my room, I shouted aloud as if addressing large crowds: Dear martyrs, compatriots! This is what we need, this is the path to our liberation."[41] Nguyen immediately threw himself into French radical circles. At the founding of the Parti Communiste Français (PCF) in December 1920, he argued that Vietnamese colonial liberation should be a central consideration in whether to join the Communist International. But his comrades in the newly formed PCF were reluctant to make colonial liberation a central concern of their work. The Comintern's response to the arguments of Asian radicals had not transformed how national Communist parties functioned. The PCF responded to Nguyen's concerns only after a Comintern directive instructed the English, French, and Italian parties to establish colonial commissions to make contact with anticolonial revolutionary organizations and "establish a closer contact with the oppressed colonial masses."[42]

When the PCF established the Union Intercoloniale in the summer of 1921 to serve as the main body for organizing colonial peoples, Nguyen found an opportunity to pursue a radical anticolonial politics with other Asian and black Communists. From 1921 to 1923, Nguyen worked in the Union Inter-coloniale with Asian, North and West African, and Francophone West Indian radicals to develop an intercolonial politics.[43] Before he left Paris for Moscow, where he would work with Sen Katayama and Roy on the Eastern Commission, Nguyen criticized the PCF for advancing colonial policies full of "purely sentimental expressions of positions leading to nothing at all." As Brent Hayes Edwards points out, Nguyen's Parisian writings offered "a remarkable 'inter-colonial' approach" that "strive[d] constantly to find links between the situation of black, brown, and yellow *indigènes* (natives)."[44] Nguyen's intercoloni-alism resonated with the ABB's growing sense of interconnected African and Asian liberation struggles. He thus captured the frustrations of U.S.-based black radicals in the orbit of the American communist movement.[45]

When ABB radicals learned of the Second Congress's "Theses on the National and Colonial Question," they believed it had reoriented organized communism around colonial liberation and broadened the realm of proletarian revolution beyond white workers. The Brotherhood was already convinced that the Bolsheviks represented a bulwark against capitalism and Western democracy and sought a political formation that linked the actions of "the darker masses" to those of "truly class-conscious white workers."[46] The Comintern now seemed to offer just such an organization.

Cyril Briggs responded to the Second Congress's resolution in much the same way as Nguyen did. "The national policy of the Russian Bolsheviks and the anti-imperialist orientation of the Soviet State" sparked his interest in communism, he recalled.[47] He urged *Crusader* readers to embrace those "forces—Socialism, Bolshevism, or what not—that are engaged in war to the death with Capitalism," since it was "under the capitalist-imperialist system that Negroes suffer." But although the ABB called the new Soviet state a "strong and fearless champion of true self-determination and the rights of weaker peoples," it had yet to fully endorse U.S. communism.[48] The November following the Second Congress, the *Crusader* praised the Socialist Party for going "out of its way to denounce the exploitation of Africa" and declaring "its belief in the right of the African to self-government."[49] The *Crusader*'s words in large part constituted an effort to promote the Socialist Party electoral ticket, but they also reflected black radicals' continued skepticism about U.S. communism.

American Communists offered mixed responses to the Comintern's theses.

The United Communist Party, which later became the Workers (Communist) Party (WP),[50] acknowledged its obligation to fight American imperialism in the Caribbean and Philippines but showed no signs of approaching the "Negro Problem" in light of the national and colonial question. While the Comintern seemed ebullient about Asian and African peoples and now vowed to unite black, Asian, and white workers, the United Communist Party remained unconvinced. A May 1921 report by the party's Central Executive Committee (CEC) went so far as to call black people "a menace in the class struggle" whom Communists would have "to enlighten" and then lead "towards class action and Communism."[51] Such a statement could hardly have gone over well with black radicals.

Overall, American Communists said rather little about Negro work. The first full article in a U.S. Communist party publication on the "Negro Problem" appeared more than a year after the Second Congress and largely recapitulated the CEC's view of black people as disorganized and needing Communists to "give a class character to their dissatisfaction."[52] But another article by John Bruce and J. P. Collins encouraged Communists to support black people's calls for "a free Africa, race equality, social equality, and better conditions" and to recognize that the "Negro struggle takes on aspects of a racial as well as a class struggle." The "freeing of Africa" would liberate large numbers of black people and "undermine one of the pillars of Capitalist Imperialism," they argued. Communists should therefore "fix responsibility for the Negro's suffering . . . on the bourgeoisie and their Capitalist-Imperialist System!"[53]

That shift in thinking resulted from the interactions between white Communists and black radicals, as over the summer of 1921, Communists began recruiting black radicals into the communist movement. Robert Minor and Rose Pastor Stokes, representing the underground and legal Communist Party factions, respectively, turned to their friend Claude McKay for introductions to Hubert Harrison, Cyril Briggs, W. A. Domingo, and other Harlem radicals. While Minor concentrated his efforts on how black radicals might redirect the UNIA toward class struggle, Stokes offered the legal party's financial support for anyone willing to promote communism. Both efforts met with little success. Harrison declined Stokes's offer, and while ABB radicals continued to meet with her, they questioned her sincerity and believed she harbored antiblack feelings. The ABB also rejected the party's financial support. Briggs, however, was convinced that Stokes was merely anxious to help the Brotherhood and ultimately joined the legal party and became a paid organizer. Though Minor found few people receptive to the idea of transforming the UNIA, he recruited several ABB radicals into the underground party.[54]

After the WP emerged at the end of 1921, its program saw Communists not as awakening black people's class consciousness but rather as aiding their "fight for economic, political, and social equality" by destroying the "barrier of race prejudice" hindering the rise of "a solid union of revolutionary forces."[55] Like the Comintern's "Theses on the National and Colonial Question," the WP's program increased U.S. communism's appeal among ABB radicals.

Bob Hardeon was one of the earliest black Communists in Chicago and was part of the ABB's Post Pushkin, which he, Edward Doty, Elizabeth Doty, and Gordon Owens established in 1920 after leaving the UNIA. Hardeon recruited many of the first blacks into the party, including Ed Doty, a plumber who led that city's independent black union movement. Post Pushkin's roughly seventy-five members participated in Marxist study groups as well as protested high rents and housing conditions. Otto Hall, who had been in the Chicago UNIA and the Industrial Workers of the World before joining the ABB in 1920, was attracted to the ABB partly by his conversations with Brotherhood members who introduced him to Marx's writings. Like so many other black radicals in Chicago, Hall became a Communist in 1921, before the consolidation of the WP. In Pittsburgh, ABB member Jim Bruce joined the WP and soon became its district organizer.[56]

None of these developments, of course, meant that black radicals no longer encountered racism or racial insensitivity from their white comrades. That June, Otto Huiswoud led Briggs, Campbell, Moore, and McKay in establishing the Harlem Branch of the WP at the American West Indian Association Hall.[57] The branch provided much-needed support for their work in the ABB, especially an office and a meeting space for the Harlem Educational Forum, the successor of the People's Educational Forum. Still, WP leaders remained largely misinformed about black radicals and the ABB and showed little real interest in Negro work. In a June 1922 report to the Comintern, the WP's James P. Cannon included a mere four sentences on the party's organizing among Negroes and mistakenly claimed that the ABB had been founded by Communists working in the UNIA.[58] More generally, white party members routinely mishandled black Communists' concerns regarding race. In Chicago, the paternalism of white Communists became so unbearable that several black Communists left the party. In the summer of 1922, black Communists refused to recruit new members, directing them instead to the ABB. The party's black members were determined to end the racial attitudes of their white comrades and planned to take their complaints to the WP's District Committee and if necessary to the Central Committee. Party leaders intervened to resolve the matter. Yet Hall revealed something of black radicals' sense of the party and the Comintern when he told his younger brother, Harry Haywood, that if they could not resolve the matter in the U.S. Party, "then there's the Communist International!" He and other black radicals felt it was "as much our Party as it is theirs."[59] It is little wonder, then, that the ABB's sole public reference to the WP came only in the *Crusader*'s final issue, which appeared in January–February 1922, when Briggs told his readers that the WP would help weaken white supremacy because of its membership in the International, which embodied "the very essence of the Negro Liberation Struggle in its program."[60]

The Negro Question and the Fourth Comintern Congress

Claude McKay's return to Harlem from London in 1921 is among the least recognized factors in the favorable response of black radicals to the international communist movement. McKay had spent a year in London's radical circles, time that played a critical role in shaping his politics.

McKay had cultivated a reputation as a poet in his native Jamaica before traveling to the United States, where he first studied agriculture. He ultimately made his way to New York, gravitating to the city's radical literary circles. In addition to publishing several articles in *Pearson's Magazine* and his poetry in the *Liberator* (including his famous "If We Must Die"),[61] McKay met various black radicals in New York, including Harrison, at that time still editor of Marcus Garvey's *Negro World*. The political ferment of the downtown literati and Harlem's black radicals combined with their excitement for the Bolshevik revolution to convince McKay that any black leader "should make a study of Bolshevism and explain its meaning to the colored masses." If Bolshevism could change the material and spiritual life of workers in Russia and make society safe for Jews, it might "make these United States safe for the Negro."[62]

In December 1919, the notoriety McKay gained from his poetry, along with his growing radicalism, led him to London, where he first worked in organized Marxist formations. Almost immediately after arriving, he encountered the diverse group of radicals at the International Socialist Club, and their intense political discussions prompted him to begin studying Marxism. Among those lecturing at the club were a number of prominent radicals, and McKay was impressed.[63] Within a couple of weeks, he wrote to Garvey about his delight at seeing "the representative organ of British Labour denouncing so strongly imperial abomination and endorsing the self-determination of Britain's subject peoples." English radicals' apparent support for colonial struggles persuaded McKay of the need to build ties between the "great destructive forces *within*" the British empire and the "subject races . . . fighting without"; black people should "let the thinking white workers of the British Isles know of the real conditions obtaining among England's subject races."[64]

But the British Left soon gave McKay reason to question its progressive potential. France's use of large numbers of African troops to occupy the German Rhineland after World War I sparked international outrage over what many perceived as the menace black men posed to white womanhood, German whiteness, and, indeed, the worldwide racial order. That outrage peaked in April 1920, when France sent an advanced guard of Moroccan troops into Frankfurt to quell local unrest. McKay was hardly surprised that the British and American governments, white suffragists, and liberals expressed anger and shock at France's use of African troops.[65] But he had not anticipated that English radicals would be among those lodging the most belligerent protests or that the *Daily Herald*, the Independent Labour Party's newspaper, would open its pages to E. D. Morel's campaign against the "Black Scourge in Europe." Morel, who had been a fierce critic of Belgian atrocities in the Congo and European imperialism generally before the war, decried the French for unleashing on German women African troops whose "barely restrainable bestiality" led them to rape white women, an act that "for well-known physiological reasons is nearly always accompanied by serious injury and not infrequently has fatal results."[66]

Only slightly more alarming to McKay was the fact that George Lansbury, editor of the *Daily Herald*, who only the previous summer had condemned white mob attacks on black maritime workers, agreed with Morel. If Morel traded in well-worn racial stereotypes by raising the specter of the savage black male preying on white womanhood, Lansbury sounded a slightly different but equally repellent alarm over the "odious outrage" of France bringing "thousands of children of the forests from Africa to Europe *without their womenfolk*." If these Africans, who were "not so advanced in the forms of civilization as ourselves," could be so easily "used against Germans, *why not against the workers here or elsewhere*."[67] According to Lansbury, African troops threatened organized labor through their potential violation of white workers' women.

A stunned and outraged McKay challenged white radicals' racial prejudices. In a letter on Morel's screed that Sylvia Pankhurst ran in the *Workers' Dreadnought*, he questioned why a proletarian paper like the *Herald* would run "all this obscene, maniacal outburst about the sex vitality of black men," appealing to "emotional prejudices" and leading to "further strife and blood-spilling between the whites and the many members of my race."[68] Lansbury never replied to McKay, and the near universal enthusiasm that white radicals had shown for Morel's pamphlet, *The Horror on the Rhine*, gave McKay the impression that racial "prejudice against Negroes had become almost congenital" among the English.[69]

Yet Pankhurst's willingness to publish his letter signaled to McKay that some whites grasped the importance of combating racial prejudice. Pankhurst stood out among British radicals in this regard. She had stridently condemned the white racial violence toward blacks the previous summer, and she recruited McKay to work for her paper and join the Workers' Socialist Federation, which led to his attendance at the founding convention of the Communist Party of Great Britain (CPGB) in the summer of 1920.[70] He likely welcomed Pankhurst's criticisms of Lansbury and of the Independent Labour Party's refusal to affiliate with the Third International,[71] as he went on to work tirelessly for the *Workers' Dreadnought* while Pankhurst was in Moscow attending the Second Comintern Congress. John Reed wrote to McKay about the discussion of the Negro question there and about Lenin's desire to see a representative of American Negroes at a future Comintern Congress.[72] McKay also read in the *Dreadnought* Roy's argument that socialism would come to Europe through "the revolution in India," as well as the Comintern's requirement that any party seeking membership in the Third International actively support "every movement for emancipation in the colonies" and carry on "agitation against all oppression of the colonials."[73]

When McKay returned to Harlem in February 1921, he brought with him a set of experiences that led him to distinguish between the limitations of an American white Left that too easily gave in to racial prejudices and the possibilities the Comintern presented for a truly radical approach to social revolution.[74] He threw himself tirelessly into radical political circles, joining the ABB and encouraging Brotherhood members to join the American communist movement. He also accepted a position on the editorial staff of the *Liberator* magazine, briefly serving as editor. One of his first articles showed his sophisticated understanding of the relationships between race, nation, and class. Despite class differences among black people, he argued, "all-white supremacy . . . places the entire race alongside the lowest section of the white working class." White supremacy thus meant that the "Negro must acquire class consciousness." McKay also implored white workers to accept and work with the Negro "whether they object to his color and morals or not."[75]

McKay's attention to race soon wore thin on his comrades at the *Liberator*, however, and they accused him with taking a "racially chauvinist" rather than a socialist approach to the Negro question. By the time McKay helped open the WP's Harlem branch, he had grown increasingly critical of the *Liberator's* editorial staff and the direction of the journal. As Wayne Cooper explains, McKay found in the *Liberator* camaraderie similar to that of the *Workers' Dreadnought* but also witnessed the lack of "foresight regarding racial matters he thought essential if radicals were to win blacks to their cause."[76] By the time he resigned from his position in August, he was disillusioned with the American Left, especially "the pretty parlor talk of international brotherhood" and "the radical shibboleth of 'class struggle'" that American Communists considered "sufficient to cure the Negro cancer along with all the other social ills of modern civilization." White radicals had repeatedly exhibited racial prejudice, and he saw little difference between his American and British comrades in the area of race, leading him to warn that race "may be eventually the monkey wrench thrown into the machinery of the American revolutionary struggle." Black radicals would hardly align themselves with the proletariat if white workers offered little to the Negro "different from the sympathetic interest of bourgeois philanthropists and capitalist politicians."[77] The Comintern's attention to the Negro question would be mere rhetoric if American Communists did not change.

McKay's resignation from the *Liberator* was not a decisive turn away from communism, even if his experiences left him questioning communism's efficacy with regard to race. Unemployed and seeking to escape Harlem and America's "suffocating ghetto of color consciousness," he planned to visit Russia and possibly to attend the Comintern's Fourth Congress. McKay found a wide array of support for his trip, which came neither at the Comintern's invitation nor with the WP's support. The NAACP's James Weldon Johnson instructed McKay to send copies of his poetry collection *Harlem Shadows* to select NAACP members and request donations, while Crystal Eastman of the *Liberator* sent letters asking radicals to help him get to Russia. For ABB radicals such as Moore and Campbell, McKay's trip offered a chance for Negroes to "investigate . . . the actual condition of the Jews and other minority groups" in Russia and to get a better sense of how communism works "in the interest of the subject peoples." If "Irish, Indian, Turk, Persian, Egyptian, all have been participating in this activity," Moore explained in a letter to Arturo (Arthur) Schomburg seeking funds on McKay's behalf, then the Negro needed "an observer there to apprise us of these events and trends which are destined to affect the status quo most profoundly."[78] Indeed, McKay hoped to study the conditions of the Russian peasantry and Jews before and after communism and to compare those conditions with what black people experienced in the southern United States. Support for McKay's trip was overwhelming: Johnson threw a farewell party at his Harlem home that was attended by W. E. B. Du Bois, Walter White, Jessie Fauset, and several prominent white writers.[79]

More than merely investigating the changes that had taken place for Russia's minority groups, McKay expressed the concerns of black radicals before the Comintern. Huiswoud, who attended the Fourth Congress as part of the American delegation, joined McKay in this effort, which presented race as an issue much broader than just the internal machinations of the WP and framed the Negro problem internationally rather than as a singularly American problem. The internationalism of this argument drew in part on the earlier work of Asian radicals.

HUISWOUD AND MCKAY WERE the first black radicals to attend a Comintern congress. Huiswoud, the ABB's national organizer, a union printer, and a charter member of the CPA, ultimately chaired the Comintern's first Negro Commission and presided over a special session on the Negro question. McKay's membership in the ABB caused considerable worry for the American delegation. As an unofficial visitor to Russia, he had to rely in part on Huiswoud's help to gain a seat as the ABB's fraternal delegate.[80] Though McKay and Huiswoud disagreed a great deal on communist work, they agreed on the Negro question, and given their experiences with white Communists, they were certain that only Comintern policies and resolutions supporting anticolonial and Negro work could alter how its member parties approached race. They also hoped to change how the Comintern itself understood race and the Negro question.[81]

Their hope for a new approach to the Negro question was probably buoyed when they learned that their old friend, Sen Katayama, was serving on the Executive Committee of the Communist International and was heading the Eastern Commission. When the Comintern had established the Eastern Commission following the Second Congress, its responsibilities included applying the "Theses on the National and Colonial Question" to the Negro question. That charge assumed even more weight when the Comintern created its Negro Department and placed it in the Eastern Commission under Katayama's direction. Katayama had been disappointed that previous discussions of the Negro question had failed to produce a clear program and consequently instructed the Negro Department to further develop the parenthetical reference to American Negroes in the Second Congress's "Theses." But most Communists rejected the Comintern's proposals on the Negro question.[82]

David Ivon Jones, a member of the South African Communist Party who

Otto Huiswoud and Claude McKay with members of the Comintern's Eastern Commission at the Fourth Congress, 1922. Seated: Huiswoud (far left), Sen Katayama (third from left), Rose Pastor Stokes (center), Ch'ü Ch'iu-Pai (third from right); Standing: McKay (third from left), Mikhail Bukharin (fourth from left), M. N. Roy (far right). From *Crisis*, December 1923.

had lived in Moscow since the Second Congress, staunchly opposed thinking about the Negro question in terms of the national question and challenged the idea of holding a World Negro Congress. He supported seeing black people in strictly class terms and urged the Comintern to focus on weakening the influence of Du Bois's PAC and Garvey's UNIA. Despite the Second Congress's theses, the Negro question was "not on a par with the Chinese question, or the Indian question," Jones insisted. It lacked their revolutionary character and could not help "accelerat[e] the collapse of capitalism." Further, the purely racial concerns of the Negro, including voting rights and an end to lynching, and racial organizations such as the UNIA typified "the immature consciousness of the Negroes in the first stage of awakening." To see race in terms of the national question, Jones continued, would foster a counterrevolutionary antiracist internationalism that might ignore the struggles of white workers to maintain a decent standard of living. Jones believed that a Negro Congress should occur only after the world proletarian revolution. Katayama, however, argued against seeing the Negro question in strictly economic terms and ultimately pushed Jones to offer tepid support for a Negro Congress. Still, Jones's belief that race was a singularly American problem led him to advise holding "a Congress of radical negroes from America and neighbouring islands" rather than an international congress.[83]

Huiswoud and McKay thus arrived in Moscow amid efforts by white Communists, convinced that race held no revolutionary potential, to disentangle the Negro question from the national question. Jones, in fact, sought to remove any basis at all for discussing race in the Comintern by insisting that such conversations would do nothing to help destroy capital. Moreover, he portrayed the ABB as a group of progressive black activists who were awakened to the supervening reality of class and who worked to move the Negro beyond race, thus legitimating his claims by grafting onto black Communists the reductionism of white Communists. That such political ventriloquism thrived reveals how misinformed white radicals were about the ABB. Katayama had raised the Brotherhood as an example of a racial organization committed to socialist revolution, and the Comintern held the ABB in high esteem, but attendees at the Fourth Congress generally failed to take seriously the ABB's program. A powerful mythology had grown up around the Brotherhood before even a single member had set foot in Moscow. But McKay and Huiswoud rearticulated race to nation in an intercolonialist framework that allowed them to emphasize precisely how struggles against racial oppression helped break down capitalism. They thus sought to move race to the fore of Comintern discussions rather than subsume it under the rubric of the national question. Their task proved difficult, however, largely because of McKay's experiences with white American Communists in Russia.

In recounting his trip to Russia, McKay juxtaposed his treatment by the American delegation with nostalgia for his experiences with white Russians: "Moscow to Petrograd and from Petrograd to Moscow I went triumphantly from surprise to surprise, extravagantly fêted on every side." He had "no fear of even the 'whitest' Russians in Russia. . . . The only persons that made me afraid in Russia were the American Communists," who had not supported his trip:

> I had been the despised brother, unwelcome at the gorgeous fête in the palace of the great. In the lonely night I went to bed in a cold bare room. But I awoke in the morning to find myself the center of pageantry in the grand Byzantine city. The photograph of my black face was everywhere among the most highest Soviet rulers, in the principal streets, adorning the walls of the city. I was whisked out of my unpleasant abode and in-

Claude McKay addressing Fourth Congress in Throne Room at the Kremlin, 1922. Claude McKay Collection, Yale Collection of American Literature, Beinecke Rare Book and Manuscript Library.

stalled in one of the most comfortable and best-heated hotels in Moscow. . . . Wherever I wanted to go, there was a car at my disposal. Whatever I wanted to do I did. And anything I felt like saying I said. For the first time in my life I knew what it was to be a highly privileged personage. And in the Fatherland of Communism![84]

McKay's reminiscence reveals something of the possibilities black radicals saw in internationalism. His juxtaposition of white Russians and white American Communists conveys his sense of an alternative to whiteness possible only through communism. When he recalled that "never in my life did I feel prouder of being an African, a black, and no mistake about it," he sounded a hopeful note about a possible future beyond the familiar habits of American and British whiteness.[85]

The American delegation's opposition to McKay's participation in the Congress nearly turned violent when American Communists had McKay ejected from his room at the Lux Hotel and then chased him from the Lux restaurant where he was dining. But then came the pageantry that surrounded him as possibly the first black person in Russia since the revolution.[86] Literary scholar Kate Baldwin suggests that McKay's reception had to do with Russian views of blackness that rendered him a stand-in for Africans, a perspective McKay apparently understood: "The Russians wanted a typical Negro at the Congress as much as I wanted to attend the Congress. . . . I had mobilized my African features and won the masses of the people." Baldwin argues that the Soviets critically misconceived race by assuming that "black Americans were . . . *ineluctably* linked to Africa," thereby obfuscating their links to other oppressed nations.[87] But McKay and other black radicals had a clear sense of their connection to both Africa and non-African peoples.

Katayama's position in the Eastern Commission and his ties to the Negro Department allowed Huiswoud and McKay to interact at the Congress with Roy and other Asian and African delegates from Egypt, India, Japan, China, and Algeria. They discussed how their respective struggles related to one another and the international significance of the Negro question, which for McKay and Huiswoud meant the international significance of race.[88] Their interactions surely proved encouraging, given American Communists' refusal to conduct meaningful Negro work and their general ignorance about black political struggles. Ludwig Katterfeld, who led the American delegation, knew surprisingly little about the activities of black radicals in the United States. Katayama criticized the racism of American delegates in section meetings and forced the issue of developing a program for Negro work.

In an untitled report written during the Congress, McKay argued that Communists should view European imperialism in Asia and Africa as part of the international dimension of racial oppression. He defined the Negro question as neither simply an American nor solely a "Negro" problem but rather as part of the international problem of race. Race, in turn, provided the basis for both African diasporic unity and unity between the diaspora and the non-African world. McKay explained that the "so-called race problem is not national and must therefore be fought with international organization." Comintern efforts at "organizing Negroes on an *international basis*," would help unite the African diaspora and contribute to the larger solidarity of "the colored races of the world," a solidarity "visible when Negroes . . . go wild over news of . . . Turkish victories over the Greek tools of Great Britain." He went on to stress the revolutionary potential of racial organizations with international networks such as the NAACP, the UNIA, and the ABB through which the Comintern could promote a "class radical" diasporic movement tied to struggles in Asia and Europe. "The possibilities for work along these lines," McKay concluded, "are enormous."[89]

This report is probably what prompted the head of the Comintern, Zinoviev, to invite McKay to address the Congress as a representative of the Negro race. Although McKay initially declined, considering himself more an artist than a politician, the opportunity was impossible to turn down. In his address, McKay elaborated on many of his ideas from the report. He described black people in classic leftist parlance as the "most oppressed, exploited, and suppressed section of the working class of the world" but added that racial oppression constituted a structural problem rather than a bourgeois ideology dividing the working class.[90] Moreover, he called the WP's failure to properly address race the Achilles' heel of Communist work among black people. An equally formidable obstacle to proletarian revolution, he assured his comrades, was the "great element of prejudice among the Socialists and Communists of America." Rather than encountering an enlightened U.S. vanguard, McKay had found "demonstrations of prejudice on various occasions when white and Negro comrades get together," noting what he considered "the greatest difficulty that the Communists of America have got to overcome— the fact that they first have got to emancipate themselves from the ideas they entertain towards the Negroes before they can be able to reach the Negroes with any kind of radical propaganda."[91] If the WP continued to ignore racism within its ranks and to overlook the marginalization of black people and their concerns, McKay warned, its claims to support black liberation would seem meaningless to the black people it hoped to organize.

Most of the American delegation responded to McKay's speech with characteristic hostility. Rose Pastor Stokes, possibly the single American delegate aside from Huiswoud who knew anything substantial about black political culture and its myriad organizations, dismissed McKay's criticisms outright. Katterfeld used a more heavy-handed approach, intervening in the translation of McKay's speech and removing important passages before its publication in a Russian-language periodical. An angered McKay accused the members of the American delegation of fearing the "truth" about their poor record on Negro work. Only Huiswoud agreed with McKay, ultimately drawing on his report to draft the Negro Commission's resolution to the Congress. Huiswoud also encountered the hostility of white comrades inside the commission, though his resolution was far less strident than McKay's speech. Huiswoud apparently had to maneuver considerably to get his document read into the Comintern's record: Stokes and McKay were the only commission members to support it.[92]

Huiswoud prided himself on being a disciplined Communist, without the desire for creative independence that made McKay a difficult comrade. He was far less likely than McKay to criticize the party openly. In his report on the Negro Commission's draft resolution, he seemed at first blush to depart sharply from McKay, discussing the racism of white labor unions rather than the racism of the Left and describing the Negro problem as fundamentally an economic problem "aggravated and intensified by the friction which exists between the white and black races." Its only solution was class struggle. But Huiswoud skillfully drew out the international character of the Negro (or race) question. Utilizing the Comintern's "Theses on the National and Colonial Question," he invoked Roy's earlier argument about European capital maintaining its power through its colonies and cautioned that American capital could very well use Negroes to suppress "a revolutionary uprising anywhere and everywhere." The problem lay in white workers' failure to show solidarity with the Negro. Beautiful theoretical phrases that encouraged black support for white workers meant nothing against the "hard concrete facts" of white workers who excluded blacks from unions and traveled in frenzied racist mobs through black communities.[93]

Huiswoud urged the Comintern to recognize the revolutionary character of "purely Negro" organizations such as the nationalist UNIA, which were "influencing the minds of the Negroes against imperialism." The UNIA, the NAACP, the ABB, and other racial organizations reflected the Negro's global vision and were already fostering linkages between Africans and American Negroes. It was inevitable, Huiswoud argued, "that the Negro population would have some sort of reaction against the oppression and the suppression to which they were subjected throughout the world." He suggested that the Comintern tap into the existing network of Negro organizations and publications with propaganda that would help link Communists with the "sort of organisation which will react against imperialism throughout the world."[94]

McKay's and Huiswoud's addresses to the Comintern drew on the earlier arguments of Asian radicals to reframe the Negro problem as a global question requiring international organization. That nascent intercolonialism shaped in important ways the Fourth Congress's "Theses on the Negro Question." The Comintern now explicitly deemed it the "special duty of Communists to apply the 'Theses on the Colonial Question' to the Negro problem" and saw "the cooperation of our Black fellow men" and liberation movements in Asia as "essential to the Proletarian Revolution and the destruction of capitalist power." And while placing American blacks at the vanguard of a worldwide Negro movement, the Comintern acknowledged a connection between black liberation struggles in Central and South America, the Caribbean, and Africa and similar struggles in "China and India, in Persia and Turkey, in Egypt and Morocco [where] the colonial peoples are rising against the same evils that the Negroes are rising against." In practical terms, the resolution affirmed the Comintern's support for "every form of the Negro movement which undermines or weakens capitalism." The Comintern also announced that it would convene a World Negro Congress, subsidize a radical black periodical in America to further black liberation worldwide, advocate racial equality, and desegregate trade unions or organize "Negroes in trade unions of their own and use united front tactics to compel their admission" to white-controlled unions. The final two points were drawn almost verbatim from the ABB's program.[95]

Black Communists and Black Radical Decline

The resolution on the Negro question passed by the Fourth Congress and its corresponding directives, the high-level participation of McKay and Huiswoud, and other accounts of the Congress helped convince ABB radicals that change was on the horizon for American communism. Not only had the Third International made Negro liberation a central concern and addressed it through a special session at one of its congresses, its "Thesis on the Negro Question" drew directly from the ABB's program, thanks to the work of Katayama, McKay, and Huiswoud. Zinoviev wrote McKay a widely circulated letter saying that the Third International sought "to bring about not only the European but also the World Revolution." The Comintern therefore called on "all Negro Workers . . . to create their own mass organization and to link up with other divisions of the fighting proletariat," including "class-conscious white workers," and struggle "to solve the racial problem in the one possible way—the proletarian [way]."[96] Discussing McKay's time in Moscow with ABB members in Chicago, Edward Doty exclaimed, "He is one of our group, and he is received with open arms, and there is no discrimination."[97] They could now see themselves as part of an international movement and as helping American communism in its threefold task: supporting black people's struggles, developing a theoretical and programmatic approach that applied the "Theses on the National and Colonial Question" to race in the United States, and organizing the masses of black people.

Although black radicals saw signs of change in American communism, they also saw evidence that many in the WP still resisted Negro work. In response to a letter from the Executive Committee of the Communist International informing the WP that it was to develop the Negro movement, party leaders expressed their disagreement with the Fourth Congress's thesis.[98] But Stokes wrote in the party's news organ, the *Worker*, that the "Theses on the

Negro Question" represented one of the most significant decisions made at the Fourth Congress and a positive step for the party. While imperialists and "Ku Kluxers" feared a rising tide of color, she assured readers and comrades that "Communists have nothing to fear from the liberation of oppressed people."[99]

Concerns about the WP's Negro work and the attention that other Communist parties gave to the Negro question remained a concern inside the Comintern as well. Katayama, along with McKay, who stayed in Russia for another six months to write *The Negroes in America* (Negry y Amerike), continued to complain about the failure of Communists to deal with race head-on. Katayama captured the central concern of many black radicals when he warned that the WP could not treat the Negro question "simply on economic ground[s]." Though that approach might work when introducing whites to the subject, the matter was ultimately far more complicated, involving interwoven social, political, and economic issues. McKay wrote more bluntly of the alarming ignorance of British, South African, and American Communists about black people in their countries, especially those from the United States, who "are woefully lacking in sympathy and understanding of the American Negroes."[100] Whatever the group or party, "every Negro worker knows . . . when it refuses to take a stand on social equality . . . it also refuses to approach the Negro question." To distinguish itself, the WP must "establish a completely clear revolutionary program . . . which first attracts to its side progressive Negro leaders and afterwards the wide masses of American Negroes."[101]

Despite party leaders' resistance to the "Theses on the Negro Question," black Communists continued to publicize the Comintern's resolution. Briggs sent reports on the Congress through the Crusader News Service to black newspapers around the country, and Du Bois's *Crisis* magazine ran a two-part article in which McKay related his experiences in Russia and repeated his call to lift black liberation "out of national obscurity" in the United States "and force it forward as a prime international issue."[102] Briggs also published in the Crusader News Service a letter from Leon Trotsky to McKay following one of their conversations about the Negro question. McKay, like other black radicals, was somewhat struck by Trotsky's notion of black people as socially, politically, and economically backward, and who, like the "economically and culturally backward colonial masses," would have to be enlightened by European workers. But McKay and others saw in this exchange — including Trotsky's declaration that the time for "resolutions on . . . self-determination [and] equality . . . regardless of colour, is over" since the "time has come for direct and practical action"—an atmosphere conducive to pushing forward with Negro work in the party.[103]

In May 1923, the ABB published a small pamphlet outlining its goals, which included undertaking an organizational drive to arouse "the race consciousness of the Negro workers and . . . their class consciousness."[104] Domingo and Huiswoud launched the initial phases of the drive with a speaking tour through New Jersey, Philadelphia, Pittsburgh, Chicago, and West Virginia and brought in a reported three hundred new members by November. In a sign of their international orientation, Huiswoud made contact with the Canadian Communist Party to try organizing Afro-Caribbean women garment workers through the Canadian branch of the International Ladies' Garment Workers' Union. The ABB also sent Huiswoud on another tour that fall as part of a full-scale membership drive focused largely on recruiting from unions, particularly the Miners' Union, resulting in sixty-five new members in the ABB's Montgomery, West Virginia, post.[105]

This expansion was encouraging, suggesting that the Brotherhood could benefit from its ties to the WP. However, these efforts coincided with the beginning of the Brotherhood's decline. In Harlem, membership dropped, and participation in local activities and meetings waned. Briggs noted that the low turnout for meetings reflected a growing apathy and that several of the ABB's charter members no longer paid dues or attended meetings. Indeed, Post Menelik regularly canceled meetings, lacked the funds to rent office space, and had difficulty carrying out its daily business.[106]

These developments combined to push the ABB toward an official affiliation with the WP. In July 1923, Briggs refuted speculation that the ABB functioned as the communist group for Negroes, but by November the Brotherhood had negotiated a formal relationship whereby the party provided financial support. According to a federal surveillance report, this agreement included a rather glaring stipulation that "in the future the Workers' Party of America would be in charge of the activities of the African Blood Brotherhood."[107] Within days, Briggs announced that the ABB's Supreme Council had agreed to merge with the Harlem branch of the WP for the purposes of securing office space and jointly sponsoring the Harlem Educational Forum to benefit both organizations. Apart from vital resources, this agreement provided the WP a desperately needed entrée into the black community. Yet there is little evidence to suggest that initially at least, the ABB ever fully integrated into the WP and relinquished its autonomy. As Joyce Moore Turner puts it, a symbiotic relationship developed where the ABB sought the support promised at the Fourth Congress and the party hoped to increase its black membership. Blacks began to enter the party in greater numbers over the next couple of years, but despite verbally relinquishing control of their organization, black radicals continued to pursue their own program.[108] Many of these radicals saw maintaining their autonomy as extremely important.

Black radicals had long contemplated the potential drawbacks of merging with the WP. Richard Moore expressed "deep regret" to Robert Minor that at the end of 1924 the party planned to discontinue the *Liberator* and launch in its stead the *Workers Monthly*. "Party control is not without grave consequences if that control be not intelligent, flexible, and dynamic," he noted, a comment informed by the WP leadership's bungling of a myriad of issues relating to Negro work.[109] On December 14, 1923, almost as soon as the ABB's formal ties to the party were established, the WP's CEC removed Huiswoud from "work among the Negroes" despite his experience with such work through the ABB. Further, when the CEC established the Negro Committee, it was headed by Minor rather than by one of the ABB's many capable activists. To his credit, Minor showed far more nuance in thinking about race and organizing black people than did most white Communists. In addition to appointing an all-black committee and running it democratically, Minor agreed with black radicals that race consciousness and "purely racial organizations" served the class interests of black workers, and he wrote articles defending Marcus Garvey, all of which unsettled the CEC.[110] Still, Minor's appointment and Huiswoud's removal made it clear that party leaders questioned whether black radicals would approach race from a proper class perspective.

Growing frustration among black radicals left many questioning the party's willingness to follow the Fourth Congress's resolution on the Negro question and doubting whether white Communists would ever alter their approach to race. As a result, many blacks either became inactive or simply left the party. To stave off a mass exodus of black members, the ABB started coordinating with the work of Minor and the Negro Committee, thereby allowing the Brotherhood to put forward proposals challenging the CEC's decisions on Negro work and criticizing the paternalism of white comrades. Minor and Gordon Owens, a member of the Negro Committee from Chicago, sent a report to the Comintern criticizing the party's "attitude that Negro work does not require full time functionaries, that it should somehow be done by communists in the their spare time," an approach that they felt merely paid "lip service to the Comintern decisions that Negro work be considered a major task of the American Party." The report confirmed that "white chauvinism," first brought to the fore by Huiswoud and McKay, was "rampant—

open and unashamed."[111] McKay noted that after "two years of talk about the Negro problem, the American Communists have little to show except bulky reports."[112] The party had conducted only "half-hearted work among Negroes" and had "no Negro organizers or officials; no Negro members on the press staff." It had also "evinced perfect indifference" to complaints about its attitude toward black people, McKay observed.[113] The ABB's Lovett Fort-Whiteman complained to Zinoviev that the "American Party does nothing practically on the Negro issues nor has it made any serious or worthwhile efforts to carry Communist teaching to the great masses of American black workers." The party's repeated refusals to move forward on a Negro conference left Katayama convinced that "the Negro question will have a very hard future."[114]

Black radicals were not content to raise their concerns solely in the Comintern, which had proven relatively powerless to assuage skepticism about the WP. Indeed, the party's constant equivocation on the Fourth Congress's resolution led to a series of intraparty confrontations. In one instance, the Negro Committee reprimanded the *Daily Worker* for failing to address police harassment or see it as "one of [the] most flagrant demonstrations of tyranny against Negroes, intended to preserve the caste system." In addition, the CEC censured Huiswoud for publicly protesting the failure of his white comrades to oppose the removal of any reference to racial equality from the Farmer-Labor Party's platform during its 1924 St. Paul convention. The members of the Negro Committee declared that in their opinion, the CEC's "uncommunistic action" had placed it "in a bad light especially with the Negro membership of the Party."[115]

The persistent problems that ABB radicals encountered with the WP bred skepticism about the possibilities of the communist movement. Though the black activists' desire to work in Lenin's Third International had prompted their membership in the WP, the Comintern seemed powerless to change how the WP carried out its Negro work. Not only was the Negro question a point of difference between competing party factions, but more important, party leaders showed a general disregard for race, even a willingness to smother Comintern policies on racial equality if they might offend southern white Communists.

IN THE FACE OF their party's intransigence, ABB radicals continued to pursue their intercolonial vision of racial liberation, which often exceeded the imagination of even the most radical of Comintern thinkers. These black radicals believed that racial oppression and the structures of white supremacy in government, unions, and society in general meant that black people, regardless of class, suffered social and political oppression that a change in the economic structure alone would never resolve. The ABB thus continued to focus on the idea of building a federation of black organizations. At the same time, the Comintern's commitment to holding an international Negro congress, in Moscow or elsewhere, met stern resistance from the Communist parties in Great Britain, France, South Africa, and especially the United States. Ironically, black radicals feared that such a congress, if organized by national Communist parties, would neglect important aspects of racial oppression, class, and black people's complex racial identities. The Negro question required international organization through attention to differences throughout the African diaspora, which by 1923 had become a critical issue confronting black radicals.

4

An Outcast Here as Outside

Nationality, Class, and Building Racial Unity

If Communist parties scoffed at the idea of a World Negro Congress, black radicals considered the possibility that those parties might organize one disastrous. While European Communists could accept, if begrudgingly, the idea of national liberation fostering proletarian revolution, they deemed heretical the claims by black radicals that race offered a similarly fertile field. Yet it was to the complexities of race that Claude McKay referred when he warned that the U.S., South African, and British Communist parties were not "class-consciously enough interested in the Negro as revolutionary material" to effectively organize such a gathering. He believed that their inadequacies turned not on their inability to organize black people but on their failure to understand the "differences existing between the American and West Indian 'Negro.'" Those differences, he cautioned, might "even spoil the preliminary arrangements" of a World Negro Congress "if they are not tactfully worked out."[1] The Negro question in proletarian struggle had sparked important discussions within international communism, though many observers still believed that the problem of the Negro was the potential threat black people posed to white workers. McKay implored Communists to consider the historical contingencies of race—that is, how the localities of race structured hierarchies of difference within the diaspora—when organizing the Negro. His warning emphasized the importance of national and class differences among black people. McKay thus captured the ABB's view that the global dimensions of race complicated any attempt to organize black people globally.

As the Comintern was turning its attention to the Negro, black radicals entering organized communism were focused on building a racial united front. Organizing a united front to fight the Ku Klux Klan and "all other organizations and tendencies antagonistic to the Negro" remained one of the ABB's goals, and Cyril Briggs continued to float the idea of federating black political organizations into a great pan-African force.[2] However, the ABB's enunciation of a political blackness intended to bring Caribbeans and African Americans together without discounting their differences. Though it firmly believed the futures of various diasporic groups were tied to one another, it did not see a single Negro problem. Intraracial conflicts in Harlem increasingly made this point obvious. As the historian Irma Watkins-Owens points out, African Americans did little formally to include Caribbean immigrants into a corporate blackness, leading Caribbeans to establish a range of cultural, civic, and political organizations that substantiated their national and Caribbean identities. Alongside the more general nativism in American society, African Americans increasingly expressed anti-Caribbean views.[3]

Class only heightened the tensions around nationality. The belief among many Talented Tenthers that they alone bore responsibility for educating, uplifting, and leading the race—their poorer, less educated brothers and sisters—prompted the NAACP and other organizations to bend their appeal to elite blacks. Black middle-class control of various community institutions and periodicals meant limited room for radical and labor organizing efforts. For ABB radicals, such differences belied the reductionist claims of white leftists that Negroes were simply workers whose problems would disappear with socialism. Indeed, the Brotherhood's desire to build racial unity confronted the conterminous foils of class and nationality. The repeated failures of their attempts to build a racial united front revealed that political blackness was not merely illusive. Its very pursuit, if it could be realized, would require black radicals to ignore national and class differences and follow the leadership of an increasingly nativist African American elite.[4]

By the time ABB radicals decided that a united front of black workers was preferable to an all-encompassing racial unity, proposing to the Comintern a congress of American Negro laborers, they had disbanded the Brotherhood and were working solely under the aegis of the WP. The proposed organizational alternative to racial unity not only offered a new approach to Negro work but also set in motion black radicals' pursuit of a black international through international communism. Yet this effort collided with the Comintern's power structure, which selected leaders, at least for black and Asian initiatives, from among those trained in Russia rather than from those with organizing experience. This system of white Communists anointing blacks to study at KUTV and then assume leadership positions after returning home implicitly saw organic local black leadership as a less capable vanguard of the race. The result was that the Comintern and/or the local party often ignored the ideas, insights, and warnings that longtime black activist-intellectuals brought to the organizing table. Indeed, it would have been impossible for black radicals to foresee that Moscow, rather than the local party alone, would constrict their ability to shape the proposed black workers' organization. Yet if by joining the American Communist Party ABB radicals joined the Comintern, they soon realized that they had given up a vehicle in which they could continue to elaborate a radical black internationalist project in a way that they believed best suited pan-African liberation. As much as they believed they gained from international communism's institutions and networks, they soon questioned their place within Lenin's international.

New Negro Anti-Caribbean Nativism

The rise of Marcus Garvey brought into stark relief the increasingly anti-Caribbean rhetoric of African American leaders in the New Negro movement. Criticisms of Garvey bolstered black intellectuals' view that Caribbeans should concentrate on the islands rather than on solving the American Negro problem. Yet while even the ABB's largely Caribbean leadership would have agreed with W. E. B. Du Bois's 1923 assessment that one of Garvey's main problems was his failure to realize that "the American Negro problem is very different from . . . the problem of the Negro in the West Indies," they rejected the corresponding belief, held by many New Negro intellectuals, that Garvey's was an inherently Caribbean flaw.[5] That Garvey did not understand the American scene seemed evident when he began attacking integration and social equality and emphasizing racial purity. Such ideas were hardly new, but they had never enjoyed such a charismatic proponent with such a vast organization as the UNIA. Still, Caribbean radicals who had been critical of Garvey were rather disturbed by other people's tendency to highlight his nationality and disparage the UNIA's membership as poor, ignorant West Indians. Even the African American radical A. Philip Randolph complained that such attacks "appeal[ed] to nationality" and a villainous "patriotism" that overlooked the fact that whatever Garvey's values or faults, they were not "lessened or increased because he is a West Indian."[6]

The acrimony toward Garvey rose sharply following his ill-advised meeting with the Ku Klux Klan in June 1922. Garvey had explained his meeting as a show of the UNIA's force and an attempt to avert future violence toward southern UNIA members by making clear that his aim was separation of the races. Yet few people outside the UNIA bought either explanation, and condemnations rained down from nearly everywhere. The NAACP's William Pickens was incredulous that Garvey now seemed to endorse "or at least conced[e] the justice of [the Klan's] aim to crush and repress colored Americans" by favorably comparing their program to his program in Africa. Walter White, Pickens's colleague in the NAACP, feared that Garvey had made an agreement to gain unfettered access to the South "in return" for "break[ing] up organisations among Negroes opposed to the klan, particularly the NAACP." Even Randolph and other radicals who had urged focusing attention solely on Garvey's program now turned to Garvey's nationality, fulminating about the "blustering West Indian demagogue who preys upon ignorant, unsuspecting poor West Indian working men and women who believe Garvey is some sort of Moses." When, in September 1922, Randolph received a post containing a severed hand and a letter purportedly from the Ku Klux Klan threatening that if he failed to join the UNIA, his hand would be mailed out next, it gave credence to White's fears. In the *Messenger*, Randolph and Chandler Owen announced they had fired "the opening gun in a campaign to drive Garvey and Garveyism . . . from American soil." Not everyone agreed with their goal, but few objected to the rhetoric when the Friends of Negro Freedom (FNF), a group established earlier by Randolph and Owen, mounted its "Garvey Must Go" campaign. At one FNF forum, the group's leaders asked whether Garvey, "who is not a citizen," should encourage American Negroes "to surrender their citizenship rights." And if Garvey were "seriously interested in establishing a Negro nation," Randolph wondered, "why doesn't he begin with Jamaica, West Indies?" The devolving discourse about Garvey reached a low point when Owen published "A Supreme Negro Jamaican Jackass," an editorial insisting that "no American Negro would have stooped to such depths."[7]

Caribbean radicals, however, complained that the focus on Garvey's nationality distracted from the reality of his movement. The radical Caribbean Unitarian minister E. Ethelred Brown lamented that coverage of Garvey in African American newspapers often portrayed his followers entirely as unnaturalized West Indians, which, he pointed out, ignored the scores of American Negroes in the UNIA as well as the Caribbeans at "the forefront of those · who opposed the aims and methods of the fallen man."[8] The *Messenger* became a clearinghouse for anti-Garvey vitriol, leaving many radical Caribbean activist-intellectuals shocked. It was here that Robert Bagnall called Garvey "a Jamaican Negro of unmixed stock, squat, stocky, fat, and sleek, with protruding jaws, and heavy jowls, small bright pig-like eyes and rather bull-dog like face," a garrulous description exceeded only by Du Bois's earlier rendering of Garvey, for the largely white readers of *Century Magazine*, as a "little fat, black man, ugly, but with intelligent eyes."[9] The *Messenger* seemed to have abandoned its long-standing internationalism to feed the general hostility toward Caribbean immigrants.

Following six months of such attacks, Owen lectured at an FNF forum on "The Problem of the Relationship between the American and West Indian Negroes." Owen attributed the tensions between the two groups to West Indians taking jobs from American Negroes and "bringing in all of [their] friends and crowding out the Americans." The differences between the groups, he claimed, were immutable, rooted in culture and nationality, and apparent in Caribbeans' sense of superiority over American Negroes and in their accents, dress, and national ideals. He also brought up Caribbeans' willingness, as British subjects, to seek redress from the British consulate, which he believed attested to their overly litigious nature, submissiveness, and inclination to "boot-licking." Owen's lecture elicited a favorable response from the African Americans in attendance, while both radical and liberal Caribbeans took exception. Several of the ministers present promised to reply from their pulpits in the coming weeks, and Domingo pointed out that Caribbean immigration was in decline and that by any measure it hardly warranted such animus. The Liberian activist and former UNIA member Edgar M. Grey found it odd that Owen's hostility toward Caribbeans did not extend to white immigrants whose businesses in Harlem rarely employed blacks.[10]

Like many Caribbean radicals, the ABB's W. A. Domingo, who served on the *Messenger*'s editorial staff, had grown unsettled by the repeated references to Garvey's nationality and the broadsides against Caribbeans in the magazine. To his mind, Randolph's and Owen's attention to Garvey's nationality fed anti-Caribbean nativism to an unprecedented degree. He first openly challenged this nativist turn in a March 1923 lecture to the FNF's forum in which he dispelled myths about Caribbean immigrants and warned that Owen's remarks threatened to exacerbate intraracial tensions and reinforce the wrongheaded idea that these "two groups of Negroes cannot assimilate."[11] His chance to debate Owen, who did not attend Domingo's lecture, came that same month in the *Messenger*'s "Open Forum" on Caribbeans. Domingo reminded his colleagues that Caribbean radicals, especially from the ABB, had been Garvey's staunchest critics. More important, Domingo was bothered that in pushing for Garvey's deportation, his *Messenger* colleagues had stressed Garvey's nationality over his faults and crimes. Along with claims that Caribbeans posed a "menace to the progress of American Negroes," the *Messenger* threatened to "extend public hostility from an individual to his group" and in turn expose Caribbean radicals to similar forms of repression from the state. Domingo lamented that once fierce advocates of "equality with white people" had traded in their internationalism for an editorial policy that threatened to "make the life of West Indians among American Negroes as unsafe and unpleasant as is the life of American Negroes among their white countrymen." In the wake of two red scares that saw several Eastern European immigrant radicals deported, Randolph and Owen knew quite well the severity of Domingo's concerns.[12]

Yet Owen dismissed Domingo's remarks as more concerned with slights against a fellow Jamaican than with racial progress. Owen rejected the idea that he and Randolph had done anything wrong and declared their intention to continue using nationality—a useful "means of explaining a certain situation"—in their political work. Garvey appealed to West Indians, Owen reasoned, because they were more emotional. They were "British subjects; they live on islands; they communicate with the outer world by shipping; they are mistress of the seas." Further, he felt that the scant Caribbean opposition to Garvey had grown from Caribbeans' overly emotional character. There was no comparison, he argued, between opposition to Garvey from American Negroes, who "are citizens and voters," and from West Indians, because "most of the West Indians opposing Garvey are *not citizens*, and *in this political minded country votes count for much.*" Furthermore, Owen claimed that the Garvey movement "does not have a large following even of ignorant American Negroes."[13]

Owen's gendered description of Caribbeans as a stateless "mistress" of the sea, a political deviant of the nation, rendered Caribbeans subordinate to manly African Americans capable of exercising the rights of state. Operating with this gender-inflected sense of national belonging, Pickens would instruct the members of a largely Caribbean crowd that their best hope was "to ally . . . with the better element of Negroes in the United States and forget where [they] came from."[14] Indeed, this sense of national deviance was at play in January 1923, when Owen led Pickens, the *Chicago Defender*'s Robert Abbott, the NAACP's Robert Bagnall, and four others in urging U.S. attorney general Harry M. Daugherty to "use his full influence . . . to disband and extirpate this vicious movement." Far from the radicalism for which he was known, Owen now appealed to the state to enforce a gendered hierarchy of diaspora. He and his group reminded Daugherty that Garvey's "followers are for the most part voteless—being either largely unnaturalized or refraining from voting."[15] Drawing on the logic of the nation, Owen's cohort believed that the alien Garvey should go somewhere else.

What struck many ABB radicals as especially peculiar about anti-Caribbean nativism was the corresponding anticommunism that portrayed Caribbeans as political deviants, outliers who were "radical beyond the rest," as one contemporary put it. Indeed, Owen insisted on calling Domingo a Communist despite knowing that Domingo was still a Socialist—as was Owen. The motif of Caribbean political deviancy suffused the writings of conservative pamphleteer and Howard University professor Kelly Miller, who believed Caribbean immigrants especially prone to embracing foreign ideologies such as Marxism that would "tear down this Temple of Freedom." If the half-educated West Indian followed Garvey, Miller argued, it was the "over-educated West Indian without a job," a consummate "conservative at home," who "becomes radical abroad." For Miller, radicals did not have a program to address the central question of race progress: how black people would "bridge the chasm between savagery and civilization" that Europeans had spanned through several millennia of evolution.[16] Not surprisingly, Miller found little favor among Caribbean and African American radicals, and he ultimately foiled their first major attempt at presenting a united racial front.

The Sanhedrin All-Race Conference and the Question of Class

Late in 1922, the Boston-based radical William Monroe Trotter met with Briggs in Harlem to outline plans for a United Front Conference (UFC). Trotter had long believed that a coordinated effort by New Negro organizations would hasten racial equality, and the defeat of the Dyer Anti-Lynching Bill earlier that year renewed his conviction. The time had come "for consultation, conference and unity," he editorialized in his *Guardian* newspaper. Trotter had previously attempted a radical-led united front in 1918 with the National Liberty Congress, a formation that included a range of moderates, that had brought Trotter into greater contact with Hubert Harrison and ABB radicals, and whose antilynching platform prompted the Dyer Bill. The UFC would be a more modest effort, involving a few key organizations representing the spectrum of New Negro thought. Trotter's National Equal Rights League, the ABB, the NAACP, Miller's National Race Congress, and the obscure International Uplift League were asked to send representatives who would "sit in Council . . . to consider the advisability of a larger call to be issued jointly . . . for the express purpose of unifying our forces."[17] Yet the sense of political possibility that existed in 1918 had by now given way to a more measured politics. The

NAACP's James Weldon Johnson initially declined the invitation, citing the group's plans for a similar, larger conference. Miller did not even reply, choosing instead to issue his own call for all national Negro organizations to "unite upon a call to consider 'The state of the Race.'"[18]

Miller's evolutionary notion of racial uplift assumed, as Kevin Gaines notes, an educated black elite leadership. While Trotter and Briggs proposed a political movement led by key activist organizations, Miller envisioned a conference centered on social betterment from which would emerge a group that could function as a Negro Sanhedrin, modeled after the biblical Jewish Sanhedrin high council. Miller eventually acknowledged that Trotter had previously issued a similar call but considered that effort limited in the "comprehensiveness of its range and scope."[19] At some point, Miller and Trotter apparently reached an agreement whereby in exchange for supporting the UFC, Miller would control the organization of what would become known as the Sanhedrin All-Race Conference. Miller thus lobbied Johnson to send NAACP delegates to the UFC, and Johnson agreed just two days before the conference was to begin. Yet Trotter and ABB radicals could not have known that Miller was maneuvering support for his racial uplift vision.[20]

On a rainy Friday evening late in March 1923, sixteen delegates made their way uptown to Harlem's Lafayette Hall for the first meeting of the UFC. In attendance along with Miller, Trotter, and Briggs were Matthew A. N. Shaw and James Neil from the National Equal Rights League; Richard Moore, Otto Huiswoud, Grace Campbell, and W. A. Domingo from the ABB; Johnson, Robert Bagnall, and Richetta Randolph for the NAACP; noted Baltimore minister William Jernigan; and FNF delegate George Schuyler. Though the delegates shared a desire for a unified movement and agreed to make the UFC a permanent organization, their political differences threatened to undermine the effort. Miller proposed that the UFC pursue racial progress by focusing on black people's political ignorance, while the ABB presented a radical internationalist platform that would link racial liberation in the United States to anticolonialism in Africa and the Caribbean. When Moore addressed the conference, he pointed specifically to independence movements in Korea, Egypt, and India and to the Russian Revolution as evidence "that all the oppressed groups of the earth have made their start towards liberation" not "merely from alien political rule" but also from exploitation and degrading poverty. Aware that there was little chance of reconciling their differences, all of the participants agreed that the UFC should function as a federation, enabling them to work in close "co-operation and the most harmonious relationship" for a racial united front committed to "one great common goal."[21]

Despite electing a slate of officers, however, the UFC never functioned as an organization. Its main purpose quickly became organizing the much broader Sanhedrin All-Race Conference. Miller's selection to chair the "committee of arrangements" and his planning of the gathering gave the UFC its dramatic purchase. But ABB and other delegates objected to Miller's role, questioning whether he would work with those from New York appointed to help plan the conference. More important, they were concerned that rather than follow the UFC's directives for the conference to focus on exploitation, lynching, discrimination, and racial pride, he would concentrate singularly on moral betterment. Their fears were soon borne out.[22]

Over the next month, Miller marginalized the UFC from the Sanhedrin. Rather than working with the other "committee of arrangements" members, he appointed a new committee drawn entirely from the black elite in Washington, D.C.—a judge, three doctors, three ministers, four Howard University professors, and Nannie Helen Burroughs and Mary Church Terrell from the National Association of Colored Women. The program drafted by this committee almost entirely disregarded the UFC's directives; the intent, as Miller saw it, was to avoid useless protestations, "vehement speeches and gushing resolutions" and to "proceed in a more comprehensive fashion."[23] To Briggs and many other UFC members, Miller's program suggested little more than a "talk-fest." But this criticism mattered little to Miller, who had built a network of support among national black religious and civic groups. Indeed, Miller was so confident in his plans that he simply declared that "the function of the [UFC] ceased, so far as the All-Race Conference was concerned," when the UFC had made him chair. Members of his D.C. committee also published articles in black newspapers calling the UFC inept and irrelevant and crediting the Sanhedrin entirely to Miller.[24]

Briggs would continue to challenge Miller's disregard for the UFC and his handling of the Sanhedrin, quickly becoming embroiled in a conflict over its direction. Miller, however, was more concerned with maintaining the NAACP's support and thus grew worried only when James Weldon Johnson, after several communications from Briggs, began to question Miller's handling of the Sanhedrin. Miller eventually agreed to a series of meetings with members of the UFC, where he agreed to follow more closely the plans outlined in March and place radicals on his committee. Such were the calculations of a shrewd politician. Miller correctly surmised that if he kept the planning committee in Washington, the radicals from Harlem (the ABB) and Boston (the National Equal Rights League) could not cover the travel costs for regular meetings. In addition, he tapped into a rampant black nativism and anticommunist sentiment when he raised concerns about "a foreign element" inciting the dispute over the conference's program. Whereas the *Messenger* had once predicted Miller's "declining prestige" as a race leader, it now praised him and criticized the ABB as a Moscow puppet seeking "to wreck all constructive, progressive, non-Communist programs." So effective were Miller's machinations that by October he exercised complete control over the Sanhedrin. Briggs and Trotter had no input in the conference, which now had as its stated purposes to "renew a right spirit of manly independence" and "effect union of aim and harmony of purpose."[25]

When the Negro Sanhedrin All-Race Conference convened on February 11, 1924, more than three hundred delegates representing sixty organizations were present at Chicago's South Side YMCA. Along with doctors, lawyers, teachers, and journalists, participants included such national figures as W. E. B. Du Bois and Ida B. Wells. Many of those in attendance shared the *Messenger*'s optimism that the Negro Sanhedrin would survey "the entire gamut of the race's economic, political and social interests and hopes," perhaps believing, as one *Chicago Defender* editorial put it, that the conference would not be another "splendid occasion of intellectual enjoyment" that failed "to do something genuinely constructive and vital." Yet labor, peonage, lynching, and the franchise were conspicuously absent from the program. Such lacunae had been expected, for Miller, just days earlier, in a formulation closely echoing Booker T. Washington's Atlanta Compromise speech, argued that since black people depended almost entirely on whites for jobs, in "all such inter-related matters the races [are] no more divorced than capital from labor."[26]

In the lead-up to the Sanhedrin, the ABB was convinced that it could challenge Miller's leadership on such issues as discrimination, racial violence, and protest. ABB officials worked with the WP's Negro Commission, then under Robert Minor's direction, to draft a pair of resolutions intended to bring these issues up for discussion. Minor was excited about the ABB's role in the Sanhedrin. For the WP, the conference answered internal criticisms about its poor record on Negro work. The ABB's resolution focused on lynching and the Klan and voiced support for Soviet Russia and for the WP's resolution on housing, education, unions, and organizing black tenant farmers and sharecroppers. By including issues that the ABB had long addressed, the WP hoped to demonstrate its commitment to racial equality. Although the ABB had worked closely with the party and ran its Harlem branch, having a WP delegate, albeit a black one, submit a resolution provided evidence in support of Miller's specious charge that white Communists stood behind black radicals' protests.

Moreover, the party made unnecessarily sectarian attacks — calling black public officials "capitalist pawns," characterizing support for black colleges as submission to Jim Crow, and proposing the *Internationale* as the "Negro's Song of Freedom."[27]

Black radicals nevertheless remained determined to push a different agenda at the Sanhedrin. Before the opening session, ABB member and WP delegate Lovett Fort-Whiteman publicly confronted Miller to demand that black laborers receive attention at the conference. Possibly caught off guard, Miller agreed that "the labor issue is the most important issue before the Race," but he opposed the "loud-voiced loquacity and sonorous silliness" that he believed attended discussions of lynching, segregation, disfranchisement, and labor. During the conference, these topics would be covered only in closed commissions. The conference itself continued with public discussions by Alain Locke on pan-Africanism and *Crisis* literary editor Jessie Fauset on the importance of literature in racial betterment. Fort-Whiteman served on the Labor Commission and occasionally addressed how class affected black people's lives. Still, four days passed without an open discussion of black workers. When again pressed publicly by Fort-Whiteman, Miller offered a side room where delegates who so desired could discuss labor. But Huiswoud, an ABB delegate, interrupted Miller, declaring from the floor, "I see labor is an outcast here as it is outside." He reminded Miller that he had "promised labor a hearing before the convention because it was the most important issue" and pointed out that most black people were workers. "We demand a hearing," he shouted, to thunderous applause. Miller relinquished the floor to an open discussion of labor led by Fort-Whiteman.[28]

Press assessments of the Sanhedrin echoed many of the complaints that Briggs and other radicals had made over the preceding several months. Many observers believed that the Sanhedrin had failed to live up to its lofty expectations. A wire from the conservative Associated Negro Press Service noted that anyone expecting "radical . . . decisions on the part of the conference must have been disappointed." Du Bois remarked that Miller put on "an interesting social occasion with no new ideas and no program"; on "every vital question," the conference "had nothing to say worth saying." Indeed, Miller's bureaucratic machinations effectively buried the Labor Commission's resolution, which included opposition to discrimination in labor unions, and the ABB's and WP's resolutions: The conference findings failed even to mention the resolutions on labor, lynching, and segregation. Even the *Messenger* had to abandon its defense of Miller, judging the Sanhedrin a useless event.[29]

Radicals in the ABB came away from the Sanhedrin confronting two incontrovertible realities. Their efforts to build a united front premised on a notion of political blackness had again fallen victim to precisely the divisions and schisms that such a concept sought to efface. Class politics and ideological differences that cast black radicals as agents of foreign ideologies who could hardly understand the American Negro problem corresponded to the national differences that rendered West Indians interlopers. Black radicals also realized that they lacked the resources and network to have effectively challenged Miller. The WP offered something of a solution for the latter problem, though in this instance association with the party only exacerbated the perception of West Indian radicals as outliers. The situation was not helped by the party's insistence that the Negro's problem lay not in race but class.

The time and energy that Briggs, Moore, Domingo, and others spent on the Sanhedrin exacted an unanticipated toll on the ABB. Although the organization grew nationally in this period, its headquarters in Harlem virtually ceased to function. Not even a month after the Sanhedrin, Edward Doty informed Chicago's Post Pushkin that he had lost all contact with Briggs and Harlem's Post Menelik. Harry Haywood remembered the ABB dissolving later that summer, though both Post Menelik and Post Pushkin continued to hold meetings into 1925.[30] By year's end, many of the ABB's leaders had joined the WP, believing that doing so would grant them access to the resources necessary to take on the national and global issues they were unable to pursue through a united front. But any enthusiasm they had for the party was tempered by a concern that giving up their organizational independence may have constituted paying too high a price. Indeed, Moore questioned the "practical effectiveness" of party control "in some cases," "though I quite see it in others, and am open to convictions as the record proves it one way or the other."[31]

The Comintern and Organizing a Race

The year 1924 proved frustrating for ABB radicals. Not only had their attempt to build a racial united front failed, but their organization had fallen into disrepair. Post Menelik rarely had a quorum for its meetings, and Post Pushkin also suffered a significant loss in membership, mainly as a consequence of the Brotherhood's role in Garvey's demise and its growing relationship with the WP. Indeed, the communist ties of ABB radicals and the perception that they had aided the government's indictment of Garvey placed them beyond the pale of acceptable New Negro thought and activism. No longer convinced that a racial united front across class lines was possible, the ABB decided to organize black workers. Such a project could have a global reach, the organization's leaders believed, if it was carried out through the party. They soon discovered, however, that the party's rank and file and officers discounted their ideas and generally hindered their work. And although discussions of their plan took place in the United States, it was formally proposed in Russia by Fort-Whiteman.

Fort-Whiteman, who had been relatively obscure, rose to prominence within the WP in the months before he left for Moscow to attend the Fifth Comintern Congress. His ascent began when he arrived in Chicago with Minor a few days before the Sanhedrin. After the conference, he remained in Chicago, working with Minor and Huiswoud on housing, residential segregation, and organizing workers on the city's South Side. Over the next four months, Fort-Whiteman had so impressed local WP officials that he emerged as a potential leader for the party's Negro work. Possibly the first African American (as opposed to Caribbean) Communist, he appeared to offer the WP something it had not found in Huiswoud, McKay, or any other ABB radical. Unlike Huiswoud, Fort-Whiteman had a dark complexion and southern roots that comported with the WP's notion of an "authentic" Negro, and while McKay was dark enough to appear a "real Negro," Fort-Whiteman had not challenged communist "science" or shown an independent streak ill-suited to party discipline.

Fort-Whiteman's route to Moscow was an improbable one. As Glenda Elizabeth Gilmore suggests, had Fort-Whiteman "let himself think too hard about it, the trek . . . might have seemed insurmountable." A tall, dark-brown man with an arresting stare, Fort-Whiteman had been born to a stable black middle-class family in Dallas, Texas, in 1889. He attended the Tuskegee Institute and studied briefly at Meharry Medical School in Nashville before going to Harlem to pursue an acting career. There, he witnessed the earliest black radical public discourses. Sometime in 1910, however, he abruptly departed for Mexico, arriving amid its revolutionary upheavals. Fort-Whiteman was impressed by the Mexican Revolution's concern with social reform and the rights of indigenous workers, leading him to join the anarcho-syndicalist Casa del Obrero Mundial (World Workers' House), an organization affiliated with the Amsterdam-based International Association of Workers. In Mexico, he witnessed the transnational institutional possibilities of a radical labor movement, insights he would carry back to Harlem.[32]

Almost immediately after returning to New York, Fort-Whiteman threw himself into Harlem's black radical network. He briefly assumed editorship of the *Colored American Review* following Briggs's dismissal, soliciting articles from Hubert Harrison and John Edward Bruce. Like many Harlem radicals, Fort-Whiteman gravitated to Harrison, joining his Liberty League and co-editing its short-lived periodical, the *Clarion*. Like Moore, Domingo, and Randolph, Fort-Whiteman also joined the SPA, where he met fellow Texan and political cartoonist Robert Minor and fell in with the SPA's left wing. By 1919, Fort-Whiteman had become an itinerant organizer for the Industrial Workers of the World, establishing chapters and focusing mainly on black workers. His speeches praised Soviet Russia and insisted that racial equality would come only with proletarian revolution, a claim that led federal and local authorities in St. Louis to arrest him on charges of sedition and inciting to riot, though the charges were later dropped.[33] Around this time, Fort-Whiteman began writing drama criticism for the *Messenger* magazine and followed the SPA's left wing into the CPA and then the WP.

Black Communists were at first skeptical of Fort-Whiteman and his rise within the WP. He had either helped establish or was an early member of the ABB, though his involvement was minimal, with his name appearing only occasionally in Brotherhood publications and federal surveillance reports. The tenuousness of this link helps to explain some black Communists' reservations about his selection to replace Minor as director of Negro work. Otto Hall later recalled that many black Communists were put off by Fort-Whiteman's superior, arrogant ways and saw him as the WP's "hatchet man," lacking the experience of other ABB members. Many also suspected Minor's hand in Fort-Whiteman's ascent, derisively referring to him as "Minor's man Friday." Moreover, they were wary of his tendency to reduce racism to a bourgeois ideology rooted "in some form of economic or industrial competition," with some black Communists concerned that his views appealed to party leaders loathe to see race in any other terms.[34] Their reservations, however, dissipated to some extent during his four months in Chicago. He participated in Negro Committee meetings, at which black members routinely discussed race as a central feature of class struggle. In addition, his experiences began to reveal problems with how the WP dealt with race. Although he was part of the American delegation to the Fifth Congress, the WP refused to pay for his travel, leaving it to "individual Negro Communists" to finance his trip.[35]

In Moscow shortly before the Fifth Comintern Congress began, Fort-Whiteman proposed to the Comintern's Far Eastern Section the idea of organizing a Negro Labor Congress. The idea was not his alone. It came from black Communists who left the Sanhedrin convinced that they could not work across class lines with black elites. That experience, he explained, had made clear that the time was "ripe for the organising of an American-Negro

Labour Congress . . . which would be an offset to the Negro petty-bourgeois reformist organisations" and lead the black liberation struggle. Its program would focus on housing, wages, working conditions, and other "social demands and grievances of the race," and it would draw its membership from independent black unions. More broadly, it would address "the aspirations of the American working class in general" and alter the WP's organizational orientation. While the small number of black Communists might make the Comintern reluctant to back such a congress, Fort-Whiteman argued that the problem was not black people's lack of class consciousness but rather "the American Communist Party's refusal to make the social demands of the Negro people an organic part of its Party programme." And as if anticipating potential objections, he invoked the Fourth Congress's resolution to declare that the "American-Negro is as much a subject of the American nation as the Indian is of England."[36] The proposed congress would help realize this goal.

The timing of the proposal was fortuitous. The Comintern had already begun to move away from the orthodoxy that had guided previous discussions of colonialism and the Negro question. Early in the Fifth Comintern Congress, the Programme Commission, led by Dmitri Manuilsky, published a report questioning "whether the slogan of the right of self-determination was sufficient for the solution of all national questions." Manuilsky had sponsored a trip to Moscow by Nguyen Ai Quoc (Ho Chi Minh) the previous year and likely drew from Nguyen's work on colonialism in Asia in rethinking the Comintern's approach. Manuilsky's Programme Commission argued that self-determination might not be as efficacious as some believed. "The slogan of the right to self-determination cannot solve all national questions," it asserted, especially in the United States, with its "extraordinarily mixed population." There, the Comintern might supplement its support of self-determination with an advocacy of "equal rights for all nationalities and races." Manuilsky even rejected the notion of a single "definition of the . . . nation" applicable to all situations, urging Communists to remain flexible enough to respond to any situation.[37]

The theoretical breach that opened in Comintern thinking about self-determination provided anticolonial radicals an opportunity to question whether European parties could lead the Comintern's efforts in Asia, in Africa, and among American Negroes. Nguyen had already questioned whether Communists fully understood "that the fate of the world proletariat, and especially the fate of the proletarian class in aggressive countries that have invaded colonies, is closely tied to the fate of the oppressed peoples of the colonies." If Communists acknowledged that capitalism's life energy rested in the colonies, it made little sense for "discussions of the revolution [to] neglect to talk about the colonies." M. N. Roy and Sen Katayama echoed this point in their presentations to the session on the National and Colonial Question at the Fifth Congress, demonstrating the extent to which others agreed with Nguyen's assessment that the work of the British and French parties in the colonial world was "almost worthless." Nguyen subsequently argued that the Comintern bore responsibility for giving greater attention to Africa and Asia and "help[ing] them to revolution and liberation."[38]

Fort-Whiteman also addressed the session on the National and Colonial Question, attempting to push Marxian analysis beyond the strict forensics of class struggle. His talk focused on the Negro's revolutionary potential, which he explained that Communists could realize only after taking seriously blacks' social demands. Communists could not continue thinking about black people as threatening white workers or, as Manuilsky warned French Communists about African soldiers on the Rhine, as tools of reaction the bourgeoisie could easily turn at "any minute against your heroic proletariat."[39] Realizing black people's revolutionary potential would require shifting the focus from their presumed lack of class consciousness to the WP's failure to recognize that "Negroes are not discriminated against as a class but as a race. Even the wealthy bourgeoisie among the Negroes suffer from persecution" under this system. The result was "a peculiar Negro culture and peculiar psychology" that neither Socialists nor Communists understood required organizing the Negro "in a specialized way."[40]

If class offered inadequate grounds on which to organize black people, Fort-Whiteman found the Comintern's habit of seeing a single Negro problem equally flawed. The limits of such an approach were apparent in the Comintern's idea of holding a World Negro Congress. "Negro," Fort-Whiteman argued in an essay on the congress, is a "very indefinite term" that misses how those West Africans taken to the Americas as slaves came "from many races" and that "has no meaning" for the Dahomians, Ashante, and Senegalese that the Comintern hoped to draw to Moscow. It also threatened to preclude drawing groups such as Moroccans struggling against French imperialism. As an alternative, he proposed calling a more expansive "International Congress of African Races," which would serve as "a corrective for the lack of work . . . in the African colonies by the respective Communist Parties of those imperialist countries holding possessions in Africa."[41]

"Negro in America," an essay that Fort-Whiteman had written earlier, while studying at KUTV, argued that the animosity directed against the Negro race as a race meant that black people—not white workers—were "historically destined to be the most revolutionary group in American society." One need only measure the WP's lack of presence in the colonial world against the Negro, who has "always regarded his social problem as a world problem" and whose most successful organizations had "a broad international programme," to see the real revolutionary potential black people offered international communism.[42] Thus, the Comintern offered black radicals an opportunity to make important connections to other anticolonial radicals. Writing to Gregory Zinoviev, chair of the Comintern's executive committee, three months after the Fifth Congress, Fort-Whiteman noted that the WP had done practically nothing "on the Negro issues" and made no serious effort to "carry Communist teaching to the great masses of American black workers." He also pointed out that the "individual Negro Communists" who had funded his trip to Russia did so believing that "by sending one of their group to Moscow" they might persuade the Comintern "to take some practical steps helpful to our work among Negroes, both in America and on a world scale."[43] In fact, at the Fifth Congress, Fort-Whiteman realized something of those global possibilities when he met the radical Guadeloupean lawyer Joseph Gothon-Lunion. Gothon-Lunion was active in the Union Intercoloniale with Nguyen, Lamine Senghor, and others and expressed the shared concerns of African diasporic and Asian radicals.

Fort-Whiteman continued working out his ideas about racial struggle with revolutionaries from around the world after the congress. The sheer force of so many challenges to his ideas may have prompted him to return to the "scientific" Marxist analysis of race that characterized his thinking in the United States. He also witnessed firsthand the Soviet experiment that many New Negro intellectuals believed offered an alternative to the racial oppression inherent in Western democracy. Given how he understood racism, the apparent cultural autonomy exercised by ethnic groups in Russia testified to the Soviets' ability to approach "racial problems with a directness and a scientific understanding." Though well aware that racist attitudes persisted in Russia—they were easily seen in the "caricatured faces of Negroes advertising cigarettes, films, pictures, etc."—he became convinced that black people were not discriminated against as a race.[44]

Fort-Whiteman returned to seeing race as a bourgeois ideology dividing the working class, a sharp change from his previous views. In the published version of "The Negro in America," he no longer claimed that black people were destined to assume revolutionary leadership in America. Invoking the trope of the unorganized black worker as potentially "a tremendous weapon for reaction," he no longer saw any revolutionary potential in black nationalism. Instead, it was an illusion spun by the black elite to convince the masses that "their social degradation flows from the mere fact that they . . . are not white." It remained imperative, he argued, that Communists take note of the international worldview and program of the "most successful organizations among the race." Rather than indicting Communist failures on race, Fort-Whiteman now suggested that the task was to "interpret [the Negro's] peculiar social situation in terms of the class struggle" and thus help black people "realize that the economic problem, the problem of exploitation and class-rule . . . lies in the heart of the race-problem."[45]

The American Negro Labor Congress

Although Comintern officials had questioned Fort-Whiteman's approach to race, they were convinced that he could lead the WP's Negro work and head the effort to organize black people globally. Yet his proposal for the Negro Labor Congress languished on the Far Eastern Section's desk for several months before the Executive Committee of the Communist International (ECCI) wrote to the WP asking for its perspective on holding a Negro Labor Congress in Chicago. That February, the ECCI informed the WP that the "Negro Question is gaining in importance for the American workers," ordering that Fort-Whiteman head a special committee to organize and convene an American Negro Labor Congress (ANLC). The ECCI instructed the ANLC to "evolve a detailed programme *of the social demands* of the Negro masses," advocate for the "complete political, economic and social equality of the Negroes," and extend the party into the U.S. South, where "the overwhelming majority of the Communist Party will be members of the Black Race." The ECCI also advised Fort-Whiteman's committee that "some well known people in the Negro movement should . . . convene the congress" to avoid giving it the appearance of Communist control. The ECCI earmarked twenty-five hundred dollars for ANLC organizers' salaries, advertisements, pamphlets, and travel expenses. Fort-Whiteman's work on the congress was to pave the way for a World Negro Congress. And to the Comintern and WP, the ANLC was a replacement for the moribund ABB.[46]

The Comintern's directives showed black radicals that they could influence their party. While working with Minor on the Negro Committee, they had tirelessly pressed the party to make it the "duty of all party members under all conditions" to demand "social equality" for Negroes, a point these activists considered "the weakest in our party practice." Many were convinced that the ANLC would place segregated housing, Jim Crow, lynching, race riots, and imperialism at the center of the wp's platform and that black radicals would control a major aspect of party organizing activities. While black radicals found working with Minor agreeable enough, they had long sought to have a black comrade head the party's Negro Committee. The Comintern's charge to Fort-Whiteman that the ANLC solve the Negro problem might have, as Gilmore argues, doomed his efforts before he began, but he shared black Communists' more general optimism about the ANLC. To many black radicals, Fort-Whiteman returned with Comintern support to organize the ANLC into a force that would transform the wp.[47]

The wp's Negro Committee scheduled the ANLC's founding convention for October 1925 on Chicago's South Side, where the ANLC had opened its national offices "in the heart of the community" it wished to serve. Given Chicago's rich history of black labor organizing, many participants considered the city ideal for building a national movement. Unlike A. Philip Randolph's Brotherhood of Sleeping Car Porters, also based in Chicago, the ANLC did not seek the black elite's support. The Negro Committee's plans for a national paper, the *Negro Champion*, and Fort-Whiteman's speaking tour to establish ANLC locals seemed poised to provide black workers a voice independent of the black elite and link black workers in the U.S. to black people worldwide.[48]

But despite the Negro Committee's internationalism and the Comintern's desire for the ANLC to organize black people globally, national Communist parties resisted the effort. wp officials had opposed the ANLC idea in Moscow, and in the United States they repeatedly voided the Negro Committee's plans and ignored Comintern instructions. Other national parties had similar responses. When Gothon-Lunion received Fort-Whiteman's invitation to the convention, he wrote back enthusiastically, pledging the Union Intercoloniale's support. But the PCF, which typically gave only minimal support to its black members, initially refused to send delegates. Relenting to Comintern pressure, French party officials eventually agreed to send Senghor and the Guadeloupean lawyer Max Bloncourt but refused to pay their travel, even advising Senghor to stow away on a boat. The South African Communist Party flatly refused to send a delegate, though the Comintern had set aside money to cover travel. Whatever the Comintern's ability to pressure its member parties, it rarely compelled them to fully follow instructions regarding issues of race and colonialism.[49]

Black Communists also came to realize that Moscow's decisions could create problems of their own. Many black Communists had been puzzled by Fort-Whiteman's selection "over such stalwarts as Moore and Huiswoud" and Briggs, figures who many activists felt "had revolutionary records superior to Fort-Whiteman."[50] Fort-Whiteman quickly became convinced of his own grandeur and largely ignored the input of others. When the Philadelphia ANLC, impressed with an electrifying speech that local longshoreman and Industrial Workers of the World organizer Ben Fletcher gave at one of their meetings, suggested him as a person from outside the party who could draw in black workers, Fort-Whiteman rejected the idea out of hand. Many cited this incident as reflecting his "leftist sectarian policies and incompetent direction," which were isolating the ANLC. And while they may have found amusing Fort-Whiteman's Russophilic habit of walking the streets of Harlem and the South Side of Chicago clad in a *robochka* (a knee-length shirt cinched with an ornate belt), high boots, and a large fur hat, they complained that it betrayed his ties to the party. Even worse, by spring, Fort-Whiteman told reporters that he was recruiting black workers to study in Moscow and that he would organize a World Negro Congress in Russia.[51]

Frustrated with Fort-Whiteman's actions, Moore, Huiswoud, Doty, and several others complained to Minor that he was dooming the ANLC, but the CEC representative paid these concerns little mind. To make matters worse, in the spring, the CEC moved the ANLC's offices from the South Side to an all-white neighborhood, where it shared offices with a popular Communist organization. Publication of the *Negro Champion* was hopelessly delayed, and literature announcing the ANLC carried the Daily Worker Publishing Company's logo. At the same time, white comrades were assuming increasingly prominent roles in the organization. Black radicals felt that Fort-Whiteman and party leaders were quite literally placing "the stamp of our Party conspicuously upon the Congress" and leaving it little chance of success. Indeed, up to that point, under Fort-Whiteman, only seven ANLC branches were functioning. Moore, Huiswoud, and two others warned that the organizing of the ANLC was playing "into the hands of our enemies" and "making the organization of such a movement very difficult in the future." They argued that the ANLC would succeed only as a mass organization that was not "narrowed down by incorrect tactics merely to communists and their close sympathizers."[52]

At summer's end, the group planning the ANLC submitted a series of resolutions to the WP in the hopes of renewing the congress's appeal to black workers. Along with moving Briggs to Chicago, where he could work on getting the *Negro Champion* off the ground and on a regular publication schedule, they identified specific black Communists to take over organizing efforts among black agricultural workers, requested that the South African party send Clements Kadalie of the Industrial and Commercial Workers Union to the founding convention and asked the French party to send Gothon-Lunion. The ANLC planners also reminded the party of the Comintern's instructions to avoid having white comrades at the forefront of the ANLC. When WP leaders still refused to act, Huiswoud and Moore decided to step into the breach, rescuing organizing of the congress from Fort-Whiteman's sectarianism and deemphasizing the WP connection. Insisting that the ANLC's success depended on a wide range of support, they solicited the participation of the NAACP, Trotter's National Equal Rights League, the Urban League, and the obscure Haiti and Santo Domingo Defense Organization. Charles Henry, the congress's chair, even wrote to Garvey, who was now in federal prison, to convey the ANLC's outrage at his imprisonment, a disingenuous gesture intended to draw the UNIA's sizable working-class rank and file to the ANLC. Fort-Whiteman, however, saw only a challenge to his leadership.[53]

But rather than attracting widespread support, the ANLC met with early responses that focused on its communist ties. American Federation of Labor president William Green warned his black members to steer clear of the ANLC or face expulsion, calling the congress a Communist ploy to instill in Negroes "the most pernicious doctrine—race hatred." While many found Green's alarm insincere, the NAACP and major black weeklies also opposed the congress, believing that the "Moscow gold" backing it would foment race hatred. A. Philip Randolph considered the congress a rival to his Brotherhood of Sleeping Car Porters and, in his pursuit of AFL affiliation, echoed Green's criticisms almost verbatim: The ANLC was "a sinister and destructive crowd" intent on destroying the labor movement. Randolph even allowed Green space in the *Messenger* to rail against the ANLC. Randolph vowed to "kill this reptile at the very outset," and his union effectively shut the congress out of some black communities: In Washington, D.C., for example, local papers, churches, and civic organizations refused to publicize a talk by Fort-Whiteman.[54]

As the convention's opening day drew near and opposition to the ANLC mounted, black Communists became convinced that Fort-Whiteman, with the WP's help, had squandered their best chance at organizing black workers. Many of these activists had seen Randolph's progress in organizing black porters, placing black workers at the center of a struggle for the race's manhood rights. But Fort-Whiteman had emphasized the ANLC's ties to Moscow, ignored important community institutions, and antagonized radical black labor organizers. His tactical mistakes were compounded by organizational carelessness—he failed to attend planning meetings in some cities and apparently never traveled to any southern city.

When the ANLC convention opened on Sunday evening, October 25, 1925, few black Communists were surprised that only a handful of delegates came from outside Chicago. But nearly five hundred black people, most of them working-class, packed a South Side auditorium, perhaps drawn more by the promise of free entertainment than by the ANLC's radical program. Nevertheless, the South Side's history of progressive labor activism among blacks made the area especially receptive to the program. The congress's founding documents suggested a balanced approach to race and class, with resolutions on lynching, Jim Crow, and equal access to public space, issues that Chicago blacks routinely confronted. The documents also gave attention to global struggle by placing the organization of black workers and support for anticolonial struggles in "Haiti, San Domingo, the Virgin Islands, Hawaii, Porto Rico, and the Philippines" at the center of racial liberation and the American labor movement. "The complete liberation of all the darker skinned peoples of Africa, Asia, North America, and South America, from the rule of imperialism," the ANLC explained, "is of life and death importance to the whole working and farming classes—colored and white—in imperialist nations, their colonies and spheres of influence."[55]

The festive mood and rapt attention of most of the South Side participants attested to the promise black radicals saw in organizing black workers. But Fort-Whiteman's ill-conceived leadership squandered the opportunity. ANLC organizers read declarations praising Toussaint Louverture, Denmark Vesey, and Nat Turner, whose portraits hung in the hall, as well as such staunch "resisters of white imperialism" as China's Sun Yat-sen and the Moroccan revolutionary Abd-el Krim. Organizers also read a cable from Clements Kadalie sending fraternal greetings from his Industrial and Commercial Workers Union into the record. A large banner hanging over the stage proclaimed, "Organization Is the First Step to Freedom." After imploring the audience to "develop a new type of leader . . . from the workers, one who will not bend the knee," and reciting with theatrical flare Claude McKay's "If We Must Die," Richard Moore turned the dais over to Fort-Whiteman. Rather than capitalize on Moore's momentum, however, Fort-Whiteman stressed socialism's singular ability to end racial oppression. Negroes "as a race . . . are of no great importance," he declared. "As a class," however, in cooperation with white workers, "we are one of the most important groups in the whole world." For a crowd used to hearing dismissive claims about race from white unions, his argument seemed to suggest that the ANLC would plunge them deeper into an interracial unionism that had yet to change their lives.[56]

But perhaps Fort-Whiteman's biggest mistake was his choice of entertainment. Instead of selecting from any number of local acts or nationally recognized black performers, he scheduled a Texas-based Russian ballet and an all-Russian theater troupe. This decision puzzled his comrades, though they would not appreciate the enormity of the misstep until it was too late. When a member of the Texas ballet realized that most of the audience was black, she drawled, "Ah'm not goin' to dance for these niggahs," after which the crowd nearly turned violent. After the audience settled down, the Russian theater troupe performed a one-act play by the famed black Russian poet Alexander Pushkin: It might have appealed to the audience's racial pride had the performance not taken place entirely in Russian.[57]

In light of these blunders, organizers were right to caution that the convention's success would depend on the number of delegates seated the next day. But only thirty-nine delegates showed up, and most were ANLC organizers, Communists, or activists in the WP's orbit. The inability to attract even a few people from opening night spoke to the magnitude of the ANLC's failure. And while the disaster was hardly the fault of Fort-Whiteman alone, it signaled to Huiswoud, Moore, and others the ineptitude of his leadership.[58]

Fort-Whiteman nevertheless portrayed the convention as a success, the start "for real revolutionary work among Negroes." He bragged to party leaders and the Comintern that no movement "in the life of the American Negro has elicited so much publicity and public attention." Minor called the gathering a "splendid foundation" from which black workers could now speak for themselves. Fort-Whiteman blamed any shortcomings on the black newspapers controlled by the "petty bourgeoisie of the American Negro."[59] Although some black papers were highly critical of the ANLC, postconvention coverage was largely positive. The *Baltimore Afro-American* considered the ANLC unprecedented, while the *Chicago Defender* argued that it was entirely reasonable for black people to turn to Bolshevism in the struggle against racial oppression. Howard University economics professor Abram Harris saw the ANLC's radicalism as "a revolt against the color psychology in the labor movement" and "race prejudice in American life." The strongest endorsement, however, came from Du Bois, who praised the effort and called it "unjust of white men and idiotic of colored men to criticize the attempt" of black workers to gravitate toward Soviet Russia. Du Bois even encouraged black people to "stand before the astounding effort of Soviet Russia to reorganize the industrial world with open mind and listening ears," advising that the Bolsheviks just might "show the world the Upward Path."[60]

Overall, however, Fort-Whiteman failed in his efforts to turn the ANLC into an international organization, and WP leaders quickly grew impatient with both him and the ANLC. Apart from his organizational mistakes, he embellished the ANLC's accomplishments, claiming at one point that 127 delegates had been seated in Chicago. In fact, the ANLC had just one fully functioning local (Chicago), its national membership numbered well under a hundred, and it had collected a mere $6.45 in total dues over two months. By January, the ANLC was so far in arrears that it could not pay organizers' salaries, cover rent, or publish a single issue of the *Negro Champion*.[61] Furthermore, the WP continued to receive complaints that Fort-Whiteman routinely missed meetings, increasing suspicions that he had not toured the South the previous summer. Though Fort-Whiteman argued that the party's revolutionary Negro work would depend "upon the ability of those who are now at the head of the American Negro Labor Congress" to build a revolutionary movement among black workers, his record and the complaints of his comrades suggested that he was not the capable leader the ANLC needed.[62]

To many white Communists, however, Fort-Whiteman represented the full potential of black leadership. John Ballam, a white CEC member who took control of the ANLC in January, felt that the party would have to "force discipline" if it hoped to "develop a Negro comrade" for leadership, though he lamented that such a comrade would likely be mulatto. Indeed, white Communists believed, like whites generally at this time, in blacks' intellectual inferiority. Their low opinion of black comrades and sense of nominal value in Negro work fostered party officials' and district organizers' hostility toward the ANLC. Communists in Cleveland, Ohio, for example, had never seriously attempted to draw black workers into their activities despite the interest that black workers there had shown in biracial unionism and their history of autonomous activism. Thus, the local district secretary's objections to a planned lecture by Fort-Whiteman—it would be useless if he "does not stop long enough . . . to work among Negroes and . . . get the organization going"— betrayed an unwillingness to pursue Negro work. So pervasive was the feeling that black comrades alone should pursue Negro work that even Ballam reminded local organizers that the Comintern considered Negro work "second only in importance to the trade union work" and proposed an internal campaign against white chauvinism.[63]

Ballam's efforts did little to stem the ANLC's increasing lethargy, prompting black Communists to propose a major overhaul of Negro work. They urged party leaders to provide black members with greater leadership opportunities as a means of challenging the thinking that marginalized blacks within the party. The general attitude among white Communists that not only forced the black radical to "enter the Party as a Negro" but compelled him or her "to remain a Negro in the Party" could easily be seen in Chicago. Black radicals there were directed to its South Side branch, which local officials referred to as "our Negro branch," a taxonomy reflecting the general sentiment that Negro work was solely the responsibility of Negro comrades. Bob Hardeon, Chicago's first black Communist and the man who recruited that city's earliest black party members, received no support from the party when his activities cost him his paying job. The party also based its judgment of the ANLC's success on its national stature, an evaluation that focused less on how well the ANLC met the needs of black workers than on how well it served the interests of white workers. In March 1926, when Minor requested increased funding for the *Negro Champion*, the party's Jay Lovestone responded by threatening to end all financial support for Negro work. He found it "disgusting and outrageous that the Negro work has not become self-sustaining in all this time" and pledged to "raise all the hell on earth to discontinue completely the subsidy." He believed that "not one cent more should be given [to Negro work] by *us*."[64]

Over the next several months, black radicals began to question the WP's ability to foster an international movement connecting them to black radicals elsewhere. Lovestone's rant only confirmed what they considered a pervasive attitude, that the party belonged to white radicals ("us") and that black radicals remained on the margins. The Comintern had proven unable to mitigate such hostility, leaving black activists to wonder if their membership in Lenin's international was more symbolic than real.

A sign of the level of discontent came with the formal requests of Fort-Whiteman and H. V. Phillips to travel to Moscow. Fort-Whiteman wanted to further the ANLC, making it "an integral part of the militant movements of the oppressed peoples of the world." Phillips's request was far more damning of the WP. Having lost all interest in the ANLC, he believed that studying in Moscow would provide him the necessary training to assume leadership within the party. The ANLC had "failed to become the organization that we pictured" because "we have such few capable leaders in the Congress group," he explained. A course of study in Moscow would transform him into a true proletarian leader among Negroes, which he believed the "Party will eventually need . . . if it intends to become an American Party."[65] While few other black radicals agreed that the ANLC's problem was a lack of leadership or that only Moscow could train effective leaders, Phillips captured their sense that if the WP hoped to succeed, it could not remain a white party and must commit to organizing black workers. Most black radicals believed that the WP would have to reinvigorate its Negro work and that the ANLC needed to establish a presence with black workers. It was not without irony that an opportunity presented itself in the form of the UNIA.

After Marcus Garvey's imprisonment in the Atlanta Federal Penitentiary in February 1925, the UNIA split between Garvey and his surrogates, on the one hand, and acting president General William Sherrill and vice president of the New York local George Weston, on the other. Garvey began to question Sherrill's and Weston's loyalty when they took out a mortgage on the vaunted Liberty Hall to pay former UNIA employees who had sued for back wages. Although Sherrill and Weston privately were growing tired of Garvey's mistakes, leadership style, and public missteps, they publicly maintained their support for him. Over the following year, however, Garvey repeatedly accused them of sabotage, removing Weston from his position in early September 1925 and six months later ordering a special meeting that removed Sherrill and elected new leadership. Weston and Sherrill responded by organizing their own elections and mounting opposition to Garvey from within the UNIA.[66]

Sherrill and Weston moved forward with the UNIA's Fifth International Convention of the Negro Peoples of the World in Harlem in August 1926. Weston invited Fort-Whiteman to attend the convention as a representative of the ANLC, leading Fort-Whiteman to believe that Weston and Sherrill represented a radical wing of the UNIA that controlled the association's "proletarian elements." At the urging of optimistic WP officials, Fort-Whiteman and Moore proposed a joint national campaign whereby members from the two groups would serve on each other's governing bodies so that they might work together toward "a common program to fight against all discrimination against the Negroes in this country." Some party officials saw this campaign as offering an inroad into urban black communities in both the South and the North; Charles Ruthenburg even suggested that this effort might replace the ANLC.[67]

Though nothing long term came of the relationship, Moore and Fort-Whiteman were key participants in the UNIA convention. Weston maneuvered to have them work on press releases attacking Garvey and to draft the UNIA's resolution on "The Social and Political Status of the Negro Peoples of the World," which advocated a class-based anti-imperialist internationalism. The document called for struggles in the United States "to secure the complete economic, political and civil equality of our people" and outlined a diasporic politics that supported "every struggle of the African Peoples to liberate themselves." For black radicals, the possibility that a radical wing of the UNIA might gain prominence hinted at a politics capable of accomplishments beyond the diminished returns that had come from working in the WP.[68]

The UNIA resolution also called for sending delegates to a November conference in Brussels called by the League against Colonial Oppression. When the German Communist Willi Münzenberg announced this inaugural meeting of the International Congress against Colonial Oppression and Imperialism, black radicals saw an opportunity to build a radical black international that might offer a broader field of struggle than did the WP. They piqued the interest of not just Weston of the UNIA but other New Negro radicals, including the NAACP's William Pickens. And the postponement of the Brussels Congress until the following February allowed them more time to try and ensure that additional U.S. black radicals could attend.[69]

The chance for practical participation in an international movement inspired new interest in the ANLC. During several meetings between December and February, the ANLC's national leaders set about reviving the organization, which now counted locals only in Philadelphia, New York, and Chicago, where the national office operated with little more than three members in a small South Side storefront. "The extreme narrowness of the base of the original conference" was also considered a problem. The national leadership urged that the ANLC return to its initial goal of building a united front of black workers that pointed to the connections among racial oppression, racial violence, and capitalism. Since Fort-Whiteman remained the public face of the ANLC, he would launch a speaking tour, but he was replaced as the group's secretary by Irving Dunjee while a temporary administrative committee oversaw the ANLC's activities. The ANLC now added to its ultimate goal of abolishing "an economic and political system that begets race hatred, discrimination, rape and murder" the goal of "bringing into the Trade Union movement . . . the great mass of unorganized Negro workers."[70]

While the WP's Political Committee (Polcom) agreed with much of the ANLC's proposal, the party's refusal to accept any responsibility for the ANLC's failures frustrated black Communists. The WP acknowledged its limited appeal to black workers and the fact that "Communist Party direction was pressed too much to the forefront," but it laid blame for the ANLC's shortcomings on the ANLC's failure to "draw in non-Party left wingers and progressives into the . . . leadership." The irony of such a charge, especially coming from the body that had ignored complaints about Fort-Whiteman, was hardly lost on black Communists.[71]

Black radicals were soon unwilling simply to accept the WP's pronouncements, announcing that they would take the necessary steps to advance the ANLC. Moore launched a speaking tour that gained the ANLC new members in Chicago; Milwaukee; Gary, Indiana; New York; Pittsburgh; and Philadelphia. In May 1927, the ANLC leadership drafted another resolution naming Moore permanent secretary, replacing Dunjee, who had abandoned the national office, and demanded that the WP provide Moore three paid organizers. Further, ANLC officials proposed a fund-raising drive for Negro work; moving the ANLC's headquarters to New York; appointing Moore and two additional black radicals to the WP's subcommittee on Negro work; placing a black comrade on the incoming CEC; and sending several black Communists to the Comintern's Sixth Congress. Proponents hoped that these ideas would increase party support for Negro work and improve the ANLC as well as effect substantive changes in the character of American communism.[72]

The Polcom largely ignored the proposal. Rather than accept Moore's selection as ANLC secretary, the committee appointed James Ford, a Fisk University graduate who had joined the party through the Chicago ANLC and had shown himself to be a promising and assiduous worker. When he took over the Chicago office, however, Ford found the organization in such shambles that he whipped off an angry missive to the Polcom, criticizing its continued neglect and warning that the party could not continue "handling the Congress with a lot of abstract supercil[i]ous ideas." Instead, he advised that the ANLC focus on organizing black barbers, porters, and laundry workers; address such issues as housing and segregation; and follow the suggestions of those who oversaw the organization's daily operations. He questioned why Moore had not yet taken over the ANLC, complaining that "after all our vaunted ostentations with all of our sincerity we only have about six locals that are really functioning." In June 1927, the ANLC's Philadelphia branch secretary, Augusto Warreno, was less forgiving when he accused party leaders of wrecking the ANLC with blunders "of the most criminal nature." "Every self-respecting Negro within and without the movement has lost every respect for you and the organization which you represent." He warned that if party leaders continued to ignore the May resolutions, he would "expose the Party to Negro workers as criminals. From now on," he declared in a parting shot at Fort-Whiteman, the ANLC would select its own representatives, "not the mad man of the Party."[73]

Writing either in late 1927 or early 1928 with H. V. Phillips and William Patterson, Fort-Whiteman proposed "A New Negro Policy" for the Comintern that departed sharply from what other black radicals had proposed. Facing accusations about his personal role in the ANLC's failures and his decline within organized communism more generally, Fort-Whiteman blamed the ANLC's failures on its attention to race. Although Fort-Whiteman, Phillips, and Patterson also criticized the tendency "to regard the Negro members of our Party" as "appendages" and to view matters pertaining to the ANLC and race as of interest solely to them rather than to white Communists, the bulk of their proposal defended Fort-Whiteman's leadership. They contended that the ANLC's overriding concern with racial violence, segregation, and social equality distracted from demonstrating to black people how communism offered a basis for activism. Northern Negroes were barely concerned with lynching and mob violence but rather were focused on "securing economic betterment," not "the attainment of political or social equality": Out of economic factors "flows the deep discontent and sore distress of the Negro masses." And without such an analysis, the ANLC was barely distinguishable from the NAACP. The ANLC had been doomed not by the WP's imprint but by its attention to race. The ANLC was beyond salvaging, and Fort-Whiteman, Phillips, and Patterson advised dissolving it.[74]

These points would have found a receptive ear in Jay Lovestone, who took control of the WP following Charles Ruthenberg's untimely death in March 1927. Lovestone, who had a well-established animus toward Negro work, delayed moving the ANLC's offices to New York, refused to pay rent for its Chicago office, and was openly contemptuous of the party's seasoned black activists.[75] Lovestone shepherded in a period of Bolshevization that plunged the party into intense factionalism. And he could now make good on his earlier threats to weaken Negro work; just as many black Communists had feared, their field of work suffered severely.

An Incessant Struggle against White Supremacy

Anticolonial Struggles and Black International Connections

By 1927, after nearly five years of working within the Workers Party, two years since disbanding the African Blood Brotherhood, and barely a year and a half after the ANLC's founding convention, black radicals found themselves without a viable organization. They had hoped that the ANLC would enable them to establish ties to other diasporic liberation struggles, but those hopes had proven false, and that failure epitomized the limitations of working in international communism. Leadership positions for black and Asian radicals in the Comintern depended largely on receiving training in Moscow—in other words, on being trained by the vanguard of the vanguard—rather than on organizing experience. Such skewed priorities had proven disastrous with the ANLC. The enthusiasm that so many black radicals had felt for the Communist International had thus waned, and many appeared prepared to leave it.

Scholars generally point to the Comintern's Sixth Congress, held in 1928, as the turning point in the approach to Negro work undertaken by the Communist Party USA (CPUSA). (By 1929, the WP had officially become the CPUSA.) At that congress, the Comintern adopted its now famous "Resolution on the Negro Question in the United States," better known as the Black Belt Nation Thesis (BBNT), which described southern blacks as an oppressed nation with the right to self-determination. Historians generally agree with Robin D. G. Kelley that the new focus on self-determination for southern blacks "opened a new chapter in CPUSA history." The party could no longer ignore the Negro question or render it a field of work reserved largely if not solely for black Communists. The Bolshevization of the party had already weakened local branches' autonomy and centralized decision making in the CEC, which answered directly to the Comintern. As Joyce Moore Turner observes, this process also ensured "an unexpected shift in Negro work because it enabled the Comintern to impose implementation of the Resolution on the Negro Question . . . on the Party."[1]

The control this resolution allowed the Comintern over how white U.S. Communists approached Negro work was not complete, and it did not extend to how its European parties approached colonial organizing in Africa and the Caribbean. Many Communists, like leaders of the PCF, regarded the BBNT and similar resolutions as instructions solely for the American party. And Comintern-controlled initiatives did not always produce the kind of political and theoretical work regarding race and black people that the Comintern envisioned. One sign of the Comintern's limitations on this score is that despite repeated attempts by black Communists to expand concern for the Negro question beyond black people to address the multiple locations of race, Moscow continued to address it largely as an American Negro problem.

When the German Communist Willi Münzenberg began organizing the first International Congress against Colonial Oppression and Imperialism, scheduled for February 1927 in Brussels, Belgium, black Communists believed they had a venue where they could pursue the internationalist politics that continued to elude them even within the international communist movement. The congress reflected the Comintern's long-standing desire to influence anticolonial struggles. Whereas the 1920 Baku Congress had focused primarily on Persia, the Brussels Congress was concerned more broadly with anticolonial struggles in Asia, Latin America, the Caribbean, Africa, and the East.[2] At Brussels, black radicals began building the kinds of ties they believed essential to pan-African liberation.

Out of the Brussels Congress would emerge the League against Imperialism (LAI), which organized a second congress in 1929 in Frankfurt, Germany. This congress produced a far more sustained organizational drive. African American Communists William Patterson, James Ford, and Williana Burroughs traveled to this congress, where they met the Sudanese radical Garan Kouyaté, future Kenyan president Jomo Kenyatta, and the Nigerian labor organizer Frank Macaulay. At the Frankfurt Congress, organizers announced the convening of the International Conference of Negro Workers (ICNW), which led to the formation of the International Trade Union Committee for Negro Workers (ITUCNW), which would develop an anti-imperialist program with black workers in the United States, South Africa, the Caribbean, and colonial Africa at its core.

African diasporic intellectuals had, of course, long been engaged in sustained exchanges. But the international congresses of the UNIA in Harlem and W. E. B. Du Bois's PACs, while important moments of black internationalism, had attracted minimal black Communist participation, and black Communists remained outside the dense networks of black intellectuals in the United States, the Caribbean, Europe, and Africa that grew from these gatherings.[3] Claude McKay was alone among U.S.-based black Communists in meeting the coterie of black radicals in France before the Brussels Congress.[4] While McKay's time in Marseilles came after he left the Comintern, travel for most black Communists would come only through the Comintern, though the interactions such travel allowed were short-lived, as with Lovett Fort-Whiteman and Joseph Gothon-Lunion. However, with Comintern backing and resources and its ability to facilitate language translations, black radicals began building long-term relationships.

The LAI congresses and the work they facilitated highlight the irony of black radicalism in the international communist movement. Black radicals believed that the Communist International would allow them to establish meaningful intellectual and organizational ties with other diasporic radicals, but the American, South African, and European parties largely blocked such efforts. As McKay had suggested and as other people often repeated by the close of the 1920s, white radicals did not seem class-conscious enough to grasp fully black people's world revolutionary potential. Hence, some black radicals had left organized communism by 1929. Yet their membership in Communist parties also put black radicals in the Comintern and thus brought them into the LAI, which facilitated their efforts to build a black international.

The Comintern's facilitation of a black intercolonialism simultaneously aided such exchanges and constricted what grew out of them. Between the first and second LAI congresses, the Comintern entered its Third Period, which was characterized by a "class-against-class" approach that called for strident attacks against those deemed reformists or collaborators with capital (that is, anyone not in or gravitating toward a communist organization). The Red International Labor Unions (RILU) would now direct global efforts to bring black people into the trade union movement. This period constricted black Communists' ability to organize around race on its own terms, stifled their intellectual creativity, and demanded a theoretical uniformity that foreclosed an approach to race that did not emphasize trade union organizing. Yet it is ironic that in a period of extremely reductive, inflexible politics dictated by Moscow, when control shifted to the Kremlin and the Comintern allowed little room for radical experimentation and when member parties continued to largely ignore Negro work, the Comintern facilitated the organization of a radical black international—the ITUCNW—that ultimately provided a rationale for its most important members to leave organized communism.

Little more than a year after the Brussels Congress, U.S. black Communists briefly revived the ANLC and pursued a range of community organizing initiatives, especially in Harlem. They also engaged in a broader range of black international initiatives in the United States. But the effects of the Comintern's Third Period policies on the WP and then the CPUSA took a tremendous toll on its black members. Factional struggles dominated internal decision-making and leadership debates, and the party exerted greater control over its members, including how they might think about revolution. Black Communists, as Mark Solomon notes, were ordered to dissociate from reformists, like those of the NAACP, and cease those activities deemed outside the realm of proletarian organizing. Theoretical dynamism and intellectual innovation virtually ground to a halt—whoever was in control at any given moment determined the correct Marxist line.[5]

This was the context in which the Sixth Congress's BBNT dictated policy and organizing activities. Whatever its efficacy, the constraints that the BBNT and the Comintern's Third Period policies in general placed on black Communists' work outside the party's orbit were considerable. Though the party would pursue organizing efforts in the areas of housing and unemployment and among black southerners, it was now clear that a radical black internationalist politics would have to take root outside both the party and the United States.

The LAI's second Frankfurt congress marked an important shift. U.S. black radicals such as James Ford and Otto Huiswoud were involved in organizing the International Conference of Negro Workers that came out of Frankfurt, and William Patterson and especially the Trinidadian George Padmore also played key roles. They established contacts with African and Caribbean activists in Europe and Africa who they hoped would become part of this new organization of black workers. However, far fewer people attended the ICNW than organizers had hoped. Opposition from colonial and European governments, the intransigence of Communist parties and organizations in Europe, and even the willingness of Ford, Patterson, and Padmore to embrace a "class-against-class" approach to organizing contributed to the low turnout. Still, black radicals drawn to the conference and to the ITUCNW maintained a vision of black radical organizing that coexisted uneasily with the Comintern's Third Period demands. They saw limited gains from a program that viewed race as a problem that could be resolved only through unity between black and white workers. For them, the anti-imperialist struggle required a much broader politics that international communism was unlikely to usher into existence.

The Brussels Congress

At Brussels, Münzenberg envisioned a world congress in which colonial peoples would denounce and embarrass France, England, America, and Belgium. He sought to have China's Chiang Kai-shek and India's Mohandas Gandhi deliver addresses and wanted the ANLC and NAACP representatives to decry racial oppression in the United States. He also proposed inviting nationalist leaders from the Congo to publicly denounce Belgian imperialism, but Belgian officials prohibited any criticism of their colonial practices in return for allowing the meeting to take place in Brussels.[6]

To realize such a gathering of anticolonial forces, Münzenberg sought to avoid any appearance of Comintern control, believing that the congress program alone would appeal to a range of progressive and radical anticolonial forces. He seemed to have judged correctly. Anticolonial radicals worldwide responded enthusiastically to the congress's proposal to establish a "permanent international organisation in order to link up all forces combating international imperialism and in order to ensure their effective support for the fight for emancipation conducted by the oppressed nations."[7] Jawaharlal Nehru and the Ghadar Party's Maulavi Barkatullah were in contact with the Comintern and met with Brussels Congress officials in Berlin in the months leading up to the congress. M. N. Roy, who by this time held a high position in the Comintern, also planned to attend, as did Indochina's Mohammad Hatta, the Mexican philosopher and radical José Vasconcelos, and several other anticolonial radicals from Latin America and the Spanish-speaking Caribbean. Messali Hadj, founder of the Paris-based radical group Étoile Nord Africaine (North African Star), would come with fellow Étoile members Chedi Ben Mustapha and Ahmed Hassan Mattar. Even George Lansbury, a member of the British Parliament from the Labour Party, was enthusiastic about the congress: he agreed with Albert Einstein, who saw in Brussels a "solidly united endeavor of the oppressed to achieve independence."[8]

Many of those planning to attend were hoping that Brussels would serve as a clearinghouse for anticolonial struggles and facilitate a global anti-imperialist movement, a goal that exceeded the visions of both the Comintern and congress organizers. ANLC organizers announced the congress through the George Weston–led faction of the UNIA. While some saw the specter of communism behind Brussels, the call elicited an enthusiastic response among U.S. black radicals, especially NAACP field secretary William Pickens.

By the mid-1920s, Pickens had exhibited increasingly radical tendencies that led him to establish working relationships with American-born black Communists, including Lovett Fort-Whiteman. With the announcement of the Brussels gathering, Pickens proposed to the NAACP's board of directors that he attend as an NAACP delegate, insisting that the future of the race lay in a worldwide struggle for freedom. The NAACP's participation could ensure that a congress that included peoples from "Hayti and the Philippines, Cuba and the Virgin Islands, Egypt and India" would not convene "with the American Negro left out." NAACP board members generally supported his proposal, though some feared that Communists would control the meeting. Despite Pickens's reasoned argument that a communist presence would not invalidate the congress, it took Du Bois's report from a meeting in Berlin with congress organizers, which assured the board that liberals would have an equal voice, to convince board members to support Pickens's attendance.[9]

The Brussels Congress had broad appeal among black radicals worldwide, who also saw it as an opportunity to establish ties with one another. Members of National Congress of British West Africa (NCBWA) and other Africans were involved in planning Brussels, and Gold Coast lawyer Joseph Casely-Hayford informed the congress that the NCBWA hoped to send delegates. The French radical Lamine Senghor and Gothon-Lunion cabled congress organizers that the Comité de Defense de la Race Nègre (Committee for the Defense of the Black Race, CDRN) would send six delegates to work with the Brussels Congress and all Negroes under French imperialism. Sierra Leonean labor organizer E. A. Richards also planned to attend, though he ultimately could not make the trip. The African National Congress sent its president, Josiah T. Gumede, and Carlos Deambrosis Martins came from Haiti representing the nationalist Union Patriotique (Patriotic Union).[10]

In March 1926, after leaving the PCF, Senghor had established the CDRN as a radical successor to the Ligue Universelle pour la Défense de la Race Noire (Universal League for the Defense of the Negro Race). Both Senghor and Gothon-Lunion had been members of the Ligue, and they conceived the CDRN as a response to the PCF's willful neglect of the Negro question.[11] Possibly as a result of conversations with Fort-Whiteman, Gothon-Lunion had written to the Comintern the previous summer to propose creating a black international centered on the CDRN, which he claimed was well placed to build an international socialist movement among colonized peoples. Though the Comintern never responded to his request, Brussels seemed to represent an opportunity to build just such an international.[12]

U.S. black Communists had similar hopes for Brussels. They attempted to get a range of black radicals to attend. Along with Pickens and Richard B. Moore, black Communists hoped they could get Hubert Harrison and George Weston to Brussels and were in contact with Casely-Hayford about the NCBWA sending delegates. At one point they proposed creating a provisional organization whose immediate focus would be getting Asian and Latin American radicals in the United States to come to Brussels.[13]

Münzenberg, however, had encountered problems convincing Moscow of the congress's value, and the Comintern was slow to send him the necessary funds. As a result, he was forced to postpone the congress three times. Only when Münzenberg warned the Comintern that without its financial support many of the Asian radicals already en route would return home disenchanted with the European Left and deprived of Bolshevism's influence, did Moscow gave him the funds he requested. But the damage was done. The date changes reduced attendance among Asian and African radicals and prevented all but one U.S. black radical from attending.[14] Indeed, when Pickens arrived in London in November 1926 to begin a speaking tour that was to end in Brussels, he had received no information on the congress. He later complained that although he had done his part to attend, the Communists had not.[15]

MOORE, THE SOLE U.S. black radical to attend, arrived in Brussels with a U.S. delegation that included Manuel Gómez of the All-America Anti-Imperialist League, the American Civil Liberties Union lawyer Roger Baldwin, Scott Nearing, and the Chinese-American Communist Chi Ch'ao-ting.[16] Though the U.S. group included nowhere near as many Asian and Latin American members as hoped, Moore interacted with an impressive array of radicals from Asia, Latin America, the Caribbean, and Africa at the congress. In addition to seeing his old friend Sen Katayama, he met M. N. Roy, Jawaharlal Nehru, Mohammad Hatta, the seventeen-member Chinese delegation, and the three Korean delegates. The congress also attracted delegates from Peru, Puerto Rica, Cuba, and Venezuela, giving it a far more internationalist cast than most of the major international black or Communist gatherings of the era.[17] Indeed, Brussels offered black radicals in international communism their first opportunity to meet on a scale approaching either Du Bois's PACs or the UNIA's international conventions.

For anticolonial radicals more generally, Brussels presented the opportunity for dialogue and to coordinate struggles. They were not about to forfeit a chance to enter a global movement whether or not Moscow was involved in the congress. Nehru captured the intercolonial mood of Brussels in an interview he gave on the eve of the congress, explaining that while Socialist and Communist parties were present, they were small and were overshadowed by the more moderate groups. Nehru echoed the hopes of many anticolonial radicals when he declared that out of the congress "a new 'Association of Oppressed Nations' will come about, if not right away then in the not-too-distant future."[18]

When the International Congress against Colonial Oppression and Imperialism opened at the Egmont Palace in Brussels on February 10, 1927, it welcomed 174 delegates from thirty-seven countries. The French novelist and Communist Henri Barbusse greeted those who had come to vindicate the "oppressed races and peoples" of the world. He decried colonialism, racism, and imperialism, insisting that colonial peoples themselves "must take . . . the right to self-determination." He also called on those in the West Indies, China, India, and Africa to join their struggles with the struggles attacking "colonization behind closed doors, such as that of the Negroes in the United States."[19] Many of those in attendance believed the anti-imperialist struggle of the day was unfolding in China. Katayama even proclaimed that China had already "struck a blow against the strongest imperialism of the world— England." Nehru raised the global importance of India while also applauding the "noble example of the Chinese nationalists," which he hoped India would one day follow.[20] Even Fenner Brockway, who headed the Independent Labour Party (ILP) delegation from Great Britain, pledged his party's support for Indian and Chinese nationalism.[21] But Africa and black people received little attention until the fifth day, when the Negro question came up for full discussion.

The speeches of the black delegates suggest that they were intent on drawing out the global contours of the Negro question and inserting race into any conception of imperialism. The African National Congress's Gumede made this connection most forcefully when he characterized antiracist struggles in South Africa as part of a larger struggle against European imperialism. Indeed, he questioned how congress organizers could display a map of the colonial world that portrayed South Africa "as if imperialism does not operate there." South Africa's troubled history, he explained, was the responsibility of "the whole of Europe."[22]

Senghor had come to Paris from Senegal, a decommissioned colonial soldier who had grown increasingly ill. By the time he arrived in Brussels, his health had deteriorated to the point that he was "afraid of the cold, and seldom went out." Nevertheless, Moore and several others remembered Senghor as intense and intelligent, with unmatched oratorical skills. Senghor referenced reports that the United States would purchase French Caribbean colonies and complained that colonial oppressors "don't sell us nowadays individually. They trade us wholesale, passing entire peoples from one to another." "They say slavery has been abolished," Senghor remarked, but it had "only been modernized."[23]

The Francophone black radicals from the Caribbean were concerned with France and the United States. Max Bloncourt detailed French atrocities in the Caribbean as well as the horrors of U.S. imperialism. In Guadeloupe and Martinique, he told the congress, black people were revolting against their limited freedoms and civil inequality. Haitian Union Patriotique delegate Carlos Deambrosis Martins highlighted brutal American practices in occupying his country, including "the murder of more than three thousand Haitians." The answer to capital's global reach, Bloncourt declared, was "the union of all oppressed peoples against imperialism."[24]

When Senghor addressed the congress, he sounded some of the same themes as Bloncourt and others but added a more pronounced intercolonial flavor. Cataloging French colonial abuses, he equated the horrors of the French empire to those of the Dark Ages. The black colonial troops France employed to maintain its hold on Morocco, Syria, Madagascar, and more recently Indochina, he argued, might come to see these colonial uprisings as essential to their own liberation. He exhorted delegates to join him in urging a joint struggle between the colonized and those in the metropole to destroy "world imperialism." But in what has been described as a moment of performative intercolonialism, in the middle of his speech Senghor turned to the Chinese delegates and expressed his desire "to embrace you, comrades, because you give a good revolutionary example to all the peoples suppressed under the colonizers' yoke. I only hope," he added, that Africans "will all take inspiration from your revolutionary spirit." Senghor removed Russia as a center of revolutionary intercolonialism by drawing a line from China to Africa. And in a final rhetorical flourish that highlighted the importance of African struggles, he declared, "Comrades, the blacks have slept too long. But beware! He who has slept long and soundly, once he has awakened will not fall asleep again."[25]

The LAI created at the Brussels gathering seemed poised to build a truly global anticolonial movement. The congress's resolutions called for a series of discrete but united struggles. Delegates from Britain, India, and China drafted a resolution calling on workers in England to support Indian and Chinese national liberation struggles and for all to commit to "unity and cooperative action." James La Guma and Daniel Colraine, the colored and white delegates of the South African Communist Party, were surprised that Gumede, who years earlier had opposed white radicals working in black struggles, now called the members of the South African party "the only people who are with us in spirit." All three worked together at Brussels to compose a resolution demanding "the right of self-determination, by the complete overthrow of capitalist and imperialist domination" in South Africa and imploring black and white workers to join in combating "world exploitation by capitalism and imperialism in colonies and semi-colonial countries."[26] Nehru, who was involved in drafting resolutions on Indian and Chinese liberation struggles, hailed the South African delegates' proposal to create an LAI branch in South Africa that could combine "the advanced wing of the white workers, the African workers, the African [National] Congress and the South African Indian Congress" in an unprecedented struggle "against all colour legislation and discrimination."[27]

But none of these resolutions focused on the Negro question. European and even Asian radicals still did not seem to see race as a central aspect of imperialism. European radicals continued to view race and nation as subsidiary concerns—if concerns at all—of socialist revolution. For example, when Britain's Lansbury arrived for the final two days of the congress, he extolled the primacy of European workers and warned that unless African and Asian nationalist leaders joined international socialism (rather than international communism), "all our work is in vain, every bit of it." And he criticized the plan to launch the LAI, arguing that rather than creating yet "another league . . . merely to extol the glories of nationalism," colonial nationalists must root their movements in class struggles.[28] The resolutions adopted at Brussels never considered the possibility that African or Caribbean liberation struggles might inform Chinese and Indian liberation movements or the struggles of British or French workers. Brussels highlighted the international Left's general inability to think creatively about race.

But the black delegates who met in Brussels as part of the Committee on the Negro Question brought race fully into their discussions of imperialism. The committee, chaired by Senghor and with Moore as secretary, also included Gumede, Bloncourt, Martins, Danae Narcisse, and St. Jacques Camille. It was one of the more geographically diverse groupings at Brussels, with members from the Francophone Caribbean and West Africa, South

Africa, the United States, and the British West Indies. By force of their global biographies and corresponding sense of race, they drafted a "Common Resolution on the Negro Question" that was not limited to any specific cultural or national group or colonial empire. Race provided an idiom through which to imagine a struggle centered on the "emancipation of the Negro peoples of the world."[29] The resolution struck a balance between the histories of racial and colonial oppression in Africa, the Caribbean, and the United States while framing struggles in these places as contingent battles central to proletarian revolution.

Moore introduced the resolution in a two-minute speech that captured the crux of the committee's approach to imperialism. One needed to realize, he began, "that the fight against imperialism is first of all an incessant struggle against imperialistic ideology," which entailed a struggle against "fascism, the Ku-Klux-Klan, chauvinism and the doctrine of the supremacy of the white race." As a result, white workers needed to understand black workers' reluctance to join their struggles, especially when "even in the more progressive groups of the labor movement we are treated as inferiors." Anti-imperialists had to "work harder to organize the Negro masses," he added, since it was "conceivable that the despised Negro peoples will be instrumental in tipping the scale of freedom in favor of the oppressed classes against the imperialistic oppressors."[30]

The Committee on the Negro Question thus situated race at the center of anti-imperialist struggle. While most delegates largely ignored race, the committee drew on it to envision a capacious notion of liberation. In the pan-African parlance of the time, their resolution demanded the complete freedom of Africa and people of African descent, African control of Africa, and "complete equality between the Negro race and all other races." Along with voicing these familiar refrains, the committee's members advocated unionizing Negro workers, forming consumer cooperatives, coordinating liberation movements throughout the diaspora, and unifying all oppressed peoples and classes for world liberation. In addition, the committee demanded independence for Haiti, Cuba, Santo Domingo, Puerto Rico, and the Virgin Islands. Such liberation, accompanied by the "confederation of the British West Indies," would help bring about "the Union of all these peoples." The "Common Resolution on the Negro Question" broke from the concern with uniting liberation struggles in a given empire to seeking ties across empires. Along these lines, Moore also worked with U.S., Latin American, and Chinese delegates on a declaration supporting "nationalists and national liberation movements [in] countries under the heel of U.S. imperialist domination" and calling for the unification of liberation struggles in Latin America with nationalist movements in the Philippines and China.[31]

Convinced that global revolution lay just over the horizon, delegates at the Brussels Congress also adopted a common resolution on the "United Front in the Struggle for Emancipation of the Oppressed Nations." The resolution claimed that national liberation depended on movements organizing "the peasants and the working masses as the basis of the national revolutionary front." This statement departed from nearly a decade of Comintern orthodoxy that routinely criticized the nationalism of oppressed "backward" peoples and claimed that the "advanced" European proletariat would bring about their liberation. Partly because Communists agreed not to push an agenda in order to avoid appearing to dominate the proceedings, the common resolution also highlighted Egypt, Mexico, and Central and South America in addition to the revolutionary example of China, with only cursory mention of Russia or European workers.[32] Anticolonial liberation would require "all oppressed peoples to assist one another in their struggle against imperialism."[33]

Delegates left Brussels excited about the possibilities. Katayama's reports to the Comintern and letters to Japanese radicals stated that the congress had fostered meaningful ties among anticolonialists. Years later, Nehru recalled that the gathering threatened to launch a great world movement against Europe.[34] Great Britain's Reginald Bridgeman worked tirelessly for the new LAI in London and refused to go along with the ILP three years later when it severed ties with the league. His expulsion from the party allowed him more time for organizing the LAI's British Section, which worked on Asia and provided critical support to black radicals during the 1930s. Indeed, the LAI in London and Berlin facilitated many exchanges between radicals, though this work was always more tenuous for blacks than for whites.

Senghor was elected to the LAI's executive branch, the only black delegate to hold such a position. He remained active until his death later in the year following his arrest and jailing, the length of which exacerbated his pulmonary problems. His position in the LAI indicated to other radicals that it would play an important role in African diasporic liberation.

Moore left Brussels with the Comité de Defense de la Race Nègre delegation, traveling through France before returning to the United States. His travel afforded him the opportunity to meet and converse with CDRN members and other black radicals in Paris and Marseilles and thus to develop a better sense of the possibility for a black international independent of the white Left. He had seen the beginnings of such an organization. In Marseilles, he tracked

Executive Council, League against Imperialism, February 1927. Seated, from left: Madame Sun Yat-sen (first), Sen Katayama (second), Chen Kuen (China, fourth), Edo Fimmen (Holland, fifth), Lamine Senghor (sixth), Lu Chung Lin (Canton government, seventh), Jawaharlal Nehru (eighth). Standing, from left: Liau Hansin (Kuomintang, first), Reginald Bridgeman (second), Manuel Gomez (eighth). From Münzenberg, *Das Flammenzeichen.*

down Claude McKay, who was living there and writing his novel *Banjo*, in desperate need of money. Moore gave McKay all the money he had. But more important, the encounter likely provided Moore with even greater insight into the life of African seamen in the port city, problems with the PCF, and the work Senghor had carried on among those seamen. McKay was even developing a character in *Banjo* based on Senghor.[35]

A Black International beyond the Party

If black radicals had gravitated to the Communist International because of its support of anti-imperialist struggles in Africa and Asia, their disappointments with it, which had led many to question the efficacy of communism for pan-African liberation, now seemed to subside. The Comintern seemed to have finally realized its potential. With the ANLC still suffering from underfunding, the inactivity of locals, inadequate leadership, and disarray in the national office, the Brussels Congress provided many black activists a reason to remain in the WP; others who had drifted away from it returned. But they continued to confront serious challenges within the party: It still resisted changing its approach to Negro work, ignored Comintern directives, and was dismissive of the ideas of its black members. Brussels, conversely, appeared to represent a real opportunity to build a black international and to offer a vehicle for black political organizing outside the party.

U.S. black radicals received scant information about Brussels, and most of it came through the party's newspaper, the *Daily Worker*, which scarcely covered the Committee on the Negro Question. When Moore returned to Harlem, however, he disseminated copies of the congress's various resolutions and its *Manifesto of the Brussels Congress against Imperialism*; he also gave speeches telling audiences across the country that the LAI had drafted "a basic program for joint action to forward the struggle for world emancipation." Moore's accounts of Brussels further substantiated the Comintern's continued value for pan-African liberation. Du Bois reprinted Moore's address at Brussels along with the Negro Committee's resolution in his *Crisis* magazine, and he described Brussels as an asset to the American Negro. Du Bois also published a passage from yet another *Manifesto to All Oppressed Peoples*, which claimed that African, Asian, Caribbean, Latin American, and working-class struggles would "abolish international capitalism and civilize the whole world."[36]

In July 1927, five months after the Brussels Congress, the Women's International Circle of Peace and Foreign Relations, a black women's club in New York led by Addie W. Hunton, Nina Du Bois, and Minnie Pickens, invited the ANLC to send representatives to the fourth PAC, scheduled for August 21–24 in Harlem. The NAACP's Pickens likely urged the invitation, as he continued to interact with Fort-Whiteman and the ANLC and maintained a membership in the LAI. However, he was unable to get Huiswoud onto the PAC's resolution committee or to have Moore speak about Brussels before the PAC. Despite failing to attend the Brussels Congress, Pickens delivered a report on Brussels to the PAC, highlighting the diverse groups of black radicals whose collaborative work had produced the resolution on the Negro question. Brussels, he told the audience, was the "first league of the economically, politically and socially oppressed" that had forcefully "called for complete racial equality throughout the world." He called on the PAC to follow suit and recognize the "common interest and make common cause with the other oppressed and exploited peoples of the world."[37] Huiswoud ultimately contributed to a resolution at the PAC supporting black workers; calling for Egyptian, Chinese, and Indian national independence; praising the Soviet Union's liberal views on race; imploring white workers to recognize their common interests with black

Hubert Harrison lecture, "World Problems of Race," at Harlem Educational Forum, September 9, 1926, Harlem, New York. Standing at far left is Richard B. Moore, who organized the session. W. A. Domingo is seated directly across from Harrison, holding a present. Williana Burroughs is seated, fourth from left, in the front row. Hubert Henry Harrison Papers, Columbia University, Rare Book and Manuscript Library, New York.

workers; and urging the West Indies to launch national liberation movements that would result in a federation.[38]

At the same time, black Communists in Harlem had been rejuvenated. In mid-April 1926, Grace Campbell reorganized the PEF as the Harlem Educational Forum (HEF), scheduling Hubert Harrison as its inaugural speaker. His topic was "Is the White Race Doomed?" Like the earlier forum, the HEF served as a vehicle for intense intellectual exchange and debate on such topics as race relations, civil liberties, and race and labor. Speakers included the prominent Communist M. J. Olgin and more mainstream New Negro intellectuals such as *Opportunity* magazine editor Charles Johnson. Campbell announced in local papers the HEF's motto: "Lay on Macbeth, and damned be he who first cries, Hold, enough!"[39] The HEF also sponsored concerts and dances, helping the organization to serve as a recruiting tool for the Communist Party. Attending Harrison's first lecture was a young teacher, Williana Burroughs, who through subsequent talks with Campbell, Cyril Briggs, and Moore joined the wp and quickly rose to prominence in its ranks. Within two years she would travel to Moscow with her family, becoming the first black woman to address a Comintern congress. She stayed for three years to study at KUTV, even running a Moscow radio program.[40]

FOLLOWING THE BRUSSELS CONGRESS, Moore expanded his range of New Negro activities. On February 12, 1928, Elizabeth Hendrickson, Captain Ely, and Victor Gasper held a mass meeting in Harlem to organize a tenants' league; spotting Moore in the audience, the organizers asked him to address the crowd. Listeners were so moved by his eloquent denunciation of exploitative landlords and the problem of soaring rents that they elected him president of the Harlem Tenants League (HTL). Campbell was also selected as one of the group's leaders. Hendrickson, a Communist and clubwoman who had previously worked with Campbell, likely had a radical organizing agenda in mind when she joined Ely and Gasper in calling the meeting. For Moore, however, the HTL represented a practical organizing effort that could mobilize a wide swath of black Harlemites.[41]

Moore drew other black Communists into the HTL, and they focused on detailing how discriminatory rents and poor housing conditions created disproportionately high death rates for the neighborhood's black families. Moore urged Harlem tenants to "form block and house committees" and "organize militant, fighting tenants leagues" that could work at the state and local levels "for the protection of the welfare and lives of the masses of the people." Otto Hall attributed a growing class consciousness in Harlem to "paying 50 percent more for rent for dirty, stuffy quarters than white residents" while "suffering a higher death rate and a tremendous rate of child mortality." Although the HTL's focus on black workers suggested an overriding concern with black men, black women were central to the organization.[42]

Moore and Campbell led the HTL in establishing tenants' committees throughout Harlem to pressure landlords to make basic repairs, lower rents, and address overcrowding. The HTL used protest marches, rent strikes, and boycotts to galvanize the community. With the impending expiration of New York City's Emergency Rent Laws in early 1929, the HTL concentrated on stemming the tide of evictions as well as gaining relief. A June march of two hundred local residents ultimately forced some property owners to withdraw rent increases and compelled the board of aldermen to enact moderate relief measures. The HTL soon claimed more than five hundred members and organized new committees in buildings across Harlem. When it announced plans to testify before the state legislature on housing, however, city officials began disrupting its activities, and police ejected the HTL from its regular meeting place at the public library at 135th Street. The repression strained the HTL, and by 1929 factional disputes within the CPUSA wreaked havoc on the group. Hendrickson and others soon grew tired of what they regarded as Moore's impractical organizing habits, his infusing of black Communists into the HTL, and the settling of party disputes at HTL meetings. When he tried to remove Campbell and Ed Welsh from the HTL, league members removed Moore as president. In turn, Campbell, Welsh, and Hendrickson left the party.[43]

Before the HTL's demise in 1929, party leaders had recognized the value of its dynamic organizing approach and considered it a potential model for organizing working-class black communities. Huiswoud suggested that the party "develop similar leagues in other large cities where Negroes are segregated and forced to pay exorbitant rents." Party leaders would hold up the HTL as a model for organizing black people at the Comintern's Sixth Congress, and the group became the template Trade Union Unity League leaders used in organizing their Unemployed Councils.[44] The HTL also attracted a number of rather important black radicals into the CPUSA. Audley Moore joined the party in the early 1930s, drawn to its work among local residents and women in the area of consumer rights. Louise Thompson Patterson recalled joining with a group of intellectuals to "establish discussion groups" and create "in Harlem a whole series of home study groups" in response to the "ferment of activity" there.[45] Amid this ferment, Malcolm Nurse, a young Trinidadian student who had recently left Nashville's Fisk University to study law in New York, also came into the party.

Nurse, who soon came to world recognition under the name George Padmore, had traveled to the United States in 1924 to study medicine. Raised in Port of Spain, he was a childhood friend of C. L. R. James. Padmore had worked as a journalist in Trinidad but left before the 1931 appearance of Albert Gomes's *Beacon*, a magazine that offered James and others in Trinidad a forum for joining politics and culture in a mode of nationalist political opposition. Padmore was well aware of the racial dynamics of Trinidadian society and seems to have had a burgeoning internationalist vision of black liberation by the time he arrived at Fisk. In Nashville, he began working with a Liberian student, Phillip Davies, on an organization of foreign black students that would not only protect Liberia's sovereignty but also raise black students' consciousness and prepare black people more generally for revolutionary struggle. As he explained to future Nigerian president Nnamdi Azikiwe, the group would replicate elements of China's Kuomintang Party.[46] No lasting organization seems to have resulted, however.

Padmore left Fisk soon thereafter for New York, where he joined the WP and was assigned to organize students on the Howard University campus in Washington, D.C. Almost immediately, Padmore established himself as a skilled organizer with a knack for drawing radical students from both the Caribbean and Africa into the party's sphere of influence. His bold involvement in protests against British ambassador Sir Esme Howard's visit to campus garnered him significant attention, as did his criticisms of key university faculty. T. Ras Makonnen recalled that Padmore encouraged his classmates to question their professors, especially Kelly Miller, rather than "treat them as gods." "You can't allow this buffoon Kelly Miller to insult Africans like this," Padmore explained. He especially protested Miller's penchant for demeaning African students by asking, "Are you from Africa? I thought so. Can't expect anything great from you."[47]

In Harlem, Padmore worked on the party's Negro Committee, participated in the ANLC, and organized local residents in the HTL with Campbell and Moore. Padmore also distinguished himself as a journalist, and his peers nominated him to serve on the editorial committee of the Negro Committee's national paper, the *Negro Champion*, and asked him to write articles for the *Daily Worker*. Padmore implored a Brooklyn crowd to give more support to the ANLC so that it might aid their "African brothers when they, taking courage from the heroic revolution of the Chinese workers, launch the inevitable revolution against white capitalist domination and exploitation." He, too, saw in organized communism the possibility of a black international.[48] Yet Padmore's time in the party was relatively short for someone who would assume leadership of the Comintern's Negro Bureau within three years and emerge as the most important black person in the history of the Third International.

An International Bureau of Negro Workers

By 1926 several black Communists were in Moscow studying at its University of the Toilers of the East, including Otto Hall; his younger brother, Harry Haywood; William Patterson; and Howard University graduate Maude White.[49] Haywood, in the spring of 1922, had followed Hall into the ABB and the WP, where he recalled his initial meetings with black Communists, "mostly workers from the stockyards and other industries" who were former Garveyites. White had joined the party in high school and come to Moscow after graduating from Howard University.[50] As the Comintern prepared to convene its Sixth Congress, scheduled to meet from July to September 1928, Patterson, Haywood, Hall, and White were joined by Ford and Burroughs on a special subcommittee charged with developing a new position on the Negro question in the United States.[51] They and other black Communists had little positive to say about the WP's record on race.

For years, black Communists had pushed the WP to organize black people, but the party had refused to work in "close co-operation" with its "Negro comrades," as Hall noted.[52] Ford brought into stark relief their central complaint: the American party's failure to follow Comintern directives. He noted that Moscow had sent the Party "no less than 19 resolutions and documents upon the Negro question," and "not a single one of them had been carried into effect." Black Communists had repeatedly raised their concern to the American party, he pointed out, but now they would "bring it before a Comintern Congress." Ford saw the problem as bigger than the American party, however. The British and French Communist parties, too, had to alter their approaches to race in colonial territories and realize that black workers globally represented the "next great revolutionary wave" in the fight "for the overthrow of capitalism and the downfall of imperialism throughout the world." Unlike black Communists, the party could not see in "the racial movement . . . a revolutionary anti-imperialist struggle" that related to "the general question of the Negroes throughout the world." In hopes of realizing this, Ford urged the organization of "trade unions among the Negro peoples of the world."[53]

Earlier in the year, the Comintern's executive committee had directed the RILU to begin trade union organizing among black industrial and agricultural workers. The RILU had adopted a resolution to that effect at its fourth congress, an unprecedented development. Through special colonial and Negro sections in various national Communist parties, the RILU was to wind its way throughout the African diaspora. Seemingly reflecting the Negro Commission's resolution from Brussels, it would reach not only major U.S. cities and South Africa but Brazil and other parts of South America, the Caribbean, West Africa, and even Portuguese colonies. Ford, the first black Communist to attend an RILU congress and an elected member of its executive bureau, proposed that several black Communists come to Moscow from the United States — Richard Moore, Edward Doty, Isaac Munsey, Lovett Fort-Whiteman, Otto Huiswoud, Charles Henry, and Cyril Briggs. He believed that these comrades' willingness to criticize the American party for its racism, failures with the ANLC, and habit of appointing inexperienced black comrades to leadership positions — and then raising them as examples that black Communists were unfit to lead—made them essential to the success of the RILU's undertaking. Yet by the end of July 1928, nearly halfway through the Comintern's Sixth Congress, there had been little movement on his recommendations: Not one of the delegates Ford named was in Moscow, and virtually no organization of black workers had occurred.[54]

At an RILU executive board meeting during the Sixth Congress, South African delegates joined U.S. delegates Ford, Patterson, Haywood, Hall, and Burroughs as well as RILU general secretary Alexander Losovsky in proposing the establishment of an International Bureau of Negro Workers (IBNW). Patterson believed that this bureau would respond to the inability of European parties to deal with the Negro question and hoped that it would advise national parties and help them "bring the Negroes into the Communist Party." Ford would chair the new IBNW and would work with several others to organize a 1929 conference that would draw black workers from around the world into a global organization for class struggle.[55] The leaders of the American delegation had little choice but to support the effort, though they rejected Ford's proposal to have a black representative on the Comintern's executive committee for discussions of the world situation and his request to appoint at least seven black members to the WP's CEC.[56]

For black Communists in the United States, France, and West Africa, the proposed IBNW carried far more weight than any other resolution or policy statement to issue from the Comintern in six years. More than a decade of calls for some sort of world meeting of black people seemed finally to have borne fruit. Over the next few years, many black Communists would shift their attention, if only for a time, from their local contexts to the world stage and the effort to build the IBNW.

Internationalizing the Negro Question

The proposed IBNW's meaning for black Communists coexisted rather uneasily with the Comintern's "class-against-class" Third Period political line. The near doctrinaire adherence to Comintern decisions that was required at the time severely constricted the activities of black Communists. In the CPUSA, internal debate was also restricted by the fact that decision making was located in the party's CEC. The results were disastrous.

Black Communists saw the BBNT that emerged from the Comintern's Sixth Congress as allowing them greater room for organizational work, but they soon realized that the Third Period mandates would weaken their ability to pursue autonomous forms of organizing. Most disagreed with the BBNT and cautioned against pursuing it too aggressively, feeling that it was, as Moore put it, "more Garveyism than Garvey himself." The ANLC, the HTL, and the *Negro Champion*, they reminded party leaders, would succeed only if they did not appear to be too closely associated with Communists. Thus, black Communists requested that the party pull John Pepper's pamphlet, *American Negro Problem*, in which the Hungarian-born Comintern representative argued that "*Negro Communists should emphasize in the propaganda the establishment of a Negro Soviet Republic.*" Black Communists considered the pamphlet a mistake and Pepper too sectarian. Pepper, however, largely disregarded their concerns and instead drew black Communists into a factional fight.[57]

Pepper took aim at Moore, whose membership in E. Ethelred Brown's Unitarian Church many party members saw as uncommunist. Though ordered to leave, Moore explained that Brown's church allowed debates among its members and that he had used such forums to argue that only communism, not Christianity, could solve the race problem. More important, he insisted that working in black churches allowed black Communists to reach the black masses in their own institutions.[58] At issue here was how party leaders responded to black Communists' methods.

Moore complained of a growing trend in the party toward a doctrinaire, antagonistic approach to decision making. The party had ignored Ford's recommendations about who to send to the Sixth Congress and increasingly resolved disputes via what Moore called a "pseudo-sophisticated dialectics" of Marxism that "begins with an analysis of objective conditions" and concludes by saying "my group had proved to be correct and always will be correct in the future." Rather than encouraging innovative ways of reaching the black masses, as Moore suggested, party leaders insisted on strict adherence to its policies, with little sense that such an approach would continue to drive away valuable black members. In an attempt to salvage his position within the party, Moore left the church and plunged into the factional fight, helping drive Campbell and Hendrickson and others from the Party and running the HTL into the ground. When the Communist Party of Great Britain's Harry Pollitt interviewed several black Communists in March 1929, nearly all of them cited the negative impact of the party's factional struggles on Negro work. Padmore believed that the Negro question was the play of the rival factions.[59]

The CPUSA's March 1929 convention exposed the continuing disjuncture between how black Communists and party leaders thought about the Negro question. Padmore challenged the party to move beyond its narrow understanding of Negro work and take up how black people were exploited as both a class and a race. The appeal of Negro work was in its internationalism, he said. If in addition to American black people the party considered the "millions of colonial blacks who have come from various . . . sections of the world," the more than "5 million Mexican workers," and the "millions of Chinese, Japanese, Koreans, Philipinos and Hindus in the United States," Padmore argued, party officials would realize that there existed within U.S. borders a powerful international force. Hall agreed, pointing out that in California, the party had carried on "very little Negro work . . . and no work among the Orientals." Whatever the motive, at the convention's end, party leaders appointed five black Communists to the CEC—Briggs, Hall, Huiswoud, John Henry, and Ed Welsh. The party also designated Huiswoud, Padmore, Patterson, Haywood, H. V. Phillips, and Ford to work on the IBNW and its forthcoming conference. But Briggs captured the sentiment of most black Communists when he claimed after the convention that much of the party's Negro work had been "of a sporadic nature intended in the main as a gesture for the benefit of the Comintern."[60]

Many black Communists in the United States and France were growing increasingly disillusioned with the prospects for international organizing. While the Brussels Congress had raised great expectations, the LAI had done little to realize its goal of a global anticolonial struggle. Ford recounted to a January 1929 meeting of the LAI's General Council in Cologne, Germany, the numerous missed opportunities to organize black industrial and maritime workers, missed opportunities that had led many blacks to lose faith in the LAI. Ford also reported his findings from two months of travel in France and Germany. In Paris, he had met with Garan Kouyaté, head of the Ligue de Defense de la Race Nègre (League for the Defense of the Black Race, LDRN), the Guadeloupean radical Stéphane Rosso, and other members of the Colonial Section of the PCF to discuss its failures to organize adequately in French colonial Africa. Ford reported that the PCF had no contact with any of the LDRN's branches in Africa, nor had German Communists made inroads with African seamen who routinely came into port in Hamburg. Ford insisted that the LAI embark on a "second period" of an "organised, systematic campaign against imperialism" and that the PCF take seriously the task of colonial organizing. The LAI and European parties had to aid the organizational work of the IBNW's conference, he stated, including helping set up branches in the United States, South Africa, and the Caribbean. Moreover, he urged the LAI to delay its upcoming second congress, scheduled for July in Frankfurt, until several other conferences had met, allowing the LAI time to "draw these broad masses into the League."[61] Although the LAI did not postpone its July meeting, it accommodated Ford's request to hold informal meetings with Negro delegates to outline the IBNW's program, with the proviso that the LAI incur no additional costs. But the Cologne meeting devoted only a single day to discussing colonial work, an odd situation for a group committed to anti-imperialist struggle.[62]

After Brussels, the LAI groped to build the kind of international organization that many black Communists had hoped would emerge. Between the February 1927 meeting in Brussels and the second congress in Frankfurt in July 1929, efforts to produce a viable group or sustain an international network of anticolonial activists largely faltered. Almost immediately after Brussels, Britain's ILP began to question the extent of Communist involvement in the LAI. Organizing the British Section of the LAI was quite slow, and ILP members hardly took colonial work seriously.[63] In the fall of 1927, when the British LAI turned its attention to colonial work, it sent John Beckett, a member of Parliament, to organize an LAI branch in South Africa. Yet according to a report by South African Communist Party founding member Sidney Bunting, Beckett carried on no work among black workers in South Africa and claimed the LAI did not want to organize black workers who had no white trade union affiliation. Bunting felt that the opportunity for LAI organizing "was wholly and entirely lost owing to [Beckett's] woeful apathy in the matter."[64] To make matters worse, the death of Senghor, the sole black delegate in the LAI executive branch, had left the LAI reeling and without a black leader. African diasporic radicals attended the LAI General Council's December conference in Brussels, but the Negro question and organizing in the colonies took up little discussion there; the Kuomintang's brutal slaughter of Chinese Communists during the December 11 Canton uprising received the most attention. From that point on, the LAI went into a steep decline, with its next General Council meeting drawing only ten members. LAI branches continued to try to establish connections with organizations in Africa and India but garnered at best mixed results. And at a February 1928 meeting, the LAI's General Council neither discussed the Negro Resolution from Brussels nor even took up the Negro question.[65]

Preparations for the LAI's Frankfurt Congress also revealed the problems besetting its organizing. In classic Third Period fashion, the Comintern moved to tightly control the activities of congress participants. At the Comintern's direction, Münzenberg pressured LAI branches to assume greater ties with Moscow and resist the socialist-led Second International. Nehru, who refused to take orders from Communists or to subordinate his work in the

Indian National Congress to the dictates of the Comintern, soon found himself marginalized.[66] Even when the Comintern found that it could not remove all "social reformists" from the Frankfurt Congress program, it still sought to dictate policy. When Münzenberg included the NAACP's Pickens among those who would address the Negro question and appointed him "reporter," the reaction was swift. Patterson wrote that appointing a representative from a "reformist" organization such as the NAACP was unacceptable and informed Münzenberg of the LAI secretariat's decision that Pickens be replaced by Ford and James La Guma of the South African Communist Party. The secretariat even considered reprimanding Münzenberg for selecting Pickens.[67] So heavy-handed was Comintern control over the planning of the Frankfurt Congress that rather than allow black delegates to meet and draft a resolution on the Negro question, as had been the case in Brussels, the resolution and similar ones on India, China, North Africa, and Latin America were drafted months before the congress.[68]

Black delegates to the Frankfurt Congress were a diverse bunch. Along with Pickens, Ford, and Kouyaté, they included Henry Rosemond, Patterson, and Burroughs from the United States and a young Jomo Kenyatta, then studying at the London School of Economics. All of these participants addressed the Negro question, but the Comintern's mandates foreclosed the kinds of deliberations that had led to innovative pronouncements on black liberation at Brussels. For the most part, their speeches struck the necessary anti-imperialist tone and attacked Negro reformist leaders and organizations, a practice that gave Pickens pause. The NAACP field secretary opposed a resolution that singled out A. Philip Randolph and Clements Kadalie as imperialist coconspirators, called Soviet Russia the "fatherland of workers and oppressed peoples," and demanded the immediate independence of Britain's and France's African colonies. Pickens warned that if the Communists "should make the anti-imperialist organization of the world synonymous with their political organization," the LAI would lose "other persons and parties, even the independents."[69] Though his arguments were generally disregarded because of his opposition to colonial independence, he may have created space in which others could deviate from the party line. Burroughs criticized the LAI for its inadequate work among African Americans and in the Caribbean, and Ford parted with the Comintern on the BBNT to insist that while African peoples would pursue national liberation, "in America . . . it was a racial question" that required racial independence. Kouyaté went further, telling the congress that the LDRN would "do everything to coordinate, centralize, unify the national emancipation movements of the Negroes of black

Africa [les Nègres de l'Afrique noire]." The "national emancipation movement of the Negroes of Africa and the Negro movement for political and social emancipation in America," he argued, "will mutually support each other."[70]

The International Conference of Negro Workers

Several of the black delegates to the Frankfurt Congress held a series of meetings on their final two days in Frankfurt to lay the basis for reviving the stalled ICNW. Along with Rosemond, Patterson, Kouyaté, Burroughs, and Kenyatta, participants included Sen Katayama, a representative from the Chinese Workers Union, and an Indian National Congress member named Gupta. The meetings conveyed a sense of the potential international reach of the proposed ITUCNW. The British member of Parliament Shapurju Saklatvala urged that the ICNW meet in London, while the Algerian Communist Abdelkader Hadj Ali, perhaps with the African radicals in France in mind, suggested Paris. The group elected Ford to chair a committee to discuss options with the LAI's Reginald Bridgeman and Labour Party member of Parliament James Maxton.[71]

To black Communists, the ICNW signaled a new turn in international communism's approach to the Negro and race. Patterson captured the feeling best when he described the conference as the "internationalisation of the Negro problem" with a program that would stress to black workers globally "the commonality of interests between their struggle and those of the oppressed toiling masses of other colonies" and of European workers.[72] The call to the conference conveyed this internationalist impulse, requesting that "all sympathizing organisations of all nationalities . . . send their fraternal delegates" and suggesting that the goals of this international organization were much broader than just organizing black workers. Indeed, the organizational participants listed included the LDRN, ANLC, and Kenyatta's Central Kikuyu Association as well as the Indian National Congress and the All-China Trade Union Federation.[73]

Over the next year, work on the ICNW proceeded at a dizzying pace. Although it was originally planned for twenty-five delegates to meet in October 1929 in Germany, it soon became clear that not enough work had been done on the conference, and it was postponed until the following July in London. In the interim, Ford returned to the United States to take control of the Trade Union Unity League's Negro Department. Black Communists in the United States selected Padmore to work on the conference organizing committee, a decision that would catapult him onto the world stage.[74]

Padmore's work over the previous year or so had caught the attention of U.S. party leaders. Along with organizing in Harlem and on Howard University's campus, he showed an expansive intellect and a grasp of world events as they related to Africa that set him apart from his fellow black Communists. Padmore was relatively inexperienced as an organizer, but he soon emerged as a competent news writer. Moreover, his ability to get black delegates to attend the Trade Union Unity League's August 1929 convention showed great promise. The CPUSA's William Z. Foster decided to take Padmore with him to Moscow, where he would give a report on the Trade Union Unity League convention. He was selected to work on the ICNW in part because of his promise; plus, he was already in Moscow. His energy and political acumen had so impressed his fellow black Communists that Ford wrote to assure the Negro Bureau secretary George Slavin that he would find in Padmore "a good, energetic and capable comrade." That his trip to Moscow would be permanent was not apparent at the time to Padmore, however, as he had planned to return to Howard in mid-October. At year's end, he remained in Moscow, meeting students at KUTV and occasionally lecturing on Africa and the world proletarian struggle.[75]

Work in the international arena would soon prove far more difficult than Padmore could have imagined. Before Ford left for the United States, he met with the French, Belgian, German, and British Communist parties about stepping up their Negro work.[76] Patterson, who remained in Europe following Frankfurt, wore a path between Hamburg and Paris, meeting with other black Communists and establishing contacts with seamen in Hamburg, London, Cardiff, and Marseilles. During his brief stay with Kouyaté in Paris, Patterson witnessed firsthand the "very unsatisfactory Negro work" of the PCF, about which Kouyaté complained while in Moscow. The PCF had no contact with the LDRN's branches outside Paris, let alone its branches in Senegal, Côte d'Ivoire, or Togo. Patterson noted the PCF's failure to give attention to the colonies or make any progress since the Comintern's Sixth Congress as well as the need for more attention from the Communist Party of Great Britain (CPGB) to organizing in British colonies and among black seamen in Cardiff.[77]

At the beginning of 1930, Padmore and Patterson intensified their organizing activities. Working closely with others in the IBNW, they helped prepare materials for work in the Caribbean and began building ties to African radicals in Europe and Africa. Their efforts were aided in part by Kenyatta and Kouyaté, who, along with Burroughs, traveled from Frankfurt to Moscow after the LAI congress. Padmore and Kouyaté began an important political and intellectual friendship. On his way to Moscow, Kouyaté accompanied Münzenberg to Berlin, meeting some of the African radicals who had worked briefly in the LAI. Kouyaté was especially drawn to a small group of Cameroonian radicals centered around Joseph Bilé, and helped them form the German branch of the LDRN, the Liga zur Verteidigung der Negerrasse. In Moscow, Kouyaté informed Padmore about the African radicals in Germany. When Padmore and Patterson arrived in Berlin in April 1930, Padmore immediately made contact with Bilé and the Gambian labor organizer Edward Small. They also met Kenyatta, black seamen from Cardiff, and the Nigerian radical Frank Macaulay.[78]

As publicity began to circulate about the ICNW, and its news organ, *Negro Worker*, began its modest circulation, many participants agreed that the conference's importance lay in potentially linking up movements in Gambia, Nigeria, Kenya, the Caribbean, and the United States. From April on, Patterson remained in Europe, making conference arrangements and awaiting word from Britain's Labour government about whether the conference could meet in London. Padmore had supplied Huiswoud and Rosemond with some contacts in Trinidad, though both would have their greatest success among Garveyites in Jamaica. Padmore traveled with Small to Sierra Leone, Gambia, Senegal, Ghana, and Nigeria to recruit delegates. He returned to London in May feeling that there were "good prospects for future work" in West Africa and a "strong anti-imperialist sentiment everywhere," views that left him convinced the conference could be a huge success "if other sectors responded" as West Africa had.[79] His enthusiasm dimmed, however, as the international communist movement's indifference became clear.

At the same time that Padmore and Patterson were making meaningful contacts with diasporic radicals, they were beginning to question what might come of those contacts, given the actions of European Communists. Patterson grew concerned that no work had been done in London, Berlin, and Paris for the conference and that issues of *Negro Worker* had neither circulated in England nor made their way to Liga zur Verteidigung der Negerrasse radicals. And not only did conference delegates have to maneuver around colonial authorities who refused them travel visas, but those who made it to Europe found the "advanced" proletariat rather unwelcoming and largely uninformed about if not hostile to the conference. As late as April, Small and other trade union leaders knew little about the conference, having received no information from the CPGB, the LAI's British section, or German Communists. In Germany, the situation was little better: The Comintern's Western European Bureau, the RILU, and the LAI were equally uninformed about the conference and had not contemplated carrying on any work among Africans in Berlin or Hamburg; Bilé knew little more than Small.[80]

The situation worsened in May, when Britain's Labour government announced that it would not allow the conference in London, forcing Patterson to move it to Hamburg at the last minute. Those already en route or, like Padmore, still in West Africa could not be informed of the change. When Gambian delegates arrived in Britain after enduring the harassment of local authorities, not only did they learn that the conference was not taking place there, but no one could give them any further information. In addition, when Patterson returned to Germany, he received no help from the German Communist Party. Worse still, when Padmore finally made his way from London to Germany with four West African delegates, German Communists refused to provide them food, financial assistance, or support of any kind, leaving Padmore to appeal to the Comintern for help. Frustrated, hungry, tired, and likely disillusioned with the international movement of which Padmore had spoken so highly, the delegates decided to return home. An exasperated Padmore remarked to Moscow, "This is a hell of a way of doing things."[81]

But Ford, Patterson, and Padmore contributed to their problems by going against their own thinking about how to build a black international. Third Period policy mandated that organizers avoid intellectuals and professionals and focus their recruitment efforts on workers considered class-conscious — that is, those already engaged in trade union work. In a pamphlet publicizing the conference, Padmore largely reiterated Comintern policy, urging black workers to unite with white workers for true freedom and describing Soviet Russia as the "fatherland of the toilers of all races." The only hint of an inter-colonialist politics came in a single line on the need to "widen the scope of the economic struggles of the Negro workers . . . into political struggles." In the United States, this approach restricted recruiting to the Trade Union Unity League and the ANLC. Ford later even criticized Rosemond's and Huiswoud's efforts in the Caribbean because they held meetings with intellectuals and sent a Jamaican delegate whom Ford considered "a petty trade union official and not a genuine worker."[82] Although Patterson made numerous complaints that European parties had failed to carry on work among Africans, he discounted his opportunities to build on the independent organizing of Africans. He came away from a meeting with Bilé and the Liga zur Verteidigung der Negerrasse unimpressed with their political consciousness. After meeting a group of about eighty African seamen and sugar refinery workers in Liverpool who had recently formed a Negro Society, he described them as a "very poor lot" with a few good elements and failed to maintain contact. As a result, the members of the Liverpool group were entirely unaware that the conference had been moved to Hamburg until they read a report in the *Daily Worker* on the day it was to have started in London. And Patterson questioned Kenyatta about an article in the *Manchester Guardian* that outlined his Kikuyu Central Association's reformist agenda, which ran afoul of the Negro Bureau's political line. In the end, he was skeptical, considering Kenyatta "an unsafe element."[83]

Under such circumstances, it is amazing that any delegates made it to the conference. Those arriving in England had to use considerable subterfuge to make their way to Hamburg, enduring intense surveillance along the way. Nineteen delegates, along with three fraternal delegates, crowded into the top floor of Hamburg's Seamen's Club. For a gathering whose organizers had at one point envisioned only twenty-five delegates, and considering the litany of problems encountered along the way, the turnout was quite promising. But when Padmore arrived in Germany after handling the ill treatment of African delegates, he realized that materials prepared in Moscow had yet to arrive. In addition, the conference was delayed because its chair, Ford, and the U.S. delegation had been held up leaving for Europe. The two Gold Coast delegates had to leave early, forcing the ICNW to open provisionally on July 6 so that they could make their presentations. Ford and the U.S. delegation arrived the following morning, and the conference opened formally that evening. However, Moscow instructed Ford that the conference would meet for only two days, rather than the week that had been planned.[84]

The conference consisted largely of reading reports on the future agenda of what now would formally be known as the International Trade Union Committee of Negro Workers. Reports and speeches were largely recitations of colonial abuses and atrocities balanced by accounts of trade union organizing and the difficulties some encountered in their work. Helen McClain, a Philadelphia Needle Trade Workers organizer, called for organizing women and paying "special attention to the position of women workers everywhere," while Small urged support for the struggle in Cameroon and for the "rights and the independence that belongs to Man and to all races." Padmore submitted a resolution on "Economic Struggles," Patterson offered one on "Forced Labour and Poll Tax," and Macaulay discussed "The War Danger." On the conference's second day, delegates had what was later described as a warm meeting with a group of Hamburg workers. In later reports to Moscow and in the published proceedings, Ford claimed that those present at the conference represented more than twenty thousand workers from different parts of Africa, the United States, and the Caribbean. Although a dubious number, it reflected the sense of possibility that many saw in what they had pulled together.[85]

While little of the dynamism and innovative thinking that had animated earlier radical black internationalist meetings were evident, some signs of independence of thought were discernable. In addition to public speeches and reports, the black delegates held meetings behind closed doors without a stenographer. Given the Communist habit of copious record keeping, this could have hardly been an oversight. Indeed, the delegates likely wanted to have frank discussions about the kind of work they envisioned the ITUCNW would carry out. Historian Holger Weiss suggests that Ford and Padmore were gently breaking from Moscow's control. Rather than functioning as mere cogs in the Comintern machinery, they and other delegates hoped to foreground questions of race and colonialism in building diasporic anticolonial movements. Indeed, the executive committee elected at Hamburg was resolutely diasporic and hardly disposed to follow orders lockstep. They likely developed a plan for responding to the troubles they had encountered in planning the conference.[86]

Ford dashed off two reports to Moscow that generally hailed the ICNW as a success, a view that contrasted widely with other contemporary observations. While the Berlin-based Indian Communist Virendranath Chattopadhyaya considered it a qualified success, a "preparatory conference" that needed greater representation, the fraternal delegate Willi Budich complained that it was neither a protest demonstration nor a strategy meeting. A representative from the Western European bureau considered its impact minimal, while others questioned its potential for launching a radical platform. In his reports, Ford reserved his criticisms largely for European Communist parties and the Comintern. He criticized organizers for failing to attract enough delegates "who had widely divergent political views," though of far greater importance were the repeated failures of the "Communist Parties who should have been most interested in our work and our programme." Ford suggested that the Comintern launch a campaign to establish parties in the Caribbean and West Africa; provide greater support to the ANLC, LDRN, and the LAI's Negro work; and have the French, British, and other European parties begin serious work among Negroes. A subsequent report by Ford was even more strident, declaring that the collective neglect and "under-estimation of Negro work" on the "part of the CPs, the unions and the sympathetic organisations" revealed their "right tendencies and opportunism in practice." Surprisingly, he also criticized the Comintern's Negro Bureau for failing to publicize the conference and compel the support of various parties.[87]

On August 23, the Comintern's Political Committee backed the ICNW's resolutions and acknowledged Ford's criticisms, sending letters of reprimand to the French and British parties and reminding them of their task to organize black workers in Europe and their countries' colonies. Kouyaté would later complain of the lack of support his LDRN received from the PCF, noting that the French party underestimated black people and the colonial masses.[88] Read as a collective complaint about the limits placed on organizing black people globally, Ford's reports expressed the continuing frustration of black Communists around the world who felt the need for a political formation capable of encompassing a range of political views. The new ITUCNW was not to be a united front in the vein of the U.S.-based ANLC or the Paris-based CDRN (or the subsequent LDRN). Those at Hamburg sought an organization encompassing a diverse range of radicals, and many saw as insurmountable and ultimately intolerable the limits posed by organized Marxism.

WHEN PATTERSON HAD FIRST taken in Leningrad's impressive architecture, smelled the wood of Pushkin's home, and walked the teeming streets of Moscow, he could hardly have imagined that he would soon help build a movement to unite black workers around the world and link their struggles with those of other colonial peoples. Leaving Moscow for Frankfurt with Ford in the summer of 1929, Patterson could not have foreseen participating in such a grand effort. It surpassed anything that had come before it and extended beyond the realm of the political possibilities of which he could conceive. It is equally unlikely that Patterson, so enamored of organized Marxism, could have imagined that communist parties would be so consistently dismissive of the work of black Communists.

Still, the black radical vision of a diasporic international essential to socialist revolution had prompted Moore and Pickens to travel to Brussels two years earlier, and prompted even more black radicals to come to Frankfurt. It had then spurred radicals from West Africa and Europe to try to take part in the ICNW. And this vision ultimately produced the ITUCNW. But while the ability to bring together black radicals from throughout the diaspora showed the international communist movement's potential, at no point did the seasoned leaders of these efforts lose sight of a fundamental irony: the national communist parties—the same parties through which radicals had to work to build the movement—were hindering if not sabotaging their work.

Such was the political cauldron that George Padmore stepped into in 1930. By the end of that year, he had assumed control of the ITUCNW, become editor of *Negro Worker* and head of the Comintern's Negro Bureau, and emerged

as the most powerful black person in the international communist movement. Of course, the efforts he led were not his alone. For all of the U.S. and
European parties' miscalculations and neglect of Negro work and despite the
Comintern's inability to compel its member parties to carry on such work
and the utterly debilitating influence of Third Period policies, the Comintern
and RILU supported their black comrades' desire to organize a worldwide
black anti-imperialist movement. Unrest in the Caribbean and various parts
of Anglophone and Francophone Africa clearly reflected a growing desire
among colonized people for national independence.

6

The Rise of a Black International

George Padmore and the International Trade
Union Committee of Negro Workers

Despite their frustrations with Communist parties and the Comintern, black Communists viewed the new International Trade Union Committee of Negro Workers as signaling a shift in how the international communist movement approached colonial work. The Negro question and all that it encompassed now carried even greater importance that could propel new forms of organizing in Africa and the Caribbean. It was thus with considerable aplomb that black Communists pursued their enormous task of building an international of black workers capable of directing anticolonial struggles. The Communist International was now asking of the ITUCNW what it had asked five years earlier of Lovett Fort-Whiteman and the ANLC—develop a solution to the Negro problem. James Ford initially led this new effort, but responsibility soon fell to George Padmore, who, convinced of his prodigious intellect and the moral and political force of his cause, took the assignment in stride, setting off with little hesitation to bring together a grouping of black men who would lead the Negro proletariat.

The imagery that would soon represent the ITUCNW, primarily in its journal, *Negro Worker*, was a familiar one, having been first used in the ANLC: a muscular, virile black worker in overalls, emerging out of the United States, breaking the chains of slavery and oppression that held down blacks not only there but also in the Caribbean and Africa. (Alluding to American empire, the image highlighted "Dixie," Cuba, Haiti, Puerto Rico, and Liberia.) In keeping

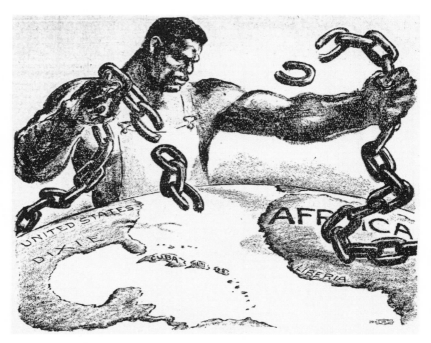

Image that appeared on ANLC letterhead, pamphlets, and flyers.

with a decade of Comintern thinking and several decades of racial uplift ideology, the image invoked the notion of a more advanced African American worker who stood at the vanguard of black liberation worldwide.

The ITUCNW made no claims that it was anything other than an effort led by black men to organize black workers. Yet Padmore's rather masculinist approach carried its own built-in constraints: Its politics and theoretical framework were prescribed by the Comintern, and the nodes of its organizing were directed largely by the same member-party structure that had proven the foil of the International Conference of Negro Workers. If Padmore was confident in his abilities to lead the ITUCNW, he was hardly indifferent to the hurdles that lay ahead.

The Comintern, with its Third Period policies, was both an ally and an albatross to Padmore and the ITUCNW. The Comintern's tight control and insistence on strict adherence to party line demanded that communist organizations give unequivocal support to Negro work. At least in theory, black Communists had the authority to compel intransigent white members and local leaders to give greater support to Negro work. But at the same time, class-against-class politics limited the range of organizing activities in which black Communists could engage. It also constricted Padmore's and the ITUCNW's ability to theorize the nature of anticolonial struggle in ways that did not rely on easy phrases and reductive notions of class struggle. Whatever the mood coming out of the July 1930 Hamburg conference, the following months would reveal continued uncertainty about Negro work within the Comintern.

The ITUCNW and Padmore's brief career as its head, as well as his corresponding position at the helm of the Comintern's Negro Bureau, reflected the potential that he and so many others saw in international communism and that drew them into the Comintern's orbit. Yet the Comintern smothered the sort of theoretical innovation and experimentation that had marked black radical participation in organized Marxism for a decade. Black Communists who would now play key roles in the International's Negro work consistently faced constraints on what they could and could not do and how they could approach race and colonialism. Their conflicted relationship with the Comintern—their ability to pursue a black international while confining themselves theoretically to the party line—was most apparent in the ITUCNW's *Negro Worker*. Unlike such earlier black radical publications as the *Crusader* and *Messenger* magazines in the United States and *La Race Nègre* in France, *Negro Worker* showed little of the imaginative thought that had theorized racial oppression as something other than a mere manifestation of class struggle. In its first year, *Negro Worker* followed a strict Comintern line, with heavy doses of the Soviet Union's importance as an exemplar. Only with Padmore's attention to the British empire in the middle of 1932 would Comintern orthodoxy give way to more nuanced approaches to colonialism, race, and socialist revolution. Also at this time, Padmore and Garan Kouyaté began to slip from Moscow's tight control and pursue more independent organizing initiatives, leading to their expulsion from the Comintern. But Padmore had already left, effectively rendering his expulsion a technical matter.

The rise to power of Hitler and the Nazis forced Padmore to flee Hamburg. He settled first in Paris, then in London. His connections with anticolonial radicals and African and Caribbean activist-intellectuals allowed him rather easily to join in London's anticolonial ferment. He maintained working relationships with black radicals across a range of political perspectives. Padmore's time in the ITUCNW, his departure from the Comintern, and his early years in London show not simply the acumen and political efficacy of a dynamic individual but also the complex choices that black radicals from across the political spectrum made in their pursuit of a liberated future for black people worldwide. Their political differences were real, but they deliberately moderated those differences, at least for a time, to pursue a common anti-colonial political project.

Building the ITUCNW

Soon after Hamburg, Padmore privately complained that the organizing of the conference had been "conducted poorly" and that Communist periodicals had barely publicized it. This neglect, he felt, reflected the long-standing problem in the communist movement of the "isolation of the Negro organizations from the International labor movement." Padmore also believed that tactical mistakes had been made, including requesting permission from Britain's Labour government to meet in London, a decision that invited surveillance and interference from colonial authorities. In addition, the denial of visas and the arrests of delegates attempting to travel to Europe resulted in unsatisfactory representation from Central and South America, the Caribbean, and Africa. And no one yet knew the fate of the South African delegates who had disappeared from a ship heading for London.[1]

At the close of the ICNW in Hamburg, Padmore informed the delegates that they were invited to attend the RILU's fifth World Congress in Moscow in August. Eleven of the delegates made the trip to Moscow, including Williana Burroughs, Padmore, Ford, Joseph Bilé, Frank Macaulay, and Edward Small. Kouyaté arrived in Moscow with several LDRN members, bringing the total number of black delegates, according to a French government surveillance report, to twenty-five.[2]

As with other Comintern meetings, the black delegates formed a Negro Commission whose members gave reports on various struggles throughout the diaspora and drafted a proposal for the RILU's future activities among black workers. Small gave a report on the Gambia Labour Union, which grew from a 1929 strike in Bathurst into a union with more than four thousand members. Such an increase, Small declared, was "proof of the claims of the revolutionary movement of the workers of the world." Macaulay discussed labor conditions in Nigeria and the Nigerian National Democratic Party, which he represented and which was widely popular among the masses. He also made an "appeal for help for a wide and extensive propaganda of the Soviet Union in these parts of the British Empire so as to bring home to the natives the real truth of the workings of the U.S.S.R." Burroughs submitted a handwritten report on trade union work in the United States to Ford and Alexander Losovsky, the RILU's general secretary, which highlighted the failures of Left-led unions and communist factions in trade unions in the area of race. On top of holding unclear objectives and engaging in segregationist practices, they had not gotten blacks jobs in shops where they exercised control, a failure that explained "in large measure the loss of membership," Burroughs wrote; black membership in trade unions had fallen from several hundred to a mere handful. She warned that to organize black workers, the CPUSA "must crush whatever white chauvinism that appears."[3]

Ford's report to the congress underscored the idea that the ITUCNW had come about in response to the past failures of RILU sections and communist unions to tap into the revolutionary potential of black workers in the United States, South Africa, West Africa, and the Caribbean. He was convinced the ITUCNW would combat the general belief that "Negroes were not a revolutionary force but reserves for capitalist reaction." Losovsky declared that it was "perfectly right" for black people to "look with suspicion upon the revolutionary trade union organizations, when it came to the racial problem." There was "tremendous political importance" in organizing Negro workers, he told the congress. Only those who understood "nothing of the class struggle or of the revolutionary movement" would miss the fact that "the revolt of the Black Continent against imperialism is only beginning, and that our job is to make use of this huge amount of combustible material" and become allies to "these vast masses seething with hatred against their oppressors."[4] Ford's and Losovsky's remarks signaled the continued importance the Comintern placed on organizing black workers, if not black people generally.

Those black radicals and Communists who came to Moscow remained cautiously optimistic about the ITUCNW. Part of their hesitancy concerned the tone of condescension that was by now commonplace in organized Marxism. Despite statements attesting to the tremendous potential of African anticolonial struggles, Communists still believed that "no Negro movement has any chance of success unless it is backed up by . . . the international proletariat," an LDRN report observed.[5] Even for Ford and other black Communists, the ability of black people to lead their own liberation struggle would depend on their "contact with an advanced movement." Ford singled out American black workers as the vanguard of the Negro struggle and said they should put forward a program that "the masses of Negro toilers," even those "in Africa where they are backward and the degree of development is not high," could easily comprehend.[6]

The black radicals who had attended the ICNW had also heard these views from African and African American students studying at KUTV, who generally viewed class as essential to understanding all social relationships. Small, Macaulay, and Bilé, however, rejected the notion that class explained all of the problems confronting Africans. To them, the students' views seemed cavalier and dismissive of race. Small believed that such views betrayed a limited racial consciousness. Bilé took particular exception to the belief among African American students that the more advanced American Negroes would necessarily lead their less modern African kin.[7] Although the ICNW delegates and their KUTV counterparts shared a general commitment to pan-African liberation, their differences about how to achieve such liberation strained relationships that seemed essential to black internationalism.

Not all black Communists agreed that a black international should follow closely the trade union model outlined by the Comintern. A report on the LDRN written during the RILU congress noted the group's anti-imperialism and Communist leadership. Yet in addition to lacking the resources to maintain contact with its sections throughout France and West Africa, the report complained of the LDRN's largely nationalist membership of lawyers, engineers, and clerical employees who were indifferent to trade union activity and believed that "Negroes must work for their liberation by their own efforts."[8]

Kouyaté, the head of the LDRN, took exception to the criticism of his organization, especially given the PCF's long history of neglect of Negro and colonial work. His report pointed out that while Ligue sections were scattered across France and in Berlin and were thriving in Togo, Cameroon, Madagascar, Senegal, and even Haiti, the only thing the PCF had ever done was provide sixteen hundred francs for the publication of La Race Nègre. Though the PCF did appoint LDRN secretary Stéphane Rosso to its executive committee, its Negro Commission subsequently stopped meeting, and its Colonial Department diminished to "a mere ornament." Even after the 1929 Frankfurt Congress, the Ligue carried out the LAI's anticolonial work; the PCF and the Confédération Générale du Travail Unitaire (General Confederation of Labor) did not.[9] The somewhat tenuous relationship between the LDRN and PCF had begun to deteriorate the preceding February, when Kouyaté organized a group of black dockworkers in Marseilles around a program supporting "the corporative claims of the black sailors." Rather than aid the effort, the PCF attacked it as a reformist "danger to the unity of the working class," while its Colonial Department and the Confédération Générale called it counterrevolutionary.[10]

Kouyaté declared that the Ligue was independent of the PCF and that it would never approach black liberation through the narrow prism of class against class. African liberation entailed a struggle involving economic, cultural, and social issues, he wrote, and the Ligue stood "against national oppression and race oppression and for social emancipation," which for Kouyaté at least meant a liberated Africa forming "a union of black soviet republics." Rather than the Soviet model, however, Kouyaté was after a mode of pan-African liberation that was global in scale. Much like Cyril Briggs's writings in the *Crusader*, Kouyaté saw a pan-African body helping to ensure the liberation of the diaspora. The LDRN's membership was therefore diasporic and included intellectuals and middle-class blacks, which the group's leaders believed essential for national liberation.[11]

In general, participants in the Hamburg conference viewed the ITUCNW as a vehicle through which they could build an international movement. Kouyaté left Moscow in full support of the ITUCNW, though he, like Padmore, was equally willing to work for African liberation through either bourgeois or proletarian nationalist movements. Macaulay considered it the first step in forming West African trade unions, while the South African radical Albert Nzula felt that the Hamburg conference surpassed any other event that year: The Communist Party of South Africa took special steps to "make the broad masses of the toiling Negroes in this country aware" of its importance. The African American Communist Harry Haywood years later captured what black radicals considered the ITUCNW's revolutionary potential when he noted that "it was the first time Black workers from Africa and the Americas had gotten together," though for many Communists it marked Africa's entrance into a revolutionary movement.[12]

Not everyone believed, however, that the Comintern finally supported building a revolutionary or even a trade union movement in Africa. In early October 1930, Kouyaté, Bilé, Small, and Macaulay traveled from Moscow to Berlin, where they held a series of meetings with members of the LAI's secretariat, Bohumil Smeral, Virendranath Chattopadhyaya, Willi Münzenberg, and B. Ferdi, to outline a program for communist work in West Africa. Kouyaté continued to push for a continent-wide focus, while Small, Macaulay, and Bilé proposed focusing on individual African independence struggles. Following the advice of a report on working in West Africa written earlier that year, the LAI secretariat proposed focusing initially on Gambia and Nigeria and then extending their resources to the rest of Africa. These meetings were generally productive, though the results were less impressive than the African radicals had hoped.[13]

The LAI secretariat remained leery of these "Negro friends," as they referred to the members of this group. Although Small and Macaulay agreed to pursue trade union organizing and to build links between existing movements and the LAI, they refused to sign any documents to that effect, leading the secretariat to question whether the two men would be useful. And the secretariat was especially troubled that Kouyaté repeatedly demanded financial support for the Ligue. The Germany-based LAI secretariat had long had problems relating to black radicals such as those in Bilé's Liga zur Verteidigung der Negerrasse. Along with failing to give institutional support, Smeral and Chattopadhyaya opposed Bilé's membership in the German Communist Party. Indeed, Chattopadhyaya's brazen dismissal of Bilé's efforts to recruit students from Cameroon led Kouyaté to warn that such an "intolerable mindset [*état d'esprit intolérable*]" would undermine the LAI by appearing to negate the importance of Africa and Africans.[14]

The problems in Germany notwithstanding, Kouyaté returned to Paris in November 1930 an enthusiastic supporter of greater ties between the LDRN and the Comintern. Whereas he had once been concerned that too close an association would infringe on the LDRN's autonomy, he now "presented the Third International as . . . a *means* toward international Negro unity, a Negro International *through* the Workers' International."[15] By the time he returned to Paris, however, the LDRN had suffered a split between those members who sought to shield the Ligue from charges of being a Communist front and the Communists Kouyaté and Rosso. Emile Faure, a French-educated Senegalese engineer who led the LDRN while Kouyaté was in Russia and Germany, did not oppose working with Communists if their program coincided with the LDRN's and did not threaten the group's autonomy. In urging closer ties to Moscow, Kouyaté stressed the ability to realize a global movement. Given "the unity and the solidarity of all black people and . . . the connection that exists" through the ITUCNW, Kouyaté explained, "the LDRN must follow an international policy if it does not want to be isolated and abandoned to its own resources."[16] However, Faure and others were concerned that Kouyaté was imposing on the LDRN a program that "went beyond a specifically black political frame." Faure was also concerned with Kouyaté's prolonged absences and had begun to question his carelessness with LDRN monies.[17] At the beginning of the new year, Kouyaté, Rosso, and the other Communists in the LDRN tried to remove Faure from leadership.[18] Faure, however, removed Kouyaté and retained control of *La Race Nègre*, leading Kouyaté and the others to create the Union des Travailleurs Nègres (Union of Negro Workers) and to publish *Le Cri des Nègres*.[19]

As Kouyaté dealt with the disintegration of the LDRN, Ford prepared to begin his assignment in Hamburg organizing the ITUCNW's offices at 8 Rothesoodstrasse, where the organization shared space in the German Communist Party's headquarters with the International of Seamen and Harbour Workers (ISH). Padmore remained in Moscow, heading the RILU's Negro Bureau and lecturing at KUTV; he would also edit the ITUCNW's organ, *Negro Worker*. But commitment to internationally oriented Negro work carried problems that would soon undermine these efforts. The RILU's logic in pursuing the ITUCNW — that it would bring the unorganized, "backward" worker in colonial Africa and the Caribbean into contact with the "advanced" European worker engaged in revolutionary trade union activity in the RILU — was not shared by those who found the RILU dismissive of questions of race. While black Communists saw the ITUCNW as a means to build a black international, the RILU did not.

The earliest directives the RILU sent to Ford and Padmore subordinated theorizing black liberation to pursuing a program of class struggle. According to these directives, the ITUCNW should emphasize the importance of the Soviet Union, improve existing contacts with black workers worldwide, develop new contacts, and fight "Negro bourgeois reformism" and white chauvinism. The RILU's directives at times contradicted themselves. On the one hand, the ITUCNW was to focus on class struggle and on bringing black trade workers and unions in line with the RILU's program; on the other, it was to appear independent of any communist organization. In a seemingly nationalist bent, the ITUCNW was to promote "independent national republics in Africa and the West Indies" and national liberation throughout Asia. Yet it was also to be a black international "based on the class struggle" rather than "conducted on racial lines."[20] It would thus focus on black seamen coming into port at Hamburg who might provide contacts in the colonies as well as pursue contacts in West Africa and the Caribbean, where no RILU section or communist party existed.[21]

Over the next year, Ford and Padmore set about carrying out the RILU's directives, with uneven success. Their work immediately proved frustrating. Ford complained regularly that he lacked supplies, resources, and trained personnel and received little support from communist organizations. More important, despite making some progress in the ports of Hamburg, where he reportedly persuaded a group of African seamen to sign a petition supporting the Scottsboro Boys (nine black men falsely accused of raping two white women in Alabama), there is no evidence that he made any contacts in Africa or the Caribbean. Part of the problem was Ford's sectarian approach to Africa. Though he had argued for a black international from across the political spectrum, he judged the continent through the prism of class struggle alone. He questioned whether nationalist-oriented groups could build a mass movement and dismissed the possibility that viable trade union activity was occurring in Africa. It soon became clear that Ford lacked the organizational acumen necessary to create a black international when the Comintern did not desire one. Padmore, conversely, seemed particularly suited to establishing contacts and building relationships with people who might not have been especially keen on aligning with Communists. His encyclopedic knowledge of Africa and the Caribbean immediately caught the Comintern's attention, and despite problems with publishing *Negro Worker* and distributing it in the colonies, he increasingly assumed greater responsibility over the ITUCNW. By August 1931, Padmore, as head of the Comintern's Negro Bureau, had begun to show his frustration with Ford, requesting that he submit a report on the ITUCNW and outline a six-month plan of action. Within a month, the RILU sent Ford back to the United States and appointed Padmore head of the ITUCNW.[22]

Padmore's Ascent

Whereas Ford was out of his depth organizing a black international, Padmore excelled at it. Rather than organizing on the ground among black maritime workers in Hamburg, he worked through the ITUCNW's *Negro Worker*, which he had begun to edit in March 1930.

The earliest available issues of *Negro Worker* that Padmore edited were little more than rough mimeographed news sheets that often went to press with last-minute handwritten corrections. The first issue reflected organized communism's decadelong emphasis on the Negro in America; the bulk of its articles described organizing among unemployed black people in major U.S. cities, the activities of the ANLC, the BBNT, and the history of the black American revolutionary tradition. Yet Padmore also gave glimpses of a global orientation. Along with the emphasis on African Americans, *Negro Worker* carried stories on labor demonstrations in Jamaica and political struggles in South Africa, Madagascar, and French West Africa and a firsthand account of Haiti under U.S. occupation. Padmore coupled these stories with brief accounts of Japanese imperialism in Korea, uprisings in Indonesia, and clashes between local police forces and revolutionaries in Nicaragua, giving *Negro Worker* a remarkably intercolonialist cast for a Comintern periodical. He also urged "all Negro workers and peasants to write us letters telling of their living conditions, wages, hours of labor, as well as their political and social problems." Padmore displayed keen editorial vision in transforming the bulletin into a proper journal that would serve as "the general *Propaganda and Organiser* of the toiling Negro masses of the world in the struggle against capitalist oppression and imperialism."[23]

In January 1931, the *International Negro Workers' Review* appeared as the "organ" of the ITUCNW. Padmore oriented the new journal toward the "day to day problems of the Negro toilers" and intended to "connect these up with the international struggles and problems of workers" generally, covering international labor movements and anticolonial struggles. It would not be yet another "theoretical" journal where Communists discussed resolutions and their opinions but instead a journal driven by "articles, letters, points of view and pictures of your daily life . . . sent in to us." And it would put forward the ITUCNW's goals and outline the RILU's program in hopes of raising "the class consciousness [and] international outlook of the Negro workers" and would attack the bourgeois black nationalism (Garveyism) and trade union reformism among black labor organizers (Clements Kadalie and A. Philip Randolph) that distracted black workers from revolutionary organizing.[24]

But the RILU restricted Padmore's ability to orient the journal as he desired. Just as the January issue appeared, the RILU changed the journal's name back to *Negro Worker* and directed that it carry short, simply written pieces which even "the most backward Negro worker could understand." As one former RILU executive board member recalled years later, the Bolsheviks believed their "greater experience" leading a revolution made them better equipped than Padmore to run a revolutionary organ.[25] Padmore dutifully followed orders. Virtually every issue carried pieces designed to introduce black workers to "the theories and practices of the International revolutionary labour movement"—presumably as embodied in the RILU. Alongside regular appeals for black workers to defend Russia, "the Fatherland of the Toilers of the World," the magazine presented the activities of Russian workers as an example of how "workers outside Russia can raise their struggles to a much higher organizational level."[26] One letter from an African sailor recalled that his brief visit to Russia convinced him that "there is only one way . . . the black slaves of Africa can free themselves, and that is, to do like the Russian workers." At one point Padmore even declared, "Let these fifteen years of Soviet power be the greatest inspiration to us in our struggle for national freedom and social emancipation."[27]

Padmore certainly considered the Bolsheviks unrivaled revolutionaries. Yet it is not clear that *Negro Worker* was ever simply "a creature of Soviet intentions," as one scholar has written, or that the general themes of Padmore's articles and editorials "were clearly prescribed by higher Comintern authority."[28] Padmore's early articles hewed closely to the party line—invoking phrases and formulations drawn from Comintern resolutions and policies, hailing the Soviet model, and relentlessly attacking black political leaders not aligned with the Comintern. But if the strictures of the Comintern hierarchy left him little room for the kind of imaginative theorizing of race, colonialism, and class struggle that had characterized earlier periods of black radical print culture, Padmore retained a core of that radical imaginary in *Negro Worker*. A close reading reveals a delicate balance Padmore struck between Moscow's mandates and an expansive coverage that had African liberation at its core.

Negro Worker's cover art conveyed the belief that American blacks stood at the vanguard of Negroes worldwide. Many of *Negro Worker*'s early issues carried the ANLC image meant to evoke a notion of American black workers leading black people everywhere. Such imagery corresponded to descriptions, both in the magazine and in internal documents, of Africans (and at times Caribbeans) as "backward." Over the course of its run under Padmore, however, the magazine offered a much different picture of the revolutionary potential of black people in Africa.

From the first issue, in fact, Padmore published articles and reports by ITUCNW members that covered labor movements, strikes and uprisings, and organizations throughout Africa and the Caribbean. Padmore considered these reports proof that revolutionary movements "have broken out in various sections of Africa" and testimony to the "extent to which the militancy and radicalisation of the Black toiling masses is taking place." Other articles covered colonial atrocities in the Belgian Congo, Liberia, Cuba, and the British Caribbean. And while Russia remained a revolutionary example for Negro workers, the ITUCNW's magazine often turned its attention to India and China, in one telling instance tweaking the call to defend Soviet Russia by urging black workers to "protect the Chinese Revolution."[29]

During Padmore's editorial tenure, tensions arose between his deep commitment to the Comintern—his sense of its importance to anticolonial struggle—and his desire to expand Comintern thinking around colonial struggles and African diasporic liberation. He thus merged Third Period rhetoric with an intercolonial focus. The ITUCNW was giving "expression to the growing revolutionary consciousness of the black masses," he wrote, "who have decided to fight under the slogan of '*Class against Class*' for national freedom and social emancipation, together with the workers in the 'mother' countries, and all other oppressed toilers."[30] Such black internationalist sentiment could effortlessly draw on Comintern policies while aligning itself with national liberation movements. Padmore's ideas about black liberation and his commitment to scientific socialism in some ways allowed for a productive tension: He could argue for the Comintern as a base from which African workers and intellectuals could receive important organizational training

THE
NEGRO WORKER

Vol. 1   June 1931   No. 6

ORGAN OF THE INTERNATIONAL TRADE UNION COMMITTEE OF NEGRO WORKERS, 8 ROTHESOODSTR., HAMBURG, GERMANY

Price 5 cents   Price 2 pence

Negro Worker, June 1931.

while also criticizing the common view many Communists held of Negro and colonial work. In the fall of 1931, Padmore called it shortsighted for Communists to complain that they could not simply "gather prepared Bolsheviks on the banks of the Congo or Nile."[31] For more than two years, he pushed to get African workers and intellectuals into KUTV, believing the goal should be "to get hold of the raw people and send them *back* 100% Bolsheviks."[32]

Africa occupied Padmore's mind, and the work of the ITUCNW turned increasingly to establishing viable connections on the continent. The Caribbean continued to receive coverage in *Negro Worker*, and Padmore had some success in recruiting Caribbean radicals into the ITUCNW. But the overwhelming focus remained African labor struggles and anti-imperialist activities. Padmore was especially concerned with the treatment of native Liberian workers by the Firestone Rubber Company and the Americo-Liberian elite. He placed the small West African country in the context of U.S. imperialism in Puerto Rico, Cuba, and the Philippines. Moreover, his articles on the British empire considered not only class but cultural dynamics and the brutal treatment and sexual exploitation of African women. He also included articles from Kouyaté on organizing "Negro-, Indo-Chinese, and Arab sailors" in French ports.[33]

Padmore toned down the magazine's African American vanguardism, replacing the recurring image of the black American worker with images of Africans who evoked a cultural African background that did not necessarily represent workers. In this image, it was not at all clear whether the person holding the rifle was a farmer or an industrial or maritime worker, though the figure seemed prepared for armed conflict. The caption "For the Freedom of Africa" suggested struggle on a continental scale.[34]

To help disseminate *Negro Worker*, Padmore used his contacts from building the ITUCNW and black sailors who traveled throughout the world. By 1932, Cyril Briggs's Crusader News Agency, with offices in New York, Cape Town, and Paris, also began helping with distribution. Though Briggs remained the agency's "director-in-chief," Kouyaté, listed as manager, devised plans to increase *Negro Worker* subscriptions around the world.[35] Black sailors and the Crusader News Agency combined to ensure a sizable readership. *Negro Worker*'s importance to anticolonial work cannot be overstated. Writing several decades later, C. L. R. James declared,

> Tens of thousands of black workers in various parts of the world received their first political education from the paper [Padmore] edited, *The Negro Worker*. It gave information, advice, guidance, ideas about black struggles on every continent. All movements need an ideology, a body

Negro Worker, June–July 1933. Courtesy of the Labour
History Archive and Study Centre.

of ideas and information to which effort can be related and which had significance beyond that which is immediately visible. This *The Negro Worker* gave to hundreds of thousands of active blacks. . . . It developed too, the consciousness among blacks that they were part of an international movement. It must be remembered that men in Mombasa, Lagos, Port of Spain, Port au Prince, Dakar struggling to establish a trade union or political organization, often under illegal conditions and under heavy persecution, read and followed with exceptional concern the directives which came from the trusted centre in Moscow.[36]

James may have exaggerated *Negro Worker*'s reach and value and Padmore's importance, but not by much. Sailors brought the magazine into the Caribbean, and while letters initially came from only the United States and South Africa, by the end of 1931 *Negro Worker* began to carry letters from Nigeria, Guadeloupe, St. Lucia, London, and Liberia. The writers enthusiastically praised *Negro Worker* and requested copies to distribute along with ITUCNW pamphlets.[37]

Within a year, Padmore had established a network of black workers that far surpassed anything previously tied to the Comintern. As late as October 1931, he remained in contact with Small's Gambia Labour Union and Macaulay. In June, Macaulay had cut ties with his father's Nigerian National Democratic Party, and with a young itinerant organizer from Sierra Leone, Isaac Theophilus Akunna (I. T. A.) Wallace-Johnson, Macaulay had established the Nigerian Workers Union, which later became the African Workers Union of Nigeria. Macaulay's sudden death in October destabilized the African Workers Union until Wallace-Johnson assumed its leadership and pursued direct ties to the ITUCNW.[38] Padmore actively sought out contacts, at one point writing to the International Seamen's Club in Amsterdam for links to black sailors from the Dutch Caribbean. On another occasion, Padmore reported that requests were coming from black workers "everywhere to have them organised." But he admitted that the ITUCNW lacked "the forces to send [people] out to all of the colonies, and it is difficult for myself alone, to stay here and organise the workers all over Africa and the West Indies."[39]

Padmore's work in Hamburg running the ITUCNW and editing *Negro Worker* was extremely difficult. After arriving in Hamburg in November 1931, he found the ITUCNW's offices in disarray; he could not locate Ford's files, and he found one German comrade's attitude toward Africans "no good at all." To make matters worse, local authorities kept the ITUCNW's headquarters under constant surveillance. One day in early December, after police had raided the

LAI offices in Berlin, they raided the ITUCNW's Hamburg offices, confiscating issues of *Negro Worker* and "about 10,000 copies of various pamphlets published by the [Negro] Committee." Adding to Padmore's frustration, in January he learned that the publication of his *The Life and Struggles of Negro Toilers* had been delayed by the Comintern's failure to pay the press in London—a press, ironically, run by the RILU.[40]

While Padmore remained a committed comrade who dove headlong into his work, he grew increasingly frustrated with the Comintern's constraints, both structural and ideological. Early in 1931, he arranged for Kouyaté to organize black maritime workers in Marseilles for the ISH. Despite Kouyaté's successes, which included leading a group of African sailors on a demonstration that summer, the PCF continued to neglect colonial work and gave no support to Kouyaté. Padmore used his position in the Comintern to admonish the PCF to provide Kouyaté better support and to integrate "black [*nègres*] dockers and sailors of French ports . . . into revolutionary unions." He also announced that the Comintern's Negro Bureau would now "assist comrade Kouyaté in the regular publication of [*Le Cri des Nègres*] in conformity with the [colonial] resolution."[41]

By year's end, however, the prospects for colonial work appeared bleak. A report by Otto Huiswoud to a December 1931 meeting of the RILU captured the frustration that both he and Padmore felt: "The national sections of the RILU in spite of the adoption of the resolutions at the 5th Congress on the work among the Negro workers have not translated this resolution into action." Consequently, there had been "practically no work on the part of the sections of the RILU, not even in the metropolitan countries." Huiswoud and others wanted the PCF "to give us an idea of what work was done among the French colonists," especially "the French section of the RILU among the 50,000 Negro workers in France.[42] Given the ITUCNW's limited resources— no travel budget for organizers or money for printing—Padmore was convinced that the ITUCNW's success would depend on collaborating with the LAI, the International Red Aid, the Western European Bureau, and the ISH. In a sign of his willingness to cultivate such relationships, he even met with Willi Budich, who had harshly criticized the Hamburg conference. Yet despite Padmore's relatively high standing, neither his diplomacy nor his repeated appeals to the Comintern could change how white Communists viewed colonial work.[43]

Soon after arriving in Hamburg, Padmore proposed that the ISH help the ITUCNW organize seamen's clubs in Dakar, Cape Town, Freetown, and the West Indies and provide financial support to Foster Jones, a sailor affiliated with the ITUCNW in Sierra Leone. Although the ISH had initially agreed, advising Padmore that such work would begin soon, it abruptly and without explanation reversed course early in the new year, leaving Padmore to scramble to salvage his reputation and connections. He maintained his correspondence with Wallace-Johnson, but by April 1932, Padmore still had not heard from Jones and E. A. Richards from Sierra Leone or from Edward Small. Even direct ties to the ITUCNW solved little, as the committee still lacked adequate resources to take advantage of them. And appeals to the Comintern for redress did nothing to compel the ISH to follow through on its promises, leaving the ITUCNW no choice but to abandon its plans.[44]

The LAI's British Section, headed by Reginald Bridgeman, had a far more productive relationship with Padmore and the ITUCNW. At some point in the summer of 1931, Bridgeman introduced Padmore to the Barbadian Communist Arnold Ward, who headed the Negro Welfare Association in London. Ward, a quarrelsome activist with little formal education and no hope of rising within the ranks of the CPGB, was thoroughly impressed with Padmore's mind and work. Early on in their correspondence, Ward urged Padmore to come help organize black workers in London and provide the British party and British labor movement with guidance on colonial work. This friendship brought Padmore into contact with a number of key black London figures and to the attention of the small group of radicals in the metropole in the early 1930s.

Black London Calls

Padmore worked at a dizzying pace in Hamburg, though he remained under the constant eye of German authorities. His letters to comrades in the United States, the Caribbean, and the Soviet Union showed an understanding of his mission that far exceeded what the Comintern had imagined for him and the ITUCNW. Though his committee would organize the black world outside the United States, he also wanted to establish a working relationship with the newly formed League of Struggle for Negro Rights (formerly the ANLC) in the United States.[45] Further, he sent ITUCNW materials to Communists in Baltimore, asking that they distribute the literature among black workers there, especially maritime workers. More important, he wrote to Robert Minor of the CPUSA with specific instructions to establish an ITUCNW subcommittee in New Orleans and New York that would in turn establish a branch in the West Indies. He also wrote to the director of the African Section of the Leningrad-based Oriental Institute praising its work and encouraging it to extend the immediate concern with Africa to the United States and to the Negro question generally. Padmore noted that while there existed a "tremendous literature" on Africa, there was "little or nothing from a Marxist point of view." But rather than insist on developing such a literature through consulting Marxist classics, he encouraged the institute to contact Bridgeman's Labour Research Department in London, which had significant information on the colonies, as well as Carter G. Woodson, head of the Association for the Study of Negro Life and History.[46]

Padmore never explained what a Marxist literature on Africa should look like. But in all likelihood he was not satisfied with what was coming out of Moscow. Nor was Albert Nzula, a South African Communist then studying in Moscow, serving on the ITUCNW's executive committee, and writing articles for *Negro Worker*. According to one of Nzula's childhood friends who also studied at KUTV, Nzula was one of the few Africans who arrived in Moscow with a keen grasp of Marxist theory, and he may have shared Padmore's disappointment with KUTV's African literature. In referencing Woodson, Padmore may have been calling for a Marxist literature that went beyond rhetorical flourishes, policy directives, and declarations of Soviet power backed by an armada of empirical data. If, as W. E. B. Du Bois put it in 1940, the world was thinking wrong about race, Padmore certainly felt that the Comintern was thinking wrong about the Negro.[47]

Padmore never exhibited such an approach in his articles for *Negro Worker* or his pamphlets. In fact, the international renown Padmore enjoyed as editor of *Negro Worker* grew with the appearance of his *The Life and Struggles of Negro Toilers*, a 126-page tract whose solemn prose fit "the fact-based utilitarianism and ideological rigidity required in institutionalized Comintern modes of knowledge production."[48] It lacked analytical value apart from its trove of empirical evidence on colonialism. But among Communists and black radicals, it showed the expansive knowledge of a colonial intellectual. In defending his book against a negative review by the British Labour Party's J. F. Horrabin, Padmore further solidified his political celebrity by attacking the Labour government's pitiable response to colonial unrest.[49] Arnold Ward told Padmore that his writings were having a major impact in Britain, making him "a very important man over here." Ward assured Padmore that a trip to London would be worth his while: "Liverpool Negroes, Cardiff Negroes, we are all looking forward for a lead." Ward and other black Communists in England were keen on Padmore because they believed he would "put forward to the white workers here" in very poignant terms "the colonial workers' plight."[50]

Padmore's relationships with Ward, Bridgeman, and the British Section of the LAI as well as his African contacts were certainly drawing his attention to the British metropole. As an organizer in Hamburg, he found that his inability to speak German limited his reach.[51] But in London, he would be able to work in the growing black immigrant population and better influence the course of anticolonial struggle.

Many of the people he met through his work in the Comintern were then making their way to London, a trek he often encouraged. He also continued to write Wallace-Johnson, hoping to put the African Workers Union of Nigeria in "close connection with the militant trade union and labour movement in England." "As a young movement you must learn from the experiences and mistakes not only of the labour movement in such countries as England and France, Germany and America," he advised Wallace-Johnson, "you must try to avoid those committed by our comrades in China, in India, in South Africa, in the West Indies, etc." But Padmore's intercolonialism and insistence that the African Workers Union of Nigeria learn from other struggles in the colonial world under the British empire was combined with more orthodox Third Period advice to distinguish only "between workers and capitalists, the rich and the poor, the exploiters and the exploited" and to send students to Moscow to learn "the science of the trade union movement." For Padmore, these were not irreconcilable tendencies, though they do suggest the fissures that would lead him away from strict adherence to the Comintern's tenets.[52]

One of Padmore's rarely noted qualities, striking in a 1930s Communist luminary, was his political open-mindedness and willingness to recalibrate his views when they proved inappropriate for the situation at hand. Over the course of 1932, as unions and activists from throughout the diaspora flooded the ITUCNW's offices with requests for issues of *Negro Worker*, pamphlets on imperialism, and membership in the organization, Padmore began to soften his once strident tone. As he witnessed various noncommunist groups giving greater attention to the Negro question and colonial work than Communist groups, Padmore, the highest-ranking black Communist in Europe, began to revaluate the people he had once derisively labeled "reformists." In a December 1931 article on "Bankrupt Negro Leadership," Padmore had lumped Arthur Cipriani, the Trinidadian mayor and labor leader, in with those "reformist trade union leaders . . . offering their services to their respective imperialist masters." Yet when British colonial authorities banned *Negro Worker* in Trinidad and Nigeria, Cipriani persuaded Labour Party member of Parliament James Maxton to raise the issue in the House of Commons (twice, for that matter). After Cipriani, the leader of the Trinidad Workingmen's Association, addressed a meeting of the Negro Welfare Association in London in

February, Ward suggested that Padmore refrain from attacking him. Taking Ward's advice, Padmore highlighted Cipriani's support for West Indian self-government and opened a correspondence with Vivian Henry, the secretary of the Workingmen's Association, eventually recruiting him into the ITUCNW. In a backhanded compliment to the ILP, Padmore noted that these "fakirs," who bore the unenviable labels "Trotskyist" and "social-chauvinist" within the Comintern, "had done more in their way than the Party or the LAI" for colonial struggles.[53]

Padmore and other black radicals remained frustrated by the minimal efforts of Communist organizing around anticolonial struggle. In March 1932, Padmore instructed James Headly of the Seamen's Minority Movement (SMM) to organize a Negro Subcommittee. The SMM was a largely white Communist-led group in the National Union of Seamen; it appealed to Indian, Chinese, Arab, and African seamen and supported colonial liberation. Black seamen in the National Union of Seamen had early on sought the LAI's aid in organizing British ports, and soon after the SMM was formed in 1929, it created a committee of "militant coloured seamen," with Headly elected secretary. But Padmore believed that the SMM should have done a better job among black seamen.[54]

When the ISH announced plans to convene a World Congress of Seamen in Hamburg, Padmore worked feverishly to get colonial delegates there. In the end, only Ada Wright, the mother of two of the Scottsboro boys, addressed the congress, as did Padmore, Kouyaté, and Harry O'Connell, a longtime Cardiff-based SMM organizer. After the congress, however, many participants openly complained that work in the SMM was going poorly. O'Connell was so irritated by his treatment that he resigned and refused even direct aid from Padmore and Kouyaté, choosing instead to form the Cardiff Coloured Seamen's Committee. Complaints about the SMM were not a new phenomenon. When James Ford first began organizing for the ITUCNW in 1931, he had worked with the SMM in British port cities "carrying out work among Negro seamen." But as he reported to Padmore, the SMM had "insufficient organizational connections in colonial countries," and Ford had grown tired of sending "Negroes on British ships to the SMM" only to have them write back "expressing disgust with the SMM as nobody met them." Ward lodged similar objections, criticizing the SMM's poor treatment of the Negro Welfare Association, which helped organize a rally for Wright in London but was not invited to participate in the rally. This incident again showed the "bad tactics" of Communists, who regularly used "Negroes when they are wanted" but at other times "put them aside," Ward wrote to Padmore.[55]

Overall, Padmore and others noticed, Communists were paying very little attention to colonial work. While the LAI's British Section passed a resolution supporting African and Caribbean independence and calling on white workers to support black workers, Ward lamented the section's failure to put forward a clear program for colonial work. By his account, the British working-class movement was falling to pieces, a catastrophe that only Padmore's coming to London could avert.[56]

Early in the summer of 1932, Padmore traveled to Moscow with Jomo Kenyatta to attend a meeting of the Comintern. From there, Padmore went to London, where he first met British heiress Nancy Cunard, members of Ward's Negro Welfare Association, and some CPGB leaders. London must have left him with mixed feelings. He learned that the party's Henry Pollitt had used *The Life and Struggles of Negro Toilers* to recruit blacks. Other black Communists joined Ward in imploring Padmore to relocate to London. Their requests revealed not merely his stature as an international revolutionary but the depth of black Communists' dissatisfaction with Comintern organizations such as the ISH, the LAI, and the CPGB. R. Brown, an organizer in Liverpool, informed Padmore that black seamen distrusted the SMM because they had been treated poorly "so often that whatever they take part in now must be able to do something for them"; otherwise, it was a waste of their time. "Before we can work with whites," Brown explained, "we'll have to educate the white worker that we have to work together in all jobs. . . . [T]hey don't want to work beside us." Padmore criticized the LAI's Berlin-based secretariat for hindering his work, as when it refused to pay for Foster Jones's travel from England to Russia to study at KUTV. Such incidents, Padmore wrote to the Berlin office in an especially terse exchange, led many Negro comrades to distrust the LAI and Communists generally. For more than a decade, the CPGB had not sent a single black person to KUTV, Padmore noted, though many people were willing and qualified to go. Padmore also pointed out that since the RILU did not give the ITUCNW a budget for student travel, his colonial work would always suffer, and comrades such as Jones would jettison communism.[57]

The dutiful, committed Communist eventually erupted in a stream of near heresy. Blame for the ITUCNW's failures in Africa and the Caribbean, Padmore asserted, lay with the Comintern's "sectarian policy" (presumably its Third Period rigidity regarding class struggle), which kept the ITUCNW from organizing progressive groups in the colonies and which "isolat[ed] us from these people." Rather than continuing to find a revolutionary example in the European proletariat, he argued, Communists in Great Britain must "give more attention, more concrete assistance, more material aid, support and advice, to the colonial victims of British Imperialism." They must also "expose before the English proletariat the vicious policy of British imperialism in India, Africa and the West Indies." Black Communists knew from experience, Padmore wrote privately, that few white workers fully grasped the plight of black workers; thus, black Communists needed to develop "international class solidarity" among class-conscious white workers. Ward, like many others, shared Padmore's dissatisfaction with organized communism, though Ward also seemed annoyed by Padmore's belief that something could be salvaged from their white comrades. "Face the situation as it is," he wrote Padmore, "these people don't like us and they only use us for a tool."[58]

Though Padmore's dissatisfaction with the Comintern led him to question its value to pan-African liberation, he remained a committed Communist for almost another year. He continued to produce *Negro Worker* and to tout the revolutionary example of Soviet Russia. He also maintained a hectic pace that included constant travel from Hamburg to Paris and London. He brought Ward's Negro Welfare Association under the ITUCNW and continued to work closely with Bridgeman's British Section of the LAI. At the same time, Padmore tried to contain an increasingly bitter Ward, whose anxieties about other black Communists encroaching on his territory led him to attack virtually everyone, including Cunard, whom Padmore had convinced to pay the Negro Welfare Association's office rent for two years.[59]

Other, less subtle signs also indicated that Padmore was moving away from Moscow. His attention turned even more to African and Caribbean liberation, and the space that *Negro Worker* devoted to the Soviet Union slowly shrank. He believed that the push for West Indian self-government and federation "arises from the widespread mass movement against the disgraceful exploitation of the workers and peasants . . . by British imperialism." He continued to emphasize class struggle, though his concern was not the European trade union movement. As Padmore told a longtime friend in New York, he was concerned largely with "getting rid of the damn white blood suckers from the W[est] I[ndies] and Africa."[60]

I Went to Hear the Great George Padmore

By the end of 1932, Padmore appeared to have made phenomenal progress building the ITUCNW. He claimed in excess of a thousand contacts throughout the diaspora and the establishment of trade union committees in Guadeloupe, Haiti, Senegal, Cameroon, Liberia, Panama, St. Lucia, and Madagascar. Moreover, the *Negro Worker*'s circulation had grown from roughly one thousand to nearly five thousand. He and Kouyaté continued to organize African and Caribbean maritime workers in French port cities, and organizing in British ports brought unprecedented success. Such achievements were all the more remarkable considering, as Padmore wrote, that various "RILU Sections, despite all the appeals of the RILU have not rendered any real assistance," especially in France and the United States, where "instead of helping they have just sabotaged and hindered us." And while the RILU acknowledged its lack of assistance, it nevertheless criticized Padmore's inability to consolidate his contacts. Moreover, the RILU reminded Padmore that it was his committee's responsibility "to render systematic assistance to the ISH in the drawing in of seamen Negro masses." But he had already tried to do so, not only with the ISH but also with various RILU sections and the SMM, and these groups had repeatedly failed to follow through on promises and agreements to organize in the colonies and European ports. Padmore had long complained that despite his willingness to aid these groups, they refused to do anything.[61]

Padmore also felt the isolation that came with working in Germany and the fatigue of his incessant travel. Yet the Comintern was not only impeding his work but also taking little heed of his problems with white racism that slowed communism's spread among black workers. When success for the ITUCNW began to look increasingly unlikely, his thoughts turned to his family, especially his daughter, Blyden (named after the Sierra Leonean writer and politician Edward Wilmot Blyden), whom he had never seen. He was also growing more open to different kinds of intellectual production. In November, he met with Cunard in Paris and began collaborating on her anthology, *Negro*, suggesting possible U.S.-based contributors and contributing several pieces himself.[62] His disillusionment with Moscow would reach a crescendo with the Comintern's failure to thwart the rise of Hitler and the Nazis in Germany.

German fascism had long concerned Padmore, though he worried little about Hitler, whom Padmore considered a demagogue "like Garvey—a has been." When the Nazis took power in January 1933, however, police raided the ITUCNW offices in Hamburg and arrested Padmore, putting him in jail briefly before deporting him to England. Back in London, he reconnected with O'Connell, whose Coloured Seamen's Committee was fighting the Cardiff City Councilors Committee's "colour-bar" means test that paid unemployed black-headed households five pounds less than white-headed households. He also met for the first time Chris Jones, the Barbadian seaman presiding over the Colonial Seamen's Association who was also in the Communist Party of Great Britain and the Negro Welfare Association. Rather than remain in London, however, by March Padmore had arranged a loan through Ward and left for Paris, where he stayed with Kouyaté and another Union des Travailleurs member, Camille St. Jacques.[63]

Paris provided Padmore even further remove from the Comintern and space to think about African diasporic liberation without its ideological constraints. He had already begun to disregard Comintern protocol by sending organizers to Africa and the Caribbean who were not Communists, and his communications with Moscow became far less frequent.[64] Comintern members suspected that Padmore's relationship with Kouyaté was to blame. Around the same time that Padmore was arrested in Germany, the PCF suspended funding for Kouyaté's Le Cri des Nègres. For more than a year, the PCF had been concerned that the publication's articles failed to cover black workers appropriately, gave too little attention to working-class life in the Soviet Union, and were far too theoretical for "backward" African workers. When an already disillusioned Kouyaté learned that the French party sought to remove Le Cri des Nègres from his control, he turned his energies elsewhere and established a West African student hostel in Paris. When he refused to attend PCF meetings, the party suspended him. Padmore, who had been shuttling back and forth between London and Paris, apparently knew little about what was going on, for when he came back to Paris in June he was surprised to learn that Le Cri des Nègres had not appeared for some time, that his friend was no longer a Communist, and that the PCF's Negro Committee was "holding everything in hand, and yet doing nothing."[65] Incredulous at the treatment of his friend and the resulting lack of Negro work, Padmore no longer felt a need to try to convince white Communists of the importance of organizing black workers in the French metropole. Just before returning to Paris, he gave a talk in London that brought him into contact with C. L. R. James and others who proved important to his continuing political transformation.

IN THE SPRING OF 1932, the thirty-one-year-old James arrived in London. His first trip to England had come at the urging of the famous Trinidadian cricketer Learie Constantine, who had moved to Nelson, Lancashire, in 1929 to join a local cricket club. James was to help Constantine write his autobiography, which would appear in 1933 as Cricket and I. James's reputation as an intellectual was well established by the time he left Trinidad; he edited local periodicals and contributed several pieces to Albert Gomes's Beacon Magazine. The previous summer, James had taken particular issue with a Beacon article by Sidney Harland that had argued for black racial inferiority. His reply to Harland, "The Intelligence of the Negro," gained James considerable notice and caused something of a stir in local intellectual circles. Gomes even wrote privately to James dismissing out of hand the suggestion that black people had contributed as much as whites to arts and letters.[66]

James's limited political activity up to that point had included work with Cipriani's Trinidad Workingmen's Association. But James felt that England offered greater possibilities for a career as a writer and a politically oriented intellectual. He had arrived with the manuscript of a novel, *Minty Alley*, and the manuscript for a biography of Cipriani, which, with Constantine's help, later appeared in Trinidad as *The Life of Captain Cipriani*. James secured the help of Leonard and Virginia Woolf, and their Hogarth Press published a portion of this biography as a pamphlet, *The Case for West Indian Self-Government*.

A voracious reader with a unique intellect, James came to England ready to measure the metropole against the lore he had learned in Trinidad. As he later put it, coming to England was a case of "the British intellectual . . . going to Britain." James spent a few months in London before heading to Nelson. In his observations, published in Trinidad's *Port of Spain Gazette* newspaper, James conveyed a sense of the limitations of the metropole. Though he found London's intellectual life stimulating, he was astonished at how few Londoners took part in it. He was unimpressed by London and Western Europe more generally. Rather than experiencing a homecoming, he grew increasingly convinced of the Caribbean's intellectual, artistic, and political potential, its modernity and coevality with Western civilization. And he hinted not at the importance of local white radicals but at the liminal bonds between the Caribbean and other nodes in the colonial world.

James gave public lectures and engaged in debates on subjects ranging from poetic form, American literature, and British imperialism to the Bolshevik revolution, sex, Abyssinia, and the Indian question. His attention to India garnered him invitations to lecture from several Indian organizations. The international orientation that James later attributed to Caribbeans, whom he saw as "essentially an international people" who constituted "a great number of disparate civilizations," might help explain his gravitation to Indian activists and radicals in London as well as his lifelong pursuit of a radical black internationalism.[67]

By summer's end, what little money James had began to thin, and he made his way to Nelson, where he stayed with Constantine. He had already begun taking notice of Britain's Labour Party, which he joined before going on to become a member of the Trotskyist Revolutionary Socialist League. In Nelson, James covered cricket matches for the *Manchester Guardian*, embarked on an intense study of Marxism, and began research for his study of Toussaint Louverture, which resulted in his classic history, *The Black Jacobins*.[68]

Just over a year later, in 1933, James was back in London, where, as during his first visit, he heard about George Padmore. He decided that it was time to hear this Padmore fellow speak and thus made his way to Grey's Inn Road. "One day," he recalled many years later, "I had heard a lot about George Padmore, the great man from Moscow who was organising black people all over the world, so I said I would go." Whatever James's expectations, he had not anticipated that Padmore would turn out to be his childhood friend Malcolm Nurse. James often recalled fondly how the two boys had bathed together in Trinidad's Arima River. But now Padmore "was tied up with Moscow, I was headed away from Moscow; I was a Trotskyist, but that didn't trouble us." Indeed, they talked almost until dawn after Padmore's speech. One exchange stood out for James. When Padmore asked James, "You came here in 1932?" James replied, "Yes, March 1932. I was here and I stayed about here in London for about three months." Taken aback, Padmore remarked, "My God, man, I was here in 1932 looking for people to carry to Moscow to help to train them to organise blacks. If I had seen you I would have asked you." James admitted that had they met then, he would have gone. "That was how we just missed one another," he recalled. "What would have happened to me I don't know," James pondered, "because by 1935 Padmore broke with them, and I remember that day very well."[69]

The next day, he and James attended a Socialist conference, where they were having a conversation and "laughing uproariously" when Padmore met C. A. Smith, who would soon become chair of the ILP. According to Smith, Padmore outlined his notion of a double revolution: a sequence by which anticolonial liberation movements would first produce national revolutions against white imperialists, which would then allow colonial proletarian revolutions to emerge against the indigenous bourgeoisie. The idea was a rather classic Leninist formulation, not a Third Period one.[70]

Padmore's formulation, his attendance with James at a Socialist conference, and the apparently positive reception of his ideas from Trotskyists, no less, were all part of the culmination of his slow march away from the Comintern and its sectarian policies. He had come to see the Comintern's class-against-class approach as a dead end, returning to a formulation that Richard B. Moore had put forward at the 1927 Brussels Congress: The struggle against imperialism was "first of all an incessant struggle against . . . the doctrine of the supremacy of the white race." Padmore was thus primed to see Russia,

Kouyaté's and St. Jacques's departures from the PCF, and the charges leveled against Kouyaté as reason enough to be skeptical of Communists. He was hardly receptive to the Comintern's request that he explain his relationship with Kouyaté or to Otto Huiswoud's visit warning him to end his association with Kouyaté, let alone a subsequent request that he come to Moscow to account for his associations in person. The final straw was the instruction from the Kremlin in mid-August 1933 to close the ITUCNW: Padmore resigned from the international communist movement and penned his "Au Revoir" editorial for the final issue of *Negro Worker*, published in August–September. Though publicly he claimed that limited resources necessitated discontinuing the journal, privately he acknowledged that Soviet efforts to "appease the British Foreign Office, which was raising hell because the Blacks in Africa were beginning to wake up," had led to his departure. "Stalin has given up the idea of support to those who are still under the row," he wrote.[71] He had been ordered "to put a brake upon the anti-imperialist work," he noted later, "and thereby sacrifice the young national liberation movements in Asia and Africa." He viewed the new Soviet Popular Front policy as "a betrayal of the fundamental interests of my people, with which I could not identify myself."[72]

Yet Padmore's articles, correspondence, and activities from the time he assumed editorial control of *Negro Worker* and stewardship of the ITUCNW reveal that he was not rejecting communism as much as trying to reconcile his commitment to organized Marxism with his evolving conception of pan-African revolution. Indeed, even while Padmore remained in the Comintern, he pushed its line, even denying that he was building a black international while pursuing the political and personal relationships essential to just such a black international.[73]

PADMORE'S RESIGNATION FROM THE Communist International marked a moment of both new possibilities and vast uncertainty. He had sacrificed family, possibly a career in law, and nearly eight years of his life for the Comintern, never even having seen his child. While for a time he had held a high position in the Comintern, directed its resources, and possessed the ability simultaneously to scold and to circumvent national parties reluctant to aid black Communists across Europe, as the head of the ITUCNW he was virtually helpless. His growing frustration with the Third International ultimately led him to question its policies, their effectiveness in organizing in the African diaspora, and Moscow's ability to compel its member groups to take colonial work seriously. In the end, even after he had made surprisingly large strides building a black international network, Moscow proved willing to sacrifice the intercolonial visions of its members when doing so served its domestic national needs.

The Comintern's machinations left Padmore disillusioned with Russia and a severe critic of Stalin. His break with the Third International, which just over a decade earlier had captured the imagination of African diasporic and Asian radicals, revolved around its retreat from anticolonial struggle. But as his public expulsion from the Communist International and exorcism in Communist periodicals reveals, his "nationalist deviation" was there all along. His formal expulsion was perfunctory, he wrote, "in keeping with the communist practice" of not allowing anyone who might embarrass communists "to make his exit without vilification."[74]

The Comintern did not announce Padmore's expulsion until the following April. In the interim, the Comintern reportedly asked him to come again to Moscow, but he refused without adequate assurances of his safe return and a very public announcement of his travels to Russia. His fears were real. His friend Albert Nzula, still at KUTV, had been labeled a Trotskyist, the single word in the international communist lexicon that could both win the argument for the person who spoke it and ensure surveillance and possibly physical reprisal—even death—for the person so labeled. Nzula, known for his excessive drinking, had openly questioned Stalin's leadership, even more brazenly when drunk. Once after drinking with a friend, or so the official report goes, he passed out in a Moscow gutter, and contracted double pneumonia. He was discovered too late for medical help and died two days later in a hospital. However, Kenyatta recalled witnessing two men from the Soviet security services come into a meeting and forcibly remove Nzula, who was never seen again. Though some observers discounted Kenyatta's account, it must have seemed entirely plausible to Padmore.[75]

When *Negro Worker* reappeared in April 1934 under Huiswoud's editorial direction, attacks on Padmore and his political character filled its pages. He was called a police agent and a "Betrayer of the Negro Liberation Struggle." His expulsion from the Comintern reportedly stemmed from his relationships with the "provocateurs" Kouyaté and St. Jacques, his "association with National Reformist and Anti-working class organizations," his weakening of "the working class movement under the slogan of race unity instead of class unity," and his taking the wrong position on national liberation. Though he largely ignored the charges, when they started to appear in the black American press, he responded by pointing out the Comintern's willingness to sacrifice African and Asian national liberation to appease France and Britain. The Comintern and its apologists also attacked those black Communists whom the CPUSA expelled for siding with Padmore or for being Trotskyists.[76] Yet the Comintern's Popular Front policy seemed to vindicate Padmore. Communist Party of Great Britain periodicals such as *Communist Review*, which rarely carried pieces on Africa and black people, ran Hugo Rathbone's 1936 article, "The Problem of African Independence," which claimed that the "backward nature of the Negro African economy may result in African independence being achieved only in parallel with the revolution in imperialist countries." This argument mirrored closely Ben Bradley's more explicit claim that avoiding war required postponing colonial independence and replacing it with Fabian-style social reforms.[77]

Padmore remained in Paris with Kouyaté, where they worked together on an abortive Negro World Congress and Padmore plugged away at his first major work after leaving the Comintern, *How Britain Rules Africa*.[78] In the summer of 1934, he stayed with Cunard in her home in Vernon, Normandy, where, Cunard later recalled, "he spent all the day and half the night writing." She was amazed at "his capacity for sheer, lengthy hard work."[79]

But London beckoned. It was the center of a burgeoning black anticolonial moment, and London activist-intellectuals were beginning to articulate a new discourse of black internationalism well outside the corridors of organized communism. In late 1934 or early 1935, Padmore, still a major figure among black people in London, returned to the independent organizing that had animated the earliest iterations of radical black internationalism in Harlem and Paris. While it would remain male-dominated organizing, African diasporic women would now play a more prominent role in public discourses and activities. And Padmore was finished with sectarian struggles.

London thus provided a unique incubator for radical black internationalist discourse and organizing in the 1930s. The Comintern was the last predominantly white political organization in which Padmore would ever hold membership. James, conversely, was moving into the international socialist movement. It would soon establish the Fourth International, in which he would play a key role. While Padmore continued to avoid abstract theorizing in favor of detailed, statistically rich explorations of imperialism, James thrust himself into an intense period of theorizing Marxism, Trotskyism, and the failures of the Third International; he also dedicated himself to a radical black tradition of self-activity and revolutionary struggle. For black radicals in London, it was a particularly vibrant moment. And George Padmore, C. L. R. James, and so many other tireless black activists provided its political vision and direction.

An International African Opinion

Diasporic London and Black Radical Intellectual Production

One wonders what George Padmore thought when he returned to London in 1935. Leaders of the Communist Party of Great Britain had led him to believe, rather falsely, that there were too few black people in England for Communists to organize. But fellow Caribbean radicals and Communists such as Chris Jones, James Headley, and Arnold Ward as well as friends settling into the metropole had told Padmore about black London's vibrant political and cultural activities. Their descriptions must have reminded him of Harlem, that most complex of U.S. black urban social scapes. In Harlem, the large northern African American community was adjusting to the constant influx of southern black migrants and an ever-growing Caribbean (and, to a lesser extent, African) immigrant population, making this Negro Mecca a uniquely diasporic city in the United States. Although London's black community was small by comparison, it was not less important to Padmore and other black radicals.

London boasted a considerable history of black political activism. Padmore knew of the Trinidadian barrister Henry Sylvester Williams (in fact, he claimed that Williams was his uncle), who had convened the first Pan-African conference in 1900 in London's Westminster Hall. Padmore also knew of Duse Mohamed Ali's *African Times and Orient Review*, which had fostered a pan-Africanist consciousness in the 1910s. Ward's Negro Welfare Association and Reginald Bridgeman's British Section of the LAI had introduced Padmore to politically minded, anticolonialist African students gathered in the West

African Students Union (WASU). He likely was impressed with their journal, *WASU*, which first appeared in March 1926. And there was the Jamaican doctor Harold Moody, who in 1931 created a politically moderate interracial organization, the League of Coloured Peoples, which put out the journal *The Keys*.[1]

Padmore may have thought little of black London politically when he settled into his flat on Cranleigh Street. More than two decades later, he recalled that "the majority of the coloured population of London and the provincial cities, apart from itinerant seamen living in the dock areas . . . was made up chiefly of students." Primarily from religious, middle-class families, these "African and West Indian intellectuals . . . were, if anything, even more conservative than English university students."[2] T. Ras Makonnen, the British Guianan radical born Thomas Griffiths, echoed this sentiment, recalling that "the existing African and West Indian organizations in England at the time were very mild."[3] Yet as one historian has observed, London's political milieu in the 1930s was one in which "many West Indian and African intellectuals embraced black internationalism for the first time."[4]

By 1935, several arrivals in the imperial capital had already helped radically alter the terms of black political discourse. C. L. R. James was now an important figure in British Trotskyism. The Jamaican writer Una Marson worked as the secretary for the League of Coloured Peoples and edited *The Keys*. T. Albert Marryshow from Grenada headed the Grenada Worker's Association; he had earlier written for Padmore's *Negro Worker* and would go on to become one of the architects of the West Indies Federation. Amy Ashwood Garvey, Marcus Garvey's first wife, ran a social parlor and a restaurant in London's West End that served as hubs of radical black activism and debate. I. T. A. Wallace-Johnson came to London in 1936, immersing himself in radical politics. Makonnen would note of this period that "England had been the executioner of its own colonial empire," for it "allowed these blacks to feel the contrast between freedom in the metropolis and slavery in the colonies."[5]

It may be that Makonnen was nearly reckless in praising England's presumed freedoms, and his "rather glib suggestion that England was the main catalyst in black anticolonialism" elides a rather long history of anticolonial politics in the Caribbean, Africa, and United States.[6] Nevertheless, blacks in London escaped the level of repression experienced in the colonies. No one had been arrested or convicted, for example, for publishing or possessing seditious literature, as had happened to Wallace-Johnson in the Gold Coast. James had felt that he could not become seriously politically active in Trinidad. If black anticolonialism grew out of a series of diasporic circuits and networks throughout the colonial world and metropole, London served as an incubator, a cauldron whose pressures Makonnen recalled forced black activists "into making alliances across boundaries that would have been unthinkable back home."[7]

When Padmore returned to London, the city pulsed with the energy of people anxious to see the British empire crumble or at least to see its treatment of colonial subjects improve drastically. He arrived with a wealth of contacts from Africa and the Caribbean, many of whom would play critical roles in anticolonial politics in the coming decades. Despite his importance, however, Padmore did not play a decisive role in that politics. He was the connective tissue, the link between Harlem and London, between the ABB and the International African Service Bureau (IASB), which he established in 1937. Padmore made these contacts because U.S. black radicals a decade earlier had pushed questions of race and black people's importance to world revolution, thereby creating a context in which organizing in Africa assumed importance within international communism; Padmore pushed Comintern thinking about Africa even further, ultimately outstripping Moscow and the white Left. London provided the unique opportunity where that political vision and project could blossom, a phenomenon that was nowhere more apparent than with the creation of radical black anticolonialist organizations.

The IASB grew out of the International African Friends of Ethiopia (IAFE), founded by James and Amy Ashwood Garvey in 1935, on the eve of Italy's invasion of Ethiopia (also called Abyssinia). In London, however, Padmore and others did not merely continue the politics of this earlier period. London's organizations, political history, and public culture presented a much different set of circumstances for black radical and intellectual culture out of which would emerge a form of radical politics that involved a score of people who would play important roles in national liberation movements over the next several decades.

James is of particular importance, for while Padmore's style continued to favor empirically dense writings that demonstrated the nature of colonial rule, James engaged the Abyssinia crisis through a prolonged effort to understand colonial Africa's role in world revolution. Part of this story involves James's participation in the ILP and British Trotskyism. As he mounted a challenge to Stalinism, James began to view the Caribbean's modernity less as testament to its fitness for self-governance and more as indicative of the limits of its revolutionary possibility. The parliamentarian radical came to view Africa as the main front of revolutionary struggle, a shift that grew out of this moment's radical black internationalism and diasporic community as well as Padmore's and Ashwood's influence, which combined to alter his worldview. The lessons James learned in London's black radical circles also shaped his understanding of Marxism. But to understand James's approach to socialism is to understand his response to Abyssinia.

While London-based black radicals agreed on the importance of Ethiopia to their liberation and the future of the British empire, they hardly agreed on what should be done. Tensions between Africans and Caribbeans were so high, years later James recalled that "by 1935 there was a definite cleavage between the two groups." Most Caribbeans, seeing themselves as modern compared with Africans, focused on the need for self-government in the Caribbean; for their part, Africans, who resented the hubris of those Caribbeans they called "white black men,"[8] insisted on the importance of Africa to the diaspora.

But the interactions in this period also fostered considerable collaborations. While Marryshow and Amy Ashwood Garvey returned to the Caribbean to carry on work in different arenas, James would not return to Trinidad for another twenty-six years. Padmore never returned, settling instead in Ghana in 1957 to help Kwame Nkrumah usher in the first independent sub-Saharan African nation. Makonnen followed Padmore there. James had met Nkrumah in the United States and wrote to Padmore introducing this young, somewhat uninformed anticolonial intellectual. Nkrumah would work with Padmore in the IASB and its successor, the Pan-African Federation, to organize the monumental fifth Pan African Congress in Manchester in 1945, a gathering attended by Jomo Kenyatta, the first president of Kenya. Nnamdi Azikiwe, Nigeria's first president after independence, was also involved in these political formations.

Britain's white Left provided critical support to the IASB but never undermined the bureau's autonomy. IASB radicals drew support from multiple, often conflicting sources, including the Communist Party of Great Britain (largely through the LAI's British Section), the ILP, progressive members of the British Parliament, and occasionally even the Labour Party. Indeed, the IASB's two major periodicals, *African Sentinel* (edited by Wallace-Johnson) and *International African Opinion* (edited by James), were funded in part by the LAI and ILP, respectively. Under James, *International African Opinion* was preoccupied with diasporic struggle and liberation movements and pitched itself as an organ of the black working class; it emphasized trade union organizing and refused to assume a vanguard role. Rather, it sought to disseminate information and draw lessons from the experiences of black workers in building an intercolonial movement to end empire and capitalism. The IASB thus represented an international black radical network largely comprised of Anglophone black radicals but also including black radicals in France and the United States.

James's work in London captures the continued importance of reconciling intradiasporic social difference with a notion of political blackness that encompassed a range of groups whose regional, national, and racial identities were often in conflict. James and Padmore ultimately envisioned the IASB as a building block for a pan-African Marxist movement that would center on African revolution. The idea was Padmore's: "He educated me," James recalled. Yet along with Padmore, Ashwood and London's dynamic if small black communities proved key to James's transformation from a parliamentarian radical insisting on a uniquely modern Caribbean vanguard of African world revolution to a Marxist who thought innovatively about class struggle and socialism and insisted on the centrality of Africa to world socialist revolution.

London, Abyssinia, and Diasporic Internationalism

On Padmore's trips to London after he left the Comintern, he regularly visited James. On one such visit in the spring of 1934, James noticed that Padmore "looked not only disheveled but his eyes were not what they ought to be." Padmore apparently had just escaped a couple of Comintern toughs intent on compelling his return to Moscow to answer for his heresy. Recalling the incident forty years later, James may have allowed a bit of intrepidness for a "West Indian of the old school" when he described Padmore as "not shaken at all by them, but he was just a little disturbed." James was being generous, for Padmore had heard that two Soviet security agents in Moscow had hauled away his friend, Albert Nzula, as well as others.[9]

Inviting Padmore in, James asked him what was the matter. Padmore gave a pithy, if opaque reply. Padmore "used a phrase which took me a long time to understand," James later recalled. "He said, 'I have left those people, you know.'" Padmore said that he had stayed in Russia, and "I saw what was going on." Padmore's tone, at least in James's rendering, hinted at the strains that the Soviet experiment placed on people's personal lives and the strains that came from the silencing of anyone critical of Stalin.[10] James's account bears quoting at length for what it forecasts about his relationship with Padmore:

He said: "I stayed there because there was a means of doing work for the black emancipation and there was no other place that I could think of.

But I had come to Moscow from the United States. They had seen me in the United States when I had worked there and I had got a good education in Trinidad." So they brought him to Moscow and Hamburg was the centre. And he moved about Europe organising the black people into the Black International Trade union Movement. So that day I asked him: "George, what has happened, why have you left them?" And he told me something of which only now, in later years, I understand the full significance. . . . In the old days, . . . when you were in the Communist Party and they gave you a line, you followed that line; you followed that line or you went out on your ears. So George packed his stuff and went away and came to London and settled down to work.[11]

As James suggests, Padmore's London work was intended to build an independent black international.

By James's account, he and Padmore "were leaders of the black movement," though he was on the "outside as a Marxist, Trotskyist." James spent much of his time in the London-based Communist League, which in 1934 joined the ILP in hopes of transforming it into a revolutionary party. James was among the Communist League members who formed the Marxist group that November, emerging as one of its most important thinkers.

Then came the Abyssinia crisis. In 1935, Italy began building up its forces in Eritrea along the Ethiopian border, providing James an occasion to rethink the racial logic of capital and make an impact on the British Left. ILP members began to debate whether to support League of Nations sanctions against Italy. Like Lenin, who dubbed the League a "Thieves Kitchen," James considered the question of sanctions a ruse for imperialist war. Instead, he proposed "workers' sanctions," an internationalist response to the Italian invasion and the rise of fascism more generally. The "workers of Europe, Peasants and workers of Africa and of India, sufferers from Imperialism all over the world, all anxious to help the Ethiopian people" rather than support their governments in war, should "organise yourselves independently, and by your own sanctions, the use of your own power, assist the Ethiopian people."[12]

That James could garner widespread support for this position, which for him had everything to do with the colonial question, spoke to his intellect and oratorical skill. He traveled throughout the British Isles (especially South Wales and Dublin), appealing for support for Ethiopia against Italian imperialism and putting forward the case for workers' sanctions. He also visited Norwich, Coventry, and Nottingham in England, and by the fall of 1935, he was chair of the ILP's Finchley branch in North London, leading a sizable group that supported his position. At the ILP's annual conference in Keighley, James gave what Fenner Brockway remembered as a "typically torrential speech." Africans would use the crisis in imperial powers to liberate themselves, he argued, but theirs was not an isolated struggle. It was central to anticolonial and workers' struggles. He repeated his appeal for support for Ethiopia through workers' sanctions, a position that brought him into conflict with ILP chairman James Maxton as well as John McGovern and George Buchanan, two ILP pacifists. Even Brockway, who before the conference had also argued for workers' sanctions, urged a more measured stance to avoid alienating Maxton, fearing that if Maxton left the ILP, it would be hopelessly weakened. James agreed only to preface his proposal for workers' sanctions with a call that it be adopted with discussion. That idea carried the day, bringing James a good deal of celebrity in London's leftist circles.[13]

If James found room in the British Left to elaborate his ideas about black liberation, London's black institutions provided fertile political ground for building a movement. One of the early arenas of his black public activism was Harold Moody's League of Coloured Peoples (LCP). The LCP was a black-led organization committed to improving race relations and had a sizable white membership. Most of the LCP's leadership was Caribbean, with some Africans and an occasional South Asian member. Moody controlled the group, molding it largely in his conservative Christian manner. Still, when the Trinidadian Cricketer Learie Constantine, an LCP member and financial supporter, introduced Moody to James, Moody immediately invited him into the organization. At the LCP's first weekend conference in the summer of 1933, James lectured on the Caribbean, almost certainly raising the issue of West Indian self-government. In the LCP, he came into contact with W. Arthur Lewis (with whom he developed a friendship), LCP secretary Una Marson, and quite likely Paul Robeson, an early LCP supporter.[14]

James was drawn into the growing discourse on race and empire among London's black population. A 1936 WASU debate took up the question of what advantages might come from "greater cooperation between Africans and West Indians"; the discussion focused specifically on what many Africans experienced as Caribbean hubris. In a lively debate, Africans criticized Caribbeans for imitating whites and for "their ignorance of the cultures of their forefathers . . . and their blindness to the advantages of mutual understanding." The debate was hailed as a sign of change. Participants agreed that Caribbeans needed to discard "the anti-African propaganda with which their educational system is saturated" and to "re-establish contact with the civilizations in which they have their roots."[15] James understood the points made that night.

James was also drawn into the orbit of Amy Ashwood Garvey. While Ashwood supported her husband's ambitions in Jamaica and the United States, her refusal to play a subordinate role contributed to their separation. She had planned to work on black women's issues in New York but in 1922 went on a speaking tour of Europe. In England, she helped the young Nigerian law student Ladipo Solanke establish the Nigerian Progress Union in 1924. After returning briefly to the Caribbean, she settled again in London in 1930 with her companion, Sam Manning, took up residence at 62 New Oxford Road, and opened the Florence Mills Social Parlour and the International Afro-Restaurant below her flat. For many black activists and local residents, her businesses provided a welcome respite from a damp, strange country.[16]

Ashwood's male peers respected her immense energy as an activist, though much of their praise betrayed the gendered structures of early-twentieth-century black radicalism. Hubert Harrison believed that Marcus Garvey owed his first wife credit for his success in the United States and saw in her "a well-spring of ambition and inspiration," once privately lamenting, "If I could get her for *my* helpmeet . . . I should rise to giddy heights of achievement!" Former students remembered Ashwood as "a mother of African and West Indian students" who was always "concerned about their behaviour." Her establishments were centers of activism. According to Makonnen, one could go to Florence Mills "after you'd been slugging it out for two or three hours at Hyde Park . . . and get a lovely meal, dance and enjoy yourself." James, who spent a great deal of time there because he could not stand English food, recalled that Ashwood was a "militant anti-imperialist . . . of tremendous force of personality." While he found her historically uninformed, James considered her "an extremely acute woman, able to see what was taking place in conversation and people's orientation—one of the brightest women I have known."[17]

The Florence Mills Social Parlour provided a political and social venue where black people could find familiar food, see familiar faces, and relax away from the gaze of white Londoners. The need for such places cannot be underestimated, for the metropole exacted quite a toll on Caribbean and African immigrants separated from friends, family, and familiar settings and always made to feel the outsider. It was natural for political discussions to thrive at Florence Mills and other West End establishments, like the Caribbean Club. As a *London Sunday Express* article noted of Ashwood's parlor, "Race intellectuals from all parts of the world [were] wont to gather" there.[18] For James, Ashwood's appeal as a political comrade was immediate, especially considering the radicals in her social network, including the Nigerian Ladipo Solanke, other WASU members, and Solanke's friend, Jomo Kenyatta, a student of anthropologist Bronislaw Malinowski at the London School of Economics. Thus, when news came of Mussolini's activities in the African horn, it was at Ashwood's restaurant and with her help that James established the International African Friends of Ethiopia in July 1935.[19]

The IAFE sought "to assist by all means in [its] power, in the maintenance of the territorial integrity and the political independence of Abyssinia,"[20] a goal that captured the sentiments of many in the diaspora. Anticolonial radicals in the Gold Coast, Nigeria, and Sierra Leone viewed Italian aggression against Ethiopia as exposing the weakness of the League of Nations and the continued view among European powers that Africa existed merely to strengthen colonial empires and home markets. For many in West Africa, the situation "could only be interpreted in terms of racial strife, cynicism, and power politics." Many people of African descent also felt that a "war with Abyssinia is our war."[21] African Americans wrote to the Ethiopian Research Council, based in Washington, D.C., that "we are Ethiopians," volunteering for military service. In Jamaica, British Guiana, Grenada, and Trinidad, Caribbeans expressed outrage at Italy's actions. Like African Americans, black people all across the Caribbean boycotted Italian businesses. The Trinidadian Negro Welfare Social and Cultural Association declared that "only the united action of all Negroes and oppressed peoples can stop this horrible mass murder," and Trinidadian and South African workers refused to service Italian ships.[22] If some on the British Left needed convincing, black workers were actively pursuing workers' sanctions.

Italy was not some minor nation overreaching. As Padmore explained in the NAACP's magazine, *Crisis*, Italy's aggression was part of a long history of European exploitation of African peoples and lands and of "white nations . . . joining hands in assigning parts of Africa to whichever one stands most in need of colonies." Race played a central role in Italy's actions, Padmore asserted, as few black activists believed that Britain, France, the United States, and the League of Nations would have tolerated such aggression toward a white nation. But Padmore, who would slowly begin to work with IAFE members, also sought to place colonialism at the core of fascism (in both its Italian and German versions) and thus to make a general critique of European empire. Although others on the British Left, especially Sir Stafford Cripps's Socialist League, had articulated a view of fascism and imperialism as interconnected, race was not taken as a central facet in thinking about Europe. For Padmore, however, fascism and empire were of a piece. "Apart from the economic motives," he noted, fascism's "racial aspect looms large." Writing as an IAFE representative in the Communist Party of Great Britain's *Labour Monthly*, Kenyatta remarked that Ethiopia was "the only independent country to which Imperialism, with its need for fresh fields and new pastures for economic exploitation, is turning to in its great international crisis." In a line profound in its simplicity, he argued, "To support Ethiopia is to fight Fascism."[23]

Kenyatta and Padmore closed the rhetorical distance European powers tried to create between empire and fascism. Padmore argued that "Hitler is a fascist dictator like Mussolini, and like the Italian, dissatisfied with Europe as it is." Italian aggression was an instance of colonialism acceptable to European powers, he maintained. Fascism was not simply the product of an abhorrent mind that deserved a unique response. The struggle for Ethiopia was a fight "against not only Italian imperialism, but the other robbers and oppressors, French and British imperialism," Padmore wrote. Fascism could not be fought on the side of imperialism. "For when it is said and done," Padmore offered in another *Crisis* editorial, "the struggle of the Abyssinians is fundamentally a part of the struggles of the black race the world over for national freedom, economic, political, social and racial emancipation."[24]

The IAFE was among a number of groups that had formed in support of Ethiopia. Both the LCP and the WASU had turned their attention to Ethiopia around the same time. The WASU passed a resolution condemning Italian aggression and British collusion and establishing ties with the African American Ethiopian Research Council and the Paris-based Comité de Défense d'Ethiope (Ethiopian Defense Committee), founded by Garan Kouyaté as an umbrella organization for colonial groups in Paris concerned with defending Ethiopia. Its secretary, the Martinican intellectual Paulette Nardal, who was fluent in English, helped maintain lines of communication with the IAFE. The IAFE also worked with white Ethiopian support groups, including the Abyssinian Association, and Sylvia Pankhurst's *New Times and Ethiopian News*.[25]

The IAFE claimed an unprecedented number of anticolonial radicals as members. Alongside James as chair, Peter Milliard from British Guiana and Grenada's Marryshow served as vice chairs; Kenyatta held the title of honorary secretary, and Ashwood was honorary treasurer. Among the other members were George Moore and Samuel Wood (Aborigines' Rights Protection Society) and Joseph B. Danquah (the Gold Coast), Samuel Manning (Trinidad), and Mohammed Said (Somalia). Padmore had come into contact with most of these activists when he headed the ITUCNW. The connection is no coincidence.[26] James credits this moment of metropolitan black anticolonialism—and diasporic liberation struggles over the next several decades more generally—to Padmore's extensive network of contacts. James and Ashwood rather than Padmore formed the IAFE, probably because Padmore was fatigued from Hamburg. But after Padmore settled in London, James recalled, "everyone who came . . . to go to the Colonial Office would call on George Padmore first."[27]

Many of the IAFE's members were or had previously been active in organized Marxist formations—the Communist International, Communist Party of Great Britain/LAI, ILP, and Fourth International. But the IAFE displayed a certain ideological ecumenicalism, with its members finding ways, for the most part, to work together in an independent black political formation. Many felt that they could do in London what was not possible in the colonies, and with good reason. They could hold forth in Hyde Park and tell whites "what we felt about their empire and about them," Makonnen recalled. "Write any tract we wanted to; make terrible speeches; all this when you knew very well that back in the colonies even to say 'God is love' might get the authorities after you!" James pointed out that in Trinidad, he "would have lost my job . . . would have been in disgrace with my family" had he pursued radical politics. As Cedric Robinson put it, these activists were part of a generation of black intellectuals who "presumed or perhaps understood that the project of anti-imperialism had to be centered in the metropole."[28]

It would be hard to overstate IAFE's importance for understanding James's political consciousness. Though he came to England concerned with West Indian self-government, he was now "meeting a lot of black people and African people in London." And what must James have thought when at Ashwood's restaurant, he met Africans such as Nigeria's Adetokunbo Adegboyega Ademola, who had studied law at Cambridge, and J. B. Danquah, the WASU's first president, who studied philosophy and law? Had Ashwood challenged his considerable hubris?[29]

London was James's uniquely diasporic moment. His interactions with African students, intellectuals, and activists informed his political activities, as was evident in the name he gave his first organization, the International *African* Friends of Ethiopia. "Gradually," he later recalled of his time in London, "I began to gain in England a conception of black people which I didn't possess when I left the Caribbean."[30]

The IAFE's work reflected James's evolving racial consciousness as his organization took full advantage of the city's wide-ranging networks and thrust itself to the center of public discussions about Ethiopia. Headquartered at Ashwood's restaurant, the IAFE tapped into a long-standing London political tradition of utilizing public spaces such as Trafalgar Square and Hyde Park's Speaker's Corner to put forward its program. The IAFE produced pamphlets calling on all peoples of African descent to pledge their support to Ethiopia. At a mid-August rally in Ludgate Circus, James informed the crowd that if Ethiopians lost their fight against Italy, "we look to them to destroy their country rather than hand it over to the invader." As if the point could have been missed, he added, "Let them burn down Addis Ababa, let them poison their wells and water-holes, let them destroy every blade of vegetation."[31] At a Trafalgar Square rally on August 25, 1935, the IAFE arranged to have the three sons of the Ethiopian ambassador to London, Dr. A. Workneh Martin, on the packed platform. Speaking to a racially mixed though largely white audience, Ashwood declared that while "no race has been so noble in forgiving," it was "now the hour . . . for our complete emancipation." In what became a common theme for IAFE activists, she insisted that Abyssinia's broader significance was that black people now stood "between [Europe] and fascism." Arnold Ward and Chris Jones also addressed the rally, while the flamboyant racetrack tipster Prince Ras Monolulu (born Peter McKay in St. Croix) carried the Ethiopian flag in the background. James assured the largely white crowd that they were not attending "an anti-white demonstration . . . but it is pro-Negro." More provocative was James's agreement that "Abyssinia is a backward nation" in need of "western civilization," though not the barbaric civilization of Italian fascism.[32]

On classic Marxist standards, James agreed with many on the British Left about Ethiopia's presumed backwardness. Indeed, Maxton and others in the ILP's Parliamentary Group reasoned that both Italy and Abyssinia were dictatorships, which in part informed their opposition to workers' sanctions. James followed this argument, but only in discussing Ethiopia's monarchical governance and slavery. And though James remained critical of Ethiopia's emperor Haile Sellasie, his sense of its backwardness came under intense scrutiny from other black radicals.[33]

Ashwood emerged as the central figure of the IAFE, speaking at both Labour Party and LAI rallies in London and connecting the IAFE to several London-based organizations that had planned a major united-front demonstration for November. She assumed much of the responsibility for the group, while James devoted his attention to struggles among British Socialists. She was a tireless organizer who quickly built the IAFE into an international net-

Amy Ashwood Garvey with three of the sons (in white pants) of Dr. A. Workneh Martin, the Ethiopian ambassador to London, at an IAFE rally, Trafalgar Square, London, August 25, 1935. Bettman/Corbis.

work. Ashwood made sure that the IAFE had a member at any demonstration on Ethiopia. And when Italy finally invaded Ethiopia in October, she ratcheted up the IAFE's work. With Padmore and Mohammed Said and in conjunction with the New York–based Friends of Ethiopia in America, she planned a fund-raising trip to New York to buy medical supplies for Ethiopia. Although the trip never materialized, she continued to press for financial support, urging attendees at an October WASU meeting to create the Ethiopian Defence Fund, which, given the IAFE's Gold Coast members, almost certainly had ties to the series of Ethiopian Defense Committees that Wallace-Johnson had created.[34]

By the end of 1935, Padmore was back in London working with Ashwood, Kenyatta, and Marryshow in the IAFE. Ashwood continued to speak at events about Ethiopia around England and drew members to the group from outside London.[35] During a brief visit to London, Makonnen, who had studied at Howard University at the same time as Padmore, heard about the IAFE and went to a rally, and afterward joined IAFE members for tea at Lyons Corner House, across from the square.[36]

Ras Monolulu holding Ethiopian flag at an IAFE rally, Trafalgar Square, London, August 25, 1935. Daily Herald Archives/SSPL.

The IAFE viewed anticolonial struggle as much more than a simple question of sanctioning Italy. James remembered that group members "wanted to form a military organisation which would go to fight with the Abyssinians against the Italians." In a letter published in the *New Leader*, James offered his services to the Ethiopian ambassador, Martin, "under the Emperor, militarily or otherwise." James viewed such service as an opportunity to work "with the masses of the Abyssinians and other Africans." It also offered the best chance "of putting across the International Socialist case" and agitating against fascism among Italian forces. At the least, serving would give him "an invaluable opportunity of gaining actual military experience" fighting in "one of the most savage battles between Capitalism and its opponents." Martin declined the offer, suggesting that James and others could better aid Ethiopia through their work in the IAFE. By James's account, IAFE radicals accepted this decision but made it clear that they opposed League of Nations sanctions.[37]

However, the IAFE was not as steadfastly opposed to League sanctions as James believed. Indeed, the IAFE began to decline largely as a consequence of leftist differences on this issue. At some point "in the excitement of forming the organisation," as James described it, the IAFE passed a resolution supporting League sanctions against Italy and the closure of the Suez Canal (thereby blocking Italy's best route to the African horn). The resolution deemed these actions "the only effective way of stopping the war in East Africa." Ashwood and Padmore began holding meetings throughout England presenting the resolution to black audiences. In Liverpool, several hundred longtime residents from the maritime-based African community came to a meeting and endorsed the resolution as well as another one that demanded that Britain lift its embargo on arms shipments to Ethiopia and allow "Africans and people of African descent to volunteer to fight in defence of Abyssinia's independence." Makonnen and Padmore spent "a good deal of time in the British Museum digging out some of the ancient history of Ethiopia" to detail its long history, social structures, and cultural practices at rallies and forums, hoping "to educate English public opinion." Later, however, James would admit that "I got myself into a blunder," as the IAFE position contradicted his arguments within the ILP for workers' sanctions. He then left the IAFE, momentarily placing himself outside the ferment of radical black internationalism. Though nearly everyone who met James recognized his brilliance, some, like Kenyatta, considered James unstable and felt that he had abandoned the organization.[38]

The loss for the IAFE was less severe than for James, who was deeply concerned about Ethiopia. Writing in *The Keys*, he showed a knack for what one scholar has called "a model of narrative economy" by covering in a mere three pages nearly a half century of European aggression against Abyssinia, teasing out the imperial intrigue leading up to Italy's invasion and situating it within the context of the French and British empires. James insisted that Abyssinia could be saved only by "the efforts of the Abyssinians themselves and action by the great masses of Negroes and sympathetic whites and Indians all over the world by demonstrations, public meetings, resolutions, financial assistance to Abyssinia, strikes against the export of all materials to Italy, refusal to unload Italian ships, etc."[39] Padmore's *How Britain Rules Africa* echoed James, warning British workers and progressives that they could hardly afford to separate the fight against fascism "from the right of all colonial peoples and subject races to Self-Determination." Africa would play a "decisive role in international affairs" in the coming years. "What India is to the British Empire," he concluded, "Africa is to world imperialism."[40]

Despite their considerable agreement, Padmore and James had often clashed in the IAFE, at times quite viciously. They had split over the question of sanctions, and James refused to give an inch. Also, James closed a largely favorable review of Padmore's *How Britain Rules Africa* by taking his friend to task for what he called a "grievously disappointing" view of Africa's future.

Though he felt that Padmore made a good Leninist argument for African self-determination, James feigned incredulity that Padmore could welcome the cooperation of "the appeal of 'enlightened far-sighted sections of the ruling classes of Europe with colonial interests' to co-operate with Africans. This is madness." Africans would "win their own freedom," James insisted, needing only the cooperation of the "revolutionary movement in Europe and Asia."[41]

James was being disingenuous. He conveyed none of the sarcasm Padmore had packed into the offending passage, and Padmore had made precisely the point that James felt needed to be made.[42] "How can there be co-operation with those who seek to destroy them?," Padmore had asked. "How can there be co-operation with imperialists . . . ?" Padmore graciously chose not to respond publicly, as he likely understood all too well his friend's troubles. In July 1936, James participated in the First International Conference for the Fourth International in Paris, and such a bold affiliation with Trotskyism left him marginalized within British socialism. When he launched the openly Trotskyist journal *Fight* in October 1936, its harsh criticisms of ILP luminaries led to his expulsion as well as that of others working on the journal. The increasingly small collective in the Marxist Group that he led was in disarray, and he was on the outside of black anticolonial agitation. Though he continued to lecture on the West Indies and imperialism to the LCP and other groups, he was a "Rudder" without a boat or even a crew.[43]

James also disagreed with Padmore and others in the IAFE regarding Ethiopian emperor Haile Selassie. James considered Selassie a feudal reactionary and argued endlessly about him with Ashwood, Padmore, and Makonnen, who considered Selassie's rule an internal matter to be worked out later. Personal animosities also arose inside the IAFE, and they, too, contributed to the group's troubles. Arnold Ward had replaced the effusive praise he once lavished on Padmore with calculated disdain, complaining that Padmore now pushed a race program and was drawing blacks from the Communist Party of Great Britain. Ironically, Makonnen accused Padmore of being "rather feeble" in dealing with the ILP, a group Makonnen found only less objectionable than the Communists. If anyone joining the IAFE had "one foot in the communist camp," he recalled, "we would deal with [them] ruthlessly." Indeed, according to a Scotland Yard report, he and Ward once came to blows over competing resolutions on Abyssinia submitted to the LAI British Section's sixth annual conference.[44] That they continued to work together is testament to their commitment to African liberation.

With Amy Ashwood Garvey slowly receding into the background of the

IAFE, however, Padmore emerged as the glue holding the group together. He regularly chaired IAFE meetings and worked tirelessly to build support among white progressives. Sundays at Hyde Park's Speaker's Corner and in Trafalgar Square now included members of Parliament Stafford Cripps and Ellen Wilkinson (both of the Parliamentary Labour Party) and William Gallacher of the Communist Party. Eric Williams, James's former student in Trinidad who in 1932 had come to read history at Oxford and who later became the first prime minister of Trinidad and Tobago, regularly attended, even appearing on the speaker's platform.

Shedding the sectarianism of his Comintern days, Padmore worked with a range of personalities. He became close with the writer and ILP anti-imperialist Reginald Reynolds and his companion (and future wife), novelist Ethel Mannin, spending weekend afternoons at their home in Wimbledon, debating politics, going to the theater, and occasionally hosting them at his flat. Padmore provided Reynolds and Mannin, who were generally disillusioned with the Left, entrée into black anticolonial circles. Through James, Padmore also met Arthur Ballard, whose Socialist Book Center was a gathering place for local radicals, among them Fenner Brockway, who introduced Padmore to various Indian radicals. Padmore became fast friends with Krishna Menon, founder in 1931 of the India League, as well as Menon's adversaries K. D. Kumira and Mulk Raj Anan. Padmore and James attended rallies, held long discussions about Indian national liberation, lectured at meetings, and even planned with Menon to organize the Colonial Marxist League.[45] Padmore also spent time with his old Howard University professor Ralph Bunche, who arrived in London in February 1937.[46]

Wallace-Johnson came to London the same month from the Gold Coast to file an appeal after being arrested and convicted for violating antisedition legislation. He had published an article in the *African Morning Post* condemning the Pope's blessing of Mussolini's troops heading to Abyssinia. Wallace-Johnson had previously come under investigation in Nigeria for distributing the banned *Negro Worker*, then fled to the Gold Coast, leaving behind books and documents that British Criminal Investigation Department agents would deem to contain "seditious sentiments and some expressing seditious intentions."[47] In the Gold Coast, as was his habit, Wallace-Johnson had met local activists and joined a select group to form the West African Youth League. But he had soon come under surveillance there as well and was the target of a 1934 Seditious Literatures Bill. He steered clear of any violations of the bill for well over a year until his "Has the African a God?" piece criticizing the

Pope and Italy's aggression, and European imperial practices in Africa more generally.[48]

After arriving in London, Wallace-Johnson immediately contacted local Communists from the LAI, including Bridgeman and Ward. According to Colonial Office records, he was soon working closely with the LAI and speaking at CPGB events. He pitched the idea of a West African bureau to Bridgeman, who showed no interest. But when Wallace-Johnson met Padmore, he listened intently. Padmore and many other people in and around the IAFE were already thinking about expanding their work beyond Ethiopia to the whole of Africa. A year earlier, James had staged his play on the Saint Domingue revolution, *Toussaint L'Overture*, starring Paul Robeson. James subsequently interested Robeson and his wife, Eslanda Goode Robeson, in organizing efforts regarding Abyssinia, and Paul Robeson was now also concerned with Africa as a whole. James agreed with Ashwood that the IAFE could easily broaden its focus to include the entire continent.[49]

During April 1937, Padmore held a series of meetings with Wallace-Johnson, James, Kenyatta, Makonnen, Ashwood, Akiki Nyabongo, and the Nigerian Louis Nwachukwu Mbanefo to discuss creating a new organization focused on Africa. All of the activists agreed that the group's program should be socialist. Mbanefo proposed creating a journal to help disseminate information on African problems and the problems of all black people. On April 23, Bunche set up a meeting between this group and the African American radical Max Yergan. Yergan was a longtime YMCA activist in Africa, and he and Bunche were key members of the U.S.-based National Negro Congress. Yergan was visiting London and had recently established with Robeson the International Committee on African Affairs, an information bureau that would carry out policy research, train select Africans, and build a cooperative movement. A major new figure in international communism, Yergan was suspicious of Padmore, whom he considered a Trotskyist, though according to Bunche, the two men "got on okay." Yergan explained the goals of his new group, and Padmore did likewise. Despite the coolness between Padmore and Yergan, they seem to have agreed to have their groups work together, with Yergan giving money to Padmore's group and Kenyatta and Wallace-Johnson joining Yergan's committee. On April 29, Padmore, Wallace-Johnson, Kenyatta, and Makonnen announced that they would call their organization the International African Service Bureau, and they immediately began raising money to rent office space and publish a journal.[50]

The International African Service Bureau

With Padmore as chair, Ashwood and Kenyatta as vice chairs, and Wallace-Johnson as general secretary, the IASB took as its motto "Educate, Co-operate, Emancipate. Neutral in nothing affecting the African people." Its executive committee included Nnamdi Azikiwe, several West African Youth League members, and Garan Kouyaté. Among the bureau's goals were "supporting the demands of Africans and other colonial people for democratic rights, civil liberties and self-determination." Rather than functioning as a diasporic vanguard that would direct colonial struggles, the bureau proposed to represent "progressive and enlightened public opinion among Africans and peoples of African descent." One of the greatest hindrances to progress, Wallace-Johnson declared in a press release announcing the group, was "the lack of direct . . . contact between the colonial peoples, the British public and interested friends, and peoples of African descent." The IASB would work through existing white radical and labor organizations and members of Parliament to address colonial policies throughout the British empire and thereby build a working-class movement centered on anticolonial struggle. An early pamphlet announced that the bureau would work with "English friends and subject races" and "co-operate with all peace-loving, democratic and working-class forces who desire to help the advancement of Africans." Programmatically, along with helping "enlighten public opinion," it would provide a "link between the Africans at home (in Africa) and the Africans abroad" through the transmission of messages, information, and views "from one to another." The IASB would pursue "a theory of colonial emancipation" that would chart a course for proletarian revolution outside both the old socialist Second International and the Stalinist Third International. The IASB would balance its theorizing of imperialism and colonial struggle with serving as a conduit for intercolonial exchange and engagement.[51]

IASB radicals actively courted the support of white radicals and white leftist formations. Nancy Cunard, who remained close friends with Padmore and in 1935 had planned to travel to Ethiopia as the IAFE's war correspondent, offered to help Wallace-Johnson with publicity for the bureau. Wallace-Johnson secured the IASB's office space at 94 Gray's Inn Road, a short walk down the road from the LAI's offices at 53 Gray's Inn Road. The Communist Party of Great Britain hoped that it might influence the bureau through Wallace-Johnson, just as the ILP hoped to gain influence through Padmore. Within months, the IASB had a cadre of white patrons that included Labour and ILP MPs, among them Reginald Sorenson, Ellen Wilkinson, and Creech

Jones. They and several other MPS among its patrons reportedly presented twenty-three questions on Britain's colonies for discussion in the House of Commons.[52]

The bureau established something of an international presence. It sent a correspondent to the World Congress against Racism and Anti-Semitism in Paris in mid-September 1937, and the correspondent established contact with William Patterson, Louise Thompson, and Francophone radicals including Emile Faure. Wallace-Johnson tried to have stories about the bureau and some of its literature published in West African papers. Padmore became the *Chicago Defender*'s London correspondent and wrote a regular column for *Crisis*, and his articles kept at least the Anglophone African world abreast of IASB activities. The St. Lucian economist and future Nobel Prize winner W. Arthur Lewis signed on as the bureau's consultant on economic research, and he explored the economic structures of colonialism and West Indies federation. The IASB's paramount concern, however, remained colonial workers, and when a wave of strikes hit the West Indies in 1937 and 1938, the IASB hailed them as marking the dawn of "a new historical epoch."[53]

On June 18, 1937, Tubal Uriah Butler, a Grenadian-born labor organizer and oil worker in Trinidad, led a sit-down strike that quickly spilled out of the oil fields and into the streets of Fyzabad, a small oil town in southwestern Trinidad. The police clashed with protestors when they tried to arrest Butler during a speech, sparking a weeklong rebellion that engulfed the island. A month later, rebellions shook Barbados for three days after police arrested the labor organizer Clement Payne in Bridgetown. Labor uprisings in St. Vincent, St. Lucia, and British Guiana soon followed. In June 1938 in Jamaica, workers led a popular uprising that brought the island's colonial government to its knees.[54]

As was its habit, the IASB organized public meetings in Trafalgar Square and Hyde Park and worked to build public support for the strikes in Trinidad and Barbados. In an "Open Letter to the Workers of the West Indies and British Guiana," the IASB hailed these revolts as giving "notice to the capitalist classes of the islands and the Imperial Power of Whitehall that coloured labour intends to obtain its just rewards." The IASB urged workers to "press forward their demands for a fundamental revolutionary change . . . with the goal towards political federation and self-determination." It also advocated establishing "an Inter-Colonial Labour Federation" to unite the colonies and push for revolutionary constitutional and political reforms. At one Trafalgar Square rally, Padmore claimed that the uprisings demonstrated that West Indian workers were "in close touch with modern developments," and he urged British trade unions to "render these coloured workers the maximum amount of support, advice and aid."[55]

By the time of the Jamaican uprising, much had changed within the IASB. The group's independence allowed it to take positions that were not supported by larger white organizations, and it openly criticized its patrons when its leaders deemed doing so appropriate. When Cripps, an apparent anti-imperialist who often appeared at IASB rallies and Abyssinia forums, suggested that Africa was less prepared than India for independence, James excoriated him as a "victim of one of the crudest of bourgeois sophistries."[56] Such criticisms occasionally made working with other groups difficult, however. Wallace-Johnson found it impossible to mediate the tension between the bureau and the LAI's Reginald Bridgeman and Ben Bradley, who considered Padmore and James little more than obstructionists. To be sure, James and Padmore were purposefully provocative. According to James, they routinely went to Communist meetings solely "to criticize their policy," with the result that Chris Jones would often work "himself into a temper and explode and make a revolution at the back of the hall." When Communists stopped calling on James and Padmore, James began showing up with his friend Gerry Bradley, "a great fighter, irrespective of the number of policemen," who would escort James to the stage, allowing James to "put the case for Trotsky, and it wrecked their meeting."[57]

These clashes eventually led the CPGB to end its financial support for the IASB, heightening Wallace-Johnson's financial difficulties. Frequently without money for food or even bus fare, he was eventually evicted from his flat for failing to pay rent, and he began sleeping in the IASB's office. Desperate, he also began dipping into the bureau's meager financial reserves. In April 1938, when the executive committee discovered that Wallace-Johnson was taking money, it expelled him, and he returned to Sierra Leone.[58]

If a Colonial Office report is to be trusted, Wallace-Johnson's departure may have left the bureau in a bit of disarray, as Padmore had to scramble for money to rent a new office. He turned to the ILP for support, moving the IASB's offices into an ILP building at 12a Westbourne Grove in West London. His relationship with the ILP had grown steadily closer over the previous year. He lectured regularly at its summer school in Glasgow, wrote articles for the *New Leader* praising the ILP for taking "a correct theoretical approach on . . . imperialist war and colonies," and later declared that only the ILP "continued to hold high the banner of Revolutionary Marxism." Padmore decided to replace the IASB's *African Sentinel* with a monthly that would cover the entire diaspora. *International African Opinion* echoed the design and editorial ori-

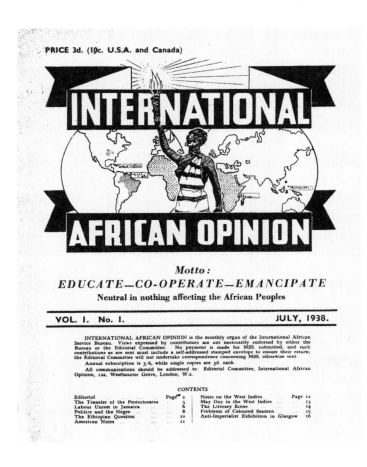

International
African Opinion,
July 1938.

PRICE 3d. (10c. U.S.A. and Canada)

INTERNATIONAL AFRICAN OPINION

Motto:

EDUCATE—CO-OPERATE—EMANCIPATE

Neutral in nothing affecting the African Peoples

VOL. I. No. I.   JULY, 1938.

INTERNATIONAL AFRICAN OPINION is the monthly organ of the International African Service Bureau. Views expressed by contributors are not necessarily endorsed by either the Bureau or the Editorial Committee. No payment is made for MSS. submitted, and such contributions as are sent must include a self-addressed stamped envelope to ensure their return; the Editorial Committee will not undertake correspondence concerning MSS. otherwise sent.

Annual subscription is 3/6, while single copies are 3d. each.

All communications should be addressed to: Editorial Committee, International African Opinion, 12a, Westbourne Grove, London, W.2.

CONTENTS

entation of *Negro Worker*, and Padmore convinced Brockway and C. A. Smith to help finance it. In a show of his and the bureau's independence, however, Padmore appointed James to edit the journal, no small irony given that he still edited *Fight*.[59]

In James's brief editorial tenure over *International African Opinion*—he would leave for the United States in October 1938—he worked to shape it into "the mouthpiece of the black workers and peasants," presenting it as a vehicle for sharing information and coordinating action in Africa and throughout the diaspora. Echoing the editorial prerogative Padmore had outlined previously in *Negro Worker*, James announced that *Opinion* would be "no literary journal or giver of advice from the mountain-tops" of the metropole. Rather, it would "stimulate the growing consciousness of the blacks" by drawing "from the black masses the lessons of the profound experiences that they accumulate in their daily toil" and by helping them mobilize "whatever assistance there is to be found in Europe for the cause of African emancipation." *Opinion* would serve as "a living weapon in the struggle, a reflection of the everyday demands of the masses as they fight their way to the larger goal."[60]

Rather than the symbol of an overall-clad African American worker that adorned *Negro Worker*, James chose for *Opinion* the image of an African woman holding a torch, seemingly stretching forth from Africa, if not Ethiopia in particular, with a world map in the background with marked diasporic nodes (West Indies, Brazil, and Africa, as well as Borneo). *International African Opinion* continued the IAFE's focus on Ethiopia while adding coverage of labor activities in West Africa and the West Indies and some political struggles by African Americans. Throughout its run, it evinced a "commitment to promoting the self-emancipation of the working classes of Africa and African descent within a broader global vision." The third issue made its working-class orientation clear, presenting the bureau's platform, which called for trade union organizing, a minimum wage, an eight-hour day, and an end to racially differentiated pay scales in the colonies. Chris Jones ran a monthly column, "Seamen's Notes," about the experiences of black workers in the shipping industry. Letters from workers in the Caribbean and West Africa appeared regularly in the journal, and it gave particular attention to workers' struggles in West Africa. It also carried pieces from the diaspora, though largely in the Anglophone world. Langston Hughes contributed a poem on the Scottsboro Boys, and the final issue carried an article by Richard B. Moore celebrating Toussaint Louverture's birthday. It also, of course, reported on the IASB's activities, including an anti-imperialist exhibit organized with the ILP on Empire Day in Glasgow. And *Opinion* covered Emile Faure's speech on French colonial policies under the Popular Front government, delivered at the India League's Conference on Peace and Empire in London, which IASB radicals also attended.[61] As a sign of the journal's appeal after only two issues, the Colonial Office placed *Opinion* on its list of periodicals banned from the colonies.[62]

James, Africa, and an Anticolonial Marxism

In his survey of African and West Indian contributions to British colonial scholarship in the 1930s and 1940s, historian Marc Matera notes that the works of many black students and intellectuals in this period foreshadowed and helped "inspire recent theoretical development" in anthropology and history. Matera charts an impressive range of scholarship produced by Africans and Caribbeans that raises critical questions about the production of knowledge, the role of alternative radical presses in social movements, and how the shifting political landscape can affect the reception of such works by later generations.[63] The theoretical reshaping of radical thought that key IASB radicals pursued was part of the production of anticolonial scholarship in this period. One of the more striking aspects of the bureau's intellectual work was its sheer volume. In a span of just four years, a core group of roughly seven members produced nine books, a novel, a play, a score of pamphlets, and three journals and a news bulletin.[64] The most prolific members of this group, James and Padmore, both of whom expended considerable energy advocating West Indian self-government and insisted on the Caribbean's modernity and enlightenment, came to argue that African liberation struggles would pave the way for world revolution. Padmore arrived at this view through his work with black radicals in international communism and his organizing in the ITUCNW. James openly admitted that Padmore "educated me" about the colonial world. Yet, James's efforts to develop a theory of the colonial origins of world revolution had everything to do with his role in the internecine struggles of the 1930s British Left.[65]

Around the time that James left the IAFE, he noticed that Victor Gollancz's Left Book Club had published several books by Communists that were highly favorable toward the Popular Front and Stalin. While James was able to read Trotsky's books in French, he realized that "there were no books in English" by Trotsky, "only pamphlets." After some conversations with other Socialists, he decided to get hold of the British publisher Fredric Warburg. Brockway had introduced James to Warburg as a young intellectual whose work he should publish. Thoroughly impressed with James, Warburg published James's largely unsuccessful novel, *Minty Alley*. James and Warburg agreed that "there was scope for the publication of books that were Marxist but not CP," James recalled. With enough money to allow him to write unfettered, James "went away to Brighton and wrote [*World Revolution*] in three or four months."[66] James later remarked that he had become a Trotskyist after reading Trotsky's *History of the Russian Revolution*, which he picked up "because I was very much interested in history and the book seemed to offer some analysis of modern society."[67] Around this time, "Moscow shifted from the 'revolutionary' policy" of self-determination, Lenin's dictum to "turn imperialist war into civil war," and abandoned proletarian struggle and, most importantly for James, Abyssinia. And at the same time, James was carrying out research for his history of the Haitian revolution and Toussaint Louverture, *The Black Jacobins. World Revolution* thus constituted a detour. Of sorts.

With *World Revolution*, James proposed a survey of "the antecedents, foundation and development of the Third International" and, most important, an analysis of "its collapse as a revolutionary force." With characteristic self-assurance, he claimed that "the ideas on which the book are based are the fundamental ideas of Marxism," which he adroitly summoned to explain "the present crisis in world affairs." James was concerned about the Soviet Union's Popular Front policy and the idea of workers aligning with their national bourgeoisie to defend Russia should Hitler's fascist Germany attack. He was also concerned about the Comintern's abandonment of Abyssinia. In an opening passage, he assailed the Comintern's failed commitment to revolution:

> Yet to-day, with the war long predicted imminent at last, with the great cracks in the imperialist structure widening day by day, with the rapacious Treaty of Versailles and its consequences, the fiasco of disarmament, the imposing assembly and pitiable collapse of the World Economic Conference, all teaching the masses the truth about Capitalism far more ably than the propaganda of the Third International; with the clash of interests over the Abyssinian question stripping to rags the drapery of the League of Nations, and exposing to millions of the most politically backward the hideous lusts and nauseating corruption of what they will be called upon to fight for, at this moment the Third International has refurbished the doctrine of national defence, is ready to fight for tricolour or stars and stripes, and clamours to defend the Union Jack.[68]

The Abyssinia reference can easily slip by as part of a catalog, but Ethiopia haunts James's text. He makes an unprecedented number of references to the African continent in plumbing Comintern history.[69] Toward the end of the penultimate chapter, "The Revolution Abandoned," James returns to Abyssinia:

> Thoughtful revolutionaries . . . realise how the [Third] International, following Stalin, missed the greatest opportunity in years of at best striking a powerful blow against the colonial policy of imperialism, and at worst rallying round itself the vanguard of the working-class movement in preparation for the coming war. Nothing was more certain than that the capitalists would ultimately do a deal at the expense, large or small, of Abyssinia. . . . The International from the first moment could have pointed out that nothing but working-class action could have saved Abyssinia, and . . . driven home nail after nail into the coffin of the League [of Nations].

The Soviet workers could have put an instant embargo on the oil that Russia sent steadily to Italy. . . . The mass feeling . . . aroused all over the world . . . could have checked Mussolini and weakened him at home.

The Third International in good Stalinist fashion had been clamouring for unity of the workers. . . . Now when there seemed a possibility of its realisation. . . . From Moscow came categorical instructions to the Communist delegates under no circumstances to support any kind of action except sanctions by the League of Nations. . . . Socialism in a single country had reached the stage where the leader of the international proletariat was as nervous of the action of the world proletariat as any Fascist dictator.[70]

It was not merely for literary effect or simply a rhetorical gesture that James would locate a major part of Stalin's abandonment of the world proletariat in the Third International's failure to seize on Abyssinia as a conflict demanding proletarian struggle.

A committed Socialist, James saw his work as serving the Fourth International's struggle against Stalinism as much as serving black anticolonial politics, though he undoubtedly would have rejected any hint of distinguishing the two. When told that his old acquaintance, Reginald Reynolds, had complained that James had turned his back "on the problems of his own people . . . to follow the barren cult of Trotskyism," he replied curtly, "It was not narrow confines. *The Black Jacobins* was not conceived within narrow confines, and neither was . . . *The History of Negro Revolt*, which was not limited to a Trotskyist position."[71] Thus, James had been rethinking Marxism precisely through the colonial question. His critique of Stalinism and the Third International hinged on Moscow's failure to recognize the potential for proletarian revolution that Abyssinia represented. Padmore seemed to agree. In his *Africa and World Peace*, also published in 1937 by Warburg, he identified the proletariat's "clear-cut unmistakable duty" as waging "the anti-imperialist fight in the rear of the enemy," not collaborating with a national bourgeoisie. The "fundamental problem of to-day" remained colonialism, Padmore wrote. Socialist struggle constituted anti-imperialist struggle, and the only way to fight fascism was "the Leninist way: 'Turn the imperialist war into civil war.'"[72]

In James's intellectual work, *World Revolution* is of a piece with *The Black Jacobins* and his larger intellectual output of the time, a robust period of intellectual activism. *World Revolution* and *The Black Jacobins* must be placed in the political context of the IASB and radical black internationalism in 1930s

London. This was the moment and milieu in which James and Padmore began to argue that Africa was the launching pad for world revolution.

The Black Jacobins further solidified James's status as a leading intellectual in London. Yet it also marked a shift in the thinking of this British intellectual who had come to Britain a parliamentarian radical committed to Caribbean self-government. In Trinidad, he had grown tired of hearing about Caribbean backwardness and inferiority, and decided he would "write a book which showed the West Indians as something else." But by the time he started to write *The Black Jacobins*, he had "reached the conclusion that the center of the Black revolution was Africa, not the Caribbean."[73] Allusions to this realization suffuse the text, particularly in the final two pages of the 1938 edition. "The imperialists envisage an eternity of African exploitation: the African is backward, ignorant. . . . They dream dreams," James wrote. Like the French rulers who would have scoffed at the idea of St. Domingue slaves emancipating themselves, white British colonial officials would never accept that among their black colonial subjects "are men so infinitely their superior in ability, energy, range of vision, and tenacity . . . that in a hundred years' time these whites would be remembered only because of their contact with the blacks." But "the blacks of Africa," James warned, "are more advanced, nearer ready than were the slaves of San Domingo."[74]

In his preface to *The Black Jacobins*, James notes without any regret that his book was written "with something of the fever and the fret" of its time, a "history of a revolution and written under different circumstances it would have been a different but not necessarily a better book."[75] Indeed, the "fever and fret" of the time had helped James abandon any notion of backward African peoples. Thus, it fit within what political theorist Anthony Bogues identifies as "radical political interventionist historical texts" that stand as "works of *historical and political theory.*" James's insistence on slavery as a modern capitalist institution and his casting the Saint Domingue slaves as the most modern proletariat of the late eighteenth century highlighted how slave rebellion undercut a major pillar of modern European empire and cut against the grain of conventional Marxist theory.[76] Still, given the uprisings that raged across the West Indies as he wrote, it is puzzling that he did not make "connections between the political present and the historical past" about which he was writing.[77]

In a series of lectures on the writing of *The Black Jacobins* that James delivered in 1971 to the Institute of the Black World, he offered something of an explanation. In London, James recalled, he first read Marx, as the circumstances required that "I thoroughly master . . . Marxism" to write *World Revolution*. "At the same time," he was also "meeting a lot of black people and African people in London," and they impressed him immensely. "I began to see these Africans around me," he recalled, and he became good friends with Louis Mbanefo. *Black Jacobins* thus was no accident: "It didn't just fall from a tree." "I had in mind writing about the San Domingo Revolution as the preparation for the revolution that George Padmore and all of us were interested in, that is, the revolution in Africa."[78]

The Black Jacobins marked not only a critical political shift by James but also a racial one, though the latter is rarely noted. While he and Padmore worked to reshape Marxism and to outline what one might call an African Marxism, and while Marxism was reshaping how James viewed history, London's diasporic community was the "seething . . . African pot" in which James thought out class struggle, world revolution, and the importance of Africa to each. But James also thought beyond class and race to point out the coloniality of knowledge dominating the Caribbean. His shift in concern to Africa was thus apparent in what he saw as Toussaint Louverture's failures in Haiti. If Toussaint's successor, Dessalines, "could see so clearly and simply" the path to full emancipation where Toussaint could not, "it was because the ties that bound this uneducated soldier to French civilisation were of the slenderest." But for Toussaint, whom James situated within the train of European Enlightenment thought, his "failure was the failure of enlightenment, not of darkness." Similarly, the failing of the Caribbean was its modernity. Caribbeans "were and had always been Western-educated," he noted in the 1963 appendix to *The Black Jacobins*, and consequently were confined "to a very narrow strip of social territory. The first step to freedom was to go abroad." The second, far more complex step involved getting "clear from [their] minds the stigma that anything African was inherently inferior and degraded. The road to West Indian national identity lay through Africa."[79]

In insisting on the indispensability of racial consciousness to colonial liberation in the Caribbean, James was not making a nationalist argument, nor had he made a claim to any biological or primordial unity between Africans and peoples of African descent. Rather, his view of the indispensability of racial consciousness to colonial liberation reflected his abiding belief in the decisive role that Africa would play in the coming global upheavals, which also involved class struggle, the nature of capital, and its historically specific racial structures. Further, the revolutionary possibilities of black self-activity were to be found not in doctors or lawyers or intellectuals but in "the quiet recruits in a black police force, the sergeant in the French native army or British police . . . reading a stray pamphlet of Lenin or Trotsky as Toussaint read the Abbé Raynal." Hence, James opposed the vanguard party, the idea that any group in the African diaspora was better suited to lead and uplift all other sections, and the notion that Marxists in a party or intellectuals on a pedestal could presume to know the course of history before the people had made it.

IN OCTOBER 1938, JAMES left England for a speaking tour through the United States, after which he made his way to Mexico, where he and Leon Trotsky famously discussed black liberation and self-determination. His departure from England marked both an ending and a beginning. Though James could not have known it when he left London, he would not return for nearly two decades. Nonetheless, his political and intellectual work with Ashwood in the IAFE and then with Padmore in the IASB had transformed him in ways that he could never have imagined and in ways that those who continue to examine James have only now begun to fully appreciate.

Despite what many people considered his unrivaled brilliance and talent, James had become a nuisance to British Socialists. Faced with a West Indian Negro of superior intellect, energy, and range of vision, those with whom he continued to work in the Trotsky Defense Group may have been annoyed to toil in his shadow.[80] Exceedingly self-assured, James certainly demonstrated his superiority. Tall and handsome, his "soft lilting English . . . was a delight to hear," and he could beguile socialists and socialites alike with his intellect, endless knowledge of English literature and Greek mythology, and mastery of Marxism and Western philosophy. Though he had helped establish the Fourth International, now even the Trotskyists wanted him out—or at least straightened out.[81]

After reaching New York, James found himself at the center of many literary and political discussions. *The Black Jacobins* had been read widely, and he was invited to lecture in Harlem, Detroit, Chicago, and Los Angeles on a range of topics, including German fascism, the future of racial minorities, and West Indian labor struggles. He even debated British philosopher Bertrand Russell on "democracy" at the University of Chicago and sought to stage his play, *Toussaint L'Ouverture*, in New York. James often asserted that "fascist conditions exist over large parts of Africa" within the British empire and boldly though rather wrongly predicted that "the world order is going to tumble to an end in the next five years." He implored black people to stay focused on their "emancipation and independence" and to use any opening to take it.[82]

If the IASB constituted the organization of black men that William Patterson, James Ford, and Garan Kouyaté had once believed essential to anticolonial struggle, James and Padmore sought to expand its goals. As his speaking tour drew down, right before he was to meet Trotsky in Mexico City, James outlined a political program that, as one scholar notes, separated James "from most Western educated socialist and communist thinkers in the 1930s and 1940s." Proposing the IASB as a mandate for a new group, the focus of this global organization would be "full economic, political, and social rights for all Negroes," national independence for African and Caribbean colonies, opposition to imperialist war, and the organization of black workers and peasants for their own liberation. This new group would also organize an interracial solidarity movement for peace.[83]

After meeting Trotsky and before returning to London, James met Rya Dunayevskaya, Trotsky's secretary, who convinced James to remain in the United States. Over the ensuing fifteen years, he engaged in some of the most important theorizing of class and Marxism in the mid–twentieth century. While working with Dunayevskaya, who assumed the nom de guerre Freddy Forest (James went by J. R. Johnson), they founded the Johnson-Forest Tendency. As a result, James met a young Chinese American philosopher, Grace Lee, who had recently left graduate school and read German. Together, they translated the classics of European radical thought from Russian, French, and German into English.[84]

In 1945, Dunayevskaya arranged for James to meet a young African student, Kwame Nkrumah, who had recently graduated from Lincoln University and was preparing to leave for London. James was immediately impressed with Nkrumah's intellect and political commitment, though Nkrumah did not know much about political struggle and revolution. James wrote a letter of introduction to Padmore, still in London, asking him to work with Nkrumah, whom James, possibly in his singular most unfortunate choice of words, described as not too bright. James later insisted that he was not calling Nkrumah unintelligent—and was impressed that Nkrumah wanted to throw the Europeans out of Africa—but that he knew little of organizing. "George understood at once," James recalled. Padmore, likely realizing that Nkrumah's was a unique mind, took this future architect of Ghanaian independence under his wing, and gave him a tattered copy of *The Black Jacobins*.[85]

Epilogue

A Vitality and Validity of Its Own

In 1958, seventy-year-old Cyril Briggs sat before the U.S. House Un-American Activities Committee (HUAC), under subpoena to answer questions about his Communist activities. Like numerous others hauled before HUAC, Briggs refused the role assigned him in what amounted to little more than a congressional show trial. Rather than play the hapless Negro seduced by a foreign ideology that he could neither fully comprehend nor resist, or cower before HUAC as so many others had, Briggs expressed his outrage at "being interrogated by a committee whose members include out-and-out white supremacists and . . . that during its 20 years has never once investigated the Ku Klux Klan." When committee chair Francis Walter accused Briggs of using a communist ploy to avoid answering questions, the defiant Briggs shot back, "I don't know what Communists or communism have to do with my position, because this has been my position since 1912 before there was, as I understand it, a Communist Party in the United States. It will continue to be my position despite any attempt by this committee to intimidate me."[1]

Briggs's retort captures a fundamental fact about black radicalism: It emerged prior to and outside of organized communism. Though black radicalism and organized Marxism converged, thereby enabling a mutual exchange, Briggs hints at the limits of that encounter, the incongruities that plagued its history and frustrated black radicals who sought to make organized Marxism address black people's concerns. Briggs explored this point more fully a few years later in a letter to Harry Haywood, lamenting that black radicals might contribute to black liberation only if they organized "an independent Negro Left which . . . can function without [the Communist Party's] restraints."[2] Black Communists commonly felt that their participation in black struggles had been hindered by the white Left. Briggs believed that the African Blood Brotherhood could have been that independent black Left had it been "better organized, had a truly mass base." Under that scenario, "things would have been different" for the high tide of black struggle in the 1960s, he thought.[3]

The Martinican radical Aimé Césaire felt the PCF's restraints when he resigned from the party over its subordination of anticolonial and antiracist struggles to working-class struggles. In his famous *Lettre à Maurice Thorez*, he criticized the PCF's paternalist approach to "backward" colonial peoples. The French party failed to recognize the historical particularities of African and Asian struggles, which could not be subordinated to the struggles of the French working class, he argued. In the most quoted line from his letter, Césaire expressed his desire that "Marxism and Communism be harnessed into the service of colored people, and not colored people into the service of Marxism and Communism." Most people writing about Césaire's letter use this passage to argue that his resignation signaled his rejection of Marxism. But he also wrote that it was "neither Marxism nor Communism I repudiate. . . . [T]he use certain people have made of Marxism and Communism is what I condemn." Césaire insisted on a Marxism that was neither pure theory nor a static series of precepts and claims to which people and movements must conform. Instead, he conceived of a dynamic theory that could be bent and reshaped to address unique historical circumstances, giving as one example Chinese communism, which had led him to envision an African communism that would move beyond the limitations of the European modes of organized Marxism.[4]

Perhaps the best argument for the importance of independent black struggle came from C. L. R. James. Speaking to the Socialist Workers Party's 1948 national convention, James delivered "The Revolutionary Answer to the Negro Problem in the United States," which in part announced a turn for his Johnson-Forest Tendency in theorizing race and class. In that resolution, he expressed apprehension with Trotsky's belief that a proletarian vanguard would have to lead the black freedom movement if that movement were to move beyond its presumed episodic character. In an elegant challenge to historicist Marxist logic that would subordinate race and black people to class and white workers, James declared,

The Negro struggle, the independent Negro struggle, has a vitality and a validity of its own; . . . it has deep historic roots in the past of America and in present struggles; it has an organic political perspective, along which it is traveling, to one degree or another.

This independent Negro movement is able to intervene with terrific force upon the general social and political life of the nation, despite the fact that it is waged under the banner of democratic rights, and is not led necessarily either by the organized labor movement or the Marxist party. . . . It is able to exercise a powerful influence upon the revolutionary proletariat, . . . it has got a great contribution to make to the development of the proletariat in the United States, and . . . it is in itself a constituent part of the struggle for socialism. In this way we challenge directly any attempt to subordinate or to push to the rear the social and political significance of the independent Negro struggle for democratic rights.[5]

James's presentation of "Negro struggle" as constitutive of socialist revolution broke with the leftist conceit of class struggle. As Bogues observes, it "opened up a new terrain for Marxist analysis," transforming it into "an analytical tool and a theory of revolutionary praxis" rather than a dogma to which social movements must conform.[6] Over this question, James and Johnson-Forest ultimately left the Trotskyist movement, moving on to engage in some of the most original theorizing in twentieth-century Marxism. James placed race on equal theoretical footing with class, even suggesting that black struggles would outstrip proletarian struggle as *the* animating or motive force of socialist revolution in the United States.[7]

Briggs, James, and Césaire viewed black struggles on a global scale, weighing specific movements in terms of their implications for struggles against racial oppression and colonialism worldwide. Though they found Marxism's focus on class struggle invaluable in theorizing race and diasporic liberation, they never accepted the doctrinaire view that the answers to all social questions lay in the collected volumes of Marx, Engels, and Lenin. Césaire imagined an African communism that might "shade or complete a good many of [Marxism's] points," an idea James and George Padmore pursued, if fleetingly. Implicit in the works of Briggs and especially Césaire and James was a challenge to the scientific pretensions of Marxism. All three men traded in the language of dialectics, none more so than James, and their challenge was not so much a critique of Marxism as a response to the effects of scientific claims elaborated within organized Marxism. As Michel Foucault observed of the

PCF's response to his work, there was (and remains to this day) a habit among Communists of "excluding from Marxist discourse everything that wasn't a frightened repetition of the already said," thereby prohibiting "the broaching of uncharted domains."[8] In the 1920s, organized Marxism showed great openness to exploring its intellectual frontiers, though it also resisted pushing too hard at the borders of what it deemed accepted "science." By the 1930s under Stalin, the avenues of exploration narrowed until they were blocked, leaving black radicals little choice but to abandon communist organizations to pursue a heretical practice. The central goals in their engagement and dialogue with organized communism were shading or completing Marxism's points, wading into the uncharted theoretical waters of race, nation, and culture, and calling into question the assumption of an infallible, objective truth.

Radicals from the ABB and the IASB extended Marxist theory to discuss Africa, Asia, colonialism, racial oppression, and fascism. In the process, they challenged the inadequacies of organized Marxist formations with regard to these questions. The activists examined in this volume refused to limit themselves to a given field, building networks and institutions in a process whereby "numerous features of Marxian analysis" were "radically revised and reformed," as the literary scholar Bill Mullen writes, so that "colored people themselves" would "supplant the international (i.e., European) working class" as the main agent of liberation.[9]

Dancing Flames

George Padmore dissolved the IASB in 1944 and then led the formation of the Pan-African Federation. Along with Peter Milliard as president and T. Ras Makonnen as general secretary, the founders included representatives from various organizations in Britain as well as Jomo Kenyatta of the Kikuyu Central Association and I. T. A. Wallace-Johnson of the West African Youth League. The following year, federation members and representatives from various organizations came to Manchester to establish a united-front movement. Following the February 1945 World Trade Union Conference in London, it had been clear that the kind of undertaking Padmore and other black radicals sought was at hand. Many of the figures who had been involved in either the ITUCNW or the IASB were present in London. Padmore had corresponded with W. E. B. Du Bois about participating in a Pan-African Conference, and when Padmore heard of the meeting in London, he invited representatives to meet with the Pan-African Federation in Manchester for a fifth PAC.[10]

That congress convened on October 15–19, 1945, representing the culmination of nearly three decades of radical political struggle and the initiation of several more decades of anticolonial struggle. The congress drew many familiar figures. Participants sought to plot a course for African liberation. Learning from the lessons of the past, the congress did not single out a specific group in the diaspora to lead pan-African struggles, nor did it draft an ambitious document that sought to capture the breadth of black political struggles. Through speeches, proposals, and resolutions, Amy Ashwood Garvey, Wallace-Johnson, Padmore, Kwame Nkrumah, Peter Abrams, Kenyatta, Makonnen, and Du Bois, among others, drafted eleven pages of resolutions on a host of issues and nodes of diasporic struggle, including different regions of Africa, British protectorates, the Caribbean, Ethiopia, Liberia, and black maritime workers. As historian Hakim Adi notes, "The Pan-Africanism of Padmore and Manchester culminated . . . in the advent to power of Nkrumah and the whole process of decolonization."[11]

The small group of largely Caribbean radicals in Harlem who formed the ABB and sought a path to African liberation were not responsible for Padmore, the IASB, or the 1945 PAC. Yet within the pantheon of international communist thinking about the Negro, their location in the United States rendered them the vanguard, a title that came with some discomfort. Still, their constant efforts to have international communism address race and anticolonial liberation, to situate Africa and Asia at the center of proletarian struggle, and to help build a world Negro movement created the context in which a dynamic personality such as Padmore could go to Hamburg and build the network that would usher in the Manchester Congress. But Adi makes a point about the limitations of the PAC that bears directly on the story told here: the possible tragedy of the postcolonial project. With decolonization, Adi points out, Frantz Fanon, Amílcar Cabral, and many others had "to develop new theoretical weapons and new forms of struggle in order to advance the cause of liberation in the African continent."[12]

In his introduction to Césaire's *Discourse on Colonialism*, historian Robin D. G. Kelley offers an appropriately surreal description of the text: "It is not a solution or a strategy or a manual. . . . It is a dancing flame in a bonfire."[13] The metaphor is compelling for the image it evokes: a chorus of flames licking the night sky, engulfing the detritus of colonialism, national and racial oppression; celebrating masses liberating themselves with what each flame illuminates in the shadows. Kelley locates Césaire in the same tradition as W. E. B. Du Bois and M. N. Roy, radicals who pursued a revision of Marxism. However, Kelley notes an incongruity in the closing paragraph of *Discourse on Colonialism*, where Césaire declares that "the salvation of Europe is not a matter of a revolution in methods." Rather, he saw it as a revolution that "until such time as there is a classless society, will substitute for the narrow tyranny of a dehumanized bourgeoisie the preponderance of the only class that still has a universal mission, because it suffers in its flesh from all the wrongs of history, from all the universal wrongs: the proletariat."[14] Kelley does not find it incongruous that Césaire, a Communist, would close by citing proletarian revolution as a savior; rather, the incongruity lies in Césaire's proposal of proletarian revolution as the final solution to a dying European civilization.[15]

I like to read Césaire differently, not to deny this incongruity but to take as part of his revision of Marxism a rethinking of the proletariat. Césaire does not so much return to European workers as the historical agents of socialist revolution as conceptualize the proletariat in much the same way that C. L. R. James, M. N. Roy, Hubert Harrison, Cyril Briggs, Nguyen Ai Quoc, and Claude McKay had earlier: no longer as simply European workers but as those engaged in anticolonial and antiracist struggles in the global South. By seeing these activist-intellectuals (and others, including Claudia Jones, Lorraine Hansberry, Frantz Fanon, Amílcar Cabral, and Angela Davis) as flames in that bonfire, it is possible to reconnect them to a longer history of black radical internationalism, an intercolonial project that viewed Marxism as a dynamic political theory capable of ushering in a future classless society. One can then begin to see that black and Asian radical traditions were not incompatible with Marxism, even if black and Asian radicals have often found organized communism a much different question. Rather than rehabilitate Marxism, however, I have approached this story by taking seriously the need for a new theoretical apparatus for the future. The task to which black radicals set themselves in imagining a path toward a liberated future took as its limit a society without racial oppression, colonialism, and capitalism. If that project—the problems black radicals took up, the questions they asked, and ultimately the answers they gave—focused more on the terms of analysis that would guide revolutionary movements and less on the futures such movements would usher into existence, the purchase in continuing to plumb this history is not merely to recoup a lost or obscured past. The historical value in such work is what it might reveal about the black radical imagination, the processes of rethinking and reshaping radical politics and conceptualizing revolution in a way that might possibly offer insight into, and thus aid in cultivating, the theoretical tools and structures of feeling with which one might imagine a reality beyond the boundaries of our liberal democratic present.

Notes

ABBREVIATIONS

AN	*Amsterdam News*
BAA	*Baltimore Afro-American*
bp	back page
CB	Cyril Briggs
CD	*Chicago Defender*
DW	*Daily Worker*
FSAA	Theodore Kornweibel Jr., ed. *Federal Surveillance of Afro-Americans (1917–1925): The First World War, the Red Scare, and the Garvey Movement*. Frederick, Md.: University Publications of America, 1986.
Garvey/UNIA	Robert Hill, ed. *The Marcus Garvey and Universal Negro Improvement Association Papers*. Berkeley: University of California Press, 1983.
GP	George Padmore
JWJ	James Weldon Johnson
KM	Kelly Miller
LAI Archives	League against Imperialism Archives, International Institute of Social History, Amsterdam
MARBL	Manuscript, Archives, and Rare Books Library, Emory University, Atlanta, Ga.
MG	Marcus Garvey
MSRK	Mark Solomon/Robert Kaufman Collection, Tamiment Institute, New York University, New York, N. Y.
NAACP Coll.	National Association for the Advancement of Colored People Manuscript Collection, Library of Congress, Manuscript Division, Washington, D.C.
NARA	United States National Archives and Records Administration, College Park, Md.
NW	*Negro Worker*
OCJ	Oakley C. Johnson
PRO	Public Records Office
RG	Record Group
RGASPI	Russian State Archive of Sociopolitical History, Moscow, Russia (followed by locator information: *fond* [collection]/*opis* [index]/*delo* [file]/*listok* [page])
SCRBC	Schomburg Center for Research in Black Culture, Manuscript,

Archives, and Rare Books Division, New York Public Library, New York, N. Y.

TD   Theodore Draper

TDC   Theodore Draper Collection, Stanford University, Hoover Institute on War, Revolution, and Peace, Stanford, Calif.

TNA   The National Archives of the UK, Kew, Surrey, England

INTRODUCTION

1. This account of Patterson comes from William L. Patterson, *Man Who Cried Genocide*, 44–49, 81, 92–93, 109–11; Hatch, "Interview," 152–69. Patterson mistakenly gives "Robert" Lansbury for George Lansbury.

2. Patterson, *Man Who Cried Genocide*, 81, 92–93.

3. Ibid., 109–11.

4. CB, "The Problem of Asia; or, Getting the Boot," *Crusader*, January 1920, 14.

5. I use "organized Marxism" for a range of communist and socialist formations that considered themselves Marxist. "Organized Left" more broadly includes formations that pushed a leftist politics but were not Marxists (e.g., labor unions and anarchists).

6. Adi, "Negro Question," 155.

7. Winston James, *Holding Aloft*, 180.

8. Much of the anticommunist historiography insists on the centrality of Kremlin intrigue and thus sees the Comintern as giving black radicals their radicalism. This view portrays black radicals as naive dupes or, worse still, as duplicitous in the moral outrages of Stalinism. For works along these lines, see Draper, *Roots*; Draper, *American Communism*; Record, *Negro and the Communist Party*; Record, *Race and Radicalism*; Glazer, *Social Basis*; Shannon, *Decline*; Klehr, *Heyday*; Klehr and Tompson, "Self-Determination"; Klehr and Haynes, *American Communist Movement*; Klehr, Haynes, and Firsov, *Secret World*; Klehr, Haynes, and Anderson, *Soviet World*; Haynes and Klehr, *Venona*; Arnesen, "No 'Graver Danger.'"

Social historians of the Left have given far more attention to the actual workings of American communism—that is, how local party branches responded to directives from Russia in light of the realities on the ground. As these works convincingly show, Comintern directives and American party activities never had a simple relationship, and the lure of Moscow gold never led these radicals to abandon their principles. For works that touch on black radicals with an eye to debating Cold War historians, see Phillip Foner, *American Socialism*; Phillip Foner, *Organized Labor*; Phillip Foner and Allen, *American Communism*; Carr, "Origins"; Naison, *Communists in Harlem*; Buhle, *Marxism in the United States*; Isserman, *Which Side?*; Isserman, *If I Had a Hammer*; Mullen, *Popular Fronts*; Horne, "Red and The Black"; Horne, *Black Liberation/Red Scare*; Susan Campbell, "'Black Bolsheviks'"; Skotnes, "Communist Party"; Maxwell, *New Negro*; Solomon, *Cry Was Unity*; Foley, *Radical Representations*; Foley, *Spectres*; Berland, "Emergence, Part I and II."

9. For a growing body of work that takes up similar concerns, see Wu, "African-Vietnamese American"; Onishi, "New Negro"; Mullen, *Afro-Orientalism*; Maeda, "Black Panthers, Red Guards."

10. This extends a point made by Patterson and Kelley that at times black interna-

tionalism "lives through or is integrally tied to other kinds of international movements." See Patterson and Kelley, "Unfinished Migrations," 27.

11. Matera, "Colonial Subjects"; Carrington, "Improbable Grounds"; Padmore, *How Britain Rules*, 8.

12. West and Martin, "Contours of the Black International," 16; Johns, *Raising the Red Flag*; Green, *Grass-Roots Socialism*; Kornweibel, *No Crystal Stair*; Edward Thomas Wilson, *Russia and Black Africa*; Hudson, *Narrative*; Kelley, *Hammer and Hoe*; Kelley, "Third International"; Moore, *Richard B. Moore*; Turner, *Caribbean Crusaders*; Sally Miller, "Socialist Party"; Henderson, "A. Philip Randolph"; Sherwood, "Comintern"; Kate A. Baldwin, *Beyond the Color Line*; Mullen, *Afro-Orientalism*; Biondi, *To Stand and Fight*; Korstad, *Civil Rights Unionism*; Smethurst, *The Black Arts Movement*; Davies, *Left of Karl Marx*; Gilmore, *Defying Dixie*; Matthew J. Smith, *Red and Black*; Pennybacker, *From Scottsboro to Munich*; McDuffie, *Sojourning*; Adi, "Pan-Africanism"; Adi, "Negro Question."

13. Kelley, *Race Rebels*, 124.

14. To my knowledge, the only scholarly treatments of James in 1930s London that broach his involvement in British Trotskyism remain Upham, "History of British Trotskyism"; Kelley, "World the Diaspora Made"; Archer, "C. L. R. James"; Alexander, *International Trotskyism*; Rosengarten, *Urbane Revolutionary*, 46–53.

15. Mignolo, "Delinking," 483. See also Mignolo, *Local Histories/Global Designs*. For a suggestive discussion of the colonial matrix of power in Marxist thought that effaces the centrality of race, slavery, and colonialism to capitalist development, see Buck-Morss, *Hegel, Haiti, and Universal History*, 56–59.

16. Padmore, *Pan-Africanism or Communism?*, 18–19. However, Padmore also criticized C. L. R. James for what Padmore considered an overly harsh and politically unnecessary (even dangerous) anticommunist attack that James launched in the concluding chapter of his *Mariners, Renegades, and Castaways*.

17. Hooker, *Black Revolutionary*; Schwarz, "George Padmore," 135–36. Hooker has given more attention to Padmore's period as a Communist than have most other scholars, but his suggestion of two distinct Padmores still influences how others have thought about Padmore. See also Thompson, "George Padmore"; Rupert Lewis, "George Padmore." For works departing from this view, see Teelucksingh, "Immortal Batsman"; Rodney Worrell, "George Padmore"; Bogues, "C. L. R. James."

18. Scott, *Conscripts*, 3–4; Scott, *Refashioning Futures*, 8.

19. To my mind, this was Kelley's intent with *Freedom Dreams*.

20. Trouillot, *Silencing the Past*, 26.

21. Ibid., 49.

22. For a representative range of such works, see Woodard, *A Nation within a Nation*; Edwards, *Practice of Diaspora*; Nikhil Pal Singh, *Black Is a Country*; Ransby, *Ella Baker*; Mullen, *Afro-Orientalism*; Stephens, *Black Empire*; Biondi, *To Stand and Fight*; Johnson, *Revolutionaries to Race Leaders*; Widener, *Black Arts West*; Gaines, *American Africans*; Rod Bush, *End of White World Supremacy*; Edwards, "Dossier"; Andrew F. Jones and Singh, "Afro-Asian Century."

23. Trouillot, *Silencing the Past*, 27. On archives structuring historical knowledge, see Burton, *Dwelling in the Archives*; Stoler, *Along the Archival Grain*. I also draw on

Foucault's discussion of the archive as a "system of statements" governing what can be said and what lies beyond "the system of its enunciability" to consider how discussions of black radicalism remain confined by a black Marxist archive. See Foucault, *Archeology of Knowledge*, 128–29.

24. Césaire, *Letter to Maurice Thorez*, 12–13.

25. Bogues, *Black Heretics*, 13.

26. Cedric Robinson, *Black Marxism*, 73.

27. Ibid., 2, 66, 72–73, 168, 175, 309, 316.

28. Cox, *Capitalism as a System*; Cedric Robinson, *Black Marxism*, 110; Cedric Robinson, "Oliver Cromwell Cox."

29. Cedric Robinson, *Black Marxism*, 66–68. Robinson never pinpoints the origins of Western civilization, and he never identifies the presence of racialism in what scholars generally consider its origins. It is thus unclear how Marxism emerged during Western civilization's "ascendancy."

30. Ibid., 2.

31. Ibid., 170.

32. One impressive display of Robinson's impression on a younger generation of scholars could be seen in an October 24, 1998, conference, Afric's Sons and Daughters with Banners Red: The History of the Black Left, organized by Erik McDuffie at Temple University.

33. Cedric Robinson, *Black Marxism*, 175–76.

34. Ibid., 68. See Cabral, *Unity and Struggle*; Chilcote, *Amílcar Cabral's Revolutionary Theory*; Masilela, "Pan-Africanism"; Nkrumah, *Consciencism*; Babu, *African Socialism or Socialist Africa?*; Davies, *Left of Karl Marx*; McDuffie, *Sojourning*.

35. Malik, "Mirror of Race," 114; Hesse, "Racialized Modernity."

36. Fanon, *Wretched of the Earth*, 40. Fanon called for a new theorizing of Marxism's terms of analysis: "The originality of the colonial context is that economic reality, inequality, and the immense difference of ways of life never come to mask the human realities. When you examine at close quarters the colonial context, it is evident that what parcels out the world is to begin with the fact of belonging to or not belonging to a given race, a given species. In the colonies, the economic substructure is also a superstructure. The cause is the consequence; you are rich because you are white, you are white because you are rich. This is why Marxist analysis should always be slightly stretched every time we have to do with the colonial problem" (ibid.). For an insightful discussion of African intellectuals "stretching" Marxism, see Masilela, "Pan-Africanism." On the Eurocentric diffusionist strain of Marxism, see Blaut, *National Question*.

37. C. L. R. James, *Black Jacobins*; C. L. R. James, *History*.

38. Moore, "Afro-Americans," 215.

39. Trotter, *Black Milwaukee*; Kelley, *Hammer and Hoe*; Green, *Grass-Roots Socialism*; Adi, *West Africans*; Johns, *Raising the Red Flag*; Hudson, *Narrative*; Phillips, *AlabamaNorth*; Cecelski, "Abraham H. Galloway"; Woodruff, "New Negro in the American Congo"; Winston James, "Being Red and Black"; Aitken, "From Cameroon to Germany."

40. Edwards, *Practice of Diaspora*, 5.

41. Brown, *Dropping Anchor*, 6.

42. Winston James, *Holding Aloft*, 54–63.

43. For an argument that Caribbean radicals envisioned a singular global blackness routed through empire, see Stephens, *Black Empire*.

44. For an excellent discussion of Liberia and arguments to recover the race's manhood through U.S. imperialism in the Philippines, see Mitchell, *Righteous Propagation*, 57–65.

45. For other examinations of intradiasporic conflict around gender and sexuality, see Neptune, *Caliban and the Yankees*; Brown, *Dropping Anchor*.

46. Dirlik, *Postmodernity's Histories*.

47. Spiegler, "Aspects," 113–24.

48. Radhakrishnan, *Diasporic Mediations*, 136.

CHAPTER 1

1. Moore, "Afro-Americans," 216.

2. Phillip Foner, *American Socialism*, 59; Winston James, "Being Red and Black," 338–49; Eugene V. Debs, "The Negro in the Class Struggle," *International Socialist Review*, November 1903, 260. In 1877, Clark joined the Workingmen's Party of the United States, which became the Socialist Labor Party a year later. He left the party in 1879.

3. Watkins-Owens, *Blood Relations*, 2, 6, 40–41, 56–74; Kasinitz, *Caribbean New York*; Nancy Foner, "West Indian Identity"; Robert Hill, "Racial and Radical," vii–ix; Ueda, "West Indians," 1022; Osofsky, *Harlem*, 3, 128–35.

4. Langston Hughes, "My Early Days," 64. I thank Frank Guridy for reminding me of this passage.

5. McKay, *Long Way from Home*, 95–96.

6. Osofsky, *Harlem*, 219–20; Hellwig, "Black Meets Black"; Keith S. Henry, "Black Political Tradition," 455–58; Watkins-Owens, *Blood Relations*, 45–53; Ueda, "West Indians."

7. Winston James, *Holding Aloft*, 2–4, 45–63.

8. Ula Taylor, *Veiled Garvey*, 39.

9. Here, I draw on the work of counseling psychologists. See, for example, Cross, *Shades of Black*; Cross, Parham, and Helms, "Stages"; Vandiver et al., "Validating"; Worrell, Cross, and Vandiver, "Nigrescence Theory."

10. C. L. R. James, *Beyond a Boundary*, 50–57; Farred, "Maple Man," 95–97.

11. C. L. R. James, *Beyond a Boundary*, 51–52. See also Neptune, *Caliban and the Yankees*, 27–35; Nielsen, *C. L. R. James*, 3–17.

12. For work on race in the West Indies that points to the differing racialized experiences of coloreds and blacks, see Horowitz, "Color Differentiation," 509–10, 531–33; Theodore Allen, *Invention*, 12–13; Nancy Foner, "Free People of Color," 406–30.

13. C. L. R. James, *Beyond a Boundary*, 49.

14. Hermes (Hermina) Huiswoud, "Biography of Otto Huiswoud," box 2, folder 8, MSRK; Turner, *Caribbean Crusaders*, 11–22.

15. Turner, *Caribbean Crusaders*, 13.

16. Ibid., 14.

17. Turner, "Richard B. Moore and His Works," 19–27.

18. CB, "Angry Blond Negro," autobiographical notes in MG Papers, University of California at Los Angeles. I thank Robert A. Hill for providing me with a photocopy of this document. This stanza generally no longer appears in published versions of "All Things Bright and Beautiful."

19. "Cyril V. Briggs," appendix 1, in *Garvey/UNIA*, 1:521–22.

20. CB to OCJ, April 18, 1962, box 8, folder 18, OCJ Papers, SCRBC; Robert Hill, "Racial and Radical," viii; Frank Smith, *Robert G. Ingersoll*.

21. This pattern was not as straightforward in New Orleans; Charleston, South Carolina; Savannah, Georgia; and parts of Mississippi. See Henry Taylor, "Spatial Organization"; Theodore Hershberg and Henry Williams, "Mulattos and Blacks," 423; Shirley Thompson, *Exiles at Home*.

22. T. Thomas Fortune, "Who Are We?: Afro-Americans, Colored People, or Negroes?," *Voice of the Negro*, March 1906, 194–98; Stuckey, *Slave Culture*, 193–244.

23. W. A. Domingo, "What Are We, Negroes or Colored People?," *Messenger*, May–June 1919, 23–25.

24. "Negro First," *Crusader*, October 1919, 9; "The African Blood Brotherhood," *Crusader*, June 1920, 7, 22.

25. Perry, *Hubert Harrison*, 3–6, 114–36, 151–57; Samuels, *Five Afro-Caribbean Voices*.

26. Watkins-Owens, *Blood Relations*, 92–93; Keith S. Henry, "Black Political Tradition," 461.

27. Phillip Foner, *American Socialism*, 216–17; Randolph and Domingo quoted in Samuels, *Five Afro-Caribbean Voices*, 130–31; "Enlightening Wall Street," *New York Times*, September 14, 1912, 16.

28. Perry, *Hubert Harrison*, 159; I. M. Robbins, "The Economic Aspects of the Negro Problem, The Solution: A Prophecy and a Remedy," *International Socialist Review*, May 1910, 1013; I. M. Robbins, "The Economic Aspects of the Negro Problem, The Solution: A Prophecy and a Remedy," *International Socialist Review*, June 1910, 1000–1117. Rubinow's *International Socialist Review* articles on "The Economic Aspects of the Negro Problem," appeared between February 1908 and June 1910 and examined topics such as slavery (February 1908, 480–88; March 1908, 548–54; April 1908, 614–21; May 1908, 691–700), the Civil War and Reconstruction (June 1908, 765–77), white supremacy (September 1908, 161–71; October 1908, 282–92), lynching (January 1909, 499–510), and black progress (September 1909, 253–65; December 1909, 527–41). I thank Robin Kelley for bringing Rubinow to my attention. See also Paul Buhle and Kelley, "Allies of a Different Sort."

29. Harrison, *Negro and the Nation*, 40. In 1917, Harrison reprinted his *New York Call* and *International Socialist Review* articles in this pamphlet.

30. Harrison, *Negro and the Nation*, 24, 28.

31. Perry, *Hubert Harrison*, 209–21.

32. Perry, *Hubert Harrison*, 226–34, 272, 314–20. Claude McKay, who entered Harlem's black radical circles in 1921, refers to Harrison's *The Negro and the Nation*

in the introduction to his 1923 Russian-language book *Negry v Amerike* (*The Negroes in America*), suggesting it continued circulating at least until that time. He likely received a copy when he joined the ABB in 1921.

33. Robert Hill, "Racial and Radical," ix.

34. Ibid., x.

35. "Does This Indict You?," *Colored American Review*, October 1, 1915, 1–2, 15; "Editorial Confidences," *Colored American Review*, October 15, 1915, n.p.

36. "Why We Should Discriminate for a Living," *Colored American Review*, October 15, 1915, 1, 2. "Don't Buy Where You Can't Work" campaigns sprang up in black communities everywhere in the 1930s, organized and led largely by black women focused on consumption, jobs, and at times radical politics. See Phillips, *AlabamaNorth*, 190–225; Crowder, "'Don't Buy'"; Greenberg, *"Or Does It Explode?,"* 114–39; Skotnes, "'Buy Where You Can Work,'" 735–61; Naison, *Communists in Harlem*, 50–51; Bates, *Pullman Porters*, 112–13; Davarian Baldwin, *Chicago's New Negroes*, 234–42.

37. Hubert H. Harrison to Editor, October 4, 1915, *Colored American Review*, October 15, 1915, n.p. Harrison's name appears as contributing editor in *Colored American Review*, December 1915, 6. The January 1916 masthead lists Bruce as contributing editor.

38. Samuels, *Five Afro-Caribbean Voices*, 28–31. In the December 1915 issue of *Colored American Review*, Lovett Fort-Whiteman, a future member of the ABB, is listed as editor.

39. Woodrow Wilson, *Papers*, 35; CB, "'Security of Life' for Poles and Serbs—Why Not for Colored Americans?" and "Liberty for All," *AN*, September 1917, transcribed copies, TDC, box 31, folder Briggs.

40. "Self-Determination," *New York Call*, November 13, 1918, 6. Briggs later claimed that self-determination was part of the ABB's platform, though Domingo and Moore dispute that claim. See Richard B. Moore, interview by TD, January 15, 1958, W. A. Domingo, interview by TD, January 18, 1958, both in box 21, folder 3, Theodore Draper Research Files, MARBL.

41. Perry, *Hubert Harrison*, 213–20.

42. Anderson, *A. Philip Randolph*, 81–82; Kornweibel, *No Crystal Stair*, 222–23.

43. "Socialist Party Congressional Program," *Liberator*, October 1918, 42–45; "Race and Class," *Liberator*, September 1919, 7.

44. Moore, "Afro-Americans," 216–17; Phillip Foner, *American Socialism*. According to Moore, Randolph and Owen devoted most of their time to the *Messenger*, were wholly committed to the SPA, and did not participate in the study group.

45. "Educational Forum Center of Light in Harlem," *Emancipator*, March 13, 1920, 1; "Speaker Draws Striking Analogy," *Emancipator*, April 3, 1920, 1; *CD*, January 29, 1921, 3, April 2, 1921, 9.

46. Moore recounted Du Bois's lecture to his daughter, Joyce Moore Turner. See Turner, "Richard B. Moore and His Works," 30; "Dr. Du Bois Addresses Forum," *CD*, October 16, 1920, 3.

47. Moore, "Afro-Americans," 217.

48. Domingo, *Socialism Imperiled*, 1492–93, 1495, 1497–1507. Domingo's pamphlet

was seized during the Palmer Raids and included in the Lusk Committee report of April 24, 1920, reproduced in *Revolutionary Radicalism*, 1489–1510. Based on textual evidence, Domingo likely circulated his pamphlet early in 1919.

49. David Berenberg to Francis Peregrino, May 16, 1919, in *Revolutionary Radicalism*, 1511.

50. Kelley, *Hammer and Hoe*, 1–10.

51. Moore, "Afro-Americans," 217; Samuels, *Five Afro-Caribbean Voices*, 44–45. Moore recounted the Lee incident to Joyce Moore Turner.

52. PEF advertisements, *Emancipator*, March 13, 1920, 1, March 20, 1920, 1, March 27, 1920, 1, April 3, 1920, 1, April 10, 1920, 1, April 17, 1920, 1, April 24, 1920, 1; "Famous Speaker Thrills Hearers," *Emancipator*, March 20, 1920, 1, 2; "Chandler Owen Stirs Audience," *Emancipator*, March 27, 1920, 1, 3; "Black Empire is Fantastic Dream," *Emancipator*, April 24, 1920, 1, 2; *CD*, February 12, 1921, 3, April 9, 1921, 9; Naison, *Communists in Harlem*, 4–5.

53. Fowler, *Japanese and Chinese Immigrant Activists*, 36–40; Turner, *Caribbean Crusaders*, 20–23; Hermes Huiswoud, "Biography of Otto Huiswoud," box 2, folder 8, MSRK; Gilmore, *Defying Dixie*, 45–47; Sen Katayama, "Capitalism in Japan," *International Socialist Review*, May 1910, 1003–6; Sen Katayama, "California and the Japanese," *International Socialist Review*, July 1913, 31–32.

54. Harrison, *When Africa Awakes*, 77.

55. Ibid., 112.

56. Ibid., 32.

57. W. A. Domingo, "Socialism the Negroes' Hope," *Messenger*, July 1919, 22; W. A. Domingo, "Capitalism the Basis of Colonialism," *Messenger*, August 1919, 26–27; W. A. Domingo, "Did Bolshevism Stop Race Riots in Russia?," *Messenger*, September 1919, 26–27; W. A. Domingo, "Private Property," *Messenger*, April–May 1920, 9–10; W. A. Domingo, "Private Property as a Pillar of Prejudice (continued)," *Messenger*, August 1920, 69–71.

58. W. A. Domingo, "Will Bolshevism Free America?" *Messenger*, September 1920, 86.

59. Winston James, *Holding Aloft*, 180.

60. See, for example, Otto Huiswoud, "Dutch Guiana: A Study in Colonial Exploitation," *Messenger*, December 1919, 22–23.

61. Turner, *Caribbean Crusaders*, 96. Black radicals continued to publicly endorse the SPA after this split, especially in elections. See W. A. Domingo, "A New Negro and a New Day," *Messenger*, November 1920, 144–45.

CHAPTER 2

1. See African Blood Brotherhood membership application, *Crusader*, October 1921, 33.

2. Important recent works along these lines include Ula Taylor, *Veiled Garvey*; Ula Taylor, "Street Strollers"; Rebecca Hill, "Fosterites and Feminists"; Edwards, *Practice of Diaspora*; Mitchell, *Righteous Propagation*; Davarian Baldwin, *Chicago's New Negroes*; Davies, *Left of Karl Marx*.

3. Said, *Representations of the Intellectual*, 11; Zeleza, *Manufacturing African Studies*, 22.

4. Robert Hill, "Racial and Radical"; Winston James, *Holding Aloft*, 155–84; Solomon, *Cry Was Unity*, 5–21.

5. C. Valentine [CB], "The Ray of Fear: A Thrilling Story of Love, War, Race Patriotism, Revolutionary Inventions, and the Liberation of Africa," *Crusader*, February 1920, 18–20, April 1920, 11–12. Briggs wrote another short story, "Secret Service," under his oft-used pseudonym, C. Valentine. See *Crusader*, May 1921, 14–15, June 1921, 11–12. For an excellent discussion of "The Ray of Fear," see Stephens, *Black Empire*, 35–38.

6. CB to TD, March 17, 1958, TDC, box 31, folder Briggs.

7. "Aims of the Crusader," *Crusader*, September 1918, 4; "Aims of the Crusader," *Crusader*, November 1918, 1.

8. CB, "Africa for the Africans," *Crusader*, September 1918, 1–4; *Crusader*, September 1918, 4, 13–14.

9. "Race Catechism," *Crusader*, September 1918, 11.

10. Shelby, *We Who Are Dark*, 209, describes racialism as a belief that race determines social traits such as "temperament, aesthetic sensibility, and certain innate talents."

11. "The American Race Problem," *Crusader*, November 1918, 12, 14; *Crusader*, September 1918, 8, November 1918, 1, 6–7. On black World War I veterans and New Negro political activism and radicalism, see Chad Williams, *Torchbearers of Democracy*; Lentz-Smith, *Freedom Struggles*.

12. Quoted in Robert Hill, "Racial and Radical," xxi.

13. Parker, "African Origin"; Moses, *Afrotopia*, 88–89.

14. Robert Hill, *Marcus Garvey*, xix–xxii; George Wells Parker, "The Children of the Sun," *Crusader*, November 1918, 11, 25. Briggs also published articles by other Hamitic League members in the *Crusader*. See Bruce Grit [John E. Bruce], "The Colonel's Narrative: A Christmas Story," *Crusader*, January 1919, 5, 27–28. The names of HLW officers (with Casely-Hayford given as "Cosely Huyfud") appear in an HLW advertisement, *Crusader*, December 1918, 18. Parker's lecture, "The African Origin of Grecian Civilization," appeared in serial form in the *Crusader*, between May and August 1919, and in the *Journal of Negro History*.

15. "Negroes of the World Unite in Demanding a Free Africa," *Crusader*, December 1918, 3.

16. Richard B. Moore, interview by TD, January 15, 1958, W. A. Domingo, interview by TD, January 18, 1958, both in box 21, folder 3, Theodore Draper Research Files, MARBL.

17. Advertisement in *Crusader*, October 1919, 27; "Correspondence," *Crusader*, December 1919, 28, 30, January 1920, 22.

18. "Correspondence," *Crusader*, January 1920, 22; "Overseas Correspondence," *Crusader*, February 1920, 31; "The African Blood Brotherhood," *Crusader*, February 1920, 31, March 1920, 22–24; "The African Blood Brotherhood: Colon, Panama," *Crusader*, April 1920, 7; Unknown to CB, *Crusader*, July 1920, 28; "Overseas Correspondence," *Crusader*, August 1920, 29; David S. Hennessey, Samuel Industrious, and

Alan Jordan to ABB Parent Body, September 12, 1920, *Crusader*, November 1920, 27; David S. Hennessey to CB, October 15, 1920, *Crusader*, January 1921, 31. Evidence suggests that Hennessey had previously organized the San Pedro de Macorís, Dominican Republic, branch of the UNIA. See [anonymous] to CB, *Crusader*, August 1920, 29.

19. Earl E. Titus, "Report on Negro Radical Activities," September 18, 1923, File 61-50-435, Joseph C. Tucker, Special Report, September 15, 1923, both in *FSAA*, reel 3. Titus reported that ABB records revealed more than seven thousand dues-paying members in September 1923.

20. Ula Taylor, *Veiled Garvey*, 2, 24–47; Chateauvert, *Marching Together*.

21. Theo Burrell, "Negro Womanhood—An Appeal," *Crusader*, July 1920, 18; Anselmo R. Jackson, "The Black Man's Burden," *Crusader*, October 1918, 9–10, 32.

22. "Helpful Hints for Woman and the Home," *Crusader*, September 1918, 26–27, October 1918, 26–27; "Women's Department," *Crusader*, March 1919, 18–19, April 1919, 18–19; "Feeding the Family in the Summer Time," 18, "The Sin of Being Unattractive," 19, and "Flat-Chested Girls," 19, all in *Crusader*, August 1919.

23. This biographical sketch of Campbell is drawn from Winston James, *Holding Aloft*, 174–75; Hicks, *Talk with You*, 161–76.

24. *CD*, April 19, 1919, 4, August 2, 1919, 3, January 3, 1920, 17, February 17, 1923, 17; Hicks, *Talk with You*.

25. *AN*, April 11, 1923, 7; *CD*, December 11, 1920, 3, November 17, 1923, 17, January 29, 1921, 3, February 12, 1921, 3, April 2, 1921, 9, April 9, 1921, 9; Winston James, *Holding Aloft*, 175.

26. Ula Taylor, *Veiled Garvey*, 64.

27. CB to TD, March 17, 1958, TDC, box 31, folder Briggs; CB, "At the Cross Roads," *Crusader*, July 1920, 5–6; *Crusader*, April 1921, 8–9; Moore, *Richard B. Moore*, 40–43.

28. "Where Glory Calls," *Crusader*, April 1919, 8; Chatterjee, *Nation and Its Fragments*, 11, chap. 1; Scott, *Refashioning Futures*, 2–5; Burton, "Introduction"; Stephens, *Black Empire*.

29. "Would Freedom Make Us 'Village Cut-Ups,'" *Crusader*, February 1919, 17.

30. "Negro First," *Crusader*, October 1919, 9.

31. Mills, *Blackness Visible*, 101; Wolfe, "Land."

32. "Negroes of World Unite in Demanding a Free Africa," *Crusader*, December 1918, 3.

33. "If It Were Only True," *Crusader*, March 1919, 10; CB, "The American Race Problem," *Crusader*, September 1918, 12; "League of Nations," *Crusader*, February 1919, 6.

34. C. Valentine [CB], "Why Lynching Persists," *Crusader*, September 1919, 7; "Out for Negro Tools," *Crusader*, May 1919, 5; CB, "The Capital and Chicago Race Riots," *Crusader*, September 1919, 3–4.

35. "Profiteering Landlords," *Crusader*, December 1918, 6; "High Rents and Bolshevism," *Crusader*, May 1919, 4; "And They Wonder at Bolshevism!," *Crusader*, September 1919, 8; "The Negro's Place Is with Labor," *Crusader*, June 1919, 7.

36. "Wage Slavery in the West Indies," *Crusader*, September 1919, 9; "One of the Effects of Alien Education," *Crusader*, September 1919, 10–11.

37. "The Problem of Asia; or, Getting the Boot," *Crusader*, January 1920, 14.

38. Hermes Huiswoud, "Biography of Otto Huiswoud," box 2, folder 8, MSRK; Turner, *Caribbean Crusaders*, 20–23; Gilmore, *Defying Dixie*, 45–47.

39. "The Problem of Asia; or, Getting the Boot," *Crusader*, January 1920, 14; "Big Hindu Leader Advises Indians to Form Unions," *Emancipator*, March 20, 1920, 1. Onishi, "New Negro," discusses this period as the moment when "trans-Pacific" alliances were forged.

40. "Bolshevism and Race Prejudice," *Crusader*, December 1919, 9; CB, "Bolshevism's Menace: To Whom and to What?," *Crusader*, February 1920, 5–6; "Self-Determination in Haiti and Santo Domingo," *Crusader*, November 1919, 10–11; "What Is Capital?," *Crusader*, December 1919, 11–12; "Not Room Enough for the Two," *Crusader*, December 1919, 8–9; "Americanism," *Crusader*, December 1919, 12; "How about Haiti?" *Crusader*, March 1919, 9–10.

41. Dirlik, *Postmodernity's Histories*, 174–75, 191, 194–95. Other works attending to the ways that social differences provide a diaspora with its ligatures include Tiffany Ruby Patterson and Kelley, "Unfinished Migrations"; Butler, "Defining Diaspora"; Tölölyan, "Contemporary Discourse"; Edwards, "Uses of *Diaspora*."

42. "Program of the A.B.B.," *Crusader*, October 1921, 15–18.

43. Ibid.

44. Guterl, *Color of Race*, 88–91.

45. C. L. R. James, "Marcus Garvey," *Labor Action*, June 24, 1940, 114.

46. For fine studies of the UNIA in the U.S. South, see Rolinson, *Grassroots Garveyism*; Harold, *Rise and Fall*.

47. Robert Hill, "Racial and Radical"; Martin, *Race First*, 231–40; Rupert Lewis, *Marcus Garvey*, 134–39; Naison, *Communists in Harlem*, 5–8; Solomon, *Cry Was Unity*, 9–10, 23–29.

48. Harrison privately begrudged Garvey his national standing and believed that he had lifted all his worthwhile ideas from the Liberty League. Yet in a sad testament to just how petty such antagonisms often became, Harrison, while in the midst of an affair with Garvey's first wife, Amy Ashwood Garvey, disparaged Garvey's ability as a leader by impugning his sexual prowess. See Hubert Harrison Diary, December 10, 1920, Hubert Harrison Papers, box 9, folder 1, Rare Book and Manuscript Library, Columbia University, New York; Harrison Diary, March 2, 5, 1925, Harrison Papers, box 9, folder 2.

49. "Domingo, W. Adolphus," in Robert Hill, *Marcus Garvey*, 378; "W. A. Domingo," appendix 1, *Garvey/UNIA*, 1:527–31; Rupert Lewis, *Marcus Garvey*, 42–44. On the National Club, see "Election of Officers of the National Club of Jamaica," *Garvey/UNIA*, 1:20–22.

50. W. A. Domingo, "Socialism the Negroes' Hope," *Messenger*, July 1919, 22; W. A. Domingo, "Capitalism the Basis of Colonialism," *Messenger*, August 1919, 26–27; "Notice," *Messenger*, September 1919, 32; Robert Hill, *Marcus Garvey*, 378.

51. "The Peace Conference," *Crusader*, January 1919, 7, 14; "British Military Intelligence Report: Negro Agitation: Universal Negro Improvement Ass'n," December 10, 1919, in *Garvey/UNIA*, 2:164–67; Anderson, *A. Philip Randolph*, 123–24; Onishi, "Giant Steps," 61–64.

52. "West Indian American Trade Opportunities," *Crusader*, June 1919, 16; "The Call for Unity," *Crusader*, June 1919, 7–8; "Worth While Publications," *Crusader*, August 1919, 8; Wells, *Crusade*, 380–81.

53. "The Jewish Massacres and Their Lesson," *Crusader*, July 1919, 6. Briggs even once posed as a white man to purchase a ship for the UNIA (CB, "Angry Blond Negro," MG Papers, University of California at Los Angeles).

54. "The Black Star Line," *Crusader*, December 1919, 9.

55. "Marcus Garvey," *Crusader*, August 1919, 9.

56. Hubert H. Harrison to Lothrop Stoddard, July 1, 1921, August 21, 1920, Harrison Papers, box 2, folder 9; "Notes on Garvey and the UNIA," Harrison Papers, box 4, folder 61. Harrison's fears were not unfounded. Domingo and other black radicals, who continued to hold Harrison in high regard, openly chided his "race-first" position and editorial work on *Negro World*. They made particular light of his byline, "H. H.," calling it his "Mr. Hyde" personality and derisively referencing him as the "Ha Ha Editor." See "Race Fist versus Class First," *Emancipator*, April 3, 1920, 4; "H. H. Challenged," *Emancipator*, April 10, 1920, 2; "Discard Ambition and Ignorance," *Emancipator*, April 17, 1920, 3; "Opinion of Randolph and Owen Editors of the 'Messenger,'" *Emancipator*, April 17, 1920, 4. For Harrison's reply, see *When African Awakes*, 79–89.

57. "Our Reason for Being," and "Bubbles," *Emancipator*, March 20, 1920, 4; "Let There Be Light," *Emancipator*, April 3, 1920, 4; "Marcus Garvey Challenged," *Emancipator*, April 3, 1920, 1, 2; W. A. Domingo to W. E. B. Du Bois, August 24, 1922, box 3, folder 10, MSRK.

58. "Marcus Garvey Challenged," and "Garvey Sues Emancipator," *Emancipator*, April 3, 1920, 1; Anselmo R. Jackson, "Analysis of the Black Star Line," *Emancipator*, March 27, 1920, April 3, 1920, 2, April 10, 1920, 2, April 17, 1920, 2, April 24, 1920, 2.

59. "African League Holds Meeting," *Emancipator*, March 13, 1920, 1, 2; "Bubbles," *Emancipator*, March 20, 1920, 4.

60. "Should Negroes Strive for Empire?," *Emancipator*, March 27, 1920, 4.

61. Frank R. Crosswaith, "Building a Negro Empire," *Emancipator*, April 10, 1920, 4; "Black Empire Is Fantastic Dream," *Emancipator*, April 24, 1920, 1, 2; "Interview with Chandler Owen and A. Philip Randolph by Charles Mowbray White," in *Garvey/UNIA*, 2:609–11.

62. "Negro First," *Crusader*, October 1919, 9; CB, "A Paramount Chief for the Negro Race," *Crusader*, March 1920, 5–6; "A Letter from Marcus Garvey," *Crusader*, April 1920, 5.

63. "Garvey's 'Joker,'" *Crusader*, July 1920, 8–9. For a sense of Briggs's growing disenchantment with Garvey, see CB, "Now for the Dirty Work," *Emancipator*, April 24, 1920, 3; CB, "Yarmouth Granted Change of Registry since Oct. 2, 1919," *Emancipator*, April 10, 1920, 1, 2; "The U.N.I.A. Convention," *Crusader*, June 1920, 5; CB to J. R. Casimir, October 11, 1921, J. R. Ralph Casimir Papers, box 1, folder 9, SCRBC.

64. W. A. Domingo, "Africa's Redemption," *Emancipator*, March 27, 1920, 4.

65. "The UNIA Convention," *Crusader*, September 1920, 8; Harrison Diary, May 24, August 28, 31, 1920, in Perry, *Hubert Harrison Reader*, 189–94; W. E. B. Du Bois to

MG, July 22, 1920, in *Garvey/UNIA*, 2:431–32; John E. Bruce to MG, August 17, 1920, in *Garvey/UNIA*, 2:601–2.

66. "The Provisional President," *Crusader*, September 1920, 10–11; Perry, *Hubert Harrison Reader*, 7.

67. Robert Hill, "Racial and Radical," xxi–xxii; "A Double Appeal," "Randolph for State Comptroller," both in *Crusader*, November 1920, 8; CB, "Heroic Ireland," *Crusader*, February 1921, 5; "Liberating Africa," *Crusader*, August 1921, 8; "The Socialist Surrender," *Crusader*, August 1921, 8–9; CB to TD, March 17, 1958, TDC, box 31, folder Briggs.

68. "The Salvation of the Negro," *Crusader*, April 1921, 8; "Program of the ABB," *Crusader*, October 1921, 15–18.

69. Winston James, *Holding Aloft*, 180; Lenin, *Collected Works*, 23:275–76.

70. "The Enemy Press within Our Ranks," *Crusader*, June 1921, 9; "Constitution of the African Blood Brotherhood," *Crusader*, June 1921, 21–23.

71. "85 Whites and Negroes Die in Tulsa Riot," *New York Times*, June 2, 1921, 1, 2; "Military Control Is Ended in Tulsa," *New York Times*, June 4, 1921, 1, 14; "Urges Race Retaliation," *New York Times*, June 20, 1921, 8; Federal Surveillance Reports, File BS 202600-667-59, File BS 202600-667-60, File BS 202600-2031-3, File BS 202600-2031-4, File BS 202600-2031-5, RG 65, NARA; Ellsworth, *Death in the Promise Land*.

72. "Denies Negroes Started Tulsa Riot," *New York Times*, June 5, 1921, 21; "Urges Negroes Here to Arm Themselves," *New York Times*, June 6, 1921, 7; Federal Surveillance Report, File 202600-2031-3, RG 65, NARA.

73. "The Tulsa Outrage," *Crusader*, July 1921, 8.

74. CB to MG, August 15, 1921, reprinted in *Crusader*, November 1921, 5; Solomon, *Cry Was Unity*, 24.

75. Robert Hill, "Introduction," xxv–xxvii.

76. *To Negroes Who Really Seek Liberation* (pamphlet), and *Negro Congress Bulletin and News Service*, August 6, 1921, both in *FSAA*, reel 4; Robert Hill, "Racial and Radical," xli; Solomon, *Cry Was Unity*, 23–25.

77. "Garvey Turns Informer," *Crusader*, November 1921, 5; CB to TD, March 7, 1958. See also Martin, *Race First*, 236–39; Winston James, *Holding Aloft*; Solomon, *Cry Was Unity*.

78. CB to TD, March 17, 1958, TDC, box 31, folder Briggs; "Crusader Warned Its Readers against Marcus Garvey," *Crusader*, January–February 1922, 8; "Editorials," *Crusader*, October 1921, 8–11; "Editorials," *Crusader*, November 1921, 8–13; "Garvey Turns Informer," *Crusader*, November 1921, 5; Martin, *Race First*, 239; Briggs's statement to the New York branch of the Department of Justice quoted in Robert Hill, "Racial and Radical," xlv.

79. "Marcus Garvey Arrested," 5, "On With the Liberation Struggle," 6, and "*Crusader* Warned Its Readers Against Marcus Garvey," 8, all in *Crusader*, January–February 1922; Cyril A. Crichlow, "What I Know about Liberia," *Crusader*, January–February 1922, 18–23.

CHAPTER 3

1. Du Bois, "African Roots," 712; Walters, *My Life and Works*, 263.

2. Geiss, *Pan-African Movement*, 241.

3. W. E. B. Du Bois, "Africa for the Africans," in *W. E. B. Du Bois*, 660–61.

4. Du Bois came into conflict with the Senegalese Blaise Diagne, a deputy in the French national parliament, over the PAC resolution condemning Belgian colonialism in Congo. Du Bois discusses the conflict in Padmore, ed., *Colonial and . . . Coloured Unity*, 13–26. See also Geiss, *Pan-African Movement*, 234–48; David Levering Lewis, *W. E. B. Du Bois: The Fight for Equality*, 37–50, 109–13. For the ABB on Du Bois, see CB, "Dr. Du Bois Misrepresents Negrodm," *Crusader*, May 1919, 3.

5. CB to OCJ, October 3, 1961, April 18, 1962, both in OCJ Papers, box 8, folder 18. Briggs cited Karl Marx's *Value, Price, and Profit* at least twice in 1919. See CB, "Andrew Carnegie—Fiend or Angel," *Crusader*, October 1919, 13; "What Is Capital?," *Crusader*, December 1919, 11.

6. CB to OCJ, October 3, 1961, OCJ Papers, box 8, folder 18.

7. Edwards, "Shadow of Shadows," 21, 41.

8. Draper, *Roots*, 176–84.

9. Hermes Huiswoud, "Biography of Otto Huiswoud," box 2, folder 8, MSRK.

10. "The Program of the Party, Adopted and Issued by the Convention of the Communist Party," *Communist*, September 27, 1919, 9.

11. "Race and Class," *Liberator*, September 1919, 7; Phillip Foner and Allen, *American Communism*, 3.

12. W. A. Domingo quote from *Emancipator* article reproduced in McKay, *Negroes in America*, 34–36. He would have written this editorial in the spring of 1920.

13. "Bolshevism and the Darker Races," *Emancipator*, March 13, 1920, 4.

14. Lenin, *Collected Works*, 31:144, 148–49.

15. Zinoviev also announced the Congress of the People of the East that would convene in Baku, Azerbaijan, after the Second Congress. The Comintern hoped that the eastern gathering would build ties to movements in the Near East (Persia, Armenia, and Turkey) and possibly Asia and India; the Comintern gave no attention to Africa in planning the Congress. Zinoviev, *Report of the Executive Committee of the Communist International*, 21–22.

16. For a notable effort along these lines, see Kate A. Baldwin, *Beyond the Color Line*. For earlier works on the Black Belt Nation Thesis, see Kanet, "Comintern and the 'Negro Question'"; Carr, "Origins of the Communist Party's Theory"; Klehr and Thompson, "Self-Determination"; Susan Campbell, "'Black Bolsheviks'"; Berland, "Emergence, Part One," and "Emergence, Part Two"; Solomon, *Cry Was Unity*, 68–91.

17. Duiker, *Ho Chi Minh*, 64–65; CB to TD, March 17, 1958, TDC, box 31, folder Briggs.

18. The best recent account of Roy's early life, his politicization, his involvement in Indian revolutionary organizations, and the failed German arms plot can be found in M. N. Roy, *M. N. Roy's Memoirs*, 1–11; Manjapra, *M. N. Roy*. For earlier accounts, see Gordon, "Portrait"; Balakrishnan, "'Silencing the Translator,'" 1–9; Ramnath, "Two Revolutions," 8.

19. Haithcox, *Communism and Nationalism*, 4–7; Saha, "Introduction," 3; Overstreet and Windmiller, *Communism in India*, 20–23.

20. M. N. Roy, *M. N. Roy's Memoirs*, 28–29; Samaren Roy, *M. N. Roy*, 12–24; Overstreet and Windmiller, *Communism in India*, 20–23. I thank David Kim for pointing out the importance of Lajpat Rai's thinking about national liberation to Roy's reevaluation of nationalism.

21. The pamphlet was eventually published in Spanish as *El Camino para la Paz Duradera del Mundo*. Samaren Roy published an English translation, M. N. Roy, *The Way to Durable Peace*.

22. M. N. Roy, *The Way to Durable Peace*, 30, 41–42.

23. Samaren Roy, *M. N. Roy*, 17–18; Samaren Roy, introduction to M. N. Roy, *Way to Durable Peace*, 10–11.

24. M. N. Roy, *M. N. Roy's Memoirs*, 350.

25. In 1919, Roy helped organize a meeting where Latin American radicals could learn more about the Comintern from Borodin. Roy and Phillips subsequently called a series of meetings that led to the formation of the Partido Comunista Mexicano. On Roy in the Mexican Communist Party, see Samaren Roy, *M. N. Roy*, 25–31; Haithcox, *Communism and Nationalism*, 9–10; Overstreet and Windmiller, *Communism in India*, 24–27; La Botz, "American 'Slackers,'" 580. For a different chronology of Borodin's time in Mexico and Roy's role in founding the Mexican party, see Spenser, "Emissaries," 152–55.

26. Seth, *Marxist Theory*, 11–12, 34–44. Chakrabarty, *Provincializing Europe*, 6–16, 47–50, 90–96, imaginatively augments Seth's discussion through an analysis of the structures of historical time permeating Marxist historiography through such terms as "precapitalist," "real" and "abstract" labor and "commodity," which more generally exist within a sense of the disciplining and modernizing function of industrial labor.

27. Frederick Engels quoted in Samaren Roy, *M. N. Roy*, 39.

28. M. N. Roy, "Hunger and Revolution in India," *Gale's Magazine*, August 1919, 25, in *Selected Works of M. N. Roy*, 158. Lynn A. E. Gale published his monthly *Gale's Magazine* in the American expatriate community in Mexico. See La Botz, "American 'Slackers.'"

29. Spenser, "Emissaries," 152–54.

30. M. N. Roy, *M. N. Roy's Memoirs*, 378–79; for Lenin's admission that he had limited knowledge on aspects of his draft theses, see 346.

31. Ibid., 369–71, 375–82; Seth, *Marxist Theory*, 34–44, 61–66.

32. M. N. Roy, "Supplementary Theses on the National and Colonial Question," in Adhikari, *Documents*, 179–88, 156–68.

33. "Supplementary Report on the National and Colonial Questions," in Riddell, *Workers of the World*, 222, 224.

34. Ibid., 238–39, 265–66.

35. Ibid., 244, 245.

36. M. N. Roy, *M. N. Roy's Memoirs*, 381; Lenin, *Collected Works*, 31:244. For the two versions of Roy's supplementary theses, see Adhikari, *Documents*, 179–88.

37. Degras, *Communist International*, 1:140–43, 163–64; Archer, *Second Congress*, 221.

38. Gregory Zinoviev, "Session 1, September 1, 1920: Tasks of the Congress of the People's of the East," in Riddell, *To See the Dawn*, 71–72. See also Mikhail Pavlovich's statement to the same effect in his address in "Session 5, September 5, 1920: National and Colonial Question," in ibid., 148–49; "Manifesto of the Congress to the Peoples of the East," in ibid., 231.

39. M. N. Roy, *M. N. Roy's Memoirs*, 381; Adhikari, *Documents*, 156–68.

40. "Speech by John Reed at Second World Congress of the Communist International on Negro Question—July 25, 1920," in Phillip Foner and Allen, *American Communism*, 5–7, 8; Degras, *Communist International*, 1:142.

41. Ho Chi Minh quoted in Duiker, *Ho Chi Minh*, 64.

42. Degras, *Communist International*, 1:327.

43. The radicals with whom Nguyen worked included Abdelkader Hadj Ali and Messali Hadj (Algeria) and Max Bloncourt (Guadeloupe). Lamine Senghor (Senegal) hovered at the margins of the Union Intercoloniale until he formally joined in 1924.

44. Duiker, *Ho Chi Minh*, 65–79; Nguyen Ai Quoc, "Some Considerations on the Colonial Question," *L'Humanité*, May 25, 1922, "Racial Hatred," *Le Paria*, July 1, 1922, "Annamese Women and French Domination," "Oppression Hits All Races," *Le Paria*, August 17, 1923, all in Ho, *Ho Chi Minh on Revolution*, 11–14, 21–22, 25–26, 52; Edwards, "Shadow of Shadows," 21.

45. Nguyen wrote at least once about racial oppression in the United States. See Nguyen-ai-Quac [Nguyen Ai Quoc], "The Martyrdom of the Negro: American Lynch-Justice," *International Press Correspondence*, October 2, 1924, 772.

46. "Summary of the Program and Aims of the African Blood Brotherhood (Formulated by 1920 Convention)," RGASPI 515/1/37. This section does not appear in the ABB's 1922 program. See "The Program and Aims of the African Blood Brotherhood, 1922," in Robert Hill, "Racial and Radical," lxvii–lxx.

47. CB to TD, March 17, 1958, TDC, box 31, folder Briggs. See also CB to OCJ, October 3, 1961, OCJ Papers, box 8, folder 18.

48. "Liberating Africa," *Crusader*, August 1921, 8; "Stand by Soviet Russia," *Crusader*, December 1921, 8. See also "Trend of World Events," *Crusader*, September 1920, 9–10.

49. "A Double Appeal," and "Randolph for State Comptroller," *Crusader*, November 1920, 8.

50. The various efforts to establish a single Communist Party in the United States and the conflicts over them are extremely complex. For a discussion of black radicals with keen attention to the various communist parties, see Solomon, *Cry Was Unity*.

51. "The Program of the American Arm of the Communist International," *Toiler*, February 12, 1921, 2, 3; "The Proceedings of the 2nd Congress of the 3rd Communist International: Moscow 1920," *Toiler*, April 23, 1921, 2, April 30, 1921, 2, June 4, 1921, 2; "The Communist Solution of the National Question," *Toiler*, August 27, 1921, 3; RGASPI 515/1/50/29–58.

52. Draper, *American Communism*, 321.

53. John Bruce and J. P. Collins, "The Party and the Negro Struggle," *The Communist*, November 1921, 15–16.

54. McKay, *Long Way from Home*, 108–9; July 13, 1921, Report, File BS 202600-2031-3, RG 65, NARA; August 10, 1921, Report, File BS 202600-2031-7, RG 65, NARA; August 22, 1921, Report, File BS 202600-2031-8, RG 65, NARA; August 26, 1921, Report, File BS 202600-2031-9, RG 65, NARA; Perry, *Hubert Harrison*, 502. Bruce and Collins mentioned Briggs in describing the ABB as the most militant black organization pushing a leftist politics. See John Bruce and J. P. Collins, "The Party and the Negro Struggle," *The Communist*, October 1921, 19. For Briggs's joining the legal party, see CB to OCJ, April 18, 1962, OCJ Papers, box 8, folder 18. McKay remembered Stokes as having "the most perfect bourgeois expression of the superior person," which likely turned off Brotherhood radicals (*Long Way from Home*, 161; Solomon, *Cry Was Unity*, 10–21).

55. "Program and Constitution, Workers Party of America, New York, 1921" (pamphlet), in Phillip Foner and Allen, *American Communism*, 9.

56. Otto Hall Memorandum, n.d., TDC, box 31, folder Otto Hall and Harry Haywood. On Doty, see Haywood, *Black Bolshevik*, 128–31; "Letter to L. E. Katterfeld in Moscow from Jay Lovestone in New York, February 11, 1922" (Comintern document), available at http://www.marxisthistory.org/history/usa/parties/cpusa/1922/0211-love stone-tokatterfeld.pdf (accessed February 24, 2009). On Hardeon, see RGASPI 515/1/1233/6–7.

57. "W.S. Harlem Branch Workers Party Meets," *Worker*, July 15, 1922, 2; "Harlem West Side Branch," *Worker*, August 5, 1922, 5.

58. RGASPI 515/1/162/108–38.

59. Haywood, *Black Bolshevik*, 121–31; Otto Hall Memorandum, n.d., TDC, box 31, folder Otto Hall and Harry Haywood; CB to Harry Haywood, June 10, 1962, Harry Haywood Papers, SCRBC. This letter is among a series of exchanges between Haywood and Briggs in the early 1960s. I thank the late Andre Elizee, the archivist at the Schomburg Center who granted me access to these letters before they had been fully processed.

60. CB, "The Workers Party, Marcus Garvey, and the Negro," *Crusader*, January–February 1922, 15–16.

61. McKay, *Long Way from Home*, 16–34; Winston James, "Race Outcast," 71–73.

62. *Negro World*, September 20, 1919, quoted in Winston James, "Race Outcast," 73.

63. McKay, *Long Way from Home*, 66–70, 75. Among the speakers McKay heard were J. T. Walton Newbold, Britain's first Communist member of Parliament; Shapurji Saklatvala, a Communist and a key Indian radical figure in London's 1930s anticolonialism; Sylvia Pankhurst, leader of the Workers' Socialist Federation and editor of *Workers' Dreadnought*; and George Lansbury, editor of the Independent Labour Party's *Daily Herald*.

64. Claude McKay to MG, December 17, 1919, Harrison Papers, box 2, folder 66.

65. On the international response from both Western governments and white radicals to France's use of African troops in Germany, see Reinders, "Racialism"; Nelson, " 'Black Horror' "; Winter, "Webbs"; Bland, "White Women," 39–41.

66. *Daily Herald*, April 10, 1920, quoted in Bland, "White Women," 40.

67. *Daily Herald*, April 10, 1920, quoted in Winston James, "Race Outcast," 81.

68. Claude McKay, "A Black Man Replies," *Workers' Dreadnought*, April 24, 1920, quoted in Winston James, "Race Outcast," 82.

69. McKay, *Long Way from Home*, 75–76.

70. Ibid., 75–85; Winston James, "Race Outcast."

71. *Workers' Dreadnought*, July 3, 1920, 4.

72. McKay, *Long Way from Home*, 206.

73. M. N. Roy, "Proletarian Revolution in India," 1, "Conditions for Admission to the Third International," 2, both in *Workers' Dreadnought*, September 11, 1920.

74. Sherwood, "Comintern," 143.

75. Claude McKay, "How Black Sees Green and Red," *Liberator*, July 1921, quoted in Cooper, *Claude McKay*, 154–55.

76. Cooper, *Claude McKay*, 162.

77. Claude McKay, "Birthright," *Liberator*, August 1922, in Cooper, *The Passion of Claude McKay*, 73.

78. Richard B. Moore to Arthur A. Schomburg, August 7, 1922, quoted in Turner, "Richard B. Moore and His Works," 47.

79. Claude McKay to H. L. Mencken, July 3, August 2, 1922, both in Cooper, *Claude McKay*, 169; McKay, *Long Way from Home*, 153–54. For more detail on McKay's conflict with *Liberator* staff and his efforts to visit Russia, see Cooper, *Claude McKay*, 134–70.

80. Robert Hill, "Huiswoud, Otto." Although in his autobiography McKay mentioned only Katayama's help in gaining a seat at the Congress, in a 1923 letter he also acknowledged Huiswoud's help (RGASPI 495/72/8/11–12; McKay, *Long Way from Home*, 159–66). RGASPI 515/1/93/73, lists both McKay and Huiswoud as fraternal delegates of the ABB.

81. McKay later claimed that Huiswoud was frustrated about not being taken as the American Negro delegate because of his complexion: "I was still everywhere demanded. When the American Negro delegate was invited to attend meetings and my mulatto colleague went, the people asked: 'But where is the *chorny* (the black)?' The mulatto delegate said: 'Say, fellow, you're all right for propaganda. It's a pity you'll never make a disciplined party member'" (McKay, *Long Way from Home*, 177; Turner, *Caribbean Crusaders*, 109–10).

82. Executive Committee of the Communist International to Reed, Farina, Gurevitch, and Hanson and Scott, n.d., RGASPI 495/155/1; RGASPI 495/155/8/1–3.

83. RGASPI 495/71/2/87–88; RGASPI 495/72/2/135–44, 145–49; RGASPI 495/155/3/7–8; D. Ivon Jones, "American Imperialism and the Negro," *International Press Correspondence*, June 30, 1922, 412–13. Despite various plans and even efforts to involve the Communist parties of Britain, Portugal, South Africa, Germany and France, the World Negro Congress never materialized. See RGASPI 495/155/3/1–3; RGASPI 495/155/4/16–26; RGASPI 495/155/14/1; RGASPI 495/155/14/14–17; RGASPI 495/155/16/1–3.

84. McKay, *Long Way from Home*, 168–69, 170–71.

85. Ibid., 168.

86. Ibid., 159–66, 169; Claude McKay, "Report on the Negro Question: Speech to the 4th Congress of the Comintern, November 1922," *International Press Correspondence*,

January 5, 1923, 16; RGASPI 495/155/17/9; RGASPI 515/1/93/92–93; Turner, *Caribbean Crusaders*, 99–110.

87. Kate A. Baldwin, *Beyond the Color Line*, 48–49.

88. McKay, *Long Way from Home*, 172–81.

89. RGASPI 515/1/93/97, 99–105. A handwritten note atop McKay's untitled report reads, "Copy of Statement Given to Billings [Huiswoud]." McKay refers to this unsigned, undated report in a letter to a Comrade Wallunyus. See RGASPI 515/1/93/81–82.

90. McKay opened his speech caustically, remarking that he would rather "face a lynching stake in civilized America than try to make a speech before the most intellectual and critical audience in the world." His words reflected his genuine concern about how the Comintern might respond to his speech. He may have also been calling into question the radicalism of his white comrades, or, as Kate A. Baldwin suggests, the speech might have reflected "McKay's awareness of his audience as at once an ally against white supremacy and perilously proximate to that very regime" (*Beyond the Color Line*, 40).

91. Claude McKay, "Report on the Negro Question: Speech to the 4th Congress of the Comintern, November 1922," *International Press Correspondence*, January 5, 1923, 16.

92. RGASPI 515/1/93/81–82; RGASPI 495/155/17/9.

93. Otto Huiswoud (Billings), "The Negro Question at the IVth World Congress," in Phillip Foner and Allen, *American Communism*, 24–27.

94. Ibid.

95. *Fourth Congress*, 30; Degras, *Communist International*,1:399–401; Turner, "Richard B. Moore and His Works," 46–48. Point 7 of the ABB's 1920 program stated, in part, "We must encourage industrial unionism among our people and at the same time fight to break down the prejudice in the unions which is stimulated and encouraged by the employers. . . . Wherever it is found impossible to enter the existing labor unions, independent unions should be formed, so that Negro Labor be enabled to protect its interests" ("Summary of the Program and Aims of the African Blood Brotherhood, Formulated by the 1920 Convention," in appendix to Robert Hill, "Racial and Radical," lxix).

96. Gregory Zinoviev to Claude McKay, May 8, 1923, quoted in Winston James, *Holding Aloft*, 181.

97. Earl E. Titus, "African Blood Brotherhood," Chicago Bureau Office, January 18, 1924, Federal Surveillance Report quoted in Winston James, *Holding Aloft*, 180.

98. RGASPI 515/1/164/1; RGASPI 515/1/174/1.

99. Rose Pastor Stokes, "The Communist International and the Negro," *Worker*, March 10, 1923, 1, 4.

100. RGASPI 495/155/17/17; RGASPI 495/155/43/160–62.

101. McKay, *Negroes in America*, 38.

102. See "Negroes' Wrongs Aired at Moscow," *AN*, December 6, 1922, 1; *Messenger*, April 1923, 653; Claude McKay, "Soviet Russia and the Negro," *Crisis*, December 1923, 64; Claude McKay, "Soviet Russia and the Negro," *Crisis*, January 1924, 114–18.

103. "To Claude McKay," in Trotsky, *First Five Years*, 355–56. McKay still considered Trotsky's the most advanced Bolsheviks on race (*Long Way from Home*, 208).

104. Turner, "Richard B. Moore and His Works," 51; "Talking Points" (ABB pamphlet), 1923, in Aptheker, *Documentary History*, 413–20.

105. Joseph C. Tucker, "Special Report on the African Blood Brotherhood, August 18, 1923, *FSAA*, reel 1; Department of Justice Surveillance File 61-50-477, Norman Amour to Mr. Burns, Director, Bureau of Investigations, Department of Justice File 61-50-401, both in *FSAA*, reel 3; Earl E. Titus, Federal Surveillance Report, August 27, November 21, 1923, Federal Surveillance File 190-17181-6, all in *FSAA*, reel 4.

106. Federal Surveillance Files 61-50-463, 61-50-469, 61-50-474, 61-50-477, 61-50-478, 61-50-482, all in *FSAA*, reel 3; Joseph C. Tucker, "Special Report on African Blood Brotherhood," August 18, 1923, *FSAA*, reel 1; Joseph C. Tucker, "Special Report: Negro Activities: African Blood Brotherhood," December 15, 1923, *FSAA*, reel 3; Earl E. Titus, Federal Surveillance Report, November 21, 27, 1923, "Special Membership Bulletin of the African Blood Brotherhood," Federal Surveillance File 190-1781-6, all in *FSAA*, reel 4; CB to TD, March 17, 1958, TDC, box 31, folder Briggs; Richard B. Moore to Members of Menelik Post, [late December 1924–early January 1925], Richard B. Moore Papers, box 4, file 1, SCRBC; Theman Ray Taylor, "Cyril Briggs," 88.

107. Federal surveillance report quoted in Winston James, *Holding Aloft*, 177.

108. Earl E. Titus, "Report: African Blood Brotherhood: Negro Radical Activities," November 21, 1923, *FSAA*, reel 3; Federal Surveillance File 190-1781-6, Earl E. Titus, "Report: African Blood Brotherhood," November 27, 30, 31, 1923, all in *FSAA*, reel 4; Haywood, *Black Bolshevik*, 128; Turner, "Richard B. Moore and His Works," 28–29, 48–51; Winston James, *Holding Aloft*, 178–82; Solomon, *Cry Was Unity*, 29.

109. Richard B. Moore to Robert Minor, November 2, 1924, box 1, folder 13, Robert Minor Papers, Communist Party USA Archives, Tamiment Library, New York University, New York.

110. Israel Amter, "Report on the Workers Party of America," February 8, 1924, RGASPI 515/1/271; Robert Minor to John Pepper, September 24, 1924, Israel Amter to John Pepper, October 9, 1924, both in RGASPI 515/1/273; Robert Minor to C. E. Ruthenberg, July 31, 1924, Robert Minor and Gordon Owens to Fourth Annual International Convention of the Universal Negro Improvement Association, August 14, 1924, both in RGASPI 515/1/359. Negro Committee members included Otto Hall, Lovett Fort-Whiteman, Edward Doty, and Gordon Owens.

111. RGASPI 515/1/359/7, 19–20, 9–18.

112. RGASPI 495/155/43/162.

113. McKay quoted in Kate A. Baldwin, *Beyond the Color Line*, 53.

114. RGASPI 495/155/17/10; RGASPI 515/1/359/8; McKay and Fort-Whiteman quoted in Kate A. Baldwin, *Beyond the Color Line*, 53.

115. Negro Committee Meeting Minutes, September 22, 1924, RGASPI 515/1/359; RGASPI 515/1/359; Robert Minor and Gordon Owens, "Report of Negro Committee," October 13, 1924, RGASPI 515/1/359; CEC Negro Subcommittee, n.d., RGASPI 515/1/183.

CHAPTER 4

1. RGASPI 495/155/43/159–60.

2. "1922 Program and Aims of the African Blood Brotherhood," appendix to Robert Hill, "Racial and Radical," lxvii–lxx.

3. Watkins-Owens, *Blood Relations*, 75–87.

4. Gaines, *Uplifting the Race*; Sullivan, *Lift Every Voice*, 50–57; Bates, *Pullman Porters*; Phillips, *AlabamaNorth*, 57–126, 190–225; Summers, *Manliness*; Mitchell, *Righteous Propagation*.

5. W. E. B. Du Bois, "Back to Africa," *Century Magazine*, February 1923, in *W. E. B. Du Bois*, 334.

6. "Garvey Unfairly Attacked," *Messenger*, April 1922, 387; Robert Hill, "General Introduction," in *Garvey/UNIA*, 1:lxxx; Watkins-Owens, *Blood Relations*, 118–19. In another instance, a *Messenger* editorial asserted the magazine's "enviable and proud record of having done more to eliminate hate between the American and West Indian Negroes than any other publication." "West Indians in Business," *Messenger*, April 1923, 653.

7. William Pickens to MG, July 24, 1922, reprinted in *Messenger*, August 1922, 471–72; "Marcus Garvey," *Messenger*, July 1922, 437; A. Philip Randolph, "A Reply to Marcus Garvey," *Messenger*, August 1922, 467–70; "Marcus Garvey Must Go!," *Messenger*, October 1922, 508; "A Supreme Negro Jamaican Jackass," *Messenger*, January 1923, 561; Anderson, *A. Philip Randolph*, 131–32, 136, 139–42. For other treatments of Garvey's tête-à-tête with the Ku Klux Klan, see Cronon, *Black Moses*, 188–92; Martin, *Race First*, 345–47; Stein, *World of Marcus Garvey*, 154–55; Ferguson, *Sage*, 72–73; Rolinson, *Grassroots Garveyism*, 143–47. Owen asked twenty-five black leaders if Garvey should "be deported as an alien creating unnecessary mischief." Of the fourteen who responded, four ignored the question, four agreed, and six opposed. See Chandler Owen, "Should Marcus Garvey Be Deported?," *Messenger*, September 1922, 479–80; "A Symposium on Garvey by Negro Leaders," *Messenger*, December 1922, 550–52.

8. E. Ethelred Brown quoted in Watkins-Owens, *Blood Relations*, 121.

9. Robert Bagnall, "The Madness of Marcus Garvey," *Messenger*, March 1923, 638; Du Bois, "Back to Africa."

10. "West Indian and American Negroes," *AN*, February 28, 1923, 2; Watkins-Owens, *Blood Relations*, 76–86.

11. "'No West Indian Problem,' Domingo," *AN*, April 4, 1923, 1.

12. "Open Forum: The Policy of the *Messenger* on West Indian and American Negroes: W. A. Domingo *vs.* Chandler Owen," *Messenger*, March 1923, 639–45.

13. Ibid.

14. Watkins-Owens, *Blood Relations*, 122–24.

15. See Chandler Owen et al. to Harry Daugherty, January 15, 1923, in Garvey, *Philosophy and Opinions*, 294–300.

16. KM, "Radicalism and the Negro," 19, Kelly Miller Papers, Box 71-6, Folder 159, Moorland-Spingarn Research Center, Howard University, Washington, D.C.; KM, Autobiography, Box 71-2, Folder 61, Miller Papers; KM, "After Marcus Garvey—What

of the Negro?," *Contemporary Review*, April 1927, 494; KM, "Watchtower," *AN*, September 15, 1934, 8; KM, "Washington's Policy,"; Gaines, *Uplifting the Race*, 138–39.

17. CB to Sheridan Johns, June 7, 1961, box 1, folder 15, MSRK; Fox, *Guardian*, 240–42; CB to TD, March 17, 1958, TDC; Crusader News Service, March 24, 1923, NAACP Coll., Administrative File C-232 (all subsequent references to material in this collection are to Administrative File C-232). On the National Liberty Congress, see Perry, *Hubert Harrison*, 366–83.

18. JWJ to Matthew A. N. Shaw, January 10, 1923, NAACP Coll.; *BAA*, January 6, 1923; CB to Sheridan Johns, June 7, 1961, box 1, folder 15, MSRK.

19. Gaines, *Uplifting the Race*, 34, 230; *BAA* February 2, 1923, 1, 5.

20. KM to JWJ, March 21, 1923, NAACP Coll.; Matthew A. N. Shaw and William Monroe Trotter telegram, March 22, 1923, NAACP Coll.; JWJ to UFC, March 22, 1923, NAACP Coll.

21. Crusader News Service, March 24, 1923, NAACP Coll.; "NAACP Participates in Conference on Civil Rights Bodies" (press release), March 30, 1923, NAACP Coll.

22. CB to TD, March 17, 1958.

23. KM to JWJ, April 11, 1923, NAACP Coll.; KM to CB, May 9, 1923, NAACP Coll.; Minutes of the Committee on All-Race Conference, May 5, 26, June 2, 1923, NAACP Coll.; Minutes of Sub-Committee on Program for All-Race Conference, May 28, 1923, NAACP Coll.; KM to JWJ, June 5, 1923, NAACP Coll.; KM to CB, July 26, 1923, NAACP Coll.

24. CB to JWJ, July 3, 12, 18, 1923, all in NAACP Coll.; KM to CB, July 26, 1923, NAACP Coll.; Norman McGhee, "Dean Kelly Miller's All-Race Conference," *Pittsburgh Courier*, June 23, 1923, 16.

25. CB to JWJ, October 19, 1923, NAACP Coll.; KM to JWJ, June 5, 1923, NAACP Coll.; KM to JWJ, October 23, 1923, NAACP Coll.; "Program of the First Meeting of the Negro Sanhedrin All Race Conference," NAACP Coll.; Department of Justice Files 61-50-410, 61-50-462, 61-50-463, all in *FSAA*, reel 1; CB to Sheridan Johns, June 7, 1961, box 1, folder 15 MSRK; Kelly Miller, *The Negro Sanhedrin: A Call to Conference* (pamphlet, 1923), 16, 22, box 71-6, folder 159, Miller Papers; *Pittsburgh Courier*, June 23, 1923, 1; Chandler Owen, "Mistakes of Kelly Miller," *Messenger*, July 1922, 443–45; "The Menace of Negro Communists," *Messenger*, August 1923, 784.

26. *Broad Ax*, February 16, 1924, 1; *BAA*, February 15, 1924, 1, 5; *CD*, February 9, 1924, 1, 4; "The Sanhedrin," *Messenger*, October 1923, 830; *BAA*, February 8, 1924, 4; Kelly Miller, *The Negro Sanhedrin*, 4, 19, box 71-6, folder 159, Miller Papers; Kelly Miller, *Radicalism and the Negro* (pamphlet, 1920), 19, box 71-6, folder 155, Miller Papers.

27. Solomon, *Cry Was Unity*, 31; handwritten notes, and "Resolution Proposed by Workers Party Delegates at the Negro Sanhedrin," both in Box 13, Negro Sanhedrin Folder, Robert Minor Papers, Rare Book and Manuscript Library, Columbia University, New York; CEC/CI Memo to Workers Party, n.d., RGASPI 515/1/164; "Report on the United States," April 9, 1924, I. Amter, "Report on the Workers Party of America," February 8, 1924, both in RGASPI 515/1/271; Department of Justice, Bureau of Investigation File 61-50-484, *FSAA*, reel 1; *DW*, February 15, 1924, 1, 3, February 18, 1924, 1, 3.

28. *CD*, February 16, 1924, 3; *DW*, February 12, 1924, 1, February 13, 1924, 1, 2, February 14, 1924, 1, 2, February 15, 1924, 1, 3, February 16, 1924, 1, 2, February 18, 1924, 1, 3; *BAA*, February 22, 1924, 1, February 29, 1924, 9.

29. *Norfolk Journal and Guide*, February 23, 1924, 1, 2; *Crisis*, May 1924, 7; *Messenger*, April 1924, 106.

30. Files 198940–983, 61-837-1, RG 60, NARA; Earl E. Titus, Department of Justice Surveillance Report, March 28, 1924, *FSAA*, reel 4; Haywood, *Black Bolshevik*, 142–43.

31. Richard B. Moore to Robert Minor, November 2, 1924, box 1, folder 13, Robert Minor Papers, Communist Party USA Archives, Tamiment Library, New York University, New York.

32. Gilmore, *Defying Dixie*, 31, 33–34; on the Casa del Obrero Mundial, see Hart, *Revolutionary Mexico*.

33. Perry, *Hubert Harrison*, 319; Kornweibel, *"Seeing Red,"* 168–71; Gilmore, *Defying Dixie*, 37–40. According to Gilmore, Fort-Whiteman returned to Harlem in 1917, though his work on the *Colored American Review* suggest a much earlier date.

34. I. Amter, "Report on the Workers Party of America," February 8, 1924, RGASPI 515/1/271; Otto Hall, interview by TD, November 29, 1958, TDC, box 31, folder Otto Hall and Harry Harwood; Haywood, *Black Bolshevik*, 145–46; Lovett Fort-Whiteman, "The Negro and American Race Prejudice," *DW*, February 9, 1924, 3.

35. Solomon, *Cry Was Unity*, 47; Kate A. Baldwin, *Beyond the Color Line*, 56.

36. RGASPI 515/1/273/168–71.

37. *Fifth Congress*, 151–52; Duiker, *Ho Chi Minh*, 98–99.

38. Nguyen Ai Quoc, "Report on the National and Colonial Questions at the Fifth Congress," in Ho, *Ho Chi Minh on Revolution*, 56–67; Duiker, *Ho Chi Minh*, 99–100.

39. Berland, "Emergence, Part One," 425–27.

40. *Fifth Congress*, 70.

41. RGASPI 496/155/25/1–4; Kate A. Baldwin, *Beyond the Color Line*, 47.

42. James Jackson [Lovett Fort-Whiteman], "Negro in America," RGASPI 515/1/360.

43. RGASPI 495/155/27/42 quoted in Kate A. Baldwin, *Beyond the Color Line*, 53, 56.

44. Gilmore, *Defying Dixie*, 44–45; Lovett Fort-Whiteman to Comintern Official, quoted in Kate A. Baldwin, *Beyond the Color Line*, 65.

45. James Jackson [Lovett Fort-Whiteman], "The Negro in America," *Communist International*, November 1924, 50–54.

46. ECCI to CEC of the Workers Party of America, January 17, 1925, RGASPI 515/1/418; ECCI to CEC of Workers Party of America, n.d., RGASPI 515/1/418; *International Press Correspondence* quoted in Berland, "Emergence, Part One," 429; Kate A. Baldwin, *Beyond the Color Line*, 55; RGASPI 515/1/360/77–78.

47. RGASPI 515/1/359/9–18; Gilmore, *Defying Dixie*, 51–52.

48. RGASPI 515/1/359/9–18, 19–20.

49. RGASPI 495/155/33/5, 6–7. Senghor subsequently resigned from the French party and formed the Comité de Défense de la Race Nègre (Committee for the Defense of the Black Race). See Edwards, "Shadow of Shadows," 22–23.

50. Haywood, *Black Bolshevik*, 139, 147.

51. RGASPI 495/1/33/23–24; RGASPI 515/1/533/1–2; RGASPI 495/155/39/4; W. A. Domingo, interview by TD, January 18, 1958, box 21, folder 3, Theodore Draper Re-

search Files, MARBL; *CD*, September 19, 1925, 10, October 17, 1925, 10; Augusto War-reno, "Benj. Fletcher Thrills Crowds in Philadelphia," *Industrial Worker*, February 16, 1929, quoted in Cole, *Ben Fletcher*, 40–41; Haywood, *Black Bolshevik*, 143–47.

52. Kate A. Baldwin, *Beyond the Color Line*, 48–49; RGASPI 515/1/504/6–6b; RGASPI 515/1/533/3, 9–10; Minutes of CEC Negro Subcommittee, April 14, 1925, RGASPI 515/1/533; Proposed Itinerary for Lovett Fort-Whiteman, RGASPI 515/1/533; RGASPI 515/1/533/18–26; RGASPI 515/1/575/61–63.

53. RGASPI 515/1/504/7–9; RGASPI 515/1/533/11–12, 13–17; RGASPI 495/155/33/3; Charles Henry to MG, n.d., untitled document, n.d., both in box 12, folder Negro–New York, Minor Papers, Rare Book and Manuscript Library, Columbia University, New York.

54. "Negroes: Warning," *Time*, August 17, 1925, 4; *BAA*, August 15, 1925, 9; *CD*, September 19, 1925, 10, October 17, 1925, 9; *Chicago Daily Tribune*, August 10, 1925, 6; *Washington Post*, October 25, 1925, 14; "The A. F. of L. and the Negro Worker," *Messenger*, September 1925, 324–25; William Green, "Our Negro Workers," *Messenger*, September 1925, 332; Anderson, *A. Philip Randolph*, 205; Bates, *Pullman Porters*, 38, 109; Gilmore, *Defying Dixie*, 52–53.

55. Constitution and Program of the ANLC, October 25–31, 1925, RGASPI 515/1/575.

56. *BAA*, November 7, 1925, 1, 3; *CD*, November 7, 1925, 2.

57. *CD*, October 31, 1925; *DW*, October 28, 1925; Haywood, *Black Bolshevik*, 144–45; Turner, "Richard B. Moore and His Works," 51–53.

58. Haywood, *Black Bolshevik*, 145; RGASPI 495/155/33/29–33; RGASPI 515/1/533/18–25.

59. RGASPI 515/1/533/13–17; Robert Minor, "First Negro Workers' Congress," *Workers Monthly*, December 1925, 70.

60. *BAA*, October 31, 1925, 9, November 7, 1925, 13; *CD*, November 7, 1925, 10, November 14, 1924, 10, November 21, 1925, 10; Abram L. Harris Jr., "Lenin Casts His Shadow over Africa," *Crisis*, April 1926, 274; W. E. B. Du Bois, "The Black Man and Labor," *Crisis*, December 1925, 60.

61. RGASPI 515/1/819/1–2; J. J. Ballam to I. Amter, February 10, 1926, RGASPI 515/1/819; RGASPI 515/1/819/92–94. Fort-Whiteman did make an initial foray into organizing a World Negro Congress, though nothing ever came of the effort. See RGASPI 495/155/33/34–37bp.

62. RGASPI 515/1/533/13–17.

63. Edgar Owens to John Ballam, January 28, 1926, RGASPI 515/1/819; RGASPI 515/1/819/5, 11, 25; J. J. Ballam to locals, April 14, 1926, RGASPI 515/1/819; Phillips, *AlabamaNorth*, 99–100.

64. RGASPI 515/1/1233/1–13; "Report on Negro Work," Otto Huiswoud, n.d., RGASPI 515/1/1574; Jay Lovestone to Robert Minor, March 22, 1926, box 1, folder 13, Robert Minor Papers, Communist Party USA Archives, Tamiment Library, New York University, New York.

65. Report of the Committee on Negro Work, February 24, 1927, RGASPI 515/1/1108; RGASPI 515/1/720/3–5, 8–9.

66. Garvey, *Philosophy and Opinions*, 291–92; MG to New York Local, Septem-

ber 4, 1925, in *Garvey/UNIA*, 6:213; George Weston to Associated Press, ca. September 27, 1925, in *Garvey/UNIA*, 6:240; George Weston and Hannah Nichols to Calvin Coolidge, November 2, 1925, in *Garvey/UNIA*, 6:260; MG Address, Detroit, 1926, in *Garvey/UNIA*, 6:381, 386; "William Le Van Sherrill," in Robert Hill, *Marcus Garvey*, 424–25; Martin, *Race First*, 241, 255; Ula Taylor, *Veiled Garvey*, 66–68; Fax, *Garvey*, 110; Cronon, *Black Moses*, 108; Colin Grant, *Negro with a Hat*, 402–3.

67. RGASPI 515/1/819/41, 55; C. E. Ruthenberg to Gitlow, Weinstone, and Krumbein, August 3, 1926, C. E. Ruthenberg to Gitlow, August 16, 1926, both in RGASPI 515/1/643.

68. Lovett Fort-Whiteman to C. E. Ruthenberg, August 21, 1926, RGASPI 515/1/720; RGASPI 515/1/819/43–44, 45–47; "Press Release of Rival UNIA Convention," August 16, 1926, in *Garvey/UNIA*, 6:431–32; Negro Committee Minutes, September 20, 1926, RGASPI 515/1/819; RGASPI 515/1/819/56–59; RGASPI 515/1/1739/37–40.

69. Item 55: "The Social and Political Status of the Negro Peoples of the World," LAI Archives.

70. Official N.O. Memorandum to Local Councils of the ANLC, [January 1927], RGASPI 515/1/819; RGASPI 515/1/819/30–31.

71. RGASPI 515/1/1108/4–6.

72. RGASPI 515/1/1108/6–15; RGASPI 515/1/1213/3.

73. RGASPI 515/1/1213/3bp; RGASPI 515/1/1067/12.

74. RGASPI 515/1/1213/4–13; Solomon, *Cry Was Unity*, 64–65.

75. RGASPI 515/1/1067/15–18.

CHAPTER 5

1. Kelley, *Hammer and Hoe*, 13–14; Turner, *Caribbean Crusaders*, 155; Naison, *Communists in Harlem*, 19; Solomon, *Cry Was Unity*, 87; Susan Campbell, "'Black Bolsheviks.'"

2. Jean Jones, *League*, esp. 14–15, 24–30; Geiss, *Pan-African Movement*, 325–37; Hooker, *Black Revolutionary*, 12–16; Marjomaa, *LACO and the LAI*.

3. Egonu, "*Les Continents*," 245–54; Langley, "Pan-Africanism"; Fabre, *From Harlem to Paris*; Stovall, *Paris Noir*.

4. Edwards, *Practice of Diaspora*.

5. Solomon, *Cry Was Unity*, 100–101.

6. McMeekin, *Red Millionaire*, 193–203.

7. Item 1: "Invitation to the International Congress against Colonial Oppression and Imperialism," Berlin, December 15, 1926, LAI Archives; RGASPI 515/1/720/11–12.

8. RGASPI 542/1/7/27; RGASPI 542/1/7/61–61bp; RGASPI 515/1/917/42; Item 2: "List of Organizations and Delegates attending the Congress against Colonial Oppression and Imperialism," Brussels, February 10, 1927, Egmont Palace, LAI Archives; Item 6: "Adressen an den Kongress gegen Kolonialunterdrückung und Imperialismus," February 10, 1927, Brussels, LAI Archives; Item 8: "Address to the Congress by George Lansbury," LAI Archives; Alba, *Politics*, 130–31. Einstein, Lansbury, and China's Madame Sun Yat-sen were listed as honorary presidents of the Congress.

9. E. Burton Ceruti to William Pickens, August 24, 1926, W. E. B. Du Bois to William

Pickens, September 10, 1926, Joel E. Spingarn to William Pickens, October 1, 1926, William Pickens, "Conference of Colonial, Semi-Colonial, and Repressed Peoples, in Belgium," September 23, 1926, Lovett Fort-Whiteman to William Pickens, September 27, 1926, untitled memo, n.d., all in box 11, folder 1, reel 11, William Pickens Papers (Additions), SCRBC.

10. CDRN delegates included Narcisse Danae, Max Bloncourt, and Eli Bloncourt from Guadeloupe and the Haitian Camille St. Jacques, a former Communist. Marjomaa, *LACO and the LAI*, 8–11, 14; Item 1: "Invitation to the International Congress against Colonial Oppression and Imperialism," Berlin, December 15, 1926, Item 2: "List of Organizations and Delegates," Item 6: "Adressen an den Kongress gegen Kolonialunterdrückung und Imperialismus," February 10, 1927, Brussels, LAI Archives; Langley, "Pan-Africanism," 84–85. I thank Sace Elder for translating the German. Weiss, *Kweku Bankole Awoonor Renner*, 36–38, shows that E. A. Richards was not a pseudonym for I. T. A. Wallace-Johnson, as claimed by Spitzer and Denzer, "I. T. A. Wallace-Johnson [Part I]," 419.

11. Langley, "Pan-Africanism," 75, 78–80; Edwards, *Practice of Diaspora*, 28–30, 98–104. Tovalou Houénou may have modeled the Ligue after the UNIA—he even spoke before the UNIA's 1924 convention, where he met Garvey. See Fabre, *From Harlem to Paris*, 64–71; Stovall, *Paris Noir*, 60–61. The Ligue went into decline later in 1924, going underground after Houénou's arrest for attempting to expel the French from Dahomey. Egonu, *"Les Continents,"* 250–52; Conklin, "Who Speaks?".

12. RGASPI 495/155/36/1–7; RGASPI 495/155/40/1.

13. RGASPI 515/1/917/43, 54, 62.

14. McMeekin, *Red Millionaire*, 193–203.

15. RGASPI 515/1/1067/13–14.

16. RGASPI 515/1/819/49; RGASPI 515/1/720/11–12; Shipman, *It Had to Be*, 162–63. Baldwin was also the National Urban League's observer (RGASPI 515/1/1212/1–2).

17. Item 2: "List of Organizations and Delegates," LAI Archives; Langley, "Pan-Africanism," 84–85; Fabre, *From Harlem to Paris*, 64–71; Stovall, *Paris Noir*, 60–61; Edwards, *Practice of Diaspora*, 18.

18. Item 44: "Interview par Daniele Martini avec Jawahar Lal Nehru," LAI Archives; Nehru, *Toward Freedom*.

19. Item 9: "Texte du Discours d'Ouverture par Henri Barbusse," LAI Archives.

20. RGASPI 542/1/77/75–81; RGASPI 542/1/69/62–64.

21. RGASPI 542/1/77/75–81; Münzenberg, *Flammenzeichen*, 31–33.

22. J. T. Gumede speech to International Congress against Imperialism, Brussels, February 10–15, 1927, available at www.anc.org.za/ancdocs/speeches/1920s/gume desp.htm (accessed January 23, 2007); RGASPI 542/1/69/28–30.

23. Spiegler, "Aspects," 118; Roger N. Baldwin, "The Capital of the Men without a Country," *Survey Graphic*, August 1927, 446.

24. Item 53: "Discours de Max Bloncourt, Délégué des Antilles" (stenographic copy), LAI Archives; Münzenberg, *Flammenzeichen*, 119–23; Geiss, *Pan-African Movement*, 328.

25. Lamine Senghor, "Au Congrès de Bruxelles du 10 au 15 Février 1927: Condamnation de L'Impérialisme et de la Colonisation," *Voix des Nègres*, March 1927, 1, repro-

duced as "Under the Dark Man's Burden," *Living Age*, May 15, 1927, 866–68; Edwards, "Shadow of Shadows," 26–27. Senghor's speech became mythic among black radicals. Writing years later, George Padmore, who did not attend the congress, described Senghor's closing declaration as *the* anticolonial moment of Brussels (*Pan-Africanism or Communism?*, 324).

26. Item 24: "Résolution Anglo-Indoue-Chinoise," LAI Archives; Item 19: "Resolution betr. Südafrika von den Delegierten der Südafrikanischen Union, D. Colraine, J. A. La Guma, J. Gumede," LAI Archives.

27. "Pandit Nehru and the Unity of the Oppressed People of South Africa," African National Congress, available at http://www.anc.org.za/ancdocs/history/solidarity/indiasa4.html (accessed May 7, 2007).

28. RGASPI 542/1/69/24–27.

29. Item 54: "Résolutions Communes sur la Question Nègre," 1927, LAI Archives.

30. Richard B. Moore, "Statement at the Congress of the League against Imperialism and for National Independence," in Moore, *Richard B. Moore*, 143–46; Item 54: "Résolutions Communes sur la Question Nègre," LAI Archives.

31. *DW*, February 11, 1927, 4, March 14, 1927, 3, March 15, 1927, 3, March 16, 1927, 3.

32. RGASPI 542/1/7/131–32; RGASPI 542/1/77/75–81.

33. Item 59: "Resolution: 'The United Front in the Struggle for Emancipation of the Oppressed Nations,'" LAI Archives; RGASPI 542/1/7/131–32; RGASPI 542/1/77/66–69.

34. Fowler, *Japanese and Chinese Immigrant Activists*, 2; Nehru, *Toward Freedom*, 123–27.

35. Turner, "Richard B. Moore and His Works," 54.

36. Flyer announcing rally, Sunday, April 10, 1927, RGASPI 515/1/1212; Flyer announcing rally, Monday Night, February 14, 1927, RGASPI 515/1/1213; "The Colonial Congress and the Negro," *Crisis*, July 1927, 165–66; "To All Oppressed Peoples and Classes," *Crisis*, October 1927, 273; W. E. B. Du Bois, "Postscript," *Crisis*, January 1928, 23.

37. William Pickens, "The Brussels Congress," address to the Fourth Pan-African Congress, New York, August 21, 1927, box 11, folder 1, reel 11, William Pickens Papers (Additions), SCRBC; "Pan-Africa," *Crisis*, October 1927, 263; RGASPI 515/1/1067/13–14; RGASPI 542/1/18/28; Turner, *Caribbean Crusaders*, 147–58; David Levering Lewis, *W. E. B. Du Bois: The Fight for Equality*, 208–11. Although Comintern records mention Moore and Huiswoud as contributors to the Fourth PAC's resolution, only Huiswoud's name is listed with the actual resolution.

38. "The Pan-African Congresses," *Crisis*, October 1927, 264.

39. The actual line from Shakespeare's Macbeth reads: "Lay on, MacDuff, and damn'd be him that first cries 'Hold, enough!'"

40. *AN*, April 14, 1926, 2, May 5, 1926, 11, February 20, 1929, 6.

41. Elizabeth Hendrickson, "Man in the Street," *AN*, January 8, 1930, 20.

42. *Liberator*, December 7, 1929, 2; CB, "High Rents and the Death Rate," *Liberator*, December 7, 1929, 3; Richard B. Moore, "Housing and the Negro Masses," *Negro Champion*, September 8, 1928, 1, 5; Otto Hall quoted in Naison, *Communists in Harlem*, 23; Solomon, *Cry Was Unity*, 97, 99.

43. *DW*, August 5, 1929, 1, August 6, 1929, 3; AN, January 1, 1930, 20, June 5, 1929, 1, 2, June 12, 1929, 3, November 27, 1929, 3; *CD*, August 3, 1929, 11; *Pittsburgh Courier*, December 21, 1929, 19; *Liberator*, December 7, 1929, 1, 2, 3, December 14, 1929, 1, December 28, 1929, 1; Elizabeth Hendrickson, "Man in the Street," *AN*, January 8, 1930, 20.

44. *DW*, March 11, 1929, 1; W. Foster, "Draft Report: The 4th Convention of the Trade Union Unity League," November 28, 1929, RGASPI 515/1/1565; "Program of Action," n.d., 515/1/3356.

45. Audley "Queen Mother" Moore, interview by Mark Naison and Ruth Prago, 1972, 10–11, Louise Thompson Patterson, interview by Ruth Prago, November 16, 1981, 30, both in Oral History of the American Left, Tamiment Library, New York University, New York; Naison, *Communists in Harlem*, 149.

46. Hooker, *Black Revolutionary*, 2, 5–7; Azikiwe, *My Odyssey*, 138–39; Neptune, *Caliban and the Yankees*, 22–32.

47. Rodney Worrell, "George Padmore," 23–24; Makonnen, *Pan-Africanism*, 101–2.

48. Minutes of the Negro Commission, January 3, 1929, RGASPI 515/1/1685; RGASPI 515/1/1366/7, 8–10, 12–13; RGASPI 515/1/1535/42; 515/1/1688/25–27; *Pittsburgh Courier*, September 1, 1928, 2; O. E. Huiswoud, "ANLC Organizes Labor Unions in West Indies," *Liberator*, December 7, 1929, 3; *Liberator*, May 10, 1930, 1.

49. RGASPI 515/1/819/8; Turner, "Richard B. Moore and His Works," 54–56.

50. Haywood, *Black Bolshevik*, 115–17, 121–22, 128–31; William L. Patterson, *Man Who Cried Genocide*, 103; Solomon, *Cry Was Unity*, 104–7. Also at KUTV were Bankole Awoonor-Renner, Oliver John Golden, and Aubrey Bailey. See McClellan, "Africans and Black Americans," 373; Turner, *Caribbean Crusaders*, 143.

51. Haywood, *Black Bolshevik*, 228–30, 232–34.

52. *International Press Correspondence*, August 8, 1928, 812.

53. Ibid., August 3, 1928, 772–73, 781–82, August 8, 1928, 811–12, August 11, 1928, 856, August 13, 1928, 872, October 25, 1928, 1345–46, October 30, 1928, 1392.

54. RGASPI 495/155/53/2, 1; RGASPI 495/155/59/2–14.

55. Adi, "Pan-Africanism," 240–41.

56. Minutes of American Delegation Meeting, August 23, 1928, RGASPI 515/1/1244.

57. Pepper, *American Negro Problems*, 12; RGASPI 515/1/1366/17–20.

58. RGASPI 515/1/1272/46–47, 17–23.

59. RGASPI 515/1/1272/46–47; RGASPI 515/1/1274/154–62, 171–76, 250–52; RGASPI 515/1/1685/1–8; RGASPI 495/155/67/7–13.

60. RGASPI 515/1/1579/165–68; RGASPI 515/1/1580/166–75; RGASPI 515/1/1583/110–12; *Negro Champion*, March 23, 1929, 2; CB, "Our Negro Work," *The Communist*, September 1929, 494, 501; Solomon, *Cry Was Unity*, 60, 96–98.

61. RGASPI 542/1/32/34–35; RGASPI 495/155/70/62–68; RGASPI 495/155/70/69–71, 72–73, 74–76; RGASPI 495/155/87/350–55.

62. RGASPI 542/1/30/48, 70; RGASPI 542/1/79/48.

63. RGASPI 542/1/16/26/32; RGASPI 542/1/18/22–24; RGASPI 542/1/20/17–19.

64. RGASPI 542/1/28/62–63. Marjomaa attributes Beckett's actions in South Africa to his antiblack views, his somewhat erratic political career, and racism, which ulti-

mately led to his membership in the British Union of Fascists. See *LACO and the LAI*, 21–27.

65. Fowler, *Japanese and Chinese Immigrant Activists*, 2; RGASPI 542/1/26/18–23; RGASPI 542/1/29/78, 77, 79, 80, 84. The British LAI's focus remained largely on China, India, the East, and Egypt, with little attention focused on colonial Africa. Furthermore, despite his failures in South Africa, Beckett still held an LAI leadership position. See RGASPI 542/1/29/12–19.

66. RGASPI 542/1/30/5–7, 9; RGASPI 542/1/29/30–31; RGASPI 542/1/14/6–8, 10–12, 15–20.

67. RGASPI 542/1/88/5–6bp; RGASPI 542/1/79/20–22, 26–27, 41; RGASPI 542/1/32/50.

68. RGASPI 542/1/79/45; RGASPI 495/155/72/59–62.

69. RGASPI 542/1/87/33–34; William Pickens to Committee Drafting the Resolution on the Negro Question, July 24, 1929, box 11, folder 2, reel 11, William Pickens Papers (Additions), SCRBC.

70. RGASPI 495/155/77/184; Kouyaté quoted in Edwards, *Practice of Diaspora*, 354.

71. RGASPI 495/155/77/184–86; Adi, "Pan-Africanism," 242.

72. RGASPI 495/155/87/28–31.

73. "An Appeal to Negro Workers of the World," *NW*, January–February 1930, 1. Curiously, the call also listed among its participants the NAACP and Kadalie's Industrial and Commercial Union, most likely in an attempt to capitalize on each organization's name recognition among black workers.

74. RGASPI 495/155/53/3; RGASPI 515/1/1688/31; Hooker, *Black Revolutionary*; Solomon, *Cry Was Unity*, 104.

75. RGASPI 534/3/450/89–90; GP, "The Trade Unity Convention and the Negro Masses," *DW*, August 27, 1929, 6; Hooker, *Black Revolutionary*, 13–14; Adi, "Pan-Africanism," 242. Padmore did not attend the Frankfurt Congress, as many have assumed based on Hooker's biography. Padmore's name does not appear in any of the rather detailed documents that recount the meetings of black delegates there.

76. RGASPI 534/3/450/89–90.

77. RGASPI 495/155/80/54–57; RGASPI 495/155/70/57–58, 59; RGASPI 495/155/77/306; Adi, "Pan-Africanism," 242; RGASPI 534/3/450/89–90; RGASPI 495/155/87/350–55.

78. Adi, "Pan-Africanism," 243; Weiss, *Road*, 88, 99–100.

79. *AN*, February 26, 1930, 20; RGASPI 495/155/89/22/27; RGASPI 534/4/330/24–25; Adi, "Pan-Africanism," 243–44; Aitken, "From Cameroon to Germany," 597, 601, 603.

80. RGASPI 495/155/87/246–47, 250; RGASPI 495/155/83/96–97; Weiss, *Road*, 88–89, 111.

81. Adi, "Pan-Africanism," 245–46; RGASPI 495/155/87/246–47, 250; RGASPI 495/155/83/96–97; Weiss, *Road*, 88–89, 111.

82. *Trade Union Programme*, 2–3, 4, 11; RGASPI 495/155/87/292; *Liberator*, May 10, 1930, 1; O. E. Huiswoud, "ANLC Organizes Labor Unions in West Indies," *Liberator*, December 7, 1929, 3; RGASPI 495/155/90/72; RGASPI 500/1/5/54–60.

83. RGASPI 495/155/87/313–15; Weiss, *Road*, 88, 99–100, 104; Johnstone Kenyatta, "Unrest in Kenya," *Manchester Guardian*, March 18, 1930, 6.

84. *Report of the Proceedings*, 1, 40; RGASPI 495/155/87/247, 295; Weiss, *Road*, 111; Spitzer and Denzer, "I. T. A. Wallace-Johnson [Part I]," 419. ICNW delegates included Bilé, Macaulay, Small, Padmore, Ford, Burroughs, Patterson, E. A. Richards (Sierra Leone), T. S. Morton (the Gold Coast), J. A. Akrong (the Gold Coast), M. De Leon (Jamaica), Helen McClain (United States), and four other African Americans. Fraternal delegates included A. Green (South Africa), Willi Budich (Germany), Budich's stenographer, and Berlin-based Communist Virendranath Chattopadhyaya.

85. RGASPI 495/155/87/248; *Report of the Proceedings*, 40; *International Press Correspondence*, July 24, 1930, 635–36.

86. *Report of the Proceedings*, 40; Weiss, *Road*, 112, 116. The ITUCNW executive committee included Ford, I. Hawkins, McClain, and Padmore (United States); Kouyaté, Macaulay, Small, and South African Albert Nzula (Africa); and E. Reid (Caribbean).

87. RGASPI 495/155/87/243–51, 290–96; *International Press Correspondence*, July 24, 1930, 635; Adi, "Pan-Africanism," 248–50; Weiss, *Road*, 117–19, 125.

88. Weiss, *Road*, 128–29.

CHAPTER 6

1. GP, "British Imperialism in Nigeria," *International Press Correspondence*, August 7, 1930, 705; Pennybacker, *From Scottsboro to Munich*, 70.

2. Edward Thomas Wilson, *Russia and Black Africa*, 185, 199; Weiss, *Kweku Bankole Awoonor Renner*, 19; *NW*, April–May 1931, 23.

3. Weiss, *Kweku Bankole Awoonor Renner*, 25–34; RGASPI 495/155/77/104–20bp.

4. "Summary of the Report of Comrade Ford to the 5th World Congress of the Red International of Labour Unions," A. Losovsky, "5th World Congress of the RILU," both in *NW*, April–May 1931, 18–21, 12–17.

5. RGASPI 495/155/77/306–8; RGASPI 495/155/87/23–27.

6. RGASPI 495/155/87/290–91.

7. Aitken, "From Cameroon to Germany," 608.

8. RGASPI 495/155/77/306–8; RGASPI 495/155/80/95–96.

9. RGASPI 495/155/87/350–55, 361–65, 380–87, 396–403; RGASPI 495/155/80/54–57, 95–96, 175. The Confédération Générale was the major French trade union organization tied to the RILU.

10. Edwards, *Practice of Diaspora*, 255; Spiegler, "Aspects," 172.

11. RGASPI 495/155/87/350–55.

12. Adi, "Pan-Africanism," 249; Weiss, *Road*, 124–25; Haywood, *Black Bolshevik*, 329.

13. RGASPI 542/1/40/73–76, 94–97; RGASPI 495/155/87/43–50.

14. RGASPI 542/1/40/73–76; RGASPI 542/1/44/75–76. I thank Charlotte Thomas and Brent Edwards for help translating this document.

15. Spiegler, "Aspects," 175.

16. Ibid.: "L'union et la solidarité de tous les nègres et . . . liaison qui été faite . . . la

LDRN doit suivre une politique internationale, si elle ne veut pas se trouver isolé et abandonné ses propres ressources."

17. Ibid., 162–63, 167–78: "Et depassant le cadre d'une politique specifiquement nègre."

18. RGASPI 542/1/49/27–27bp, 28 (translated by Matthew Friedman).

19. Edwards, *Practice of Diaspora*, 259–60; Turner, *Caribbean Crusaders*, 195.

20. RGASPI 495/155/87/434–35; RGASPI 495/155/96/2–3.

21. RGASPI 495/155/62/5; RGASPI 495/155/98/31–32, 27–28; Turner, *Caribbean Crusaders*, 193–94.

22. Weiss, *Kweku Bankole Awoonor Renner*, 3–4; RGASPI 495/155/96/2–5; Turner, *Caribbean Crusaders*, 194–95.

23. *NW*, March 15, 1930, RGASPI 495/155/92/7–23. In November 1930, Padmore and a Cuban Communist, G. Hernandez, published a special French version with reports and speeches from the Hamburg conference and the Negro Bureau's program. See *L'Ouvrier Negre*, November 1, 1930, RGASPI 495/155/92/39–54bp.

24. *International Negro Workers' Review*, January 1931, 3, February 1931, 9.

25. RGASPI 495/155/96/4; I. I. Potekhin, interview by Rold Italiaander, quoted in Edward Thomas Wilson, *Russia and Black Africa*, 214.

26. *International Negro Workers' Review*, January 1931, 25, February 1931, 22; J. W. Ford, "In the War Drive against the Soviet Union of Russia," *NW*, March 1931, 7–9; "Facts about the Soviet Union," *NW*, July 1931, 14–16; "Facts about Soviet Russia," "Declaration of the Rights of the Working and Exploited Peoples," both in *NW*, September 15, 1931, 14–17; "War in the East," *NW*, October–November 1931, 2–4; J.B., "The Land of Socialist Construction," *NW*, December 1931, 13–15.

27. I. Amter, "The Land of Socialist Construction," "Negro Workers, Fight against the War!," "African Sailor Tells His Impression of Soviet Russia," all in *NW*, January–February 1932, 22–25, 28, 32; GP, "Fifteen Years of Soviet Russia," *NW*, November–December 1932, 28.

28. Edward Thomas Wilson, *Russia and Black Africa*, 214.

29. E. F. Small, "Situation of Workers and Peasants in Gambia, West Africa," "Appeal to the Black Soldiers of France," both in *International Negro Workers' Review*, January 1931, 22–24, 20–22; Albert Nzula, "Native Workers Make Organizational Advances in South Africa," *International Negro Workers' Review*, February 1931, 14–15; Albert Nzula, "Conference of the African Federation of Trade Unions," *NW*, April–May 1931, 5–6; GP, "The Revolutionary Movement in Africa," *NW*, June 1931, 3–5; Moreau, "White Terror in Cuba," *NW*, April–May 1931, 6–7; Wang, "Development of the Chinese Workers' Movement," *NW*, March 1931, 12–14; Foster Jones, "Situation of Native Workers in Sierra Leone," *NW*, April–May 1931, 3–5; Mansy, "Bloody Suppression of Native Rising in the Belgian Congo," *NW*, August 1931, 5–8; GP, "Hands Off Liberia!," "Force Labour under the British Flag," both in *NW*, October–November 1931, 5–11, 12–13; "Workers, Defend Your Colonial Brothers!," "New Revolt in India," both in *NW*, December 1931, 3–4, 10.

30. "Workers, Defend Your Colonial Brothers!," *NW*, December 1931, 4.

31. Turner, *Caribbean Crusaders*, 197.

32. Pennybacker, *From Scottsboro to Munich*, 75.

33. GP, "The Revolutionary Movement in Africa," *NW*, June 1931, 3–5; GP, "Hands Off Liberia,", "Under the Banner of the Red Aid," both in *NW*, October–November 1931, 5–13, 31–37; GP, "Workers, Defend Liberia!," "The War Is Here," both in *NW*, January–February 1932, 3–10; GP, "War in the East," "How the Imperialists Are 'Civilizing' Africa," both in *NW*, March 1932, 4–9, 11–14; GP, "What Is Empire Day?," *NW*, June 1932, 1–3; GP, "How the Empire Is Governed," *NW*, July 1932, 1–6; G. Kouyatte [Kouyaté], "Black and White Seamen Organize for Struggle," *NW*, December 1931, 19–20; G. Kouyatte [Kouyaté], "Solidarity between White and Coloured Sailors," *NW*, March 1932, 27–28.

34. For *NW* articles on the Caribbean, see Otto Huiswoud, "Imperialist Rule in British Guiana," *NW*, August 1931, 3–5; Charles Alexander, "For a Revolutionary Trade Union Movement," *NW*, March 1932, 14–18; "Self-Determination for the West-Indies," *NW*, April 1932, 19; T. Albert Marryshow, "Appeal to the West Indian Overseas," *NW*, May 1932, 12–14; Charles Alexander, "Against Illusions in the West Indian Masses," *NW*, July 1932, 12–15.

35. Mass Mailing addressed to Dear Friend, n.d., Crusader News Agency letterhead, LP/ID/CI/36/39ii, Labour Party Papers, Labor History Archive and Study Center, People's History Museum, Manchester, England.

36. C. L. R. James, "Notes on the Life of George Padmore," in *C. L. R. James Reader*, 290.

37. Mackenzie, "Radical Pan-Africanism," 71; "Workers Correspondence," *NW*, October–November 1931, 38–42, March 1932, 29–32; RGASPI 534/3/754/2, 3, 157; RGASPI 534/7/74/20–20bp, 30–30bp; Weiss, *Kweku Bankole Awoonor Renner*, 33, 55–57, 59.

38. Weiss, *Kweku Bankole Awoonor Renner*, 29, 33, 38; Spitzer and Denzer, "I. T. A. Wallace-Johnson [Part I]," 419.

39. Foster Jones, "Situation of Native Workers in Sierra Leone," *NW*, April–May 1931, 3–5; RGASPI 534/3/754/19, 27.

40. RGASPI 534/3/754/21; RGASPI 534/3/754/20; Hooker, *Black Revolutionary*, 24; Turner, *Caribbean Crusaders*, 195; Pennybacker, *From Scottsboro to Munich*, 72.

41. Turner, *Caribbean Crusaders*, 211; Padmore quoted in Edwards, *Practice of Diaspora*, 259, 263–64; RGASPI 495/155/99/53–55.

42. Turner, *Caribbean Crusaders*, 195–96.

43. RGASPI 534/3/754/20; Weiss, *Kweku Bankole Awoonor Renner*, 21.

44. Weiss, *Kweku Bankole Awoonor Renner*, 36, 38, 40, 43–44; Pennybacker, *From Scottsboro to Munich*, 30.

45. At its 1930 St. Louis convention, the ANLC renamed itself the League of Struggle for Negro Rights, which was to assume responsibility for Negro work in the United States. See Solomon, *Cry Was Unity*, 190–91.

46. RGASPI 534/3/754/3, 21–22; RGASPI 534/3/755/111. For reference to the missive from GP to Robert Minor, December 10, 1931, see RGASPI 538/1/12/77–78.

47. Edgar, "Notes," 677–78; Du Bois, *Dusk of Dawn*, 58.

48. Padmore, *Life and Struggles*; Edwards, "Shadow of Shadows," 20.

49. GP, "'Left' Imperialism and the Negro Toilers," *Labour Monthly*, May 1923, 319.

50. RGASPI 534/3/754/151.

51. RGASPI 534/3/754/186.

52. Rohdie, "Gold Coast Aborigines," 389, 392–98; Weiss, *Kweku Bankole Awoonor Renner*, 23, 41–42, 45–46.

53. GP, "Bankruptcy of Negro Leadership," *NW*, December 1931, 5; "Self-Determination for the West Indies," *NW*, April 1932, 19; RGASPI 534/3/754/136–136bp, 159; RGASPI 534/3/755/100–100bp, 110, 127–30, 147, 148; Memo from Superintendent Caning, n.d., TNA: PRO MEPO 38/9; Report on British Section of the League against Imperialism, July 18, 1932, IOR/L/PJ/12/272/76–78, Asia, Pacific, and African Collection, British Library, London; Pennybacker, *From Scottsboro to Munich*, 75.

54. RGASPI 534/3/754/159, 154; RGASPI 534/3/755/91, 110; RGASPI 534/3/755/127–30; St. Clair Drake, Cardiff Diary, 5, box 62, folder 3, St. Clair Drake Papers, SCRBC; "Appeal to the Negro Seamen and Dockers!," *NW*, April 1932, 20–24; "World Congress of Seamen," *NW*, 23–29. On the SMM, Jones, and Headley, see Sherwood, "Comintern," 152–53; Pirio, "Note"; Rich, *Race and Empire*, 129–30; Tabili, *"We Ask,"* 158.

55. RGASPI 534/3/755/148–148bp; RGASPI 538/1/12/28–31.

56. LAI British Section, Report of the 2nd Annual Conference, May 21–22, 1932, Friars Hall, London, LP/ID/CI/36/34, Labour Party Papers; Edwards, *Practice of Diaspora*, 259.

57. RGASPI 534/7/50/93; Sherwood, "Comintern" 155; RGASPI 534/3/755/145, 152, 159–61; RGASPI 538/1/12/16–18; Pennybacker, *From Scottsboro to Munich*, 76.

58. RGASPI 534/3/755/151; RGASPI 534/3/756/6–7; GP, "Negro Toilers Speak at the World Congress of ILD," *NW*, February–March 1933, 4; RGASPI 538/1/12/58–61.

59. Superintendent Canning Report, December 13, 1932, TNA: PRO MEPO 38/11A. Ward's letters to Padmore contained various negative references to Foster Jones, Chris Jones (aka Braithwaite), James Headly, and Jomo Kenyatta. Ward's tone suggests less a principled criticism of their failings than a misguided attempt to make himself appear at the political fore of London black radicals. See RGASPI 534/3/755/100–100bp, RGASPI 534/7/50/93, RGASPI 534/3/756/6–7.

60. GP, "Nationalist Movement in West Indies," *NW*, November–December 1932, 6–7; GP to Cyril Ollivierre, September 26, 1932, George Padmore Letters, SCRBC.

61. RGASPI 495/155/100/29–31; RGASPI 542/1/54/92; Turner, *Caribbean Crusaders*, 197.

62. GP to Cyril Ollivierre, July 5, September 26, 1932, Padmore Letters; Canning Report, November 7, 1932, TNA: PRO MEPO 38/8A; Canning Report, November 11, 1932, TNA: PRO MEPO 38/9A; Hooker, *Black Revolutionary*, 27.

63. Hooker, *Black Revolutionary*, 30–31; Turner, *Caribbean Crusaders*, 197–98; Pennybacker, *From Scottsboro to Munich*, 77; Tabili, *"We Ask,"* 158; Henry O'Connell to the Editor, *NW*, April–May 1933, 24–25.

64. Turner, *Caribbean Crusaders*, 199–200; Edgar, "Notes," 677–78; Cohen, "Introduction," 15.

65. Turner, *Caribbean Crusaders*, 212–13; Edwards, *Practice of Diaspora*, 265–67.

66. C. L. R. James, *Letters*; Mackenzie, "Radical Pan-Africanism"; Richardson, Chrysostom, and Grimshaw, *C. L. R. James*; Nielsen, *C. L. R. James*; Neptune, *Caliban and the Yankees*, 22–31.

67. C. L. R. James, *Letters*, 22–33, 44, 97; C. L. R. James, *At the Rendezvous*, 143.

68. Mackenzie, "Radical Pan-Africanism"; Richardson, Chrysostom, and Grimshaw, *C. L. R. James*.

69. C. L. R. James, *At the Rendezvous*, 254.

70. C. A. Smith, interview by James R. Hooker, September 18, 1964, cited in Hooker, *Black Revolutionary*, 26–27; Upham, "History of British Trotskyism."

71. GP, "Au Revoir," *NW*, August–September 1933, 18; GP to Cyril Ollivierre, July 28, 1934, Padmore Letters; Turner, *Caribbean Crusaders*, 213.

72. Hooker, *Black Revolutionary*, 31.

73. RGASPI 534/3/754/27–29.

74. RGASPI 534/3/754/32.

75. Cohen, "Introduction," 15; Edgar, "Notes," 677–78. See C. L. R. James, "Notes on the Life of George Padmore," 24–25, for a slightly different secondhand account from Kenyatta of this incident.

76. "Expulsion of George Padmore from the Revolutionary Movement," *NW*, June 1934, 14–15; "A Betrayer of the Negro Liberation Struggle," *NW*, July 1934, 6–10; Helen Davis, "The Rise and Fall of George Padmore as a Revolutionary Fighter," *NW*, August 1934, 15–17; *AN*, June 16, 1934, 3, July 28, 1934, 1, 2, August 11, 1934, 1, 15, September 15, 1934, 1, 2, December 8, 1934, 1, 4; *Pittsburgh Courier*, June 23, 1934, 10, September 22, 1934, A7; GP, "An Open Letter to Earl Browder," *Crisis*, October 1935, 302, 315; Hooker, *Black Revolutionary*, 32–35. On other black Communists expelled for siding with Padmore, see *AN*, October 20, 1934, 15, January 19, 1935, 3, June 30, 1934, 8, July 14, 1934, 8.

77. Sherwood, "Comintern," 145–47, 149; Hugo Rathbone, "The Problem of African Independence," *Labour Monthly*, March 1936, 161–71; Hugo Rathbone, "The Problem of African Independence (Conclusion)," *Labour Monthly*, April 1936, 237–49.

78. On the Negro World Congress, see Edwards, *Practice of Diaspora*, 261–82.

79. Nancy Cunard quoted in Hooker, *Black Revolutionary*, 34.

CHAPTER 7

1. Killingray, "'To Do Something'"; Adi, *West Africans*, 58–61, 76–78.

2. Padmore, *Pan-Africanism or Communism?*, 329.

3. Makonnen, *Pan-Africanism*, 117.

4. Matera, "Black Internationalism," 2.

5. Makonnen, *Pan-Africanism*, 155.

6. Edwards, *Practice of Diaspora*, 241–42; Cedric Robinson, *Black Marxism*, 267.

7. Makonnen, *Pan-Africanism*, 155. See also Edwards, *Practice of Diaspora*; Stephens, *Black Empire*.

8. C. L. R. James, "Notes on the Life of George Padmore," 31a–32.

9. Padmore also had probably heard C. A. Smith recount Trotsky's version of German Communist Party leader Heinrich Brandler's years as an "honorary prisoner" in Moscow between 1924 and 1928, when he was living in the famed Lux Hotel but unable to leave Russia. See C. A. Smith, "Can Comintern Be Reformed?," *New Leader*, October 13, 1933, 6–7; Deutscher, "Record," 53, 55. Only later, in 1935, was Lovett Fort-Whiteman sentenced to a Russian prison for the crime of Trotskyism (officially, "anti-Soviet agitation"), and he died a violent death in 1939. Klehr, Haynes, and Anderson,

Soviet World, 218–27. For personal accounts of the circumstances surrounding Fort-Whiteman's death, see Homer Smith, *Black Man*, 78, 81; Robert Robinson, *Black on Red*, 361.

10. For a look at Russians' inner lives under Stalin, see Hellbeck, *Revolution*.

11. C. L. R. James, *At the Rendezvous*, 254–56.

12. Richardson, Chrysostom, and Grimshaw, *C. L. R. James*; C. L. R. James, "Is This Worth War?," *New Leader*, October 4, 1935, 5; Alexander, *International Trotskyism*, 442–43; Upham, "History of British Trotskyism."

13. Richardson, Chrysostom, and Grimshaw, *C. L. R. James*; Archer, "C. L. R. James," 61–63; Brockway, *Inside the Left*, 326–27; Corthorn, *In the Shadow*, 69–70; Penny-backer, *From Scottsboro to Munich*, 92.

14. "Conference Report," *The Keys*, July 1933, 3–8; "'*The Keys*' Disclose," *The Keys*, July 1933, 9; Killingray, "To Do Something," 62–63; Barbara Bush, *Imperialism*, 220; Ralph Bunche Diary, April 12, 1937, box 279, folder 1, Ralph J. Bunche Papers, Department of Special Collections, Charles E. Young Library, University of California at Los Angeles (hereafter, Bunche Diary); Donnell, "Una Marson," 116.

15. *The Keys*, December 1936, 16, quoted in Matera, "Black Internationalism," 160–61.

16. Martin, *Amy Ashwood Garvey*, 136–41; Adi and Sherwood, *Pan-African History*, 69–70.

17. Hubert Harrison Diary, March 5, 1925, Hubert Harrison Papers, box 9, folder 2, Rare Book and Manuscript Library, Columbia University, New York; Makonnen, *Pan-Africanism*, 130; James quoted in Martin, *Amy Ashwood Garvey*, 140–42, 144.

18. *Sunday Express* quoted in Martin, *Amy Ashwood Garvey*, 140.

19. Ibid., 141; C. L. R. James, "Black Intellectuals," 160; Asante, *Pan-African Protest*, 45. The group originally was called the International African Friends of Abyssinia, but it quickly substituted "Ethiopia" in its name. An August 14, 1935, letter from Jomo Kenyatta to Sylvia Pankhurst suggests that the group had just formed, though it was publicly active by late July and holding public meetings at the time of this letter. Pad-more later claimed the IAFE grew out of his Gold Coast ad hoc committee formed in 1934 to aid the Aborigines' Rights Protection Society. See *Daily Herald*, August 19, 1935, 2; Esedebe, *Pan-Africanism*, 98; Padmore, *Pan-Africanism or Communism?*, 144–45; Barbara Bush, *Imperialism*, 222; Martin, *Amy Ashwood Garvey*, 141.

20. J. M. Kenyatta, "Hands Off Abyssinia," *Labour Monthly*, September 1935, 532.

21. Langley, *Pan-Africanism*, 326–37.

22. Harris, *African-American Reactions*, 26, 25–28; *Daily Herald*, September 2, 1935, 7; Kelley, *Race Rebels*, 123–58.

23. Corthorn, *In the Shadow*, 2–6, 62–63, 73–83; Owen, *British Left and India*, 209; J. M. Kenyatta, "Hands Off Abyssinia," *Labour Monthly*, September 1935, 536; GP, "Ethiopia and World Politics," *Crisis*, May 1935, 139, 157.

24. GP, "Ethiopia and World Politics," *Crisis*, May 1935, 139; GP, "The Missionary Racket in Africa," *Crisis*, July 1935, 214.

25. Adi, *West Africans*, 68–69; Padmore, *Pan-Africanism or Communism?*, 144–45; Edwards, *Practice of Diaspora*, 298; Barbara Bush, *Imperialism*, 222–23. The Comité included Emile Faure, Messali Hadj, and Stéphane Rosso.

26. Rohdie, "Gold Coast Aborigines," 397–402; Asante, "Neglected Aspects," 34–35.

27. Mackenzie, "Radical Pan-Africanism," 72.

28. Makonnen, *Pan-Africanism*, 123, 147; Hall, "Conversation," 21; Cedric Robinson, *Black Marxism*, 262.

29. C. L. R. James, "Lectures," 69.

30. Ibid.

31. James quoted in Asante, *Pan-African Protest*, 46.

32. *Daily Herald*, August 26, 1935, 3; Martin, *Amy Ashwood Garvey*, 142–44, 150; Adi, *West Africans*, 68; Ben Bradley to Secretary of the National Joint Council of the Labour Party and T[rade] U[nion] C[ommittee], October 13, 1935, LP/JSM/CP/144i, and James Maxton to Ben Bradley, October 16, 1935, LP/JSM/CP/144ii, Labour Party Papers. On the tradition of public political speeches in Trafalgar Square and Hyde Park's Speaker's Corner, see Keller, *Triumph*. Monolulu was arrested at a September 15, 1935, IAFE rally in Hyde Park for "using indecent expressions." See *Times* (London), September 24, 1935, 11.

33. Corthorn, *In the Shadow*, 69–72.

34. Martin, *Amy Ashwood Garvey*, 144–45; Harris, *African-American Reactions*, 65–66; Adi, *West Africans*, 68; Adi and Sherwood, *Pan-African History*, 71.

35. Martin, *Amy Ashwood Garvey*, 150.

36. Adi and Sherwood, *Pan-African History*, 71; Makonnen, *Pan-Africanism*, 113–14.

37. *New Leader*, June 5, 1936, 5. C. L. R. James reprints this letter in "Black Intellectuals," 158–59. James and the IAFE's plan anticipated the successful efforts of Amílcar Cabral and the Partido Africano da Independência da Guiné e Cabo Verde to agitate among Portuguese soldiers against the Portuguese empire and dictatorship, efforts that led to the bloodless military coup in Portugal on April 25, 1974. See Chabal, *Amilcar Cabral*, 143–54.

38. C. L. R. James, "Black Intellectuals," 159–60; Adi and Sherwood, *Pan-African History*, 71; Bunche Diary, April 7, 1937; Makonnen, *Pan-Africanism*, 114–15.

39. C. L. R. James, "Abyssinia and the Imperialists," *The Keys*, January–March 1936, 40; Scott, *Conscripts*, 123.

40. Padmore, *How Britain Rules*, 4, 8.

41. C. L. R. James, "'Civilising' the 'Blacks,'" *New Leader*, May 29, 1936, 5.

42. Based on James's review of *How Britain Rules Africa*, the edition referenced here, published in 1969, differs from the 1936 edition only in that the chapters lack the subheadings that appeared in the original edition.

43. Padmore, *How Britain Rules*, 391–92; Alexander, *International Trotskyism*, 447–49; Upham, "History of British Trotskyism"; C. L. R. James, "The Workers and Sanctions," *New Leader*, October 25, 1935, 4; C. L. R. Rudder [C. L. R. James], "Popular Fronts in Past Times," *Fight*, December 12, 1936, 16; "The Annual Conference," *The Keys*, July–September 1936, 4; Corthorn, *In the Shadow*, 124, 140. In *Fight*, James took to signing his articles with the humorous byline C. L. R. Rudder. Rudder was actually his maternal grandfather's surname. See Rosengarten, *Urbane Revolutionary*, 11.

44. Makonnen, *Pan-Africanism*, 114, 117, 179, 184; extract from Scotland Yard Report 85, March 10, 1937, TNA: PRO IOR/L/JP/12/257, 18–24; Bogues, "C. L. R. James," 196; Pennybacker, *From Scottsboro to Munich*, 85.

45. Hooker, *Black Revolutionary*, 45–47; Owen, *British Left and India*, 203–39; Surveillance Report, June 29, 1938, TNA: PRO KV 2/1824, 28A; Metropolitan Police Report, September 12, 1938, TNA: PRO KV 2/1824, 34A. Bunche records Padmore entertaining the grandson of the famed Bengali poet and intellectual Rabindranath Tagore. See Bunche Diary, March 24, 1937.

46. Palmer, *Eric Williams*, 16; Mackenzie, "Radical Pan-Africanism," 72; Richardson, Chrysostom, and Grimshaw, *C. L. R. James*; Reynolds, *My Life*, 117; C. L. R. James, *At the Rendezvous*, 257; Bunche Diary, March 31, April 5, 25, 1937; Urquhart, *Ralph Bunche*, 64–66; Charles P. Henry, *Ralph Bunche*, 77–78. On Indian radicals in London at this time, see Owen, *British Left and India*.

47. Wallace-Johnson was never arrested or charged, though the Colonial Office waited until March 1934 to drop the matter. Spitzer and Denzer, "I. T. A. Wallace-Johnson [Part I]," 419–25; A. C. Burns Report, December 5, 1933, TNA: PRO CO 583/195/4, 11; Reginald Bridgeman to Undersecretary of State for the Colonies, Colonial Office, London, January 8, 1934, TNA: PRO CO 583/195/4, 11A; Alex Fiddian to Reginald Bridgeman, February 6, 1934, TNA: PRO CO 583/195/4, 8; A. C. Burns to I. T. A. Wallace-Johnson, March 29, 1934, TNA: PRO CO 583/195/4, 6.

48. Azikiwe, the paper's editor, was also arrested, though only Wallace-Johnson was tried and convicted. See *Times* (London), May 27, 1938, 4; Spitzer and Denzer, "I. T. A. Wallace-Johnson [Part I]," 428, 433, 440–45; Nkrumah, *Ghana*, 22–23.

49. Colonel Sir Vernon Kell to F. J. Howard, June 21, 1937, TNA: PRO CO 323/1517/2, 9; "Secret: Wallace Johnson and the International African Service Bureau," n.d., TNA: PRO CO 323/1610/2. In Gold Coast, Wallace-Johnson had conceived a "Pan-West African organization." See Spitzer and Denzer, "I. T. A. Wallace-Johnson [Part I]," 433.

50. Bunche Diary, April 5, 12, 18, 23, 24, 29, 1937; Mbinga Koinange to Ralph Bunche, April 23, 1937, box 10b, folder 14, Ralph J. Bunche Papers, General Correspondence, SCRBC; Asante, *Pan-African Protest*, 206; Azikiwe, *My Odyssey*, 193, 197–98; Matera, "Black Internationalism," 159. Yergan's International Committee on African Affairs would come under Robeson's leadership in 1942, when Robeson changed its name to the Council on African Affairs. See Von Eschen, *Race against Empire*, 17–18; Anthony, *Max Yergan*, 167–84.

51. IASB Press Release, n.d., "The International African Service Bureau for the Defense of Africans and Peoples of African Descent" (pamphlet), both in box 10b, folder 13, Bunche Papers, General Correspondence, SCRBC; "What Is the International African Service Bureau?" (pamphlet), n.d., TNA: PRO MEPO 38/91; C. L. R. James, "Notes on the Life of George Padmore," 38; "Our Policy," *African Sentinel*, October–November 1937, 1; Makonnen, *Pan-Africanism*, 117; Padmore, *Pan-Africanism or Communism?*, 147; Hooker, *Black Revolutionary*, 49; Edwards, *Practice of Diaspora*, 303.

52. Metropolitan Police Report, July 6, 1937, TNA: PRO MEPO 38/91; Bunche Diary, May 1, 1937; "Secret: Wallace Johnson and the International African Service Bureau," n.d., TNA: PRO CO 323/1610/2; Colonial Office Report, September 16, 1935, TNA: PRO MEPO 38/9, 34A; PF.40304/DS9, July 2, 1937, TNA: PRO MEPO 38/9, 40a; Owen, *British Left and India*, 243; Von Eschen, *Race against Empire*, 18. Other IASB patrons included Ethel Mannin, Geraldine Young, Cunard, Sylvia Pankhurst, Communist Victor Gollancz of the Left Book Club, and Max Yergan.

53. *African Sentinel*, October–November 1937, 2; *Jewish Record*, September 27, 1937, 2; "Secret: Wallace Johnson and the International African Service Bureau," n.d., TNA: PRO CO 323/1610/2; *CD*, October 2, 1937, 24; *AN*, September 3, 1938, 1; GP, "A Negro Looks at British Imperialism," *Crisis*, December 1938, 397; *Gold Coast Spectator*, July 13, 1937, TNA: PRO CO 323/1517/2, 15; MetPol Report, August 17, 1937, TNA: PRO MEPO 38/91; "Manifesto of the Second World Congress against Racism and Anti-Semitism (Paris, September 10–13, 1937)," "Copie d'un Ordre du Jour Vote à Dakar (Sénégal)," both in box 10, folder 10, Louise Thompson Patterson Papers, MARBL; "Paris Conference and Spain," chap. 7, Unpublished Memoirs, box 20, folder 6, Patterson Papers.

54. Arthur Lewis, *Labour*, 21–38; Reddock, *Women*, 155–61; MacDonald, *Trinidad and Tobago*, 57–60; Bolland, *On the March*, 113–20; Schwarz, "C. L. R. James," 43–46; Kelvin Singh, *Race and Class Struggles*, 158–72.

55. *Africa and the World*, July 27, 1937, 9, 10, August 14, 1937, 1–4; *African Sentinel*, October–November 1937, 10; Surveillance Report, August 8, 1937, TNA: PRO KV 2/1824, 13A; Rupert Lewis, *Marcus Garvey*, 269–70; Schwarz, "C. L. R. James," 49; *Pittsburgh Courier*, August 28, 1937, 7; *AN*, July 16, 1938, 4; *CD*, September 11, 1937, 24, July 23, 1938, 24; "An Open Letter to the Workers of the West Indies and British Guiana," June 26, 1938, TNA: PRO MEPO 38/91; Teelucksingh, "Immortal Batsman," 9–10.

56. Bunche Diary, March 24, April 5, 15, June 15, 1937; IASB Executive Committee, "Sir Stafford Cripps and 'Trusteeship,'" *International African Opinion*, September 1938, 3.

57. Bunche Diary, June 24, July 7, 1937; Mackenzie, "Radical Pan-Africanism," 72, 73; Richardson, Chrysostom, and Grimshaw, *C. L. R. James*; Martin, *Amy Ashwood Garvey*, 145. James and Padmore also routinely heckled Garvey when he spoke at Speaker's Corner. Nonetheless, Padmore and Garvey had developed a mutual respect, visiting one another's flats, and Garvey donated money to the IASB. See C. L. R. James, "Notes on the Life of George Padmore," 31a; Bunche Diary, April 23, June 3, 1937; Martin, *Amy Ashwood Garvey*, 146.

58. M. M. Milne-Thomson to Major W. H. A. Bishop, April 14, 1938, TNA: PRO CO 323/1610/2, 26; M. M. Milne-Thomson to R. J. D. Lamont, May 8, 1938, TNA: PRO CO 323/1610/2, 29; D. J. Jardine to O. G. R. Williams, May 12, 1938, TNA: PRO CO 323/1610/2, 31; Surveillance Report, June 8, 1938, TNA: PRO KV 2/1824, 24A; E. B. Boya to R. H. Drayton, n.d., TNA: PRO CO 323/1610/2, 43; Spitzer and Denzer, "I. T. A. Wallace-Johnson [Part I]," 450–52.

59. *CD*, October 25, 1938; GP, "Fascism in the Colonies," *Controversy*, February 1938, 94–97; GP, "Hands Off the Colonies!," *New Leader*, February 25, 1938, 5; TNA: PRO CO 323/1518/9, 11; Hooker, *Black Revolutionary*, 46; Mackenzie, "Radical Pan-Africanism," 72; E. B. Boya to R. H. Drayton, n.d., TNA: PRO CO 323/1610/2, 43.

60. "Editorial," *International African Opinion*, July 1938, 2–3.

61. *International African Opinion*, July 1938, 26, August 1938, 5; Langston Hughes, "August 19th: Scottsboro Death Date," *International African Opinion*, August 1938, 7; Richard B. Moore, "Toussaint — The Black Liberator," *International African Opinion*, May–June 1939, 4–5; Invitation from "Indian Swaraj League, London," to tea party at

Taj-Mahal Restaurant, West Street, Cambridge Circus, May 29, 1937, box 10b, folder 14, Bunche Papers, General Correspondence, SCRBC; Quest, "George Padmore's and C. L. R. James's *International African Opinion*," 104.

62. H. R. Oke to Malcolm MacDonald, July 1, 1938, TNA: PRO CO 323/1610/2, 51; Colonel Sir Vernon Keel to F. J. Howard, September 1938, TNA: PRO CO 323/1610/2, 55.

63. Matera, "Colonial Studies," 388–90.

64. Though some of these works were written before the creation of the IASB, all were published and/or written in England in the 1930s. See Padmore, *How Britain Rules*; Padmore, *Africa*; Kenyatta, *Facing Mount Kenya*; C. L. R. James, *Minty Alley*; C. L. R. James, *Case for West Indian Self-Government*; C. L. R. James, *World Revolution*; C. L. R. James, *Black Jacobins*; C. L. R. James, *History*; Arthur Lewis, *Labour*. The periodicals included *Fight* and *International African Opinion* (edited by James), *African Sentinel* and *Africa and the World* (edited by Wallace-Johnson). The play was James's *Toussaint L'Overture*, which ran in mid-March 1936. For this play, see C. L. R. James, *C. L. R. James Reader*, 66–111.

65. Rosengarten, *Urbane Revolutionary*, 52.

66. Richardson, Chrysostom, and Grimshaw, *C. L. R. James*; Reynolds, *My Life*, 116, 141; Warburg, *Occupation*, 185, 211.

67. James quoted in Cedric Robinson, *Black Marxism*, 265.

68. C. L. R. James, *World Revolution*, xxv, 12–13.

69. Ibid., 55, 65, 115, 312. All but one of James's references to "Africa" and "Africans" concerned the failure of the Second International with regard to colonialism or concerned colonialism more generally, while he summoned "Abyssinia" specifically to criticize the Comintern (86, 103, 230, 170).

70. Ibid., 386–89.

71. Mackenzie, "Radical Pan-Africanism," 70.

72. Padmore, *Africa*, 3, 5, 257–58, 263–64. Padmore quotes a 1915 pamphlet by Gregory Zinoviev and V. I. Lenin. See Lenin, *Collected Works*, 21:295–338.

73. Mackenzie, "Radical Pan-Africanism," 70.

74. C. L. R. James, *Black Jacobins*, 376–77.

75. In a testament to James's heft and complexity, postcolonial theorist David Scott (*Conscripts*) took this declaration as inviting an interrogation of how the seven paragraphs that James added to beginning of the 1963 edition's last chapter completely altered the book's narrative structure from a vindicationist romance in order to address the tragedy of postcolonial governance.

76. Bogues, *Black Heretics*, 78, 81; Buck-Morss, *Hegel, Haiti, and Universal History*, 56–58. It is important to note Bogues's observation that James premised his argument for the Saint Domingue slaves' humanity on their ability to struggle, which Bogues considers a "failure to rework the premodern/modern divide in ways which would have been more reflective of African realities." Bogues, *Black Heretics*, 80.

77. Schwarz, "C. L. R. James," 50.

78. C. L. R. James, "Lectures," 69, 71, 72.

79. C. L. R. James, *Black Jacobins*, 197–98, 239–240, 288, 402.

80. Surveillance Report, February 10, 1937, TNA: PRO KV 2/1824, 5B.

81. Warburg, *An Occupation*, 214; Fenner Brockway, "The Rise and Fall of the Com-

munist International," *New Leader*, April 16, 1937, 2; C. L. R. James to *New Leader*, April 23, 1937, 2.

82. *AN*, November 5, 1938, 17, December 17, 1938, 4, 24; *Pittsburgh Courier*, December 17, 1938, 2; *CD*, February 4, 1939, 3, February 11, 1929, 6.

83. C. L. R. James to unknown, February 28, 1939, Leon Trotsky Exile Papers (MS Russ 13.1), Series I:2069, Houghton Library, Harvard University, Cambridge, Mass.; Rosengarten, *Urbane Revolutionary*, 51–52.

84. Boggs, *Living*, 45–116.

85. James later remarked that his and Padmore's greatest achievement was "the working out of the theory which shaped the revolution in the gold coast . . . and with this the total rout of all imperialist pretensions to continue to rule in Africa." James, "Notes of the Life of George Padmore," 38.

EPILOGUE

1. CB, testimony, in *Hearings*, 78.

2. CB to Harry Haywood, July 22, 1962, Harry Haywood Papers, SCRBC.

3. Ibid. Briggs especially lamented what he considered the gulf between New Negro movement radicals and civil rights and Black Power activists. But this view misses the connections that New Negro movement radicals made with subsequent radical formations. The involvement of former Communist organizer Audley Moore in the defense campaign for Robert F. Williams in Monroe, North Carolina, demonstrates the existence of such ties. Moore had also worked with Malcolm X and Black Power activists connected to Maxwell Stanford (Muhammad Ahmad) in the Revolutionary Action Movement. See Ahmad, *We Will Return*, 7–13, 104. For an insightful study of Moore and other radical black women in the American Communist Party, see McDuffie, *Sojourning*. For a discussion of Cold War black women radicals, see Gore, *Radicalism*.

4. Césaire, *Letter to Maurice Thorez*, 6, 12–13.

5. McLemee, *C. L. R. James*, 139.

6. Bogues, *Caliban's Freedom*, 94–96. For James's participation in the socialist movement and the Fourth International in the United States, see Le Blanc, "Introduction."

7. Students of James and the Johnson-Forrest Tendency will recognize this as a major point over which James would later break with Grace Lee Boggs and James Boggs, though in that instance he rejected the suggestion that black people would replace workers as the ushers of socialism. For a recounting, see Boggs, *Living*, 107–9.

8. Foucault, *Power/Knowledge*, 110–11. See also Foucault's January 7, 1976, lecture in *Power/Knowledge*, esp. 83–89.

9. Mullen, *Afro-Orientalism*, xxiv–xxv.

10. Padmore, *Colonial and . . . Coloured Unity*; Adi, "George Padmore," 71–90.

11. Adi, "George Padmore," 89.

12. Ibid.

13. Kelley, "Poetics," 10.

14. Césaire, *Discourse*, 78.

15. Kelley, "Poetics," 24.

Bibliography

A NOTE ON SOURCES

A good deal of research material used in this work came from archives in Moscow, Russia, in the Russian State Archive of Sociopolitical History (RGASPI), formerly the Russian Center for the Preservation and Study of Documents of Recent History (RTsKhIDNI). My work has been aided by the opening of the Russian archives in the mid-1990s and by a 1998 agreement between the Library of Congress and RTsKhIDNI to microfilm the records of the Communist Party of the United States of America and make them available to U.S.-based researchers. This microfilm collection is available at the Library of Congress as well as at the Yale University Library Microfilm Room. Equally invaluable was the work of the International Committee for the Computerization of the Comintern Archive (INCOMKA), a project established by the International Council on Archives to facilitate access to the Comintern's archival materials. Those materials can be accessed at a workstation in the Library of Congress European Reading Room. (INCOMKA workstations are also available at the Archives Nationales in France; the Federal Archives in Germany; the State Archives in Italy; the National Archives in Sweden; the Federal Archives in Switzerland; the Ministry of Education, Culture, and Sport in Spain; and the Open Society Archives in Hungary.) Though this archive includes only part of the vast collection from the RGASPI, it contains a great deal of material from the Negro Bureau (fond 495) and the League against Imperialism (fond 542) that proved essential to writing chapters 5 and 6. Susan Pennybacker graciously shared with me her extensive research from Moscow for her *From Scottsboro to Munich*. For a historian working in the especially contentious field of Comintern history and in an era of increasingly hypercompetitive, almost proprietary disputes over sources, Susan easily shared the results of her years of hard labor in the rather unwieldy Moscow archives, when there were no INCOMKA or microfilm collections in the Library of Congress. Her generosity made writing chapter 6 possible. Meredith Roman helped me identify important files in fond 534, which my colleague, Jochen Hellbeck, helped me access through a researcher in Moscow. Though I could only get a few of the more than one thousand pages of documents Meredith suggested I consult, those materials still proved invaluable.

Research in the League against Imperialism Archives, held at the International Institute of Social History in Amsterdam, Netherlands, turned up several documents in French. Christiana Oladini-James translated all of these documents into English. Unless otherwise noted, Comintern (INCOMKA) documents in French were translated by myself (with help from numerous friends, especially Brent Edwards and Charlotte Thomas).

MANUSCRIPT COLLECTIONS

England

British Library, London
  Asia, Pacific, and Africa Collection
People's History Museum, Labour History Archive and Study Center, Manchester
  Labour Party Papers
Public Records Office, National Archives, Kew Gardens, London
  Colonial Office
  Metropolitan Police

Netherlands

International Institute of Social History, Amsterdam
  League against Imperialism Archives

United States

Chicago Historical Society, Manuscript Collection, Chicago
  Claude A. Barnett Papers
Columbia University, Rare Book and Manuscript Library, New York
  Hubert Henry Harrison Papers
  Robert Minor Papers
Emory University, Manuscript, Archives, and Rare Books Library, Atlanta
  Theodore Draper Research Files
  Louise Thompson Patterson Papers
Harvard University, Houghton Library, Cambridge, Mass.
  Leon Trotsky Exile Papers (MS Russ 13.1)
Howard University, Manuscript Division, Moreland-Spingarn Research Center,
    Washington, D.C.
  Kelly Miller Papers
Library of Congress, Manuscript Division, Washington, D.C.
  Communist Party of the United States of America Records
  National Archives of the Department of Justice
  National Association for the Advancement of Colored People Manuscript
    Collection
New York University, Tamiment Library and Robert F. Wagner Labor Archives,
    New York
  Communist Party USA Archives
    James Ford Papers
    Robert Minor Papers
  Mark Solomon and Robert Kaufman Research Files on African Americans
    and Communism
Schomburg Center for Research in Black Culture, Manuscript, Archives, and Rare
    Books Division, New York Public Library, New York
  Egbert Ethelred Brown Papers

Ralph J. Bunche Papers, General Correspondence
J. R. Ralph Casimer Papers
Frank Crosswaith Papers
St. Clair Drake Papers
Harry Haywood Papers
Oakley C. Johnson Papers
Richard B. Moore Papers
George Padmore Letters
William Pickens Papers (Additions)
George Schuyler Papers
Stanford University, Hoover Institute on War, Revolution, and Peace, Stanford, Calif.
    Theodore Draper Collection
United States National Archives and Record Administration, College Park, Md.
    General Records of the Department of Justice, Record Group 60
    Records of the Federal Bureau of Investigation, Record Group 65
University of California at Los Angeles, Department of Special Collections,
        Charles E. Young Library, Los Angeles
    Ralph J. Bunche Papers

NEWSPAPERS AND MAGAZINES

Africa and the World
African Sentinel
Amsterdam News
Atlanta Daily World
Baltimore Afro-American
Chicago Daily Tribune
Chicago Defender
Cincinnati Commercial
Communist (newspaper)
The Communist (monthly journal)
Controversy
Crisis
Crusader
Daily Herald
Daily Worker
Emancipator
Fight
Harlem Liberator
International African Opinion
International Press Correspondence
International Socialist Review

Jewish Record
Liberator
Living Age
Manchester Guardian
Messenger
Modern View
Negro Champion
Negro Worker
New Leader
New York Times
Norfolk Journal and Guide
Pittsburgh Courier
Survey Graphic
Time
Times (London)
Voice of the Negro
Washington Post
Worker
Workers Dreadnaught
Workers Monthly

MICROFILM

Kornweibel, Theodore, ed. *Federal Surveillance of Afro-Americans (1917–1925): The First World War, the Red Scare, and the Garvey Movement.* Frederick, Md.: University Publications of America, 1986.

BOOKS

Adhikari, G., ed. *Documents of the History of the Communist Party of India.* Vol. 1, 1917–22. New Delhi: People's Publishing, 1971.

Adi, Hakim. *West Africans in Britain, 1900–1960: Nationalism, Pan-Africanism, and Communism.* London: Lawrence and Wishart, 1998.

Adi, Hakim, and Marika Sherwood. *Pan-African History: Political Figures from Africa and the Diaspora since 1787.* London: Routledge, 2003.

Ahmad, Muhammad (Maxwell Stanford Jr.). *We Will Return in the Whirlwind: Radical Organizations, 1960–1975.* Chicago: Kerr, 2007.

Alba, Victor. *Politics and the Labor Movement in Latin America.* Trans. Carol de Zapata. Palo Alto, Calif.: Stanford University Press, 1968.

Alexander, Robert Jackson. *International Trotskyism, 1929–1985: A Documented Analysis of the Movement.* Durham, N.C.: Duke University Press, 1991.

Allen, Theodore. *The Invention of the White Race.* Vol. 1. New York: Verso, 1994.

Anderson, Benedict. *Imagined Communities: Reflections on the Origin and Spread of Nationalism.* New York: Verso, 1983.

Anderson, Jarvis. *A. Philip Randolph: A Biographical Portrait.* New York: Harcourt Brace Jovanovich, 1973.

Anthony, David Henry, III. *Max Yergan: Race Man, Internationalist, Cold Warrior.* New York: New York University Press, 2006.

Aptheker, Herbert, ed. *Documentary History of the Negro People in the United States.* Vol. 3, *From the NAACP to the New Deal, 1910–1932.* New York: Citadel, 1990.

Archer, Bob, trans. *Second Congress of the Communist International: Minutes of the Proceedings, Volume Two.* London: New Park Publications, 1977.

Asante, S. K. B. *Pan-African Protest: West Africa and the Italo-Ethiopian Crisis, 1934–1941.* London: Longman, 1977.

Azikiwe, Nnamdi. *My Odyssey: An Autobiography.* New York: Praeger, 1970.

Babu, Abdul Rahman Mohamed. *African Socialism or Socialist Africa?* London: Zed Press, 1981.

Baldwin, Davarian. *Chicago's New Negroes: Modernity, the Great Migration, and Black Urban Life.* Chapel Hill: University of North Carolina Press, 2007.

Baldwin, Kate A. *Beyond the Color Line and the Iron Curtain: Reading Encounters between Black and Red, 1922–1963.* Durham, N.C.: Duke University Press, 2002.

Bates, Beth Tompkins. *Pullman Porters and the Rise of Protest Politics in Black America, 1925–1945.* Chapel Hill: University of North Carolina Press, 2001.

Biondi, Martha. *To Stand and Fight: The Struggle for Civil Rights in Postwar New York City.* Cambridge: Harvard University Press, 2003.

Blaut, James M. *The National Question: Decolonising the Theory of Nationalism.* London: Zed, 1987.

Boggs, Grace Lee. *Living for Change: An Autobiography*. Minneapolis: University of Minnesota Press, 1998.

Bogues, Anthony. *Black Heretics, Black Prophets: Radical Political Intellectuals*. New York: Routledge, 2003.

———. *Caliban's Freedom: The Early Political Thought of C. L. R. James*. Chicago: Pluto, 1997.

Bolland, O. Nigel. *On the March: Labour Rebellions in the British Caribbean, 1934–1939*. Kingston, Jamaica: Ian Randle, 1995.

Bracey, John, August Meier, and Elliot Rudwick, eds. *Black Nationalism in America*. Indianapolis, Ind.: Bobbs-Merrill, 1970.

Braziel, Jana Evans, and Anita Mannur, eds. *Theorizing Diaspora: A Reader*. Malden, Mass.: Blackwell, 2003.

Brockway, Fenner. *Inside the Left: Thirty Years of Platform, Press, Prison and Parliament*. London: New Leader, 1947.

Brown, Jacqueline Nassy. *Dropping Anchor, Setting Sail: Geographies of Race in Black Liverpool*. Princeton: Princeton University Press, 2005.

Buck-Morss, Susan. *Hegel, Haiti, and Universal History*. Pittsburgh, Pa.: University of Pittsburgh Press, 2009.

Buhle, Mari Jo, Paul Buhle, and Dan Georgakas, eds. *Encyclopedia of the American Left*. Urbana: University of Illinois Press, 1992.

Buhle, Paul. *C. L. R. James: The Artist as Revolutionary*. New York: Verso, 1988.

———. *Marxism in the United States*. New York: Verso, 1987.

Burton, Antoinette, ed. *After the Imperial Turn: Thinking with and through the Nation*. Durham, N.C.: Duke University Press, 2003.

———. *Dwelling in the Archives: Women Writing House, Home, and History in Late Colonial India*. New York: Oxford University Press, 2003.

Bush, Barbara. *Imperialism, Race, and Resistance: Africa and Britain, 1919–1945*. London: Routledge, 1999.

Bush, Rod. *The End of White World Supremacy: Black Internationalism and the Problem of the Color Line*. Philadelphia: Temple University Press, 2009.

Cabral, Amílcar. *Unity and Struggle: Speeches and Writings*. New York: Monthly Review Press, 1979.

Césaire, Aimé. *Discourse on Colonialism*. 1955; New York: Monthly Review Press, 2000.

———. *Letter to Maurice Thorez*. Paris: Présence Africaine, 1957.

Chabal, Patrick. *Amilcar Cabral: Revolutionary Leadership and People's War*. Trenton, N.J.: Africa World, 2003.

Chakrabarty, Dipesh. *Provincializing Europe: Postcolonial Thought and Historical Difference*. Princeton: Princeton University Press, 2000.

Chateauvert, Melinda. *Marching Together: Women of the Brotherhood of Sleeping Car Porters*. Urbana: University of Illinois Press, 1998.

Chatterjee, Partha. *The Nation and Its Fragments: Colonial and Postcolonial Histories*. Princeton: Princeton University Press, 1993.

Chilcote, Ronald H. *Amílcar Cabral's Revolutionary Theory and Practice: A Critical Guide*. Boulder, Colo.: L. Rienner Publishers, 1991.

Cohen, Robin. *Global Diasporas: An Introduction.* Seattle: University of Washington Press, 1997.

Cole, Peter, ed. *Ben Fletcher: The Life and Times of a Black Wobbly.* Chicago: Kerr, 2007.

Communist Party USA. *The Communist Position on the Negro Question.* Intro. Nathan Ross. New York: New Century, 1947.

Cooper, Wayne. *Claude McKay: Rebel Sojourner in the Harlem Renaissance.* New York: Schocken, 1987.

———, ed. *The Passion of Claude McKay: Selected Poetry and Prose, 1912–1948.* New York: Schocken Books, 1973.

Corthorn, Paul. *In the Shadow of the Dictators: The British Left in the 1930s.* London: Tauris, 2006.

Cox, Oliver Cromwell. *Capitalism as a System.* New York: Monthly Review Press, 1964.

Cronon, E. David. *Black Moses: The Story of Marcus Garvey and the Universal Negro Improvement Association.* Madison: University of Wisconsin Press, 1969.

Cross, William E., Jr. *Shades of Black: Diversity and African-American Identity.* Philadelphia: Temple University Press, 1991.

Crossman, Richard H. *The God That Failed.* 1949; New York: Columbia University Press, 2001.

Cruse, Harold. *The Crisis of the Negro Intellectual: From Its Origins to the Present.* New York: Morrow, 1967.

Davies, Carol Boyce. *Left of Karl Marx: The Political Life of Black Communist Claudia Jones.* Durham, N.C.: Duke University, 2007.

Degras, Jane T., ed. *The Communist International, 1919–1943.* 3 vols. London: Oxford University Press, 1956–65.

Dirlik, Arif. *Postmodernity's Histories: The Past as Legacy and Project.* Lanham, Md.: Rowman and Littlefield, 2000.

Domingo, W. A. *Socialism Imperiled or, the Negro—A Potential Menace to American Radicalism.* (Pamphlet) In *Revolutionary Radicalism: Its History, Purpose and Tactics, with an Exposition and Discussion of the Steps Being Taken and Required to Curb It.* Pt. 1, vol. 2, 1489–1510. Albany, N.Y.: Lyon, 1920.

Drake, St. Clair, and Horace R. Cayton. *Black Metropolis: A Study of Negro Life in a Northern City.* Chicago: University of Chicago Press, 1993.

Draper, Theodore. *American Communism and Soviet Russia: The Formative Period.* New York: Oxford University Press, 1960.

———. *The Roots of American Communism.* New York: Viking, 1957.

Du Bois, W. E. B. *Autobiography: A Soliloquy on Viewing My Life from the Last Decade of Its First Century.* New York: International, 1968.

———. *Dusk of Dawn: An Essay toward an Autobiography of a Race Concept.* 2nd ed. New Brunswick, N.J.: Transaction, 1991.

———. *W. E. B. Du Bois: A Reader.* Ed. David Levering Lewis. New York: Holt, 1995.

Duiker, William J. *Ho Chi Minh: A Life.* New York: Hyperion, 2000.

Edwards, Brent Hayes. *The Practice of Diaspora: Literature, Translation, and the Rise of Black Internationalism*. Cambridge: Harvard University Press, 2003.

Ellsworth, Scott. *Death in a Promised Land: The Tulsa Race Riot of 1921*. Baton Rouge: Louisiana State University Press, 1982.

Esedebe, P. Olisanwuche. *Pan-Africanism: The Idea and Movement, 1776-1991*. Washington, D.C.: Howard University Press, 1994.

Fabre, Michel. *From Harlem to Paris: Black American Writers in France, 1840-1980*. Chicago: University of Illinois Press, 1993.

Fanon, Frantz. *The Wretched of the Earth*. New York: Grove Weidenfield, 1923.

Fax, Elton C. *Marcus Garvey: The Story of a Pioneer Black Nationalist*. New York: Dood, Mead, 1972.

Ferguson, Jeffrey. *The Sage of Sugar Hill: George Schuyler and the Harlem Renaissance*. New Haven: Yale University Press, 2005.

Fierce, Milfred C. *The Pan-African Idea in the United States, 1900-1919: African-American Interest in Africa and the Interaction with West Africa*. New York: Garland, 1993.

Fifth Congress of the Communist International: Abridged Report of Meetings held at Moscow June 17-July 8, 1924. London: Communist Party of Great Britain, 1923.

Foley, Barbara. *Radical Representations: Politics and Form in U.S. Proletarian Fiction, 1929-1941*. Durham, N.C.: Duke University Press, 1993.

———. *Spectres of 1919: Class and Nation in the Making of the New Negro*. Urbana: University of Illinois Press, 2003.

Foner, Phillip. *American Socialism and Black Americans: From the Age of Jackson to World War II*. Westport, Conn.: Greenwood, 1977.

———. *Organized Labor and the Black Worker, 1619-1981*. New York: International, 1982.

Foner, Phillip, and James Allen, eds. *American Communism and Black Americans: A Documentary History, 1919-1929*. Philadelphia: Temple University Press, 1987.

Foucault, Michel. *The Archeology of Knowledge and the Discourse on Language*. New York: Pantheon, 1972.

———. *Power/Knowledge: Selected Interviews and Other Writings, 1927-1977*. New York: Pantheon, 1980.

Fourth Congress of the Communist International: Abridged Report of Meetings held at Petrograd and Moscow, November 7-December 3, 1922. London: Communist Party of Great Britain, 1923.

Fowler, Josephine. *Japanese and Chinese Immigrant Activists: Organizing in American and International Communist Movements, 1919-1933*. New Brunswick, N.J.: Rutgers University Press, 2007.

Fox, Stephen R. *The Guardian of Boston: William Monroe Trotter*. New York: Athenaeum, 1971.

Gaines, Kevin K. *American Africans in Ghana: Black Expatriates and the Civil Rights Era*. Chapel Hill: University of North Carolina Press, 2006.

———. *Uplifting the Race: Black Leadership, Politics, and Culture in the Twentieth Century*. Chapel Hill: University of North Carolina Press, 1996.

Garvey, Marcus. *Philosophy and Opinions of Marcus Garvey; or, Africa for the Africans.* Ed. Amy Jacques-Garvey. New York: Routledge, 1967.

Gatewood, Willard B. *Aristocrats of Color: The Black Elite, 1880–1920.* Bloomington: Indiana University Press, 1990.

Geiss, Imanuel. *The Pan-African Movement: A History of Pan-Africanism in America, Europe, and Africa.* New York: Africana, 1974.

Gilmore, Glenda Elizabeth. *Defying Dixie: The Radical Roots of Civil Rights, 1919–1950.* New York: Norton, 2008.

Glazer, Nathan. *The Social Basis of American Communism.* New York: Harcourt, Brace, and World, 1961.

Gore, Dayo F. *Radicalism at the Crossroads: African American Women Activists in the Cold War.* New York: New York University Press, 2011.

Grant, Colin. *Negro with a Hat: The Rise and Fall of Marcus Garvey.* New York: Oxford University Press, 2008.

Grant, JoAnne. *Black Protest: 350 Years of History, Documents, and Analyses.* New York: Ballantine, 1996.

Green, James. *Grass-Roots Socialism: Radical Movements in the Southwest, 1895–1943.* Baton Rouge: Louisiana State University Press, 1978.

Greenberg, Cheryl Lynn. *"Or Does It Explode?": Black Harlem in the Great Depression.* New York: Oxford University Press, 1991.

Guterl, Matthew Pratt. *The Color of Race in America, 1900–1940.* Cambridge: Harvard University Press, 2001.

Haithcox, John. *Communism and Nationalism in India: M. N. Roy and Comintern Policy, 1920–1939.* Princeton: Princeton University Press, 1971.

Hanchard, Michael, ed. *Racial Politics in Contemporary Brazil.* Durham, N.C.: Duke University Press, 1999.

Harold, Claudrena N. *The Rise and Fall of the Garvey Movement in the Urban South, 1918–1942.* New York: Routledge, 2007.

Harris, Joseph E. *African-American Reactions to War in Ethiopia, 1936–1941.* Baton Rouge: Louisiana State University Press, 1994.

———, ed. *Global Dimensions of the African Diaspora.* Washington, D.C.: Howard University Press, 1982.

Harrison, Hubert H. *The Negro and the Nation.* New York: Cosmo-Advocate, 1917.

———. *When Africa Awakes: The "Inside Story" of the Stirrings and Strivings of the New Negro in the Western World.* 1920; Baltimore, Md.: Black Classic, 1997.

Hart, John Mason. *Revolutionary Mexico: The Coming and Process of the Mexican Revolution.* Berkeley: University of California Press, 1997.

Haynes, John Earl, and Harvey Klehr. *Venona: Decoding Soviet Espionage in America.* New Haven: Yale University Press, 1999.

Haywood, Harry. *Black Bolshevik: Autobiography of an Afro-American Communist.* Chicago: Liberator, 1978.

Hearings before the Committee on Un-American Activities, House of Representatives, Eighty-fifth Congress, Second Session, Part 1, September 2 and 3, 1958. Washington, D.C.: U.S. Government Printing Office, 1959.

Hellbeck, Jochen. *Revolution on My Mind: Writing a Diary under Stalin.* Cambridge: Harvard University Press, 2006.

Henry, Charles P. *Ralph Bunche: Model Negro or American Other?* New York: New York University Press, 1999.

Hicks, Cheryl D. *Talk with You Like a Woman: African American Women, Justice, and Reform in New York, 1890–1935.* Chapel Hill: University of North Carolina Press, 2010.

Hill, Robert, ed. *Marcus Garvey: Life and Lessons: A Centennial Companion to the Marcus Garvey and Universal Negro Improvement Association Papers.* Berkeley: University of California Press, 1987.

————. *The Marcus Garvey and Universal Negro Improvement Association Papers.* Berkeley: University of California Press, 1983.

Ho Chi Minh. *Ho Chi Minh on Revolution: Selected Writings, 1920–1960.* Ed. Bernard B. Fall. New York: Praeger, 1967.

Hooker, James R. *Black Revolutionary: George Padmore's Path from Communism to Pan-Africanism.* New York: Praeger, 1967.

Horne, Gerald. *Black and Red: W. E. B. Du Bois and the Afro-American Response to the Cold War, 1944–1963.* Albany: State University of New York Press, 1986.

————. *Black Liberation/Red Scare: Ben Davis and the Communist Party.* Newark: University of Delaware Press, 1994.

Hudson, Hosea. *The Narrative of the Life of Hosea Hudson: His Life as a Negro Communist in the South.* Ed. Nell Irvin Painter. Cambridge: Harvard University Press, 1979.

Hughes, Langston. *The Big Sea.* New York: Hill and Wang, 1940.

Isserman, Maurice. *If I Had a Hammer: The Death of the Old Left and the Birth of the New Left.* New York: Basic Books, 1987.

————. *Which Side Were You On?: The American Communist Party during the Second World War.* Urbana: University of Illinois Press, 1993.

James, C. L. R. *At the Rendezvous of Victory: Selected Writings.* London: Allison and Busby, 1984.

————. *Beyond a Boundary.* Durham, N.C.: Duke University Press, 1993.

————. *Black Jacobins: Toussaint L'Ouverture and the San Domingo Revolution.* New York: Vintage, 1989.

————. *The C. L. R. James Reader.* Ed. Anna Grimshaw. Oxford: Blackwell, 1992.

————. *The Case for West Indian Self-Government.* London: Hogarth Press, 1933.

————. *A History of Pan-African Revolt.* 1937; Chicago: Kerr, 1995.

————. *Letters from London: Seven Essays by C. L. R. James.* Oxford: Prospect Park, 2003.

————. *The Life of Captain Cipriani: An Account of British Government in the West Indies.* Nelson, Lancashire: Coulton, 1932.

————. *Mariners, Renegades, and Castaways: The Story of Herman Melville and the World We Live In.* Hanover, N.H.: University Press of New England, 2001.

————. *Minty Alley.* 1936; Jackson: University Press of Mississippi, 1997.

————. *World Revolution, 1917–1936: The Rise and Fall of the Communist International.* 1937; Atlantic Highlands, N.J.: Humanities, 1993.

James, Winston. *Holding Aloft the Banner of Ethiopia: Caribbean Radicalism in Early Twentieth-Century America*. New York: Verso, 1998.

Johnpoll, Bernard K., and Harvey Klehr. *Biographical Dictionary of the American Left*. Westport, Conn.: Greenwood, 1986.

Johns, Sheridan. *Raising the Red Flag: The International Socialist League and the Communist Party in South Africa, 1914–1932*. Belleville, S.A.: Mayibuye, UWL, 1955.

Johnson, Cedric. *Revolutionaries to Race Leaders: Black Power and the Making of African American Politics*. Minneapolis: University of Minnesota Press, 2007.

Jones, Jean. *The League against Imperialism*. Socialist History Society Occasional Papers Series 4. London: Socialist History Society, 1996.

Kasinitz, Philip. *Caribbean New York: Black Immigrants and the Politics of Race*. Ithaca: Cornell University Press, 1992.

Kaye, Sir Cecil. *Communism in India, with Unpublished Documents from the National Archives of India, 1919–1924*. Compiled and edited by Subodh Roy. Calcutta: Editions Indian, 1971.

Keller, Lisa. *Triumph of Order: Democracy and Public Space in New York and London*. New York: Columbia University Press, 2009.

Kelley, Robin D. G. *Freedom Dreams: The Black Radical Imagination*. Boston: Beacon, 2002.

———. *Hammer and Hoe: Alabama Communists during the Great Depression*. Chapel Hill: University of North Carolina Press, 1990.

———. *Race Rebels: Culture, Politics, and the Black Working Class*. New York: Free Press, 1996.

Kenyatta, Jomo. *Facing Mt. Kenya*. New York: Vintage, 1965.

Klehr, Harvey. *The Heyday of American Communism: The Depression Decade*. New York: Basic Books, 1984.

Klehr, Harvey, and John Earl Haynes. *The American Communist Movement: Storming Heaven Itself*. New York: Twayne, 1992.

Klehr, Harvey, John Earl Haynes, and Kyrill Anderson. *The Soviet World of American Communism*. New Haven: Yale University Press, 1998.

Klehr, Harvey, John Earl Haynes, and Fridrikh Igorevich Firsov. *The Secret World of American Communism*. New Haven: Yale University Press, 1996.

Kornweibel, Theodore, Jr. *No Crystal Stair: Black Life and "The Messenger," 1917–1928*. Westport, Conn.: Greenwood, 1977.

———. *"Seeing Red": Federal Campaigns against Black Militancy, 1919–1925*. Bloomington: Indiana University Press, 1998.

Korstad, Robert. *Civil Rights Unionism: Tobacco Workers and the Struggle for Democracy in the Mid-Twentieth-Century South*. Chapel Hill: University of North Carolina Press, 2003.

Kurashige, Scott. *The Shifting Grounds of Race: Black and Japanese Americans in the Making of Multiethnic Los Angeles*. Princeton: Princeton University Press, 2008.

Langley, J. Ayodele. *Pan-Africanism and Nationalism in West Africa: A Study in Ideology and Social Classes*. Oxford: Clarendon Press, 1973.

Lemelle, Sidney, and Robin D. G. Kelley, eds. *Imagining Home: Class, Culture, and Nationalism in the African Diaspora*. New York: Verso, 1994.

Lenin, V. I. *Collected Works*. Vols. 5, 20, 21, 22, 23, 31. Moscow: Progress, 1964–77.

———. *National Liberation, Socialism, and Imperialism: Selected Writings*. New York: International, 1970.

Lentz-Smith, Adriane. *Freedom Struggles: African Americans and World War I*. Cambridge: Harvard University Press, 2009.

Lewis, Arthur. *Labour in the West Indies: The Birth of a Workers Movement*. 1939; London: New Beacon, 1977.

Lewis, David Levering. *W. E. B. Du Bois: Biography of a Race*. New York: Holt, 1993.

———. *W. E. B. Du Bois: The Fight for Equality in the American Century, 1919–1963*. New York: Henry Holt and Company, 2000.

———. *When Harlem Was in Vogue*. New York: Oxford University Press, 1989.

Lewis, Rupert. *Marcus Garvey: Anti-Colonial Champion*. Trenton, N.J.: Africa World Press, 1998.

Locke, Alain, ed. *The New Negro*. New York: Atheneum, 1992.

MacDonald, Scott B. *Trinidad and Tobago: Democracy and Development in the Caribbean*. New York: Praeger, 1986.

Makonnen, T. Ras. *Pan-Africanism from Within*. London: Oxford University Press, 1973.

Manela, Erez. *The Wilsonian Moment: Self-Determination and the International Origins of Anticolonial Nationalism*. New York: Oxford University Press, 2007.

Manjapra, Kris. *M. N. Roy: Marxism and Colonial Cosmopolitanism*. Delhi: Routledge, 2010.

Mannin, Ethel. *Comrade O Comrade; or, Low-Down on the Left*. London: Jerrolds, 1947.

Marjomaa, Risto. *The LACO and the LAI: Willi Münzenberg and Africa*. Comintern Working Paper 4. 2005. Available online at https://www.abo.fi/student/media/7957/cowopa4marjomaa.pdf. Accessed December 1, 2010.

Martin, Tony. *Amy Ashwood Garvey: Pan-Africanist, Feminist, and Mrs. Marcus Garvey no. 1; or, A Tale of Two Amies*. Dover, Mass.: Majority, 2007.

———. *Race First: The Ideological and Organizational Struggles of Marcus Garvey and the Universal Negro Improvement Association*. Dover, Mass.: Majority, 1986.

Marx, Karl. *Capital*. Vol. 1, *A Critical Analysis of Capitalist Production*. New York: International, 1987.

———. *The First International and After: Political Writings*. Ed. David Fernbach. Vol. 3. London: Penguin, 1992.

Maxwell, William J. *New Negro, Old Left: African-American Writing and Communism between the Wars*. New York: Columbia University Press, 1999.

Mbembe, Achille. *On the Postcolony*. Berkeley: University of California Press, 2001.

McDuffie, Erik. *Sojourning for Freedom: Black Women, American Communism, and the Making of Black Left Feminism*. Durham, N.C.: Duke University Press, 2010.

McKay, Claude. *A Long Way from Home*. New York: Harcourt, Brace, 1970.

———. *The Negroes in America*. Trans. Robert Winter. 1923; Port Washington, N.Y.: Kennikat Press, 1979.

McLemee, Scott, ed. *C. L. R. James on the "Negro Question."* Jackson: University Press of Mississippi, 1996.

McMeekin, Sean. *The Red Millionaire: A Political Biography of Willi Münzenberg, Moscow's Secret Propaganda Tsar in the West.* New Haven: Yale University Press, 2003.

Mignolo, Walter D. *Local Histories/Global Designs: Colonality, Subaltern Knowledges, and Border Thinking.* Princeton: Princeton University Press, 2000.

Miller, James A. *Remembering Scottsboro: The Legacy of an Infamous Trail.* Princeton: Princeton University Press, 2009.

Mills, Charles W. *Blackness Visible: Essays on Philosophy and Race.* Ithaca: Cornell University Press, 1998.

———. *From Class to Race: Essays in White Marxism and Black Radicalism.* Lanham, Md.: Rowman and Littlefield, 2003.

Mitchell, Michelle. *Righteous Propagation: African Americans and the Politics of Racial Destiny after Reconstruction.* Chapel Hill: University of North Carolina Press, 2004.

Moore, Richard B. *Richard B. Moore, Caribbean Militant in Harlem: Collected Writings, 1920–1972.* Ed. W. Burghardt Turner and Joyce Moore Turner. Bloomington: Indiana University Press, 1992.

Moses, Wilson J. *Afrotopia: The Roots of African American Popular History.* New York: Cambridge University Press, 1998.

———. *The Golden Age of Black Nationalism, 1850–1925.* Hamden, Conn.: Archon, 1978.

Mullen, Bill V. *Afro-Orientalism.* Minneapolis: University of Minnesota Press, 2004.

———. *Popular Fronts: Chicago and African-American Cultural Politics, 1935–46.* Urbana: University of Illinois Press, 1999.

Münzenberg, Willi. *Das Flammenzeichen vom Palais Egmont: Offizielles Protokoll des Kongresses Gegen Koloniale Unterdrückung und Imperialismus, Brüssel, 10–15, Februar 1927.* Berlin: Neuer Deutscher, 1927.

Naison, Mark. *Communists in Harlem during the Depression.* New York: Grove, 1984.

Nehru, Jawaharlal. *Toward Freedom: The Autobiography of Jawaharlal Nehru.* Boston: Beacon, 1967.

Neptune, Harvey. *Caliban and the Yankees: Trinidad and the United States Occupation.* Chapel Hill: University of North Carolina Press, 2007.

Nielsen, Aldon Lynn. *C. L. R. James: A Critical Introduction.* Jackson: University Press of Mississippi, 1997.

Nkrumah, Kwame. *Consciencism: Philosophy and Ideology for De-Colonization.* New York: Monthly Review, 1970.

———. *Ghana: The Autobiography of Kwame Nkrumah.* New York: International, 1957.

Okpewho, Isidore, Carole Boyce Davies, and Ali A. Mazrui, eds. *The African Diaspora: African Origins and New World Identities.* Bloomington: Indiana University Press, 2001.

Osofsky, Gilbert. *Harlem, the Making of a Ghetto: Negro New York, 1890–1930.* Chicago: Dee, 1996.

Overstreet, Gene D., and Marshall Windmiller. *Communism in India.* Berkeley: University of California Press, 1959.

Owen, Nicholas. *The British Left and India: Metropolitan Anti-Imperialism, 1885–1947.* Oxford: Oxford University Press, 2007.

Padmore, George. *Africa and World Peace.* 1937; London: Cass, 1972.

———. *Haiti, An American Slave Colony.* (Pamphlet) Moscow: Centrizdat, 1931.

———. *How Britain Rules Africa.* 1936; New York: Negro Universities Press, 1969.

———. *Labour Imperialism in East Africa.* (Pamphlet) Moscow: Centrizdat, 1931.

———. *The Life and Struggles of Negro Toilers.* London: Red International Labour Union, 1931.

———. *Pan-Africanism or Communism?: The Coming Struggle for Africa.* 1956; New York: Doubleday, 1971.

———. *Trade Union Programme of Action for Negro Workers.* (Pamphlet) Moscow: International Propaganda and Action Committee of Transport Workers, 1931.

———, ed. *Colonial and . . . Coloured Unity: A Program of Action: History of the Pan-African Congress.* London: The Hammersmith Bookshop LTD, 1963.

Palmer, Colin A. *Eric Williams and the Making of the Modern Caribbean.* Chapel Hill: University of North Carolina Press, 2006.

Patterson, William L. *The Man Who Cried Genocide: An Autobiography.* New York: International, 1971.

Pennybacker, Susan. *From Scottsboro to Munich: Race and Political Culture in 1930s Britain.* Princeton: Princeton University Press, 2010.

Pepper, John. *American Negro Problems.* New York: Workers Library, 1928.

Perry, Jeffrey B. *Hubert Harrison: The Voice of Harlem Radicalism, 1883–1918.* New York: Columbia University Press, 2009.

———, ed. *A Hubert Harrison Reader.* Middletown, Conn.: Wesleyan University Press, 2001.

Phillips, Kimberley L. *AlabamaNorth: African-American Migrants, Community, and Working-Class Activism in Cleveland, 1915–1945.* Urbana: University of Illinois Press, 1999.

Plummer, Brenda Gayle. *Rising Wind: Black Americans and U.S. Foreign Affairs, 1935–1960.* Chapel Hill: University of North Carolina Press, 1996.

Prashad, Vijay. *The Darker Nations: A People's History of the Third World.* New York: New Press, 2007.

Radhakrishnan, R. *Diasporic Mediations: Between Home and Location.* Minneapolis: University of Minnesota Press, 1996.

Ransby, Barbara. *Ella Baker and the Black Freedom Movement: A Radical Democratic Vision.* Chapel Hill: University of North Carolina Press, 2003.

Ray, Sibnarayan, ed. *Selected Works of M. N. Roy: Volume 1, 1917–1922.* New York: Oxford University Press, 1987.

Record, Wilson. *The Negro and the Communist Party.* New York: Atheneum, 1971.

———. *Race and Radicalism: The NAACP and the Communist Party in Conflict.* Ithaca: Cornell University Press, 1964.

Reddock, Rhoda E. *Women, Labour, and Politics in Trinidad and Tobago.* London: Zed, 1994.

Report of the Proceedings and Decisions of the First International Conference of Negro Workers. Hamburg: International Trade Union Committee of Negro Workers, 1932.

Revolutionary Radicalism: Its History, Purpose and Tactics, with an Exposition and Discussion of the Steps Being Taken and Required to Curb It. Albany, N.Y.: Lyon, 1920.

Reynolds, Reginald. *My Life and Crimes*. London: Jerrolds, 1956.

Rich, Paul B. *Race and Empire in British Politics*. New York: Cambridge University Press, 1990.

Richardson, Al, Clarence Chrysostom, and Anna Grimshaw. *C. L. R. James and British Trotskyism: An Interview with C. L. R. James*. June 8 and November 16, 1986, South London. Available online at http://workersrepublic.org/Pages/Ireland/Trotskyism/clrjames.html. Accessed January 20, 2010.

Riddell, John, ed. *To See the Dawn: Baku, 1920—First Congress of the Peoples of the East*. New York: Pathfinder, 1993.

———. *Workers of the World and Oppressed Peoples, Unite! Proceedings and Documents of the Second Congress, 1920, Volume 1*. New York: Pathfinder, 1991.

Robinson, Cedric. *Black Marxism: The Making of the Black Radical Tradition*. Chapel Hill: University of North Carolina Press, 2000.

Robinson, Robert. *Black on Red: My Forty-four Years inside the Soviet Union*. Washington, D.C.: Acropolis, 1988.

Rolinson, Mary G. *Grassroots Garveyism: The Universal Negro Improvement Association in the Rural South, 1920-1927*. Chapel Hill: University of North Carolina Press, 2007.

Rosengarten, Frank. *Urbane Revolutionary: C. L. R. James and the Struggle for a New Society*. Jackson: University Press of Mississippi, 2008.

Roy, M. N. *M. N. Roy's Memoirs*. Bombay: Allied, 1964.

———. *The Way to Durable Peace*. Ed. Samaren Roy. Calcutta: Minerva, 1986.

Roy, Samaren. *M. N. Roy: A Political Biography*. New Delhi: Orient Longman, 1997.

Said, Edward. *Representations of the Intellectual: The 1993 Reith Lectures*. New York: Vintage, 1996.

Samuels, Wilfred D. *Five Afro-Caribbean Voices in American Culture, 1917–1929*. Boulder, Colo.: Belmont, 1977.

Scott, David. *Conscripts of Modernity: Tragedy of Colonial Enlightenment*. Durham, N.C.: Duke University Press, 2004.

———. *Refashioning Futures: Criticism after Postcoloniality*. Princeton: Princeton University Press, 1999.

Seth, Sanjay. *Marxist Theory and Nationalist Politics: The Case of Colonial India*. Delhi: Sage, 1995.

Shannon, David A. *The Decline of American Communism: A History of the Communist Party of the United States since 1945*. New York: Harcourt, Brace, and World, 1959.

Shelby, Tommie. *We Who Are Dark: The Philosophical Foundations of Black Solidarity*. Cambridge: Harvard University Press, 2005.

Sherwood, Marika. *Claudia Jones: A Life in Exile*. London: Lawrence and Wishart, 1999.

Shipman, Charles. *It Had to Be Revolution: Memoirs of an American Radical*. Ithaca: Cornell University Press, 1993.

Singh, Kelvin. *Race and Class Struggles in a Colonial State: Trinidad, 1917–1945*. Calgary: University of Calgary Press, 1994.

Singh, Nikhil Pal. *Black Is a Country: Race and the Unfinished Struggle for Democracy*. Cambridge: Harvard University Press, 2004.

Smethurst, James. *The Black Arts Movement: Literary Nationalism in the 1960s and 1970s*. Chapel Hill: University of North Carolina Press, 2005.

Smith, Frank. *Robert G. Ingersoll: A Life*. Buffalo, N.Y.: Prometheus, 1990.

Smith, Homer. *Black Man in Red Russia*. Chicago: Johnson, 1964.

Smith, Matthew J. *Red and Black in Haiti: Radicalism, Conflict, and Political Change, 1934–1957*. Chapel Hill: University of North Carolina Press, 2009.

Solomon, Mark. *The Cry Was Unity: Communism and African Americans, 1917–1936*. Jackson: University Press of Mississippi, 1998.

Stein, Judith. *The World of Marcus Garvey: Race and Class in Modern Society*. Baton Rouge: Louisiana State University Press, 1986.

Stephens, Michelle. *Black Empire: The Masculine Global Imaginary of Caribbean Intellectuals in the United States, 1919–1962*. Durham, N.C.: Duke University Press, 2005.

Stoler, Laura Ann. *Along the Archival Grain: Epistemic Anxieties and Colonial Common Sense*. Princeton: Princeton University Press, 2009.

Stovall, Tyler Edward. *Paris Noir: African Americans in the City of Light*. New York: Houghton Mifflin, 1996.

Stuckey, Sterling. *Slave Culture: Nationalist Theory and the Foundations of Black America*. New York: Oxford University Press, 1987.

Sullivan, Patricia. *Lift Every Voice: The NAACP and the Making of the Civil Rights Movement*. New York: The New Press, 2010.

Summers, Martin. *Manliness and Its Discontents: The Black Middle Class and the Transformation of Masculinity*. Chapel Hill: University of North Carolina Press, 2004.

Tabili, Laura. *"We Ask for British Justice": Workers and Racial Difference in Late Imperial Britain*. Ithaca: Cornell University Press, 1994.

Taylor, Ula. *The Veiled Garvey: The Life and Times of Amy Jacques Garvey*. Chapel Hill: University of North Carolina Press, 2002.

Thompson, Shirley Elizabeth. *Exiles at Home: The Struggle to Become American in Creole New Orleans*. Cambridge: Harvard University Press, 2009.

A Trade Union Programme of Action for Negro Workers. Hamburg: International Trade Union Committee of Negro Workers, n.d.

Trotsky, Leon. *The First Five Years of the Communist International*. Vol. 2. New York: Pathfinders, 1972.

———. *A History of the Russian Revolution*. Vols. 1–3. London: Sphere Books, 1967.

Trotter, Joe William. *Black Milwaukee: The Making of an Industrial Proletariat, 1915–45*. Urbana: University of Illinois Press, 1985.

Trouillot, Michel-Rolph. *Silencing the Past: Power and the Production of History*. Boston: Beacon, 1995.

Turner, Joyce Moore. *Caribbean Crusaders and the Harlem Renaissance*. Urbana: University of Illinois Press, 2005.

Urquhart, Brian. *Ralph Bunche: An American Life*. New York: Norton, 1993.

Von Eschen, Penny. *Race against Empire: Imagining Political Culture beyond the Color Line*. Cambridge: Harvard University Press, 2000.

Walters, Alexander. *My Life and Works*. Chicago: Fleming H. Revel Company, 1917.

Warburg, Fredric. *An Occupation for Gentlemen*. 1959; Boston: Houghton Mifflin, 1960.

Watkins-Owens, Irma. *Blood Relations: Caribbean Immigrants and the Harlem Community, 1900–1930*. Bloomington: Indiana University Press, 1996.

Weiss, Holger. *Kweku Bankole Awoonor Renner, Anglophone West African Intellectuals, and the Comintern Connection: A Tentative Outline, Part 2*. Comintern Working Paper 10. 2007. Available at https://www.abo.fi/student/media/7957/cowopa10weiss.pdf. Accessed December 1, 2010.

———. *The Road to Hamburg and Beyond: African American Agency and the Making of a Radical African Atlantic, 1922–1930, Part Three*. Comintern Working Paper 18. 2009. Available at https://www.abo.fi/student/media/7957/cowopa18weiss.pdf. Accessed December 1, 2010.

White, E. Frances. *Dark Continent of Our Bodies: Black Feminism and the Politics of Respectability*. Philadelphia: Temple University Press, 2001.

Widener, Daniel. *Black Arts West: Culture and Struggle in Postwar Los Angeles*. Durham, N.C.: Duke University Press, 2010.

Williams, Chad L. *Torchbearers of Democracy: African American Soldiers in the World War I Era*. Chapel Hill: University of North Carolina Press, 2010.

Wilson, Edward Thomas. *Russia and Black Africa before World War II*. New York: Holmes and Meier, 1974.

Wilson, Woodrow. *The Papers of Woodrow Wilson*. Ed. Arthur S. Link. Vol. 44. Princeton: Princeton University Press, 1983.

Woodard, Komozi. *A Nation within a Nation: Amiri Baraka (LeRoi Jones) and Black Power Politics*. Chapel Hill: University of North Carolina Press, 1999.

Worcester, Kent. *C. L. R. James: A Political Biography*. Albany: State University of New York Press, 1996.

Zeleza, Paul Tiyambe. *Manufacturing African Studies and Crises*. Dakar: CODESRIA, 1997.

Zinoviev, Gregory. *Report of the Executive Committee of the Communist International to the Second World Congress of the Communist International*. Petrograd: Communist International, 1920.

ARTICLES

Adi, Hakim. "George Padmore and the 1945 Manchester Pan-African Congress." In *George Padmore: Pan-African Revolutionary*, ed. Fitzroy Baptiste and Rupert Lewis, 66–96. Kingston, Jamaica: Ian Randle, 2009.

————. "The Negro Question: The Communist International and Black Liberation in the Interwar Years." In *From Toussaint to Tupac: The Black International since the Age of Revolution*, ed. Michael O. West, William G. Martin, and Fanon Che Wilkins, 155–75. Chapel Hill: University of North Carolina Press, 2009.

————. "Pan-Africanism and Communism: The Comintern, the 'Negro Question' and the First International Conference of Negro Workers, Hamburg 1930." *African and Black Diaspora Journal: An International Journal* 1, no. 2 (2008): 237–54.

Aitken, Robbie. "From Cameroon to Germany and Back via Moscow and Paris: The Political Career of Joseph Bile (1892–1959), Performer, 'Negerarbeiter' and Comintern Activist." *Journal of Contemporary History* 43, no. 4 (2008): 597–616.

Archer, John. "C. L. R. James and Trotskyism in Britain: 1934–1938." *Revolutionary History* 6, no. 2/3 (1996): 58–73.

Arnesen, Eric. "No 'Graver Danger': Black Anticommunism, the Communist Party, and the Race Question." *Labor* 3, no. 4 (2006): 13–52.

Asante, S. K. B. "The Neglected Aspects of the Activities of the Gold Coast Aborigines Rights Protection Society." *Phylon* 36, no. 1 (1975): 32–45.

Bair, Barbara. "Pan-Africanism as Process: Adelaide Casely Hayford, Garveyism, and the Cultural Roots of Nationalism." In *Imagining Home: Class, Culture, and Nationalism in the African Diaspora*, ed. Sidney Lemelle and Robin D. G. Kelley, 121–44. New York: Verso, 1994.

————. "True Women, Real Men: Gender, Ideology, and Social Roles in the Garvey Movement." In *Gendered Domains: Rethinking Public and Private in Women's History*, ed. Dorothy O. Helly and Susan M. Reverby, 154–66. Ithaca: Cornell University Press, 1992.

Baptiste, Fitzroy. "The African Conferences of Governors and Indigenous Collaborators, 1947–1948: A British Strategy to Blunt the 1945 Manchester Pan-African Congress." In *George Padmore: Pan-African Revolutionary*, ed. Fitzroy Baptiste and Rupert Lewis, 37–65. Kingston, Jamaica: Ian Randle, 2009.

Berland, Oscar. "The Emergence of the Communist Perspective on the 'Negro Question' in America: 1919–1931, Part One." *Science and Society* 63, no. 4 (1999–2000): 411–32.

————. "The Emergence of the Communist Perspective on the 'Negro Question' in America: 1919–1931, Part Two." *Science and Society* 64, no. 2 (Summer 2000): 194–217.

Bland, Lucy. "White Women and Men of Colour: Miscegenation Fears in Britain after the Great War." *Gender and History* 17, no. 1 (2005): 29–61.

Blaut, James M. "Marxism and Eurocentric Diffusionism." In *The Political Economy of Imperialism: Critical Appraisals*, ed. Ronald M. Chilcote, 127–40. Boston: Kluwer Academic, 1999.

Bogues, Anthony. "C. L. R. James and George Padmore: The Ties that Bind— Black Radicalism and Political Friendship." In *George Padmore: Pan-African Revolutionary*, ed. Fitzroy Baptiste and Rupert Lewis, 183–202. Kingston, Jamaica: Ian Randle, 2009.

Buhle, Paul, and Robin D. G. Kelley. "Allies of a Different Sort: Jews and Blacks in the American Left." In *Struggles in the Promised Land: Toward a History of Black-Jewish Relations in the United States*, ed. Jack Salzman and Cornel West, 197–229. New York: Oxford University Press, 1997.

Burton, Antoinette. "Introduction: On the Inadequacy and the Indispensability of the Nation." In *After the Imperial Turn: Thinking with and through the Nation*, ed. Antoinette Burton, 1–26. Durham, N.C.: Duke University Press, 2003.

Butler, Kim. "Defining Diaspora, Refining a Discourse." *Diaspora* 10, no. 2 (2001): 189–219.

Campbell, Horace. "Pan-Africanism and African Liberation." In *Imagining Home: Class, Culture, and Nationalism in the African Diaspora*, ed. Sidney Lemelle and Robin D. G. Kelley, 285–307. New York: Verso, 1994.

Campbell, Susan. "'Black Bolsheviks' and the Recognition of African-America's Right to Self-Determination by the Communist Party USA." *Science and Society* 58, no. 4 (1994–95): 440–70.

Carr, Leslie G. "The Origins of the Communists Party's Theory of Black Self-Determination: Draper vs. Haywood." *Insurgent Sociologist* 10, no. 3 (1981): 35–49.

Carrington, Ben. "Improbable Grounds: The Emergence of the Black British Intellectual." *South Atlantic Quarterly* 109, no. 2 (2010): 369–89.

Cecelski, David. "Abraham H. Galloway: Wilmington's Lost Prophet and the Rise of Black Radicalism in the American South." In *Time Longer Than Rope: A Century of African American Activism, 1850–1950*, ed. Charles M. Payne and Adam Green, 37–67. New York: New York University Press, 2003.

Cha-Jua, Sundiata Keita. "C. L. R. James, Blackness, and the Making of a Neo-Marxist Diasporan Historiography." *Nature, Society, and Thought* 11, no. 1 (1998): 53–89.

Clifford, James. "Diaspora." *Cultural Anthropology* 9, no. 3 (1994): 302–38.

Cohen, Robin. "Introduction." In *Forced Labor in Colonial Africa*, by I. I. Potekhin, A. Z. Zusmanovich, and Robin Cohen, 1–19. London: Zed, 1979.

Conklin, Alice. "Who Speaks for Africa? The René Maran–Blaise Diagne Trial in 1920s Paris." In *The Color of Liberty: Stories of Race in France*, ed. Sue Peabody and Tyler Stovall, 302–37. Durham, N.C.: Duke University Press, 2003.

Cross, William E., Jr., Thomas Parham, and Janet Helms. "The Stages of Black Identity Development: Nigrescence Models." In *Black Psychology*, ed. Reginald Jones, 319–38. Berkeley, Calif.: Cobb and Henry, 1991.

Crowder, Ralph L. "'Don't Buy Where You Can't Work': An Investigation of the Political Forces and Social Conflict within the Harlem Boycott of 1934." *Afro-Americans in New York Life and History* 15, no. 2 (1991): 7–44.

Deutscher, Isaac. "Record of a Discussion with Heinrich Brandler, 15 February 1948." *New Left Review* 1, no. 105 (1977): 47–55.

Donnell, Alison. "Una Marson: Feminism, Anti-Colonialism and a Forgotten Fight for Freedom." In *West Indian Intellectuals in Britain*, ed. Bill Schwarz, 114–31. Manchester, U.K.: Manchester University Press, 2003.

Du Bois, W. E. B. "The African Roots of the War." *Atlantic Monthly*, May 1915, 712.

Edgar, Robert. "Notes on the Life and Death of Albert Nzula." *International Journal of African Historical Studies* 16, no. 4 (1983): 65–79.

Edwards, Brent Hayes. "Dossier on Black Radicalism." *Social Text* 19, no. 2 (Summer 2001): 1–13.

———. "The Shadow of Shadows." *positions* 11, no. 1 (2003): 11–49.

———. "The Uses of *Diaspora*." *Social Text* 19, no. 1 (2001): 45–73.

Egonu, Iheanachor. "*Les Continents* and the Francophone Pan-Negro Movement." *Phylon* 42, no. 3 (1981): 245–54.

Farred, Grant. "The Maple Man: How Cricket Made a Postcolonial Intellectual." In *Rethinking C. L. R. James*, ed. Grant Farred, 165–86. Cambridge, Mass.: Blackwell Publishers, 1996.

Foner, Nancy. "The Free People of Color in Louisiana and St. Domingue: A Comparative Portrait of Two Three-Caste Slave Societies." *Journal of Social History* 3, no. 4 (1970): 406–30.

———. "West Indian Identity in the Diaspora: Comparative and Historical Perspectives." *Latin American Perspectives* 25, no. 3 (1998): 173–88.

Gordon, Leonard A. "Portrait of a Bengal Revolutionary." *Journal of Asian Studies* 27, no. 2 (1968): 197–216.

Guarnizo, Luis Eduardo, and Michael Peter Smith. "The Locations of Transnationalism." In *Transnationalism from Below*, ed. Michael Peter Smith and Luis Eduardo Guarnizo, 3–34. New Brunswick, N.J.: Transaction, 1998.

Hall, Stuart. "A Conversation with C. L. R. James." In *Rethinking C. L. R. James*, ed. Grant Farred, 15–44. Cambridge, Mass: Blackwell, 1996.

Hatch, James V. "Interview with Louise Thompson Patterson and William L. Patterson, April 26, 1975." *Artist and Influence* 19 (2000): 153–69.

Hellwig, David J. "Black Meets Black: Afro-American Reactions to West Indian Immigrants in the 1920s." *South Atlantic Quarterly* 77, no. 2 (1978): 206–24.

Henderson, Jeff. "A. Philip Randolph and the Dilemmas of Socialism and Black Nationalism in the United States, 1917–1941." *Race and Class* 20, no. 2 (1978): 143–60.

Henry, Keith S. "The Black Political Tradition in New York: A Conjunction of Political Cultures." *Journal of Black Studies* 7, no. 4 (1977): 455–84.

Hershberg, Theodore, and Henry Williams. "Mulattos and Blacks: Intra-Group Color Differences and Social Stratification in Nineteenth-Century Philadelphia." In *Philadelphia: Work, Space, Family, and Group Experience in the Nineteenth Century*, ed. Theodore Hershberg, 392–434. New York: Oxford University Press, 1981.

Hesse, Barnor. "Racialized Modernity: An Analytics of White Mythologies." *Racial and Ethnic Studies* 30, no. 4 (2007): 643–63.

Hill, Rebecca. "Fosterites and Feminists, or 1950s Ultra-Leftists and the Invention of AmeriKKKa." *New Left Review* 1, no. 228 (1998): 67–90.

Hill, Robert. "Huiswoud, Otto (1893–1961)." In *Biographical Dictionary of the American Left*, ed. Bernard K. Johnpoll and Harvey Klehr, 219–21. Westport, Conn.: Greenwood, 1986.

———. "Introduction: Garvey's Gospel, Garvey's Game." In *Philosophy and Opinions of Marcus Garvey*, ed. Amy Jacques Garvey, v–lxxix. New York: Macmillan, 1992.

―――. "Racial and Radical: Cyril V. Briggs, *The Crusader Magazine*, and the African Blood Brotherhood, 1918–1922." In *The Crusader*, ed. Robert A. Hill, v–lxx. New York: Garland, 1987.

Horne, Gerald. "The Red and the Black: The Communist Party and African-Americans in Historical Perspective." In *New Studies in the Politics and Culture of U.S. Communism*, ed. Michael E. Brown, Randy Martin, Frank Rosengarten, and George Snedeker, 199–237. New York: Monthly Review Press, 1993.

Horowitz, Donald L. "Color Differentiation in the American Systems of Slavery." *Journal of Interdisciplinary History* 3, no. 3 (1973): 509–41.

Hughes, C. Alvin. "The Negro Sanhedrin Movement." *Journal of Negro History* 69, no. 1 (1984): 1–13.

Hughes, Langston. "My Early Days in Harlem." In *Harlem: A Community in Transition*, ed. John Henrik Clarke, 62–64. New York: Citadel, 1964.

James, C. L. R. "Black Intellectuals in Britain." In *Colour, Culture, and Consciousness: Immigrant Intellectuals in Britain*, ed. Bhikhu Parekh, 154–63. London: Allen and Unwin, 1974.

―――. "Lectures on the Black Jacobins." *Small Axe* 8, no. 2 (2000): 65–112.

―――. "Notes on the Life of George Padmore." Typescript on Microfilm, Schomburg Center for Research in Black Culture, New York.

James, Winston. "Being Black and Red in Jim Crow America." *Souls* 1, no. 4 (1999): 45–63.

―――. "Being Red and Black in Jim Crow America: On the Ideology and Travails of Afro-America's Socialist Pioneers, 1877–1930." In *Time Longer Than Rope: A Century of African American Activism, 1850–1950*, ed. Charles M. Payne and Adam Green, 336–99. New York: New York University Press, 2003.

―――. "A Race Outcast from an Outcast Class: Claude McKay's Experience and Analysis of Britain." In *West Indian Intellectuals in Britain*, by Bill Schwarz, 71–73. Manchester, U.K.: Manchester University Press, 2003.

Jones, Andrew F. and Nikhil Pal Singh, eds. "The Afro-Asian Century." *positions: east asia cultures critique* 11, no. 1 (2003).

Jung, Moon-Kie. "Interracialism: The Ideological Transformation of Hawaii's Working Class." *American Sociological Review* 68, no. 3 (2003): 373–400.

Kanet, Roger E. "The Comintern and the 'Negro Question': Communist Policy in the U.S. and Africa, 1921–41." *Survey* 19, no. 4 (1973): 86–122.

Kelley, Robin D. G. "'But a Local Phase of a World Problem': Black History's Global Vision, 1883–1950." *Journal of American History* 86, no. 3 (1999): 1045–77.

―――. "Introduction to the Charles H. Kerr 150th Anniversary Edition." In Karl Marx and Frederick Engels, *The Communist Manifesto: 150th Anniversary Edition, 1848–1998*, v–xii. Chicago: Kerr, 1998.

―――. "A Poetics of Anticolonialism." In Aimé Césaire, *Discourse on Colonialism*, 7–28. 1955; New York: Monthly Review Press, 2000.

―――. "The Third International and the Struggle for National Liberation in South Africa, 1921–1928." *Ufahamu* 15, nos. 1–2 (1986): 99–120.

―――. "The World the Diaspora Made: C. L. R. James and the Politics of History."

In *Rethinking C. L. R. James*, ed. Grant Farred, 103–30. Cambridge, Mass: Blackwell, 1996.

Killingray, David. "'To Do Something for the Race': Harold Moody and the League of Coloured Peoples." In *West Indian Intellectuals in Britain*, ed. Bill Schwarz, 51–70. Manchester, U.K.: Manchester University Press, 2003.

Klehr, Harvey, and William Tompson. "Self-Determination in the Black Belt: Origins of a Communist Policy." *Labor History* 30, no. 3 (1989): 354–66.

La Botz, Dan. "American 'Slackers' in the Mexican Revolution: International Proletarian Politics in the Midst of a National Revolution." *The Americas* 62, no. 4 (2006): 563–90.

Langley, J. A. "Pan-Africanism in Paris, 1924–1936." *Journal of Modern African Studies* 7, no. 1 (1969): 69–94.

Le Blanc, Paul. "Introduction: C. L. R. James and Revolutionary Marxism." In *C. L. R. James and Revolutionary Marxism: Selected Writings of C. L. R. James, 1939–1949*, ed. Scott McLemee and Paul Le Blanc, 1–37. Atlantic Highlands, N.J.: Humanities, 1994.

Lee, Christopher Joon-Hai. "The 'Native' Undefined: Colonial Categories, Anglo-African Status and the Politics of Kinship in British Central Africa, 1929–38." *Journal of African History* 46, no. 3 (2005): 455–78.

———. "The Uses of the Comparative Imagination: South African History and World History in the Political Consciousness and Strategy of the South African Left, 1943–1959." *Radical History Review* 92 (April 2005): 31–61.

Lewis, Linden. "Richard B. Moore: The Making of a Caribbean Organic Intellectual: A Review Essay." *Journal of Black Studies* 25, no. 5 (1995): 589–609.

Lewis, Rupert. "George Padmore: Towards a Political Assessment." In *George Padmore: Pan-African Revolutionary*, ed. Fitzroy Baptiste and Rupert Lewis, 148–61. Kingston, Jamaica: Ian Randle, 2009.

Mackenzie, Alan J. "Radical Pan-Africanism in the 1930s: A Discussion with C. L. R. James." *Radical History Review* 24 (Fall 1980): 68–75.

Maeda, Daryl J. "Black Panthers, Red Guards, and Chinamen: Constructing Asian American Identity through Performing Blackness, 1969–97." *American Quarterly* 57, no. 4 (2005): 1079–1103.

Malik, Kenan. "The Mirror of Race: Postmodernism and the Celebration of Difference." In *In Defense of History: Marxism and the Postmodern Agenda*, ed. Ellen Meiksins Wood and John Bellamy Foster, 112–33. New York: Monthly Review Press, 1997.

Mann, Kristin. "Shifting Paradigms in the Study of the African Diaspora and of Atlantic History and Culture." *Slavery and Abolition* 22, no. 1 (2001): 3–21.

Masilela, Ntongela. "Pan-Africanism or Classical African Marxism?" In *Imagining Home: Class, Culture and Nationalism in the African Diaspora*, ed. Sidney Lemelle and Robin D. G. Kelley, 308–30. New York: Verso, 1994.

Matera, Marc. "Colonial Subjects: Black Intellectuals and the Development of Colonial Studies in Britain." *Journal of British Studies* 49, no. 2 (2010): 388–418.

McClellan, Woodford. "Africans and Black Americans in the Comintern Schools,

1925–1934." *International Journal of African Historical Studies* 26, no. 2 (1993): 371–90.

Mignolo, Walter D. "Delinking: The Rhetoric of Modernity, the Logic of Coloniality, and the Grammar of De-Coloniality." *Cultural Studies* 21, no. 2 (2007): 449–514.

Miller, Kelly. "Washington's Policy." In *Booker T. Washington and His Critics: Black Leadership in Crisis*, ed. Hugh Hawkins, 87–94. Lexington, Mass.: D. C. Heath and Co., 1974.

Miller, Sally. "The Socialist Party and the Negro, 1901–1920." *Journal of Negro History* 56, no. 3 (1971): 220–29.

Moore, Richard B. "Afro-Americans and Radical Politics." In *Richard B. Moore, Caribbean Militant in Harlem: Collected Writings, 1920–1972*, ed. W. Burghardt Turner and Joyce Moore Turner, 215–21. Bloomington: Indiana University Press, 1988.

Morris, Aldon. "Reflections on Social Movement Theory: Criticisms and Proposals." *Contemporary Sociology* 29, no. 3 (2000): 445–54.

Nelson, Keith L. "The 'Black Horror on the Rhine': Race as a Factor in Post–World War I Diplomacy." *Journal of Modern History* 42, no. 4 (1970): 602–27.

Neptune, Harvey. "Manly Rivalries and Mopsies: Gender, Nationality, and Sexuality in United States–Occupied Trinidad." *Radical History Review* 87 (Fall 2003): 78–95.

Nonini, Donald M., and Aihwa Ong. "Chinese Transnationalism as an Alternative Modernity." In *Underground Empires: The Cultural Politics of Modern Chinese Transnationalism*, ed. Aihwa Ong and Donald M. Nonini, 3–33. New York: Routledge, 1997.

Onishi, Yuichiro. "The New Negro of the Pacific: How African Americans Forged Cross-Racial Solidarity with Japan, 1917–1922." *Journal of African American History* 92, no. 2 (2007): 191–213.

Painter, Nell Irvin, and Hosea Hudson. "Hosea Hudson: A Negro Communist in the Deep South." *Radical America* 11, no. 4 (1977): 7–23.

Palmer, Colin A. "Defining and Studying the Modern African Diaspora." *Journal of Negro History* 85, nos. 1–2 (2000): 27–32.

Parker, George Wells. "The African Origin of the Grecian Civilization." *Journal of Negro History* 2, no. 3 (1917): 334–44.

Patterson, Tiffany Ruby, and Robin D. G. Kelley. "Unfinished Migrations: Reflections on the African Diaspora and the Making of the Modern World." *African Studies Review* 43, no. 1 (2000): 11–45.

Pease, Donald E. "C. L. R. James's Mariners, Renegades, and Castaways and the World We Live In." In *Mariners, Renegades, and Castaways: The Story of Herman Melville and the World We Live In*, vii–xxxiii. Hanover, N.H.: University Press of New England, 2001.

Pirio, G. Alonso. "A Note: Minorities' Responses to Racism in the British Seamen's Union." *South Asia Bulletin* 4, no. 2 (1984): 56–58.

Quest, Matthew. "George Padmore's and C. L. R. James's *International African Opinion*." In *George Padmore: Pan-African Revolutionary*, ed. Fitzroy Baptiste and Rupert Lewis, 105–32. Kingston, Jamaica: Ian Randle Publishers, 2009.

Ramnath, Maia. "Two Revolutions: The Ghadar Movement and India's Radical Diaspora, 1913–1918." *Radical History Review* 92 (Spring 2005): 7–30.

Reinders, Robert. "Racialism on the Left: E. D. Morel and the 'Black Horror on the Rhine.'" *International Review of Social History* 13, no. 1 (1968): 1–28.

Rohdie, Samuel. "The Gold Coast Aborigines Abroad." *Journal of African History* 6, no. 3 (1965): 389–411.

Robinson, Cedric. "Oliver Cromwell Cox and the Historiography of the West." *Cultural Critique* 17 (Winter 1990–91): 5–19.

Roy, Samaren. "M. N. Roy and Comintern's Colonial Policy." In *Political Thinkers of Modern India*, vol. 5, *M. N. Roy*, ed. Verinder Grover, 666–74. New Delhi: Deep and Deep, 1990.

Safran, William. "Comparing Diasporas: A Review Essay." *Diaspora* 8, no. 3 (1999): 255–91.

Saha, Mahadevaprasad. "Introduction." In Sir Cecil Kaye, *Communism in India, with Unpublished Documents from the National Archives of India, 1919–1924*, 1–24. Compiled and edited by Subodh Roy. Calcutta: Editions Indian, 1971.

Samuels, Wilfred D. "Hubert H. Harrison and 'The New Negro Manhood Movement.'" *Afro-Americans in New York Life and History* 5, no. 1 (1981): 29–41.

Schwarz, Bill. "C. L. R. James and George Lamming: The Measure of Historical Time." *Small Axe* 7, no. 2 (2003): 39–70.

———. "George Padmore." In *West Indian Intellectuals in Britain*, by Bill Schwarz, 135–36. Manchester, U.K.: Manchester University Press, 2003.

Sherwood, Marika. "The Comintern, the CPGB, Colonies, and Black Britons, 1920–1938." *Science and Society* 60, no. 2 (1996): 137–63.

Skotnes, Andor. "'Buy Where You Can Work': Boycotting for Jobs in African-American Baltimore, 1933–1934." *Journal of Social History* 27, no. 4 (1994): 735–61.

———. "The Communist Party, Anti-Racism, and the Freedom Movement: Baltimore, 1930–1934." *Science and Society* 60, no. 2 (1996): 164–94.

Spenser, Daniela. "Emissaries of the Communist International in Mexico." *American Communist History* 6, no. 2 (2007): 151–70.

Spitzer, Leo, and LaRay Denzer. "I. T. A. Wallace-Johnson and the West African Youth League [Part I]." *International Journal of African Historical Studies* 6, no. 3 (1973): 413–52.

———. "I. T. A. Wallace-Johnson and the West African Youth League. Part II: The Sierra Leone Period, 1938–1945." *International Journal of African Historical Studies* 6, no. 4 (1973): 565–601.

Taylor, Henry L. "Spatial Organization and Residential Experience: Black Cincinnati in 1850." *Social Science History* 10, no. 1 (1986): 45–69.

Taylor, Ula. "Street Strollers: Grounding the Theory of Black Women Intellectuals." *African Americans in New York Life and History* 30, no. 2 (2006): 153–71.

Teelucksingh, Jerome. "The Immortal Batsman: George Padmore the Revolutionary, Writer, and Activist." In *George Padmore: Pan-African Revolutionary*, ed. Fitzroy Baptiste and Rupert Lewis, 1–20. Kingston, Jamaica: Ian Randle, 2009.

Thompson, Vincent B. "George Padmore: Reconciling Two Phases of

Contradictions." In *George Padmore: Pan-African Revolutionary*, ed. Fitzroy
Baptiste and Rupert Lewis, 133–47. Kingston, Jamaica: Ian Randle, 2009.

Tölölyan, Khachig. "The Contemporary Discourse of Diaspora Studies."
Comparative Studies of South Asia and the Middle East 27, no. 3 (2007): 647–55.

———. "Rethinking *Diaspora*(s): Stateless Power in the Transnational Moment."
Diaspora 5, no. 1 (1996): 3–36.

Tyrrell, Ian. "Making Nations/Making States: American Historians in the Context
of Empire." *Journal of American History* 86, no. 3 (1999): 1015–44.

Tuner, Joyce Moore. "Richard B. Moore and His Works." In *Richard B. Moore,
Caribbean Militant in Harlem: Collected Writings, 1920-1972*, ed. W. Burghardt
Turner and Joyce Moore Turner, 19–108. Bloomington: Indiana University Press,
1988.

Ueda, Reed. "West Indians." In *Harvard Encyclopedia of American Ethnic Groups*,
ed. Stephan Thernstrom, 1021–27. Cambridge: Harvard University Press, 1980.

Vandiver, Beverly, William E. Cross Jr., Frank Worrell, and Peony Fhagen-Smith.
"Validating the Cross Racial Identity Scale." *Journal of Counseling Psychology* 49,
no. 1 (2002): 71–85.

Vincent, Ted. "The *Crusader* Monthly's Black Nationalist Support for the Jazz Age."
Afro-Americans in New York Life and History 15, no. 2 (1991): 63–76.

Watkins-Owens, Irma. "Early-Twentieth Century Caribbean Women: Migration
and Social Networks in New York City." In *Islands in the City: West Indian
Migration to New York*, ed. Nancy Foner, 31–33. Berkeley: University of California
Press, 2001.

West, Michael O., and William G. Martin, "Contours of the Black International:
From Toussaint to Tupac." In *From Toussaint to Tupac: The Black International
since the Age of Revolution*, ed. Michael O. West, William G. Martin, and Fanon
Che Wilkins, 1–44. Chapel Hill: University of North Carolina Press, 2009.

Winter, J. M. "The Webbs and the Non-White World: A Case of Socialist Racialism."
Journal of Contemporary History 9, no. 1 (1974): 181–92.

Wittner, Lawrence S. "The National Negro Congress: A Reassessment." *American
Quarterly* 22, no. 4 (1970): 883–901.

Wolfe, Patrick. "Land, Labor, and Difference: Elementary Structures of Race."
American Historical Review 106, no. 3 (2001): 866–905.

Woodruff, Nan Elizabeth. "The New Negro in the American Congo: World War I
and the Elaine, Arkansas Massacre of 1919." In *Time Longer than Rope: A Century
of African American Activism, 1850-1950*, ed. Charles M. Payne and Adam Green,
150–78. New York: New York University Press, 2003.

Worrell, Frank, William E. Cross Jr., and Beverly Vandiver. "Nigrescence Theory:
Current Status and Challenges for the Future." *Journal of Multicultural
Counseling and Development* 29, no. 3 (2001): 201–13.

Worrell, Rodney. "George Padmore: Pan-Africanist Par Excellence." In *George
Padmore: Pan-African Revolutionary*, ed. Fitzroy Baptiste and Rupert Lewis,
22–36. Kingston, Jamaica: Ian Randle, 2009.

Wu, Judy Txu-Chun. "An African-Vietnamese American: Robert S. Browne, the Antiwar Movement, and the Personal/Political Dimensions of Black Internationalism." *Journal of African American History* 92, no. 4 (2007): 491–515.

Wynter, Sylvia. "Beyond the Categories of the Master Conception: The Counterdoctrine of Jamesian Poises." In *C. L. R. James's Caribbean*, ed. Padget Henry and Paul Buhle, 63–91. Durham, N.C.: Duke University Press, 1992.

Zeleza, Paul Tiyambe. "Rewriting the African Diaspora: Beyond the Black Atlantic." *African Affairs* 104, no. 414 (2005): 35–68.

THESES AND DISSERTATIONS

Balakrishnan, Anand. "'Silencing the Translator': Uncovering the Indian Nationalist Imagination in America, 1893–1917." B.A. thesis, Brown University, 2003.

Hughes, Cicero Alvin. "Toward a Black United Front: The National Negro Congress Movement." Ph.D. diss., Ohio University, 1982.

Matera, Marc. "Black Internationalism and African and Caribbean Intellectuals in London, 1919–1950." Ph.D. diss., Rutgers University, 2008.

Onishi, Yuichiro. "Giant Steps of Black Freedom Movements: Trans-Pacific Connections between Black America and Japan in the Twentieth Century." Ph.D. diss., University of Minnesota–Twin Cities, 2004.

Spiegler, J. S. "Aspects of Nationalist Thought among French-Speaking West Africans, 1921–1939." Ph.D. diss., Nuffield College, Oxford University, 1968.

Taylor, Theman Ray. "Cyril Briggs and the African Blood Brotherhood: Another Radical View of Race and Class during the 1920s." Ph.D. diss., University of California–Santa Barbara, 1981.

Upham, Martin Richard. "The History of British Trotskyism to 1949." Ph.D. diss., University of Hull, 1980. Available online at http://www.socialist.net/the-history-of-british-trotskyism-to-1949-part-1.htm. Accessed May 3, 2010.

Index

Ashwood, Amy: and IAFE, 9, 197, 203, 206–7, 207 (ill.), 209; and IASB, 213; London activism, 6, 196, 202–3

Asian radicals: influence on Comintern, 5, 73–74, 76, 81, 94; interaction with black radicals, 25, 42, 58, 74, 94

Azikiwe, Nnamdi, 150, 198, 213

Bagnall, Robert, 106–7

Barbusse, Henri, 140

BBNT. *See* Black Belt Nation Thesis

Bhattacharya, Narendra Nath. *See* Roy, Manabendra Nath

Bilé, Joseph, 159, 160, 168, 169–70, 171–72

Black agricultural workers: and ABB Sanhedrin agenda, 112; and BBNT, 133–34; as focus of black Socialists, 40–42

Black Belt Nation Thesis (BBNT): constraints on black Communists, 136, 152–54; European parties' concept of, 134; impact on CPUSA, 133–34, 136; and Lenin's "Draft Theses," 77. *See also* Comintern—Third Period of

Black Communists: and ANLC, 116–17, 120–23, 128–30; Comintern Third Period constraints on, 135–36, 152–54, 160–61, 166–68, 171, 181; criticism of Fort-Whiteman, 116, 121–23; disillusion with LAI, 154–55, 186; disillusion with WP, 85–86, 126–27, 129–30; dissatisfaction with Comintern organizations, 186; and Harlem Tenants League, 148–49; hopes for Brussels Congress, 134; ideological differences within, 169–70; local leadership devalued, 105; as outsiders, 135, 168

Black internationalism: and ABB, 4–5, 7–9, 16–17, 48–49, 55–60, 72–74; and Brussels Congress, 134–35, 138–39, 144, 146; and CDRN, 138–44; and Frankfurt Congress, 2–3, 134–35; and IASB, 7–8, 213; and ITUCNW, 3, 6, 16, 187–88; and LDRN, 138–44; overview, 3–4. *See also* Intercolonialism

The Black Jacobins (James), 191, 220–22, 269 (n. 75)

Black liberation: combined with Comintern policies, 176, 178, 184; Garvey's pro-capitalist approach to, 60–61; linked with Asian liberation, 4, 42–44, 55–60, 72–74; subordinated to class struggle, 83, 173; and vanguardism, 165–66, 166 (ill.), 169–70, 176, 222–23, 229. *See also* Pan-African liberation

Black Marxism, 11–14, 234 (n. 36)

Black Marxism (Robinson), 12–13

"Blackness": as political notion, 17–19, 104; vs. "colored," 27–28

Black radicalism: and colonial fracture, 8, 11–12; expansion of Marxist theory, 12–14, 73–74, 225–30; global outlook, 16–17; and limitations of organized Marxism, 9–11, 135, 226–28; Moore's analysis of, 14–15; Robinson's analysis of, 12–14

Black radicals: attitudes toward ABB/WP affiliation, 100; and Comintern, 4–7, 74, 90–97, 104–5; criticism of American Communists, 5, 73, 74–76, 83–86, 100–101; criticism of Du Bois, 40, 72; criticism of Garvey, 62–63, 72, 105–7; enthusiasm for Brussels Congress, 137–39

—Caribbean: influence of, 16–17, 229; perspective of, 24–25; as political deviants, 109, 114; "racial downgrading" of, 17, 27–29; racial hierarchies in, 17–18, 27–29, 32–33, 57–58; response to anti-Garvey rhetoric, 106–9

—Harlem: African American/Caribbean conflicts, 26–27, 104–9, 114; and Briggs's radical journalism, 37–39; characteristics of, 4–6; as diasporic community, 25–33, 195; influence of Harrison on, 33–35; internationalism of, 42–44

—London: anticolonial scholarship, 217–18; anti-fascism as focus of, 6–7, 203–4, 209; collaborations among, 198; conflict between Africans and Caribbeans, 19, 198; internationalism, 194–97, 201–3; self-determination as focus of, 7

Black reformism: attacked at Frankfurt Congress, 156; and Comintern Third Period policy, 160–61; and NAACP, 104, 136, 156

"Black scourge," 87–88

Black seamen: Ford's work with, 173; ICNW's work with, 158, 159; and *International African Opinion*, 217; ISH's non-support of, 181–82, 185, 188; Kouyaté's work with, 170, 181, 188; as *Negro Worker* distributors, 189; Senghor's work with, 145; SMM's treatment of, 185, 186

Black separatism, 38–39, 48–49, 50, 56

Black Socialists: break with SPA, 40–41, 44; and class, 24, 34–35, 57–60; communism's appeal to, 65, 237 (n. 44); frustration with white Left, 23–24; internationalism, 42–44, 55–60. *See also* Socialist Party of America

Black Star Line, 62, 63, 68, 242 (n. 53)

Black struggle vs. class struggle in revolution, 226–27

Black women: and ABB's program, 48, 52–54; role in Harlem Tenants League, 148; role in London radicalism, 194

Black workers: ABB focus on, 59–60, 68, 112–13; and ANLC agenda, 120–23, 126–30; IASB as voice for, 213–14, 216–17; ITUCNW network of, 180, 187–88; revolutionary potential of, 118–19; and RILU, 151–52; and Sanhedrin agenda, 112–14

Bloncourt, Max, 141

Borodin, Mikhail, 78–79

Bridgeman, Reginald, 144, 182, 215

Briggs, Cyril Valentine: and anticolonialism/anti-imperialism, 31, 37–39, 55–60, 63–65; on black business, 36–37; on black international, 225–26; criticism of U.S. foreign policy, 38, 49, 56–57, 237 (n. 40); and diasporic identity concept, 55–56; and Garvey, 61–68, 242 (n. 53); and HUAC, 225; immigrant experience, 30–32; influence on Patterson, 2; interest in Marxist theory, 73; internationalism of, 18, 55–60; and race/class link, 47–50, 57–60; as radical journalist, 36–39, 46–51; response to Comintern Second Congress's "Theses," 83; on self-determination, 38, 56–57, 237 (n. 40); and SPA, 50, 60, 65; support of black separatism, 38–39, 48–49, 50, 56; and UFC, 11, 109; view of Soviet Russia, 58–59, 83; and WP, 84–85. *See also* African Blood Brotherhood for African Liberation and Redemption

Brockway, Fenner, 140, 211

Brotherhood of Sleeping Car Porters, 123

Brown, E. Ethelred, 106, 153

Brussels Congress: anticolonialism/anti-imperialism as issue at, 134, 137–42; and black internationalism, 138–39, 146; impact in United States, 146–48; resolution on Negro question, 142–44; resolution on worker/peasant unity, 144

Bunche, Ralph, 211, 212

Burrell, Theo, 52–53

Burroughs, Williana, 134, 156, 157, 158

Campbell, Grace: as ABB leader, 33, 53–54, 110; and Harlem Tenants League, 54, 148–49; and organized communism, 73; as PEF/HEF founder, 39, 147; as secretary of 21st Assembly District, 39; and SPA, 34, 44, 54, 65; and WP, 85

Cannon, James P., 85

Capitalism: linked with racism, 48–49, 64; linked with slavery, 221, 269 (n. 76); and Venetian empire, 13

CDRN. *See* Comité de Defense de la Race Nègre

Césaire, Aimé, 12, 226, 227, 229–30

Cipriani, Arthur, 184–85

Clark, Peter H., 24

Class: as ABB focus, 45–46; and color in Caribbean, 57–58; as factor in African American/Caribbean conflict, 104; and race linked, 34–35, 47–50, 57–60, 81; race made equivalent to, 226–27, 270 (n. 7)

"Class-against-class" approach. *See* Comintern—Third Period of

Class struggle: black liberation subordinated to, 83, 173; linked with anti-colonialism/anti-imperialism, 3–4, 59–60, 80; and racial unity, 57–60; vs. black struggle in revolution, 226–27, 270 (n. 7); white Left focus on, 23–24, 74–75

Colored American Review, 36–37, 237 (n. 37)

Comintern: and ABB, 5, 7; and ANLC, 120; and anticolonialism/anti-imperialism, 5, 73, 186–87, 192–94; appeal to black radicals, 4–6, 7; attitude toward Brussels Congress, 139; criticism of Socialist Second International, 76, 81; Eastern Commission, 90, 91 (ill.), 94; Ford's criticism of, 162–63; and Harlem cultural institutions, 4–5; influence of Asian radicals on, 5, 73–74, 76, 81, 94; influence of black radicals on, 7–8, 74; interest in Negro work, 98, 104–5, 120; and ITUCNW, 6; James's criticism of, 219–20; and KUTV, 1; Padmore's break with, 9, 167, 186–89, 191–94; and pan-African liberation, 5, 72–73; Popular Front policy, 192–94, 218–20

—Third Period of: constraints on black

Communists, 135–36, 152–54, 160–61, 166–68, 171, 181; focus on trade union organizing, 135, 166, 169; and Frankfurt Congress, 155–56; impact on American parties, 136; and Padmore's intercolonialism, 176, 178, 184. *See also* Black Belt Nation Thesis

Comintern Second Congress (1920): Asian radicals' impact on, 81; and Lenin's "Draft Theses," 76–77, 79–80, 82; and the Negro question, 82, 86, 90–91; and John Reed, 82, 88; and Roy's supplementary theses, 79–81; "Theses on the National and Colonial Question," 81, 90–91

Comintern Third Congress (1921), 73

Comintern Fourth Congress (1922): ABB and Asian radicals' impact on, 74; intercolonialism as mandate, 96–97; and the Negro question, 74, 90–97; "Theses on the Negro Question," 96–97

Comintern Fifth Congress (1924), 116–19

Comintern Sixth Congress (1928), 133–34, 136

Comité de Defense de la Race Nègre (CDRN): and black international concept, 138, 144; and Brussels Congress, 138, 256 (n. 11); as response to PCF failures, 138–39, 253 (n. 49). *See also* Ligue de Defense de la Race Nègre

Comité de Défense d'Ethiope (Ethiopian Defense Committee), 204

"Common Resolution on the Negro Question" (Brussels Congress), 143

Communist International. *See* Comintern

Communist Labor Party, 74

Communist Party of America (CPA): black radicals' doubts about, 73–76; focus on class struggle, 74–75; membership, 74

Communist Party of Great Britain

(CPGB): and IASB, 215; resistance to Negro work, 158, 159

Communist Party USA (CPUSA): factional struggles, 149, 152–53; impact of BBNT on, 133–34, 136; 1929 convention, 153–54. *See also* American Communists; Workers Party

Constantine, Learie, 201

CPA. *See* Communist Party of America

CPGB. *See* Communist Party of Great Britain

CPUSA. *See* Communist Party USA

Le Cri des Nègres (Kouyaté), 189

Cripps, Stafford, 211, 215

Crisis, 203, 204

Crusader: as ABB's organ, 66, 98; approach to American communism, 83; and Asian radical movements, 58; criticism of Garvey and UNIA, 68; focus on black women's beauty, 52–53, 53 (ill.); as HLW's organ, 51, 65; racialist focus on culture, 46–50; support of SPA, 50, 65, 83; treatment of Tulsa race riot, 66; on WP, 86

Cunard, Nancy, 186, 188, 194, 213

Debs, Eugene V., 24, 31

Diaspora: African linked with Asian, 9, 58–59, 73–74, 94; concept of, 17–19; IASB as representing, 213; *International African Opinion* as voice for, 216–17

Diasporic identity: and diversity of experience, 17–19; and hierarchies, 55–59

Diasporic projects: "blackness" as unifying concept, 17–19, 114; class in, 57–60

Discourse on Colonialism (Césaire), 229–30

Domingo, Wilfred Adolphus (W. A.): challenge to anti-Caribbean nativism, 107–8; criticism of American Communists, 75–76; debate with Chandler Owen, 107–9; focus on black agri-

cultural laborers, 40–41; and Garvey, 61–62, 63, 64; on Harrison, 34; internationalism of, 18, 40–41, 43–44; organizational work, 99; rejection of Caribbean racial hierarchies, 32–33

Doty, Edward, 85, 97, 114

Doty, Elizabeth, 85

Du Bois, W. E. B.: on African self-government, 72; on ANLC convention, 125; black radicals' criticism of, 40, 72; as Marxist, 13; Pan-African Congresses, 7, 56, 71, 72; at PEF, 40; on Sanhedrin, 113

Dunayevskaya, Rya (aka Freddy Forest), 224

Emancipator, 40, 63

Ethiopia: IAFE support of, 206–9; and James's "workers' sanctions," 200–201; LCP's support of, 204; WASU's support of, 204

European Communists: concept of BBNT, 134; resistance to Negro work, 117–18, 121, 158–60, 162–63

Fanon, Frantz, 14, 229, 230, 234 (n. 36)

Faure, Emile, 172, 217

Fight, 210, 266 (n. 43)

Fletcher, Ben, 122

Florence Mills Social Parlour, 202–3

Ford, James: on African American vanguardism, 169; on ANLC's failures, 130; and Brussels Congress, 2–3; at Comintern Sixth Congress, 151–52; criticism of Comintern, 162–63; and Frankfurt Congress, 134, 156; and IBNW, 152; and ICNW, 136, 157, 158, 160, 162; as ITUCNW leader, 172–74; on LAI failures, 154–55

Fort-Whiteman, Lovett: as ANLC leader, 120–26, 128; biographical details, 115–16, 233 (n. 33); at Comintern Fifth Congress, 116–19; criticism of American Communists, 101, 117, 118, 119; focus on race, 118–19; return to Marxist orthodoxy, 119–20, 130; and Sanhedrin, 113; as WP Negro work director, 115, 120–23

Frankfurt Congress: and black internationalism, 2–3; Comintern control of, 155–56; focus on intercolonial organizing, 134–35

Friends of Negro Freedom, 106–7

Garvey, Amy Ashwood. *See* Ashwood, Amy

Garvey, Marcus: African empire concept, 60, 62–65; anti-radical shift, 67; arrest of, 68, 72; black radicals' criticism of, 62–63, 72, 105–7, 241 (n. 48), 242 (n. 56); and Briggs, 61–68; and Domingo, 32, 61–62, 64; pro-capitalist approach, 61–62; and UNIA factional split, 128. *See also* Universal Negro Improvement Association

Ghadar Party, 58, 77, 78

Goode, Eslonda, 2, 212

Gothon-Lunion, Joseph, 20, 119, 121, 123, 138

Griffiths, Thomas. *See* Makonnen, T. Ras

Gumede, Josiah T., 138, 140

Hall, Otto, 85, 86, 116, 154

Hamitic League of the World (HLW), 50–51, 56

Hardeon, Bob, 85, 127

Harlem Educational Forum (HEF), 85, 99, 147–48. *See also* People's Educational Forum

Harlem Tenants League (HTL), 54, 148–49, 153

Harrison, Hubert Henry: as activist-intellectual, 33–34; on Ashwood, 202; criticism of Garvey, 62–63, 65, 241 (n. 48), 242 (n. 56); criticism of SPA, 34–35; internationalism of, 43; and race/class link, 34–35

Haywood, Harry, on ITUCNW, 171

Hendrickson, Elizabeth, 54, 148, 149

Hierarchies: and diasporic identity,

55–59; as fault lines of diasporic populations, 18

Hindu Conspiracy case, 77–78

HLW, 50–51, 56

Ho Chi Minh. *See* Nguyen Ai Quoc

How Britain Rules Africa (Padmore), 194, 209

HUAC (U.S. House Un-American Activities Committee), 225

Hughes, Langston, 25–26

Huiswoud, Otto: as ABB/Communist organizer, 74, 85, 90, 99, 113; and ANLC, 122, 123; as chair of Comintern Negro Commission, 90, 92, 95–97, 248 (n. 81); criticism of RILU national sections, 181; and ICNW, 136; immigrant experience, 29–30; as *Negro Worker* editor, 193; at PAC, 146; on race/class link, 74–75; and Sanhedrin, 113; warning to Padmore, 192

IAFE. *See* International African Friends of Ethiopia

IASB. *See* International African Service Bureau

IBNW, 152, 158

ICNW. *See* International Conference of Negro Workers

Independent Labor Party (ILP): Bridgeman's expulsion from, 144; at Brussels Congress, 140; and IASB, 215; and James, 197, 200–201, 209, 210; and LAI, 144, 155; support for IASB, 198

Indian radicalism, 77–79, 245 (n. 28)

Industrial Workers of the World (IWW), 40, 116

Intercolonialism: and ABB, 55–60, 101–2; and Asian/black radical interaction, 73–74, 81; and Brussels Congress, 137–41; as Comintern Fifth Congress issue, 117–19; as Comintern Fourth Congress mandate, 96–97; and Comintern Third Period, 176, 178, 184; IASB as conduit for, 213; and ICNW, 157–62; in *Negro Worker's* news coverage, 174–80, 261 (n. 23); of Nguyen Ai Quoc, 82–83, 117–18, 246 (n. 43); of Padmore, 153–54, 176, 178, 182–85, 187, 192, 267 (n. 45). *See also* Black internationalism

International African Friends of Ethiopia (IAFE): and anticolonialism/antiimperialism, 9, 203–5, 208; and Ashwood, 197, 203, 206–7; disagreements within, 210; and IASB, 6; ideological ecumenicalism, 205; and James, 6, 9, 197, 203–6, 208–9, 265 (n. 19); and League of Nations sanctions, 208–9; and Padmore, 205, 207, 209–11; potential for broader focus, 212; as response to Italian aggression, 197, 203; support of Ethiopia, 206–9; and I. T. A. Wallace-Johnson, 207

International African Opinion, 198, 215–17, 216 (ill.)

International African Service Bureau (IASB): anticolonialism/antiimperialism, 6–7, 213; and black internationalism, 7–8; collaborations, 198–99; as conduit for intercolonialism, 213; continuity with ABB, 7–8, 9; goals, 212–13, 217; and ILP, 198, 215; independence of, 215–16, 268 (n. 57); intellectual contributions, 6–7, 218–24; and James, 197–98, 212, 215, 216–17, 270 (n. 85); Marxist theory expanded by, 226–28; and Padmore, 3, 6, 9, 197, 199, 212, 213, 215–16; support of West Indies revolts, 214–15; and I. T. A. Wallace-Johnson, 212, 213, 215; and white Left, 6, 198, 213–14, 267 (n. 52)

International Bureau of Negro Workers (IBNW), 152, 158

International communism. *See* Comintern

International Conference of Negro Workers (ICNW), 3, 136, 157–62, 259 (n. 75), 260 (n. 84)

International Congress against Colonial Oppression and Imperialism (1927). *See* Brussels Congress

International Congress against Colonial Oppression and Imperialism (1929). *See* Frankfurt Congress

International Convention(s) of the Negro Peoples of the World, 64–65, 67, 128, 157–62

International of Seamen and Harbour Workers (ISH), 181–82, 185, 188

International Trade Union Committee of Negro Workers (ITUCNW): and African American vanguardism, 165–66; and black internationalism, 3, 6, 16, 187–88; and Comintern Third Period policies, 165–67, 173; intercolonial black worker program, 134–35, 180, 187–88; and I. T. A. Wallace-Johnson, 180–82

ISH. *See* International of Seamen and Harbour Workers

ITUCNW. *See* International Trade Union Committee of Negro Workers

Jackson, Anselmo, 51, 63

Jacques, Amy, 27

James, C. L. R.: on a black international, 226–27; and British Socialists, 210, 220, 223; as Caribbean intellectual, 189–90; on Caribbean racial distinctions, 28–29; as editor of *International African Opinion*, 215–17; focus on Africa, 19, 197–98, 209, 221–22; and IAFE, 6, 9, 197, 203–6, 208–9, 265 (n. 19); and IASB, 197–98, 215, 216–17, 224, 270 (n. 85); and ILP, 197, 200–201, 209, 210; influence of, 8; as J. R. Johnson, 224; as Marxist, 190–91, 194, 196–98, 200, 210, 218–24, 226–28, 266 (n. 43), 269 (n. 76), 270 (n. 7); move to England, 190–91; opposition to vanguardism, 222–23; relationship with Padmore, 149, 191, 199–200, 209–10; on UNIA, 60; U.S. tour, 223–24; "workers' sanctions" proposal, 200–201, 209; written works, 6–7, 218–23, 269 (n. 75)

Johnson, James Weldon, 89, 110–11

Johnson-Forrest Tendency, 224, 226, 270 (n. 7)

Jones, David Ivon, 90–92

Jugantar Party, 77

Katayama, Sen: as bridge between black and Asian radicals, 58; at Brussels Congress, 139, 140; as chair of Comintern Eastern Commission, 90–92, 94; at Comintern Fifth Congress, 118; expansion of Marxist theory, 42; and ICNW, 157; influence on Huiswoud, 30; on Negro question, 98

Katterfeld, Ludwig, 94, 95

Kenyatta, Johnstone (Jomo): on fascism, 204; and fifth Pan African Congress, 198; at Frankfurt Congress, 2–3, 134, 156; and IAFE, 207; and IASB, 212, 213; and ICNW, 157, 158, 159; in London, 7; on Nzula's death, 193; and Pan-African Federation, 228

The Keys, 196, 209

Kouyaté, Garan: break with Comintern, 167, 189, 192–94; collaborationist approach, 170–71; at Frankfurt Congress, 3, 134, 156–57; and IASB, 213; and ICNW, 157, 158–59; and LDRN, 154, 156–57, 170–71; support of Ethiopia, 204

Ku Klux Klan, 104, 105–6, 225

KUTV. *See* University of the Toilers of the East

La Guma, James, 142, 156

LAI. *See* League against Imperialism

Lansbury, George, 1, 87

LCP. *See* League of Colored Peoples

LDRN. *See* Ligue de Defense de la Race Nègre

League against Imperialism (LAI): and African Communists, 155, 171–72, 258 (n. 64); and black internationalism, 2–3, 134–35, 144; Executive Council, 145 (ill.); failures in Negro work, 154–55, 185, 186, 259 (n. 65); and IASB, 215; and ILP, 144, 155; and ITUCNW, 182; and Senghor, 144, 155. *See also* Anticolonialism/anti-imperialism

League of Colored Peoples (LCP), 196, 201

League of Nations: Briggs's criticism of, 49, 56–57; IAFE response to proposed sanctions by, 208–9; James's view of sanctions by, 200–201, 209, 220

Lenin, V. I., 73, 76–82

Lettre à Maurice Thorez (Césaire), 226

Lewis, W. Arthur, 201, 214

Liberator, 75, 88–89

Liberty League, 35, 39, 61, 116

The Life and Struggles of Negro Toilers (Padmore), 183, 186

Ligue de Defense de la Race Nègre (LDRN): and black international concept, 138, 144; indifference to trade union organizing, 170; and Kouyaté, 154, 156–57, 170–71; split over Comintern ties, 172. *See also* Comité de Defense de la Race Nègre

Lovestone, Jay, 131, 137

Macaulay, Frank, 134, 159, 161, 168, 169–70, 171

Makonnen, T. Ras: on black London, 196; on Florence Mills Social Parlour, 202; and IAFE, 207, 209; and IASB, 212; and Pan-African Federation, 228

Manuilsky, Dmitri, 117, 118

Marryshow, T. Albert, 196, 207

Marson, Una, 196, 201

Marxist theory: Asian radicals' expansion of, 42, 73–74, 80–81; black radicals' expansion of, 12–14, 73–74, 225–30; colonial fracture in, 8, 11–12; and Harrison, 34; and race, 5, 8, 13–14, 34, 41; Robinson's critique of, 12–14; Roy's reformulation of, 78–79; and Zinoviev, 81

Mbanefo, Louis Nwachukwu, 212, 222

McKay, Claude: as ABB Communist, 74, 135; as Comintern Fourth Congress attendee, 89–95, 93 (ill.), 248 (nn. 80–81), 249 (n. 90); on diasporic differences and Negro work, 103; on Harlem, 26; impact of British radicals on, 86–88, 247 (n. 63); and *Liberator*, 88–89; and Trotsky, 98–99, 249 (n. 103); and white Left, 88–89, 92–94; and *Workers' Dreadnought*, 87–88

Menon, Krishna, 211

Messenger: anti-ANLC rhetoric, 123; anticommunist rhetoric, 112; anti-Garvey campaign, 106–7; Domingo's contributions to, 43, 61–62, 107–8; on Sanhedrin, 112, 113

Mexican Communist Party (Partido Comunista Mexicano), 77, 78–79, 245 (n. 25)

Miller, Kelly: on Caribbean political deviancy, 109; Padmore on, 150; and Sanhedrin, 110–14

Minor, Robert: on ANLC convention, 125; collaboration with Fort-Whiteman, 116; and Sanhedrin, 112; as underground leader, 84; as WP Negro Committee head, 100, 112, 120–22, 127

Monolulu, Ras, 206, 208 (ill.), 266 (n. 32)

Moody, Harold, 196, 201

Moore, Richard B.: analysis of black radicalism, 14–15; and ANLC, 122, 123, 128, 129–30; collaborative approach, 153; as delegate to Brussels Congress, 2, 139, 143–44; dispute with John Pepper, 153; and French radicals, 144–45; immigrant experience, 30; influence on Patterson, 2; as member of E. Ethelred Brown's Church, 153; on PEF's significance, 40; as president of Harlem Tenants League, 148–49; UFC address, 110; on white supremacy, 191

Morel, E. D., "Black Scourge," 87–88

Münzenberg, Willi, 134, 137, 155–56

NAACP (National Association for the Advancement of Colored People): and ANLC, 123; and Brussels Congress, 138–39; and Comintern Third Period, 136; and Frankfurt Congress, 156; and Garvey, 106; as reformist, 104, 136, 156; and Sanhedrin, 109–11

National liberation: as Brussels Congress issue, 140–44; and Indian radicalism, 77–79; and Lenin's "Draft Theses," 76–77; and national Communist parties, 83; vs. nationalism, 80

National separation, 38–39, 48–49, 50, 56

Nation-state concept, and pan-African liberation, 55

The Negro and the Nation (Hubert Henry Harrison), 35

Negro Champion, as ANLC organ, 121, 122, 127

The Negroes in America (McKay), 98

Negro question: Brussels Congress resolution on, 142–44; and Comintern Second Congress, 82, 86, 90–91; and Comintern Fourth Congress, 74, 90–97; and Comintern Sixth Congress, 133–34, 136; Domingo on, 75; internationalized by ICNW, 157–62; David Ivon Jones on, 90–92; Katayama on, 98; and Lenin, 76, 81; noncommunist attention to, 184–85; and SPA, 24, 35, 41–42, 65. *See also* Negro work; Race

Negro work: and ABB's organizational drive, 99; American Communists' resistance to, 84–86, 94–95, 97, 100–101, 126–27, 131, 145–46, 151; black Communists' ideas on, 126–29; Comintern's interest in, 98, 104–5, 120; complicated by national/class differences, 103–5, 114; CPUSA's approach to, 133–34, 136; European Communists resis-

tance to, 117–18, 121, 158–60, 162–63;
Fort-Whiteman's approach to, 118–20;
Harlem Tenants League as model,
149; and ITUCNW, 134–35, 180, 187–
88; LAI failures regarding, 154–55, 185,
186; and Sanhedrin agenda, 112–14.
See also Negro question; Race

Negro Worker: attacks on Padmore, 193;
circulation, 187–88; Comintern influence on, 175–76; as ICNW organ, 159;
imagery in, 165–66, 176, 177 (ill.), 179
(ill.); and intercolonialism, 174–80,
261 (n. 23); as ITUCNW organ, 3, 167,
174–80, 192; shift in editorial policy,
187

Negro World, as UNIA's organ, 61

Nehru, Jawaharlal, 137, 139–40, 142

New Negro movement: ABB role in,
45–46; African American/Caribbean
tensions in, 105–9; anti-Caribbean
nativism in, 105–9; and color question, 32–33; criticism of ABB, 114;
Harlem as Mecca of, 25–26; and
Harlem Tenants League, 148–49; Harrison's significance in, 34; internationalism, 9; and meaning of "radical," 15

Nguyen Ai Quoc: at Comintern Fourth
Congress, 74; influence on Comintern
Fifth Congress, 117; intercolonialism,
82–83, 117–18, 246 (n. 43); on Lenin's
"Draft Theses," 82

Nkrumah, Kwame, 198, 224

Nurse, Malcolm. See Padmore, George

Nzula, Albert, 3, 171, 183, 193, 199

Owen, Chandler: anticommunism, 109;
anti-Garvey campaign, 106, 107–9;
debate with Domingo, 107–9; as SPA
member, 44, 50, 109

Padmore, George: on black London,
196; break with Comintern, 9, 167,
186–89, 191–94, 199–200, 233 (n. 16),
264 (n. 9); as central figure, 8–9; col-

laborative approach, 167, 181, 184–85,
211, 267 (n. 45), 268 (n. 57); early
work, 149–50; on fascism, 7, 203–4,
209; as Harlem-London link, 197; as
head of Comintern's Negro Bureau,
167, 172–74; as head of ITUCNW, 3,
6, 8, 167, 180–83, 187–88, 262 (n. 45);
and IAFE, 205, 207, 209–11; and IASB,
3, 6, 9, 197, 199, 212, 213, 215–16; and
ICNW, 136, 157–62, 259 (n. 75); intercolonialism, 153–54, 176, 178, 182–85,
187, 192, 267 (n. 45); invited to London, 182, 183; and KUTV, 158, 178; as
Negro Worker editor, 174–80, 182, 192;
and Pan-African Federation, 228; relationship with James, 149, 191, 199–
200, 209–10; written works, 7

Pan-African Congresses (PAC), 71, 72,
146, 198, 228–29

Pan-African Federation, 198, 228

Pan-Africanism or Communism? (Padmore), 9

Pan-African liberation: and Brussels
Congress, 134, 143–44; as goal of
ABB, 45–46, 51, 55–60; and IASB, 199;
and international communism, 5,
72–73; linked with Asian liberation,
4, 42–44, 55–60, 72–74; linked with
proletarian revolution, 4, 24, 42, 43,
45–46, 59–60, 213; and London political scene, 195–96; and nation-state
concept, 55; and Padmore, 9, 187, 199.
See also Black liberation

Pankhurst, Sylvia, 87–88

Parker, George Wells, 50

Parti Communiste Français (PCF): and
anticolonialism/anti-imperialism,
81–82; Kouyaté's break with, 189; resistance to Negro work, 121, 134, 154,
158, 170, 181; and Senghor, 121, 253
(n. 49), 256 (n. 11)

Partido Comunista Mexicano (Mexican Communist Party), 77, 78–79, 245
(n. 25)

Patterson, William: on ANLC failure,

130–31; evolving radicalism, 1–3; and Frankfurt Congress, 2–3, 134, 156; and ICNW, 3, 136, 157, 158, 160–61 PCF. *See* Parti Communiste Français

People's Educational Forum (PEF), 39–42, 147 (ill.). *See also* Harlem Educational Forum

Pepper, John, 153

Phillips, Charles Francis, 79

Phillips, H. V., 127–28, 130, 130–31, 154

Pickens, William: and anti-Garvey campaign, 106, 108; and Brussels Congress, 138, 139; and Frankfurt Congress, 156

Pollitt, Henry, 186

Post Menelik, 45, 99, 114

Post Puskin, 85, 114

Proletarian revolution: black liberation through, 74, 83, 116, 173; and Césaire, 230; and IASB, 226–28; linked with anticolonialism/anti-imperialism, 59, 80, 213, 218; linked with pan-African liberation, 4, 24, 42–43, 45–46, 59–60, 213; Roy's approach to, 79–80

Race: and class linked, 34–35, 47–50, 57–60; as component of colonialism, 4, 8, 16, 38, 42; as international problem, 94–95, 157–62; introduced into international communism, 5, 8, 73–74, 197; made equivalent to class, 226–27, 270 (n. 7); as political, 17–18, 55–58; and SPA, 23–24, 34–35, 41–42, 65; white Left disregard of, 23–24, 34–35, 41–42, 74–75. *See also* Negro question

"Racial downgrading," 17, 27–29

Racial hierarchies, 17–18, 27–29, 32–33, 57–58

Racialism/racism: black radicalism as response to, 12–14; capitalism linked with, 48–49, 64; as determinant of Western civilization, 12–14; of white Left, 34–35, 85–89, 90–96

Racial oppression: and Caribbean racial hierarchies, 32–33; linked with capitalism, 48–49; linked with colonialism, 4, 8, 16, 38, 42; Socialists' failure to address, 23–24, 34–35; as species of national oppression, 77; as structural problem, 95

Racial unity: through black separatism, 38–39, 48–49, 50, 56; and class struggle, 57–60; limited by hierarchies, 18, 57–59, 114

Racial uplift ethos: and ABB, 55; and Briggs, 36, 55; and Domingo, 64; and Du Bois, 72; and Miller, 110–11; and NAACP, 104

Radical Forum, 35

Rai, Lala Lajpat, 78

Randolph, A. Philip: anti-ANLC rhetoric, 123; Brotherhood of Sleeping Car Porters, 121, 123; and Domingo, 32; on Garvey, 105–6; on Harrison, 34–35; on SPA ticket, 65

Rand School for Social Science, 30, 41, 42, 58

Red International Labor Unions (RILU): and black workers, 151–52; directives to ITUCNW, 173; Fifth World Congress, 168–69; focus on trade union organizing, 135, 151–52; restrictions on *Negro Worker*, 175

Reed, John, 82, 88

"Resolution on the Negro Question in the United States" (Comintern Sixth Congress). *See* Black Belt Nation Thesis

Reynolds, Reginald, 211

RILU. *See* Red International Labor Unions

Robeson, Paul, 201, 212, 267 (n. 50)

Robinson, Cedric, 12–14, 205

Rosemond, Henry, 156, 157

Roy, Manabendra Nath (M. N.): approach to national liberation, 79–80, 245 (n. 28); and Brussels Congress, 137, 139; at Comintern Fifth Congress, 118; reformulation of Marxist theory,

78–79; response to Lenin's "Draft Theses," 79–80; as revolutionary conspirator, 77–78
Rubinow, Isaac M. (aka I. M. Robbins), 34
Ruthenburg, Charles, 128, 131

Sanhedrin All-Race Conference, 110–14
Seamen's Minority Movement (SMM), 185, 186
Selassie, Haile, 206, 210
Self-determination: Briggs's views on, 38, 56–57, 237 (n. 40); Comintern Fifth Congress's views on, 117; as focus of London black radicals, 7; John Reed's views on, 82
Senghor, Lamine: at Brussels Congress, 140–41, 144; and CDRN, 138–39, 256 (n. 11); and intercolonialism, 74; and LAI, 144, 155; and PCF, 121, 253 (n. 49), 256 (n. 11); work with black seamen, 145
Sherill, General William, 128
Small, Edward, 159, 161, 168, 169–70
Smith, C.A., 191
SMM, 185, 186
Socialism. *See* Socialist Party of America
Socialism Imperiled (Domingo), 40–41
Socialist Fourth International, 8
Socialist Party of America (SPA): *Crusader*'s support of, 50, 65, 83; Domingo's criticism of, 40–41; Harrison's role in, 34–35; Huiswoud's activism in, 74; PEF attempts to transform, 40–42; and race, 24, 35, 41–42, 65. *See also* Black Socialists
Socialist Second International, 76, 81
SPA. *See* Socialist Party of America
Stalinism: James as critic of, 197; Padmore as critic of, 192–93, 199–200, 219–20
Stokes, Rose Pastor, 84, 95, 97, 247 (n. 54)

Third International. *See* Comintern
Toussaint L'Overture (James), 212
Trotsky, Leon, 75, 98–99, 223–24, 249 (n. 103)
Trotter, William Monroe, 109, 110
Truth Seeker, 33
Tulsa race riot, 66–67, 75
21st Assembly District, 39, 54

UNIA. *See* Universal Negro Improvement Association
Union Intercoloniale, 83, 246 (n. 43)
Union organizing: and Comintern Third Period, 135, 166; as focus of IASB, 198; and RILU, 135, 151–52
United Communist Party. *See* Workers Party
United Front Conference (UFC), 109–12
Universal Negro Improvement Association (UNIA): ABB's criticism of, 61, 66–68, 72; factional split, 128; International Convention of the Negro Peoples of the World (1920), 64–65, 67, 128–29; James on, 60; *Negro World* as organ of, 61; promotion of Black Star Line, 62; as working-class organization, 60. *See also* Garvey, Marcus
University of the Toilers of the East (KUTV): as Comintern school, 1, 2, 105, 150, 169; differences with ICNW, 170; and Padmore, 178

Vanguardism and black liberation, 165–66, 166 (ill.), 169–70, 176, 222–23, 229

Wallace-Johnson, Isaac Theophilus Akunna (I. T. A.): as *African Sentinel* editor, 198; Gold Coast arrest of, 196, 211–12, 267 (nn. 47–48); and IAFE, 207; and IASB, 212, 213, 215; and ITUCNW, 180, 182; and Padmore, 184, 212; and Pan-African Federation, 228
Warburg, Frederic, 218

Ward, Arnold, 182–83, 185–87, 263
(n. 59)
Warreno, Augusto, 130
Washington, Booker T., 33, 36, 37
West African Students Union (WASU),
6, 195–96, 201, 204, 210
West Indies Federation, 196
Weston, George, 128
When Africa Awakes (Hubert Henry
Harrison), 43
White Left: black Socialists' frustra-
tion with, 23–24; challenged by Asian
radicals, 5; class struggle as focus of,
23–24, 74–75; devaluation of black
leadership, 105; disregard of race
issue, 23–24, 34–35, 41–42, 74–75; and
IASB, 6, 198, 213–14, 267 (n. 52); and
internationalism, 8; paternalism of,
85; racism of, 34–35, 85–89, 90–96
Wilson, Woodrow, 38, 49, 56–57
The Worker, 97–98
Workers' Dreadnought, 87–88
Workers Party (WP): ABB affiliation
with, 99–100, 112–14; and ANLC,
120, 122–23, 126–27; approach to

race issue, 84, 85, 95; disillusionment
of black Communists with, 85–86,
126–27; Harlem Branch, 85; marginalization of black Communists, 126–27,
146; Negro Committee, 100, 112, 120,
121, 122, 127; resistance to Negro work,
100–101, 126–27, 131, 145–46, 151; and
Sanhedrin agenda, 112–14. *See also*
American Communists; Communist
Party USA
World Negro Congress: black radicals'
fears concerning, 102, 103; Comintern
support of, 97; opposed by Jones, 91;
proposals for, 16
World Revolution (James), 218–20

Yergan, Max, 212, 267 (n. 50)

Zinoviev, Gregory: concern with Asian
radicalism, 76, 244 (n. 15); as head of
Comintern Executive Committee, 76,
94–95; on Negro/proletarian collaboration, 97; recognition of race/class
link, 81